WOMEN'S WAYS OF MAKING

WOMEN'S WAYS OF MAKING

EDITED BY
MAUREEN DALY GOGGIN
AND SHIRLEY K ROSE

UTAH STATE UNIVERSITY PRESS
Logan

© 2021 by University Press of Colorado

Published by Utah State University Press
An imprint of University Press of Colorado
245 Century Circle, Suite 202
Louisville, Colorado 80027

All rights reserved

 The University Press of Colorado is a proud member of
the Association of University Presses.

The University Press of Colorado is a cooperative publishing enterprise supported, in part, by Adams State University, Colorado State University, Fort Lewis College, Metropolitan State University of Denver, Regis University, University of Colorado, University of Northern Colorado, University of Wyoming, Utah State University, and Western Colorado University.

ISBN: 978-1-64642-037-7 (paperback)
ISBN: 978-1-64642-038-4 (ebook)
https://doi.org/10.7330/9781646420384

Library of Congress Cataloging-in-Publication Data

Names: Goggin, Maureen Daly, editor. | Rose, Shirley K, editor. | Feminisms and Rhetorics Conference (10th : 2015 : Tempe, Ariz.)
Title: Women's ways of making / edited by Maureen Daly Goggin and Shirley K Rose.
Description: Logan : Utah State University Press, [2020] | Includes bibliographical references and index.
Identifiers: LCCN 2021001135 (print) | LCCN 2021001136 (ebook) | ISBN 9781646420377 (paperback) | ISBN 9781646420384 (ebook)
Subjects: LCSH: Rhetoric—Social aspects. | Feminism and literature. | Feminist theory. | Women—Psychology.
Classification: LCC P301.5.S63 W66 2020 (print) | LCC P301.5.S63 (ebook) | DDC 808—dc23
LC record available at https://lccn.loc.gov/2021001135
LC ebook record available at https://lccn.loc.gov/2021001136

Cover illustration by Michael Dambrowski

The University Press of Colorado gratefully acknowledges the support of Arizona State University toward the publication of this book.

To all the women makers who have been invisible.

CONTENTS

List of Figures ix
Acknowledgments xi

Women's Ways of Making as Embodied Epistemic Acts: An Introduction
   Maureen Daly Goggin and Shirley K Rose   3

SECTION 1: WOMEN'S WAYS OF EMBODYING RHETORIC

1. Remaking the Female Reproductive Body in *Saga*
   Rachael A. Ryerson   17

2. The Woman Rhetor and Her Body: A Case-Study Analysis of How a Feminist Zinester Constructs Ethos as Corporeal Experiential Authority
   Christine Martorana   40

3. Ripped Goddess: New Ways of Making Women's Fitness
   Holly Fulton-Babicke   57

4. Building Embodied *Ethe*: Brandi Chastain's Goal Celebration and the Problem of Situated Ethos
   Lorin Shellenberger   73

5. Posed to Emote: Making the Emotional-Embodied Work of Rhetorical Training Observable through Yoga Practice
   Jacquelyn E. Hoermann-Elliott   95

6. Yoga as Feminist Techne: Making Space for Administrative Well-Being
   Kathleen J. Ryan and Christy I. Wenger   115

SECTION 2: WOMEN'S WAYS OF MAKING ARGUMENTS TOGETHER USING WORDS AND DEEDS

7. Elizabeth I and the Rhetoric of the Marriage Crisis: Making Arguments
   Jane Donawerth   135

8. Fleur de Force: Beauty, Creativity, and YouTube
   Andrea J. Severson   150

9. A Study of Making-ness: Texts, Memory, and Art
   Kathleen Blake Yancey   162

10. Red Tent: Creating Art and Our Lives in Jail through Feminist Rhetorics
    Jill McCracken, Amanda Ellis, Melissa Greene, and Charlese Trower   177

SECTION 3: WOMEN'S WAYS OF MAKING THE ACADEMY

11. Renewing Feminist Perspectives on Women WPAs' Service and Leadership
    Hui Wu and Emily Standridge   203

12. Other Ways of Making It: Transcending Traditional Academic Trajectories
    Theresa M. Evans, Linda Hanson, Karen S. Neubauer, and Daneryl Weber   221

13. Making It as a Female Writing Program Administrator: Using Collective Action and Feminist Mentoring Practices to Transgress Gendered Boundaries
    Angela Clark-Oates, Bre Garrett, Magdelyn Hammond Helwig, Aurora Matzke, Sherry Rankins-Robertson, and Carey Smitherman Clark   245

About the Authors   265
Index   271

FIGURES

1.1. Marko holding his newborn child, Hazel, from *Saga*   24
1.2. Princess Robot giving birth, from *Saga*   26
1.3. Alana holding Hazel alongside Hazel's father, Marko, from *Saga*   30
1.4. Hazel breastfeeding, from *Saga*   32
1.5. Alana breastfeeding Hazel, from *Saga*   33
2.1. In Here, *In My Head*: Cath describes her early experiences with menstruation   43
4.1. Chastain's goal celebration, 1999   81
10.1. Coauthors after Feminisms and Rhetorics conference presentation in Phoenix, Arizona   182
10.2. Red Tent setup in PCJ   187
10.3. Coauthors at the top of Mt. Pima, Phoenix, Arizona   193
10.4. On top of the world, Phoenix, Arizona   193
10.5. Display of Red Tent participants' artwork at December 2015 Community Fundraiser, St. Petersburg, Florida   195

ACKNOWLEDGMENTS

As with any publication, many hands contributed to the appearance of *Women's Ways of Making* in print. We gratefully acknowledge Rachael Levay, acquisitions editor at the University Press of Colorado and Utah State University Press, for her guidance, kindness, and wisdom in bringing this collection to light. Laura Furney, assistant director and managing editor at University Press of Colorado and Utah State University Press, shepherded our project gracefully and expeditiously through the production process. Many thanks to Kami Day for copyediting work that understood our intentions and caught our errors. The enthusiasm for our project and encouragement from everyone we worked with at the press has meant so much to us. We also want to thank two anonymous reviewers for suggestions that helped us clarify the coherence of the collection. Finally, we acknowledge Cheryl Glenn and Shirley Wilson Logan for their support for this project in its very early stages.

WOMEN'S WAYS OF MAKING

WOMEN'S WAYS OF MAKING AS EMBODIED EPISTEMIC ACTS
An Introduction

Maureen Daly Goggin and Shirley K Rose

> I think every act of making is an act of revolution.
> —Betsy Greer

In October 2015, national and international scholars came together for the Tenth Biennial Feminisms and Rhetorics Conference held at Arizona State University in Tempe, Arizona, to share their work on the theme of women's ways of making, exploring the implications of claims like Greer's, in the epigraph above, for rhetorical studies. This volume emerged out of selected and revised presentations from that event. *Women's Ways of Making* calls attention to all those who identify as women as active poly-knowledge makers in a variety of fields, with a primary focus on feminist rhetoric and writing studies. In *The Nicomachean Ethics*, Aristotle distinguished among three types of knowledge: episteme, techne, and phronesis. Episteme is scientific or theoretical knowledge—a *knowing that*. Techne is a skill or craft knowledge (craftsmanship, craft of art)—a *knowing how*. Phronesis[1] is practical wisdom—a *knowing what to do in a particular situation*. Although knowledge (both episteme and techne) can exist without wisdom (phronesis), it cannot happen the other way around. One cannot be wise without both *knowing that* and *knowing how*. Phronesis requires understanding a situation, reflecting critically, and scrutinizing knowledge systems, practices, and impacts of goals. We argue that the essays in this collection demonstrate that the three ways of knowing emerge from experience and work in harmony as embodied acts.

To put it another way, resonating as it does with the influential *Women's Ways of Knowing* by Mary Field Belenky, Blythe McVicker Clinchy, Nancy Rule Goldberger, and Jill Mattuck Rule, published more than three decades ago in 1986, the focus of this volume draws attention to *making* as three epistemologies: an episteme, a techne, and a phronesis that together give pointed consideration to making as a rhetorical embodied endeavor. That is to say that material practices, those the hands[2] perform, are a form of *knowing that* (episteme), *knowing how* (techne), and *wisdom making* (phronesis). However, since the Enlightenment, embodied knowledge creation has been overlooked, ignored, or disparaged as inferior to other forms of expression or thinking that seem to leave the material world behind.[3] Making as embodied knowledge has been, in a word, gendered, rendering it as ostensibly inept. Yet, as Maureen Johnson, Daisy Levy, Katie Manthley, and Maria Novotny argue, "If we are as much physical as we are intellectual, then research must be undertaken with attention to bodies and practices, not just artifacts and textual residue" (2015, 40). Privileging the hand over the eye, as we do here, thus problematizes the way the eye has been co-opted by thinkers as the mind's tool of investigation. Though eyes are just as embodied as hands, philosophy has managed to elevate the status of eyes by making them central to the way we conceive of knowing (*I see* equals *I understand*). Patricia Spyer (2006) has aptly called this privileged focus on the eye "ocularcentrism." Here we argue for other senses—touch, taste, smell, hearing—as keys to knowing one's materials; and for the dexterity of the practiced hand, or body, for knowing how to transform those materials; and for reflecting on that work of transforming as contributing to defining experience as knowing when and where to do something.[4] Only when all these ways of knowing are engaged can *making* be understood as a rhetorical practice.

John Dewey's analysis of the way we tend to value the immaterial over the material aptly points out what is at stake in this argument:

> The depreciation of action, of doing and making, has been cultivated by philosophers. . . . There is also the age-long association of knowing and thinking with immaterial and spiritual principles, and of the arts, of all practical activity in doing and making, with matter. For work is done with the body . . . is directed upon material things. The disrepute which has attended the thought of material things in comparison with immaterial thought has been transferred to everything associated with practice. (1929, 5)

In other words, the mundane procedures and concrete materials that are the essence of what gets made are usually overlooked or, if acknowledged, perceived as debased or beneath what is considered that which is disembodied or abstract—that which ostensibly "rises above" its circumstances of production. Not coincidentally, these practices and materials are typically gendered as feminine. Yet, as historian Laurel Thatcher Ulrich has demonstrated with her own work on women and textiles, the ways women have manipulated the material world bear scrutiny as legitimate subjects of social, cultural, and economic history. The work featured in this collection then challenges this hierarchy of eye over hand and body separated from mind and calls for attending to embodied knowledge, and doing that helps rescue women from obscurity. Indeed, we concur with Greer, who notes, "Creativity [is] a force to be reckoned with" (2007, 401). She pushes further to suggest, as she does in the epigraph, that "every act of making is an act of revolution" (2008, 55).

What about the objects of making? In the *Power of Making*, Rosy Greenlees and Mark Jones argue that "handmade objects have a story. They have been touched, manipulated, hammered, thrown, carved by another human hand. They connect us to our past and to our familial and cultural histories" (2011, 5). Things, that is to say, are existentially central to who we are and who we have been. *Made things* are worth our attention, and because they are worth our attention, their making is worth our attention. And the intention and attention required in the making of things is worth our attention as well.

In working with the contributors to this collection, we have been struck by how often they turn to material metaphors for characterizing even the work of making more conventionally linguistic texts as rhetorical practice. For example, Jane Donawerth describes the "*mesh*" (chapter 7; emphasis added) Queen Elizabeth I created as she presented arguments and in turn responded to advisors, Parliament, suitors, poets, and the public in order to effect her agency. Similarly, Jill McCracken, Amanda Ellis, Melissa Greene, and Charlese Trower describe how they "*weave* new knowledge about and a greater understanding of ourselves by paying attention to our voices, perspectives, and experiences—personal, professional, painful, and joyful [emphasis added]" (chapter 10). Similarly, in this volume, Angela Clark-Oates, Bre Garrett, Magdelyn Hammond Helwig, Aurora Matzke, Sherry Rankins-Robertson, and Carey Smitherman-Clark use metaphors that call to mind using their whole bodies, writing of "*navigat[ing]* the landscapes of [their] respective institutions" (chapter 13; emphasis added), a metaphor that incorporates both the physical body and the mind, working together with a tool such as a compass.

Kathleen Blake Yancey writes eloquently of the process of making a very material "artist's book" but also calls attention to her loss of control of the meaning-making process in very material and physical terms (chapter 9). She draws attention to the contrast between giving a typical conference paper she might hold in her own hand and stand to read and interacting with the visitors who picked up and handled her artist's book at the Feminisms and Rhetorics conference exhibit. She also attends to the way new materials—"paper and markers and highlighters"—allowed her to make a "new kind of meaning." Her narrative of creating the book emphasizes the work of her hands in "tearing pages out and then bundling pages together," "drawing on the book pages," and "cutting the text into squares," and she compares this to our usual lack of involvement in the decision-making process that determines where text appears on the page in our physical texts.

Together, these and other contributions to the collection demonstrate the challenges of rendering in conventional, abstract textual form the insights from reflection on material making. These challenges call attention to the ways *Women's Ways of Making* seeks to collapse several impoverished binaries: mind/body, producer/consumer, passive recipients/active agents, public/private, craft/art, and man/woman. Our intention is to challenge gendered notions of making, of artifacts, of practices, of innovation, of digital spaces, and of applied/theoretical research, as well as more conventional notions about ways of making arguments, making knowledge, and making sense. Dissolution of these static binaries is part of the work feminists have undertaken over the last twenty years and thus informs the contributions this collection offers to this ongoing conversation in feminist rhetoric.

Working together to articulate a multivocal sense of all women's ways of making, the essays in *Women's Ways of Making* value and emphasize different ways of innovating, composing, creating, translating, using, reusing, repurposing, recycling, researching, remixing, and working in history and today. Thus, the things they address are quite varied. Collectively, this rhetorical scholarship across these multiple areas of women's work represents the generative outcomes that result from acknowledging women's rhetorical agency as makers.

The essays included in the collection demonstrate a range of scholarly approaches, including historiographies, ethnographies, rhetorical analyses, and reflective personal narratives. Many of the essays use transdisciplinary approaches. Our twenty-nine contributors (including ourselves) are a diverse group representing scholars at every stage of making their scholarly lives in the academy, from graduate students through established senior faculty members, as well as those outside academia. Contributors work in diverse institutional settings where their embodied experiences shape the knowledge they make (see brief biographical statements in "Contributors" section). That diversity is purposeful and celebrated here.

ORGANIZATION OF CHAPTERS

There are many ways to order and arrange essays in edited collections. In making decisions about the organization of the chapters in this collection, we've mused on multiple occasions about the ways putting together the text as an imagined physical thing has made us aware of the ways we make arguments through these acts of arrangement and rearrangement, clustering, juxtaposing, and ordering. Consulting our experiences as readers of edited collections, we simultaneously imagine the whole as a narrative with an arc the reader experiences as they make their way from first page to last, and we acknowledge it must be more like an assemblage of parts, each of which can be picked up and examined more or less carefully than the others, with and without reference to the rest.

Women's Ways of Making is divided into three sections: "Women's Ways of Embodying Rhetorics," "Women's Ways of Making Arguments together Using Words and Deeds," and "Women's Ways of Making the Academy." The first section, "Women's Ways of Embodying Rhetoric," offers six chapters in which authors examine embodied rhetoric, the ways women make meaning, as well as signify it with their bodies, in a variety of media and means including comics, zines, and participation in online communities and athletic performance. Rachael Ryerson's chapter, "Remaking the Female Reproductive Body in *Saga*," examines the ways the *Saga* comic series reworks comics industry norms for gendered bodies by representing childbirth and breastfeeding in ways that are abject but visually resituates them at the center of action, disrupting hegemonic discursive practices and thus making those gendered bodies rhetorical.

Christine Martorana's chapter, "The Woman Rhetor and Her Body: A Case-Study Analysis of How a Feminist Zinester Constructs Ethos as Corporeal Experiential Authority" (chapter 2), examines how women have devised and enacted creative ways of re-presenting their bodies, offering case-study analysis of the feminist zine *Here. In My Head.* Focusing on the ways these zine authors create their rhetorical ethos, which she describes as "corporeal experiential authority," Martorana demonstrates how the woman rhetor can re-present her physical body as a site of authority beyond the adversarial framework. Corporeal experiential authority is cultivated when a rhetor explicitly references the physicality of their own body and then uses these physical experiences to connect with and offer guidance to their audience. Martorana concludes by considering what corporeal experiential authority suggests for a feminist re-visioning of ethos and our understanding of the rhetorical strategies available to feminist rhetors.

Holly Fulton-Babicke's chapter, "Ripped Goddess: New Ways of Making Women's Fitness" (chapter 3) places the Ripped Goddess online women's fitness community's practices in conversation with theory on the disciplining and definition of the female body and literature discussing the function of embodiment in online environs. Fulton-Babicke explores how women in this community articulate new, richly nonmonolithic ways of imagining physical fitness in the context of femininity using the affordances of virtual social media. She explores the ways members of the Ripped Goddess community "remix" elements of female embodiment, showing a community-wide tendency to claim both traditional feminine and resistant and/or feminist traits in their identities as "ripped goddesses" and craft "visions" of feminine embodiment that move beyond binary conceptions of male/female, subject/object, and strong/weak through ownership of women's strength, right to occupy physical space, and adroitness in crafting unique articulations of femininity.

Loren Shellenberger's chapter, "Building an Embedded Êthe: Performances of Ethos in Elite Female Athletes" (chapter 4) analyzes the ways elite female athletes build and shape the physical self, relating this process of self-creation to ethos. Through a rhetorical analysis of the performances of ethos by soccer player Brandi Chastain, Shellenberger demonstrates the dynamic interplay among race, class, gender, and embodiment, suggesting not only the interrelatedness of these elements and one's ability to shape or construct the self but also that a contemporary account of ethos must acknowledge identities as fluid and must account for these facets of identity as parts of an interlocking system of representation.

Feminist writing instructor Jackie Hoermann-Elliott examines in her chapter, "Posed to Emote: Making the Emotional-Embodied Work of Rhetorical Training Observable through Yoga Practice" (chapter 5) how contemplative practices enhance the writing process of first-year college students by supporting the embodied and emotional work of writing. An established yoga practitioner, Hoermann-Elliott analyzes the reflective narratives and final projects developed by students enrolled in her Yoga-Zen Writing class in spring 2015. Her findings demonstrate that first-year writing courses can be enhanced and even revitalized by contemplative writing practices developed through yoga and meditation experiences that support the embodied and emotional work of making that writing requires contemporary students to engage in.

In the final chapter of this section devoted to examining women's ways of making bodies rhetorical, Kathleen J. Ryan and Christy I. Wenger reimagine women's work as writing program administrators through the contemplative practice of yoga in their chapter, "Yoga as Feminist Techne: Making Space for Administrative Well-Being" (chapter 6). They argue that yoga is a *techne* that offers a way of doing and making in feminist administration. Yoga provides not only a way of (re)making administrative narratives but also actionable strategies that unsettle the mind/body binary in order to work toward the well-being of WPAs and the programs they lead. Employing a dialogue through which they enact the discursiveness at the heart of feminism and at the heart of *Women's Ways of Making*, they explore the ways through which conscious and deliberate yoga practice helps us craft new ways of being, of making and enacting knowledge, and of shaping writing programs—all embodied acts.

The second section, "Women's Ways of Making Arguments together Using Words and Deeds," is comprised of four essays that, though diverse in topical focus and methodology, all demonstrate how making arguments and making meaning are collaborative processes. In these chapters, media and genre are understood as material resources for making meaning. In "Elizabeth I and the Rhetoric of the Marriage Crisis" (chapter 7) Jane Donawerth examines the ways Queen Elizabeth I made arguments as she engaged in the debate over her possible marriage, a debate that was carried on through twenty years across multiple court and public genres (petitions, speeches, councilors' letters, sermons, plays, and pamphlets). Donawerth also addresses how the Queen's initiation of and responses to arguments enabled her to test rhetorical strategies and flex her complicated agency as a female ruler. Donawerth demonstrates that Elizabeth achieved agency as a maker of arguments in an ecology of writing that took into account shifting political exigencies, constructing her ethos not only from her own desires and individual style but also from collaboration with previous speakers.

Examining the markedly different discursive space of YouTube beauty vlogs in "Fleur de Force: Beauty, Creativity, and YouTube" (chapter 8), Andrea Severson argues that YouTube video bloggers are active producers and creators of original content that constructs a unique and empowering space for women in both their individual videos and their larger channels and online identities. Severson examines how, rather than simply accepting mainstream ideals, beauty vloggers often promote messages that counter those from the mainstream beauty industries, engaging in a wide variety of ways of making through the way they construct their channels and the content they feature, as well as in community-making practices with their viewers. Severson's rhetorical analysis of the *Fleur de Force* vlog not only pays attention to the content of Fleur's videos but also attends to Fleur's work of making the video—considering the rhetorical effects of choices made in sound recording, lighting, and editing and examining Fleur's explicit discussion of this work on camera.

In "A Study of Making-ness: Texts, Memory, and Art" (chapter 9), Kathleen Blake Yancey reflects on what she learned in the process of creating an artist's book to commemorate the loss of several pieces of heirloom jewelry during a burglary in her home. Yancey observes that choices of discursive genres and media made in the acts of planning and creating the commemorative project contributed to the process of making meaning from a confusing and disorienting personal experience. She further reflects on the ways her discussions with the 2015 Feminisms and Rhetorics conference participants who visited her exhibit of the commemorative book required her to cede some of the control over meaning making she is accustomed to in more conventional conference presentations and engaged her in unanticipated collaborations in making meaning.

In the final chapter of this second section, the authorial team of Jill McCracken, Amanda Ellis, Melissa Greene, and Charlese Trower examines the ways of making arguments for valuing women's lives employed by the Red Tent Women's Initiative (Red Tent) in the project of sponsoring a weekly support group for nonviolent female offenders within the Pinellas County Jail in Clearwater, Florida. Their chapter, "Creating Art and Our Lives in Jail through Feminist Rhetorics" (chapter 10), argues that the Red Tent is a site whereby community is made, examining how the acts of creating art, connecting women in the community, offering acceptance, healing, sharing wisdom and compassion, and empowering participants make active meaning and knowledge.

In section three, "Women's Ways of Making and Remaking the Academy," our contributors discuss women's ways of making the academy through remaking a variety of roles—transforming traditional or conventionally gendered roles of students, teachers, scholars, and administrators. Hui Wu and Emily Standridge's "Renewing Feminist Perspectives on Women WPAs' Service and Leadership" (chapter 11) draws parallels between challenges to higher education in the twenty-first century and in the late nineteenth century. The authors point out that as demands for graduates with writing abilities have created a favorable job market for WPAs, female WPAs have benefitted from these positions' focus on service and women's commonly perceived ability to "serve." However, these gendered perceptions of their positions can also serve to feminize their labor, leading to gender inequity. The authors present a study in which they reconceptualize WPA work as "public service" through a renewed feminist approach that reveals the patriarchal ideologies that determine values of academic work. The authors conclude that women WPAs' transcendence of traditionally defined gender traits and labor divisions demonstrates their readiness for higher university leadership as part of public service. By "remaking" administration as public service, the authors seek to change the exchange value of the "hands-on" work women administrators do in their daily embodied encounters with others.

In the next chapter, "Other Ways of Making It: Transcending Traditional Academic Trajectories" (chapter 12), Tess Evans, Linda Hanson, Karen S. Neubauer, and Daneryl Weber report on a pilot survey exploring nontraditional academic women's reasons for pursuing graduate study later in life: the kinds of support they received as well as the kinds of obstacles they encountered, and their reflections on whether they would make the same choice again. Their study showed that while tenure-track jobs are attainable for nontraditional academics, and most nontraditional academic women would choose again to pursue degrees, the financial costs and the ambiguities of ageism are especially troubling. These researchers discuss their findings that survey respondents valued the emotional and intellectual satisfaction of fulfilling work more than money, recognition, or status and conclude that nearly 90 percent of their survey participants were "making it" in ways that challenged the system to go beyond traditional measurements of success. The authors' examination of the ways lived experience embodied by their older respondents allowed them to transform the exchange value of graduate study helps us understand that experience as a substantial resource for making and remaking.

The final chapter explores feminist pedagogies from both student and teacher perspectives. In their chapter, "Making It as a Female Writing Program Administrator: Using Collective Action to Transgress Gendered Boundaries" (chapter 13), the six-member authorial team of Angela Clark-Oates, Bre Garrett, Magdelyn Hammon Helwig, Aurora Matze, Sherry Rankin Robertson, and Carey Smitherman-Clark offer brief labor narratives of the ways they have learned about their environments in the process of negotiating a multiplicity of identities. Each of their vignettes showcases lived experience through which the authors confirm research showing that women in academia are treated differently than men are. Strategically placed in the chapter to interrupt the scholarly text, these vignettes evoke for the reader the abrupt and disruptive experiences of the authors, demonstrating that these experiences have happened to physical bodies and have had physical consequences.

Then, speaking collectively, the authors synthesize their vignettes to show how they have made sense of their local experience, making bodies whole by making meaning toward what they describe as a "pedagogy of administration" for mentoring other female administrators.

As readers will see, most of the essays grapple with contemporary issues, but one, Jane Donawerth's "Elizabeth I and the Rhetoric of Marriage Crisis: Making Arguments," transports us back to ancient times, reminding us that feminist rhetorical practices have a long, unbroken history and that embodiment has been a central focus. Although these thirteen chapters are only a small fraction of the exciting work of feminist rhetoric generated, shared, and developed at the Tenth Biennial Feminisms and Rhetorics Conference: "Women's Ways of Making," they offer provocative glimpses through powerful lenses for understanding women's embodied ways of making meaning and knowledge together. We invite you to experience these women's ways of making through your body and soul.

NOTES

1. Aristotle distinguished between two types of wisdom: *phronesis* (φρόνηση) and *sophia* (σοφία). Whereas *phronesis* is practical wisdom, *sophia* is understood as theoretical wisdom. In common parlance the difference between the two is the difference between book smart and common sense. We are not making this fine distinction here, though an argument could be made for doing so.
2. We use *hands* somewhat metaphorically here; any body part can make something (e.g., painting with a brush in one's mouth, doing pottery with one's feet, and so on), and many body parts are involved in the work of making accomplished by yoga or running, as contributions to this volume demonstrate.
3. Michel Foucault's work on the body as a site for disciplinarity has been foundational in bringing the body back into cultural history. See *Discipline and Punish* (1995) and *The History of Sexuality (1988)*. For an overview of Foucault's impact on embodied knowledge, see Arthur Frank (1990) and Felix Driver (1994). Also see Elizabeth Spelman, "Woman as Body: Ancient and Contemporary Views" (1982). For work on rhetoric and the body, see Debra Hawhee, *Bodily Arts* (2004) and *Moving Bodies* (2009), as well as Jack Selzer and Sharon Crowley, *Rhetorical Bodies* (1990).
4. Pamela Smith's concept of material literacy as an artisanal epistemology whereby one gains "knowledge neither through reading nor writing but through a process of experience and labor. Rather than producing a 'lettered man,' such literacy has the goal of making knowledge productive" (2001, 76) and comes close to what we are arguing here. However, we see no need to disconnect reading and writing practices from experience and labor practices; indeed, the knowing hand is central to writing practices.

WORKS CITED

Aristotle. 2009. *The Nicomachean Ethics.* Translated by David Ross. Rev. with an introduction and notes by Lesley Brown. New York: Oxford University Press.

Belenky, Mary Kay, Blythe McVicker Clinchy, Nancy Rule Goldberger, and Jill Mattuck Tarule. 1986. *Women's Ways of Knowing: The Development of Self, Voice, and Mind.* New York: Basic Books.
Dewey, John. 1929. *The Quest for Certainty: A Study of the Relation of Knowledge and Action.* New York: Minton.
Driver, Felix. 1994. "Bodies in Space: Foucault's Account of Disciplinary Power." In *Reassessing Foucault: Power, Medicine, and the Body*, edited by Colin Jones and Roy Porter, 113–31. Abingdon, England: Routledge.
Geer, Betsy. 2007. "Craftivism." In *Encyclopedia of Activism and Social Justice*, edited by Gary L. Anderson and Kathryn G. Herr. Newbury Park, CA: SAGE.
Geer, Betsy. 2008. *Knitting for Good: A Guide to Creating Personal, Social, and Political Change, Stitch by Stitch.* Boston: Trumpeter Books.
Greenlees, Rosy, and Mark Jones. 2011. Foreword to *Power of Making: The Importance of Being Skilled*, edited by Daniel Charny, 5. V&A and Crafts Council.
Foucault, Michel. 1995. *Discipline and Punish: The Birth of a Prison*, 2nd ed. Translated by Alan Sheridan. New York: Vintage.
Foucault, Michel. 1978–1988. *The History of Sexuality.* Translated by Robert Hurley. Vols. 1, 2, and 2. New York: Pantheon.
Frank, Arthur. 1990. "Bringing Bodies Back In: A Decade Review." *Theory, Culture and Society* 7 (1): 131–62.
Hawhee, Debra. 2004. *Bodily Arts: Rhetorics and Athletics in Ancient Greece.* Austin: University of Texas Press.
Hawhee, Debra. 2009. *Moving Bodies: Kenneth Burke at the Edges of Language.* Columbia: University of South Carolina Press.
Johnson, Maureen, Daisy Levy, Katie Manthley, and Maria Novotny. 2015. "Embodiment: Embodying Feminist Rhetorics." *Peitho Journal* 18 (1): 39–43.
Selzer, Jack, and Sharon Crowley, eds. 1999. *Rhetorical Bodies.* Madison: University of Wisconsin Press.
Smith, Pamela H. 2001. "Giving Voice to the Hand: The Articulation of Material Literacy in the Sixteenth Century." In *Popular Literacy: Studies in Cultural Practices and Poetics*, edited by John Trimbur, 74–93. Pittsburgh: University of Pittsburgh Press.
Spelman, Elizabeth. 1982. "Woman as Body: Ancient and Contemporary Views." *Feminist Studies* 8 (1): 109–31.
Spyer, Patricia. 2006. "The Body, Materiality and the Senses." In *Handbook of Material Culture*, edited by Christopher Tilley, Webb Keane, Susanne Küchler, Michael Rowlands, and Patricia Spyer, 125–29. Newbury Park, CA: SAGE.
Ulrich, Laurel Thatcher. 2001. *The Age of Homespun: Objects and Stories in the Creation of an American Myth.* New York: Vintage Books.

SECTION 1

Women's Ways of Embodying Rhetoric

1
REMAKING THE FEMALE REPRODUCTIVE BODY IN *SAGA*

Rachael A. Ryerson

For those who read comics, and even for those who do not, it hardly comes as a surprise that women's bodies in comics are typically portrayed in hypersexualized, fetishized ways. As Jennifer Stuller points out, "The bodies of women in mainstream comics tend to be fetishized, receive more focus than their narrative, are shown as parts rather than an active whole . . . and are typically drawn in physically impossible positions that manage to display both their breasts and their rear ends" (2012, 237). Women's bodies are visually rendered for the heterosexual male gaze, and they are often posed to lead this gaze to their sexualized parts, that is their breasts, vagina, or buttocks. For some time now, the trend in mainstream comics has been to hypersexualize, yet reduce in complexity and agency, the female body, all in an effort to cater to the mostly male comics consumer (Brown 2011, 77).

Despite the frequency with which women's bodies cater to the heterosexual male gaze in Western, mainstream comics, many comic artists, writers, and fans challenge those representations. For example, websites such as the Hawkeye Initiative disrupt the sexual objectification of women through parody: they replace the female bodies with male bodies in the same pose and clothing, and in doing so, reveal and resist hegemonic discursive practices within the comics industry (Scott 2015). In her comics, Julie Doucet also uses parody to challenge normative notions of the female body through grotesque female materiality, a misogynistic concept typically used to discipline and marginalize women's bodies. Her comic *Heavy Flow* is a good example; Doucet illustrates her cartoon self as a hyperbolic, menstruating King Kong in search of Tampax. Doucet represents the female body as a grotesque, abject body, and in doing so, "challenges cultural norms through a process of resignification based on the production of parodic excess" (Køhlert 2012, 20). This comic forces an encounter with an abject

DOI: 10.7330/9781646420384.c001

body, "leaking" as it is from an orifice often characterized in comics as monstrous.

Likewise, Fiona Staples (artist) and Brian K. Vaughan's (writer) sci-fi comic, *Saga*, challenges cultural, comic industry norms around the female reproductive body by representing and glorifying abject representations of those bodies. Western mainstream comics avoid or downplay visual representations of female bodies that emphasize their reproductive and maternal capabilities. In addition, such comics tend to portray these bodes as abject, as monstrous feminine bodies that should be visually marginalized, ignored, or erased altogether because of the psychological horror they inspire in the assumed-male spectator (Brown 2011). *Saga* contests these representations of women's bodies by normalizing the abject through visual depictions of childbirth, public breastfeeding, and miscarriage. As this essay shows, *Saga* illustrates the female reproductive body in abject ways, but instead of sequestering, erasing, or vilifying these bodies, this comic visually centers and celebrates them, and, in the process, ultimately reworks discursive norms for these bodies.

ABJECT THEORY AND CRITICISM

Unequivocally, Julia Kristeva helped establish the theory of abjection, and often scholars draw upon her work to analyze phenomena through this theoretical lens. While a full explication of Kristeva's theory of abjection is outside the scope of this essay, a brief introduction to abjection, especially its connection to the female reproductive body, warrants explanation. At its core, Kristeva's theory responds to Freudian and Lacanian schools of thought about subjectivity and marks an affective turn toward ontology, a perspective that situates bodily experience as substantive of subjectivity. According to Kristeva, the abject stands for that which we most dread, the hidden, feared parts of being and knowing that "disturb identity, system, order" (1982, 4). Kristeva cites phenomena like excrement, vomit, and the corpse as examples of abjection because they represent a threat to bodily integrity, from within and without, and "these body fluids, this defilement, this shit are what life withstands" (3). Abjection, then, is "sickness at one's own body" and is "the result of recognizing that the body is more than, in excess of, the 'clean and proper'" (Grosz 1990, 78). Rina Arya clarifies that "abject things cross boundaries, making their states indeterminate and it is this in-between state that renders the object abject" (2014, 27). As a result, "the abject is radically excluded" because it highlights "the place where meaning collapses" (Kristeva 1982, 2). To maintain subjectivity and identity, the individual disavows the abject because it is a reminder of disorder and death, of the body's ambiguity and fluidity.

For Kristeva, abjection first occurs when the infant separates from the mother. Imogen Tyler summarizes Kristeva's model of subjectivity: "The infant's bodily attachment to his/her maternal origins must be successfully and violently abjected in order for an independent and cogent, speaking human subject to 'be born.' Any subsequent 'abjections' must therefore be understood as repetitions that contain an echo of this earlier cathartic event—the first and primary abject(ion)—birth and the human infant's separation from the maternal body/home" (2009, 80). Following Kristeva, to expel the mother the infant makes the mother abject, developing feelings of horror and fear in order to establish bodily boundaries and a singular identity separate from the mother. Together, the matricide Kristeva's theory calls for along with the feelings of disgust and horror that become attached to the maternal, both theoretically and physically, lead to monstrous-feminine representations of maternal and reproductive female figures throughout culture. Indeed, the pregnant body, as a soon-to-be maternal figure in excess of its physical boundaries and with many leaking orifices, is a prime example of the abject.

Although Kristeva never claims to be a feminist and never labels her theory of abjection as feminist, the concept of abjection has been a compelling and productive one for feminist scholars and rhetoricians. Feminists draw on this theory with the hope that cultural representations of the abject can be "read against the grain in ways that will destabilize and/or subvert misogynistic representations of women" (Tyler 2009, 82–83). Tyler does not wholeheartedly disagree with this application of abject theory, but she does worry that this form of criticism, in reaffirming the link between the maternal and the monstrous, becomes "another site in which a narrative of acceptable violence is endlessly rehearsed until we find ourselves not only colluding with but more fundamentally believing in our abjection" (87). Tyler calls for a more enriched understanding of abject theory that does not simply reaffirm the maternal, reproductive figure as horrific and/or disgusting. But, what if a popular culture text used abject representations of the fecund female body to normalize those bodies? The comic series *Saga* accomplishes as much by centralizing the abject female reproductive body, representing its panoply—pregnant, birthing, breastfeeding, miscarrying—naturalizing its chaotic excess and reworking norms for such figures in the comic genre.

ABJECTION OF MATERNAL AND FEMALE REPRODUCTIVE BODIES IN MAINSTREAM COMICS

Comic scholars have noticed that mainstream comics tend to portray maternal and pregnant figures as abject. Indeed, very few superheroines are both positive maternal figures and adept heroines—maternal superheroines often fail as mothers, become an obstacle for their superhero male counterparts, or are depicted as "inherently evil, neglectful, or absent" (Brown 2011, 82). The maternal figure in comics has not always been abject—indeed, Laura Mattoon D'Amore's examination of superhero comics from 1963 to 1980 shows how the feminist movement heavily impacted the comics of this time period. As a result, the "superheroine's performance of maternity empowers the maternal, accepting motherhood—and the feminized qualities associated with it—as an asset, rather than a liability" (2012, 1226). Yet, D'Amore's finding seems more the exception than the norm. More often, as Anne Marie O'Brien discovered in analyzing Jack Kirby's 1970–73 superhero comic series *Fourth World*, mainstream comics depict a "problematic rejection of the female reproductive body" (2014, para. 7). For instance, two main female mother figures, Granny Goodness and Motherbox, reiterate the monstrous/selfish versus pure/selfless mother trope. Granny Goodness is characterized as a cruel and terrible mother, whose "defining trait of selfishness is matched with her exaggeratedly aged physical features" (para. 10). Her visual appearance reinforces her characterization as a grotesque maternal figure—she is abject. In contrast, Motherbox, a sentient portable supercomputer that can heal and help many of the characters in Fourth World, is defined as a sexless, selfless entity whose "clean" and "secure" physical boundaries mark her as a safe and acceptable maternal figure.

Like maternal figures, and perhaps more so, pregnant bodies in comics are often overlooked or erased because they visually and physically embody that which has been defined as abject: "The pregnant body itself represents a threatening dissolution of bodily boundaries and serves as a symbol of femininity as monstrous" (Brown 2011, 81). In the superhero comic genre specifically, the female reproductive body is represented as abject because these bodies defy the bodily norms for the genre. What is more, "in a genre obsessed with armoring, containing, and defending the integrity of self-sufficient and powerful bodies, a pregnant body is troublesome because it evidences the inherent fluidity and penetrability of the superheroine" (79). As a result, pregnant bodies in this genre, as well as other comic genres, are portrayed in abject, monstrous ways because they disturb the ideal boundaries and containment mainstream comics foist on the female body. Jane Ussher explains that "the corporeality of the changing pregnant body, the act of birth, the amniotic fluid, afterbirth, and blood, and the hormonal changes and lactation which follow, stand as the pinnacle of that which signifies abjection" (2006, 86), and thus it makes sense that a genre bent on representing the female body in its ideal form would make visual representations of pregnancy abject.

To be fair, feminist underground comix from the 1970s to present day visually represent and frankly discuss female reproductive bodies. Indeed, Chin Lyvely and Joyce Farmer Chevely's 1973 comic, *Abortion Eve*, openly discusses abortion and female reproductive bodies in/through the comics medium. Likewise, Lynn Johnston, in her long-running comic strip, *For Better or For Worse*, illustrates and describes pregnancy not as idyllic or as monstrous but in its actuality (1981, 1983, 1989). Women in Johnston's comics about pregnancy complain about nausea, swollen feet, discomfort, fear, and weight gain, even offering feminist comments like, "Why is it that a paunch is fine on a man but is ugly on a girl who's had two kids!" (1981). Comic strips like Johnston's, as well as feminist underground comix, represent the lived, personal, political experiences of female reproductive bodies, but this is not the case for many mainstream superhero/action comics.

In contrast, mainstream comics rarely show the pregnant female body, often alluding to pregnancy only in flashbacks (as is the case with Black Widow) or preferring to speed up the pregnancy (as is the case with Invisible Girl). Indeed, Sue Storm (Invisible Girl/Woman) takes maternity leave from the Fantastic Four team and is replaced by another female superheroine figure until she can reappear, svelte in her skin-tight leotard. Power Girl, another example, reveals she is pregnant in *Justice League International*, issue 52, but she does not appear pregnant in subsequent issues, and she disappears from the series after issue 67, only to reappear in *Zero Hour: Crisis in Time* heavily pregnant and ready to give birth. The comic visually skips her pregnancy and offers a truncated view of the actual birth of the baby. This comic series, along with many mainstream Western comics, refuses to show the female reproductive body at its most abject—pregnant, giving birth, breastfeeding, miscarrying—because such bodies are "not the ideal well protected impervious body valorized in comics" (Brown 2011, 80).

Altogether, existent comics scholarship on abjection and the maternal and/or female reproductive body does well to identify how and when these bodies become abject and astutely highlights why these representations are problematic. However, rarely discussed are the ways abject female bodies might productively challenge discursive norms for such figures in comics. Frederik Byrn Køhlert, in his article on carnivalesque subversion in Julie Doucet's comics, demonstrates how the abject can be used to critique norms for the female body in comics. Although Køhlert reads Doucet through the lens of Bakhtin's concept of the carnivalesque, he echoes Kristeva's theory of abjection in his focus on the grotesque body as one that emphasizes the openings and protrusions of the body, as well as the "processes of becoming such as intercourse, giving birth, and dying" (2012, 21). With its capacity for menstruation and lactation, the female body becomes the grotesque (read: abject) body. However, Køhlert suggests such bodies have subversive potential, and in Doucet's comics specifically, "the misogynistic concept of grotesque female materiality [is] a generative principle from where she articulates a critique in both form and content of the normative and restricting representations of the female body" (19). Doucet visually re-presents abject female bodies to rework the hegemonic, regulatory frame for those bodies.

To do more than synonymize female reproductive bodies with abjection, comics readers and scholars must attend to those comics that use abjection to remake sociocultural conceptions of such bodies. How might comics recast female figures of abjection to disrupt industry practices and simultaneously introduce a new level of acceptance for visual representations of the female reproductive body? A good example can be found in the recent comics series *Saga*, which centralizes abject, visual representations of the female reproductive body. In addition to seeing pregnant bodies, readers of *Saga* also see main characters giving birth (including crowning), breastfeeding, and miscarrying. Instead of allocating these abject figures to the margins or background or making them into villains and thereby reifying these bodies' association with the monstrous-feminine, *Saga* naturalizes these abject figures, and in the process, disrupts comic-industry norms for the female reproductive body.

DISRUPTING TABOOS OF CHILDBIRTH

Heavily influenced by *Star Wars* and described as an epic space opera, *Saga* is the collaborative result of Brian K. Vaughan's writing and Fiona Staples's artistry. This comic series, first issued on March 14, 2012, follows two lovers, Alana from the technologically advanced Landfall Coalition, and Marko, from the poorer Wreath, the only satellite of Landfall. These two planets are at war with each other, making Marko and Alana Romeo and Juliet figures, star-crossed lovers on the run from authorities on both sides of the galactic war, hunted for breaking social taboos by being together. They are mainly pursued because they have given birth to a daughter, Hazel, our narrator of the series, who is a blend of the two parents, with Alana's wings and Marko's horns. Characters in the comics call Hazel a half-breed, revealing the racial commentary running throughout this series. In addition to addressing issues related to race, class, drugs, sexuality, violence, and parenting, *Saga* remakes the abject female reproductive body by visually re-presenting pregnancy, childbirth, breastfeeding, and miscarriage.

The *Saga* series begins with Alana giving birth to Hazel in the opening few pages and in this way disrupts norms around the way female reproductive bodies are portrayed in comics. Issue 1 of *Saga* opens with a profile view of Alana's face, flushed red and sweat clad, as she asks Marko, "Am I shitting? It feels like I am shitting" (figure 1.1). Readers discover in the following panels that she is giving birth, a scene that culminates with the squalling Hazel covered in the blood of her birth. Although Alana's vagina is screened off from the viewer, what remains important is that this comic, produced by a mainstream comic publisher like Image Comics, shows childbirth in the opening pages of its inaugural issue. Imogen Tyler and Lisa Baraitser observe that there has been a dramatic increase in media representations of childbirth in the last three decades, specifically in film, reality television, video-sharing platforms like YouTube, and fine-art practice. Tyler and Baraitser explain that taboos of childbirth, "especially the moment of crowning, and the maternal experiences of pain and pleasure at childbirth," are being broken as "birth is becoming routinely witnessed and represented in more graphic and public ways" (2013, 1). Alana's birth narrative does not show the moment of crowning, and in this way, this scene fails to challenge taboos around visual representations of childbirth. However, these panels do reference the bodily fluids that often accompany birth, forcing an encounter with the abject that does not inspire fear or disgust because the moment (and its fluids) are taken as givens, as norms, instead being marginalized or erased because they are associated with the abject.

Like Julie Doucet, Staples and Vaughan do not shy away from including what some would consider a taboo not only for women in comics but also for visual representations of childbirth in general: a laboring woman (possibly) shitting and the blood associated with childbirth. Barbara Creed, in her influential work on abjection of the female body and the maternal in the horror-film genre, contends that "images of blood, vomit, pus, shit, etc., are central to our culturally/socially constructed notions of the horrific" (1986, 51) and are thus images

Figure 1.1. Marko holding his newborn child, Hazel. (Illustrated by Fiona Staples. Saga 1 [March 14, 2012]: 4. Published by Image Comics. Permission from Image Comics.)

of abjection. Comics may show blood, vomit, excrement, and other notions of the horrific but not as they are connected to the fecund female body. Comics categorize the pregnant body as an abject body because it "violates principles of discipline and containment in that it becomes a body that bursts forth with increased mass and with various leaking fluids" (Brown 2011, 79). By including this normal excretion of bodily fluids—blood and excrement—during childbirth, *Saga* radically (re)presents the abject female reproductive body in the comic-book space. This visual, visceral representation of childbirth reworks, similar to Doucet's comics, grotesque female materiality to critique the regulatory, normative frame constructing/constraining how the female reproductive body can be portrayed. No longer is the abject female reproductive body linked to the horrific, inspiring disgust, despite the shock value of these visual depictions. Alana's excrement and Hazel's birth blood clearly link the female reproductive body with the abject, and in so doing, shift norms for female bodies in mainstream comics.

Perhaps more interesting is how these first few pages reunite the female reproductive body with the act of producing thought. Tyler and Baraitser notice that from Plato to Nietzsche, "reproductive metaphors, carefully parsed from their feminine form, are mobilized to describe capacities for producing thought, and for the engendering and reproduction of philosophy itself" (2013, 4). For example, when someone says they gave birth to an idea, they rely on a reproductive metaphor. Notably, these metaphors are separated from the female reproductive body, which suggests philosophy has "consistently eviscerated and/or appropriated women's reproductive capacities" (4). *Saga* reconnects the reproductive female body with the act of producing thought by pairing Hazel's narration about "this is how an idea becomes real" with a visual depiction of her birth. Brian Vaughan specifically speaks about pairing childbirth with the birth of an idea, remarking "that is how ideas are born. Sometimes you do not know if you are taking a shit, or if you are bringing a beautiful, 8-pound baby into the world, because they feel *very* similar" (Edgar 2014, para. 3). Instead of divorcing the reproductive metaphor inherent in birthing an idea, Staples and Vaughan link thought production with the female reproductive body and in this way valorize that body; where many comics would portray the pregnant or birthing body in abject, marginalized ways, *Saga* celebrates the female reproductive body by visually capturing its natural functions during childbirth and by attaching that body to thought creation.

Saga uses abject representation to remake the female reproductive body to a greater degree in issue 19. Upon opening the comic, one immediately encounters an up-close view of Princess Robot's crowning baby, awash in birth fluid (figure 1.2). A crowning baby surprises viewers because this view is almost always left out of visual depictions of childbirth in any given genre. Despite the rise of graphic representations of childbirth, showing a crowning baby is still considered taboo (Tyler and Baraitser 2013, 11). For example, even in the Birth Rites collection, a collection of artwork on childbirth, the image of "Terese crowning in ecstatic birth" has a shock value that has prompted curators to request the image be hidden or sequestered away. The image is currently housed in the University of Salford Midwifery Department

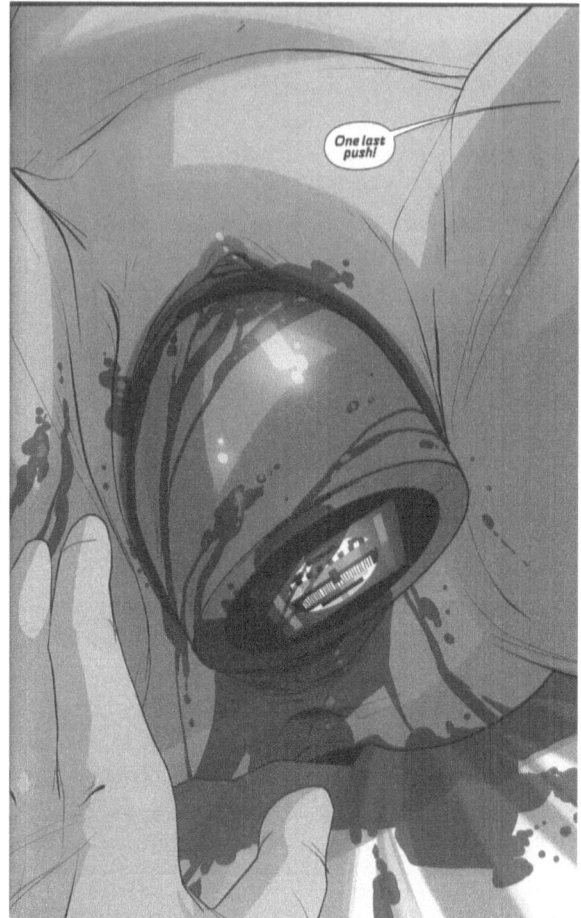

Figure 1.2. Princess Robot giving birth. (Illustrated by Fiona Staples. Saga 19 [May 21, 2014]:1. Published by Image Comics. Permission from Image Comics.)

in the United Kingdom, and even in this space, the midwives cover the emerging baby's head with Post-It notes (12–13). For some, this moment of childbirth might recall the figure of the monstrous maternal because "we don't know what, or rather who that 'thing' is" (13), while others might feel discomfort at the sight of Terese's ecstasy, a moment "disconcerting because of the double-reading of childbirth and sexual pleasure it suggests" (13). For Tyler and Baraitser, this image remakes the female reproductive body by naturalizing and normalizing an abject representation of the female reproductive body often associated with the monstrous-feminine.

Likewise, *Saga* breaks one of the major visual taboos of childbirth in illustrating the moment when the baby is crowning and by including the fluids that normally accompany that moment. To be fair, however, this baby is a robot baby instead of a human child and those birth fluids are blue instead of red, which may make this crowning view more palatable. Regardless, this view of the female reproductive body is atypical for comics, and for media in general, because it highlights those aspects of the female body media tend to make monstrous: the vagina and the womb. The vagina has been depicted as a monster with teeth, as in the 2007 film *Teeth (Lichtenstein)*, and it has been allegorically linked with the monstrous, as in medieval art illustrating a knight spearing a gaping dragon's mouth (Ussher 2006, 1). Creed links the monstrous vagina and womb with horror films like *Jaws*, *The Thing*, and *Poltergeist* because these films feature images of "the voracious maw, the mysterious black hole which threatens to give birth to equally horrific offspring as well as threaten to incorporate everything in its path" (1986, 63). If the vagina is already monstrous, the crowning child makes this space more horrific because it literally collapses the boundaries between the known and the unknown.

Yet, *Saga* provides an up-close view of this very moment, forcing an encounter with the abject female body. In choosing to portray this particular moment in childbirth, and on the opening page of an issue no less, Staples and Vaughan disrupt socially constructed taboos around visual representations of childbirth, and they disrupt hegemonic discursive practices of the comics industry. If, as Jeffrey Brown contends, the pregnant body in comics "can be monstrous precisely because it indicates a collapse between inside and outside, and self and other" (2011, 80), then *Saga*'s singular focus on a female reproductive image that visually represents that collapse has the effect of moving the abject pregnant body away from the margins. Although many comics reject, marginalize, or erase the abject from their pages, and in particular the female reproductive body, *Saga* centralizes an abject body and in the process remakes social norms that constrain what can(not) be visually shown about childbirth.

NORMALIZE BREASTFEEDING

If Kristeva's theory of abjection associates the abject with "those aspects of bodily experience which unsettle singular bodily integrity: death, decay, fluids, orifices, sex, defecation, vomiting, illness, menstruation, pregnancy, and childbirth" (Tyler 2009, 80), then the lactating body embodies the abject on a number of levels. First, the "leaking, seeping body of the new mother, milk swelling in her swollen breasts, issuing forth without restraint if she does not regularly feed her child is a further sign of women's abjection of her unruly, uncontained boundaries" (Ussher 2006, 94). Like pregnant superheroines, the lactating body is made abject in comics because it produces fluids that cross boundaries; it is not a contained, clean unit. In addition, the breastfeeding mother, in creating milk and nursing her child, emphasizes an opening that recalls pregnancy and childbirth. Breastfeeding becomes a reminder of an infant's dependency on the mother figure, when to "be born," "the child must abject the maternal body so that the child itself does not become abject by identifying with the maternal body" (Arya 2014, 18).

Furthermore, the nipple, which (along with breasts) is highly sexualized in Western culture, becomes associated with that which is abject. The muddying of the abject with the erotic has the cultural effect of producing disgust in some viewers (largely male viewers). As a result, these spectators either look away or seek to discipline the body that is disrupting their sociocultural values for performance and representation of the female body. When people (again, often men) shame women for breastfeeding in public, they not only reveal that breastfeeding uncovered and in public is coded as abject, they affirm Tyler's claim that making abject the female reproductive body has repercussions in real-world situations. For Tyler (2009), it becomes acceptable to enact a certain level of violence and abuse on these women's bodies. However, sociocultural norms that shun women nursing uncovered in public spaces have come under fire in recent years, sparking the #normalizebreastfeeding movement. This movement has helped make public, uncovered breastfeeding more socially acceptable, with the social media hashtag, #normalizebreastfeeding, tagging a number of photos, memes, inspirational sayings, and anecdotes about breastfeeding in public. These visual depictions of breastfeeding disrupt cultural norms that shun or socially discipline women who breastfeed in public. *Saga* has become a part of that movement in featuring a breastfeeding superheroine on the cover of its very first issue.

As the pregnant female body is made abject in mainstream comics, particularly in superhero comics, so too is the lactating body. Typically, women in comics are not visually depicted breastfeeding their children, although there are a few exceptions. For example, a 1985 issue of *Sabre* shows the main female character, Melissa, breastfeeding in front of the main male character, Sabre (McGregor et al. 1985). Not only is her nipple exposed, but Sabre comments that "these guys [babies] are the lucky ones," and "looks good to me," signaling his acceptance of public breastfeeding (1). In Frank Miller's *Batman: Dark Knight III: The Master Race*, readers also see Wonder Woman breastfeeding her son. What makes this reproductive representation atypical for comics is that Wonder Woman's full nipple is shown, albeit in shadow. More recently, Jessica Drew (Spider-Woman) publicly breastfeeds her child without exposing her nipple, but readers do see pumped and bottled breastmilk, and the abjection attached to that milk is a highly unusual representation for a mainstream Marvel comic series. These depictions of breastfeeding in *Sabre*, *Dark Knight III*, and *Spider-Woman* normalize public breastfeeding for a medium known for eliding female reproductive bodies, and yet, such representations are rare in comics. *Saga* is adding to this small list of mainstream comic books that represent breastfeeding, and this comic specifically normalizes breastfeeding through abject visual representation, as evidenced on the cover of their first issue, in some of the early pages of this same issue, and on the hardcover trade paperback cover.

Alana's pose on the cover of the first issue shows her casually breastfeeding Hazel as she is holding a pistol in her other hand (figure 1.3). She is not passive and vulnerable while breastfeeding but in an active pose and able to both nurse her child and fend off an attack. In other words, she is not a sex object incapable of action but a maternal figure capable of caring for herself and her offspring. She is not pictured in a serene setting, quietly nursing her child away from public eyes, considered the "ideal" breastfeeding scenario in Western culture. Staples and Vaughan challenge industry norms in visually representing breastfeeding, and they further push at these norms by illustrating a fierce, independent maternal figure as opposed to a submissive, passive one. To be fair, as far as images of public breastfeeding are concerned, this one is modest. Alana is not covering her breast entirely, but the viewer sees no nipple and they certainly do not see any fluid. According to Rina Arya, "The sight of a woman breastfeeding in public is still widely viewed as abhorrent, and if tolerated, as a practice needing to be discretely conducted, with the nipple, and the abject bodily fluid, the breast milk, most definitely concealed" (2014, 94). In a way, this breastfeeding image is not as abject as it could be in that it keeps discreet the most abject elements of breastfeeding: the nipple and the fluid. Yet, while this comic cover may be tolerable for some, many found it unsettling.

Despite being a more palatable image of public breastfeeding, this image disrupts discursive norms for reproductive bodies in the comics medium, and as a result has sparked controversy. Dave Dorman, an illustrator whose work includes covers for *Heavy Metal*, *Star Wars*, and

Figure 1.3. Alana holding Hazel alongside Hazel's father, Marko. (Illustrated by Fiona Staples. Saga 1 [March 14, 2012]: Cover. Published by Image Comics. Permission from Image Comics.)

Aliens, found the cover offensive, commenting on his blog that "it seems that in today's desperate-for-sales comic book market, nothing is sacred. In the midst of world-saving adventures, today's modern heroine breast feeds her child with zero modesty" (Melrose 2012, para. 1). This statement reveals much about cultural attitudes toward public, uncovered breastfeeding. Notice that Dorman not only attaches religious rhetoric to breastfeeding in using words like sacred and modesty but he also uses such rhetoric to chastise Staples and Vaughan. He sees them as using breastfeeding to sell comic books and, in the process, make immodest the modern superheroine. He defines immodesty as showing a partial breast during breastfeeding, and yet he has illustrated several pieces that eroticize women's breasts by making them the center of the image, barely clothing them, and connecting them to a sexualized pose or facial expression. Apparently, there is nothing immodest about using women's breasts to satisfy the male, heterosexual gaze; it is only in connecting a woman's breasts to her reproductive function that they somehow become immodest, or better yet, abject. And he is not the only one to take offense, as many comic book stores refused to rack this first issue on their shelves, or they covered it or turned it over. Again, this move is more surprising considering that comic book stores proudly display comics with covers that hypersexualize women and draw attention to their sexualized parts.

Saga's artist Fiona Staples personally answered Dorman's comments with "I find it a little hard to fathom why anyone would object to a depiction of breastfeeding" (Wheeler 2012, para. 4). Both Staples and Vaughan responded to Dorman in a more public, visual way when they released their hardcover *Saga Deluxe Edition, Book One*, which collects the first three trade paperbacks, or issues 1–18. As Vaughan explains in an interview with *Verge*, he and Staples decided to "have the most gigantic, in-your-face Hazel breastfeeding" (Duhaime-Ross 2014, para. 6) for the cover of this collection (figure 1.4). As this statement reveals, they intended this image be disruptive, to challenge norms for how the female reproductive body can be portrayed. Noticeably, they show more breast in this image than they do in the image for the cover for issue 1—it dominates a quarter of the cover page. They chose a more revealing view of breastfeeding to emphasize the abject while refusing to apologize for its appearance in their comic. Similar to the up-close view of Princess Robot giving birth, Staples and Vaughan's images zoom in on a taboo, abject visual representation of the female reproductive body, and they do so as a means of critiquing comics' portrayal of female bodies.

These two covers alone challenge comic-industry norms for the female body, but Staples and Vaughan further contest these boundaries in the early pages of issue 1. Immediately following the birth of Hazel are panels showing Alana breastfeeding (figure 1.5). In addition to breastfeeding uncovered in public, Alana even reveals her entire breast as she prepares to breastfeed Hazel. In panel 3 we see the nipple, and panel 4 zooms in for a closer view. Visually representing a woman breastfeeding uncovered in public is unusual for mainstream comics, but to show her nipple in direct association with its reproductive function is downright taboo for this medium. In comics, women's breasts are

Figure 1.4. Hazel breastfeeding. (Illustrated by Fiona Staples. Saga, Deluxe Edition, 1 [November 19, 2014]: Cover. Published by Image Comics. Permission from Image Comics.)

almost always sexualized, but *Saga*'s view takes a sexual object and makes it abject and in the process remakes the female reproductive body in this discourse. In her article that analyzes representations of breastfeeding in prime-time fictional television, Katherine Foss notices that "most breastfeeding representations consisted of a mother calmly nursing her newborn, at home or in the hospital, covered by a blanket or clothing" (2013, 334). What is more, "in the six portrayals in which women nurse in public, their actions are heavily criticized and conveyed as inappropriate" (334). Overall, Foss's study suggests that breastfeeding is socially coded as normal and abnormal depending on the mother's location or

Figure 1.5. Alana breastfeeding Hazel. (Illustrated by Fiona Staples. Saga *1 [March 14, 2012]: 5. Published by Image Comics. Permission from Image Comics.)*

level of exposure. When women were covered or in a private space, their nursing was deemed beautiful and natural, but when characters in the television shows were nursing in public and/or uncovered, they were portrayed as deviant or inappropriate. If breastfeeding in public and uncovered is socially taboo for prime-time television, how much more so is it for a genre that showcases breasts as sexual objects only? In visually representing breastfeeding as they do, Staples and Vaughan question social norms attached to nursing and, in the process, radically remake the female reproductive body, suggesting these bodies are appropriate and beautiful in their reproductive form.

REMAKING MISCARRIAGE

Readers familiar with *Saga* have come to expect surprising, and somewhat shocking, images and storylines from this series, but perhaps most unexpected is Alana's miscarriage at the end of issue 42. Alana is pregnant with her second child, but when her ship is violently knocked sideways midlaunch, she is thrown against a wall and afterward no longer feels the fetus moving. Readers hoped that the baby was still alive, but later issues proved this was not the case. Instead, Alana travels to a distant planet where she can obtain an abortion because she is far enough along in her pregnancy that she needs to have the deceased fetus removed. She travels to the Badlands after Abortion Town turns her away, and once there, an upright, dog-like creature with long, bloody fingers removes the dead baby from Alana.

While the comic offers commentary on abortion rights, especially in situating Alana next to an elephant character who has recently had an abortion for nonmedical reasons, more pertinent to this essay is *Saga*'s treatment of miscarriage. Miscarriage is not common in comics, but it is not entirely uncommon either, especially in superhero(ine) comics in which it is more convenient for characters to be childless. In the 2014 comic *Batman Beyond 2.0*, Barbara (Batgirl) discovers she is pregnant with Bruce Wayne's (Batman's) child, only to have a miscarriage by the end of the issue (Higgins et al. 2014); ultimately, this miscarriage quickly resolves the anger Dick Grayson (Robin) feels toward Bruce for sleeping with Barbara, and the writers avoid storylines that include superhero(ine)es and their children. In a different DC comic, Linda Park, an investigative reporter and wife to The Flash, miscarries twins when The Flash and Zoom battle in issue 199, but when The Flash and Zoom travel back in time in issue 225, Linda is protected from Zoom's blast. As a result, her pregnancy is miraculously restored, and she gives birth a few panels later. The miscarriage is erased, as is Linda's nine-month pregnancy. In contrast, Alana is pregnant over a swath of *Saga* issues, and she carries within her person her dead child across four issues of the series. This representation of miscarriage is an abject one, but instead of maligning such bodies, *Saga* remakes the female reproductive body by making it both abject and powerful.

In showing Alana carrying her dead child within her body over time and space, Staples and Vaughan make an abject figure the focal point of the comic series. Alana is an ambiguous reproductive body, neither subject nor object, and thus she is abject. No separation or clear-cut border exists between Alana and the child, and Alana and death. Alana is pregnant, but she is not. She is carrying a child, but it is dead. She has miscarried, and yet she continues to carry. She is contradiction without resolution, and it is this ambiguity that most disturbs our systems of order and knowing. As Kristeva reminds us, "Abjection is above all ambiguity" (1982, 9), and what causes abjection is "what disturbs identity, system, order. What does not respect borders, positions, rules. The in-between, the ambiguous, the composite" (4). In making Alana such an indefinite and borderline figure, Staples and Vaughan increase the abjection attached to their superheroine.

Alana is further linked to the abject in being both pregnant and in carrying death in her body. She refers to herself at one point as "a fucking coffin" (Staples and Vaughan 2017b, issue 43, 10), enclosing a corpse within her own person. Kristeva explains that the "corpse, without God and outside science, is the utmost of abjection. It is death infecting life" (1982, 4), which is what is happening to Alana. While readers do not see the corpse of the dead child, they know Alana is carrying a corpse, which adds another layer of abjection onto her person, her body—she is abject as pregnant and as a "coffin." Add to these layers the fact that Alana also projectile vomits a black liquid in issue 3, signaling she needs to have the dead fetus removed before it kills her. Vomit, like excrement and blood, are abject because they traverse the boundary of the body (Kristeva 1982, 69), and the black color of Alana's vomit only intensifies readers' revulsion. Thus, Alana is pregnant, carrying a corpse in her body, and spewing black bile, all of which make this female reproductive body most abject, and yet Staples and Vaughan remake such bodies for the comics medium by showing their power, quite literally.

As Alana is traveling to the Badlands to obtain an abortion, she and her traveling party are attacked by dung people, and at the moment they are about to be overtaken, Alana suddenly shoots magic out of her hands, decimating the dung people. Everyone is surprised, and the issue ends with Alana asking "Wait, what?" because her people have wings and are not spellcasters like her husband's people. In the following issue, readers learn Alana has gained the power from the dead child, who would have inherited both wings and magical abilities from his parents. Not only is Alana a central, abject figure in a mainstream comic series, she actually gains strength from her miscarriage, a point reinforced by the narrative text that accompanies Alana's defeat of the dung people. It reads, "Here's the thing about miscarriages. They are painful, they are horrific, and they are very, very common. . . . But while a miscarriage may feel like the end of the world . . . it's actually just the beginning of a new one" (Staples and Vaughan 2017b, issue 43, 20–22).

Other comic superheroines have gained power from their pregnancies, like Powergirl, who, while pregnant, produces a magical protective shield and bubble, respectively, but in that instance, a live child equals supernatural powers. In contrast, *Saga* shows the *loss of life* as positive and powerful, and in recasting miscarriage as such, it reworks female reproductive bodies through abject, visual representations.

In addition to possessing supernatural abilities as a result of her miscarriage, Alana also projects her dead child, Kurti, as he would appear if he were the same age as her daughter, Hazel, who at this point in the series is probably six to eight years old. Projecting Kurti drains Alana's energy, and she faints at one point, but in seeing her son, Alana also struggles with having the abortion. She senses that removing Kurti from her body will result in the disappearance of his projection, and it would mean losing him all over again. In fact, readers know the abortion Alana undergoes is successful, not because the removal of the fetus is shown but because, over the course of five panels, the Kurti projection gradually disappears. Showing Alana's abortion from this poignant perspective is more emotional than it is abject because Alana's body is not the focal point. No longer pregnant, and no longer carrying a corpse, Alana is no longer abject, but this shift occurs only after her extreme abjection has reworked norms for female reproductive bodies in mainstream comics.

Saga is not the only recent comic series to challenge norms for the female reproductive body. In 2016, *Spider-Woman: Shifting Gears, Volume 1: Baby Talk*, by Dennis Hopeless (w) and Javier Rodriguez (a), had a heavily pregnant Jessica Drew on the cover, and on the first issue no less. Drew, a private investigator and a superheroine, struggles with being a first-time mother, showing the realities and imperfections of superheroine mothers without making them abject. Although this Marvel comic does not show a vaginal view of Jessica's child being born, it does show her breastfeeding the newborn. Including a pregnant, breastfeeding superheroine in a mainstream comic series challenges industry norms for female reproductive bodies, and that disruption is made apparent in fans' responses to *Spider-Woman*.

In a discussion forum titled "Really Marvel? A Pregnant Superhero?" on ComicVine, a user-created comic encyclopedia site, readers reveal their resistance to a pregnant superheroine. Comments like "marvel comics are going down the drain," "she's already a bad mother," "all they need now is a transgender superhero," and "marvel is just starting to shit out any content that can be seen as progressive, politically correct, or just flat out pandering to anyone who isn't white or a male," highlight some readers' opposition toward a pregnant superheroine on a mainstream comic cover ("Really Marvel?," n.d.). One commenter suggests the writer must have brain cancer to write Jessica Drew as pregnant, and when one person asks, "What happened to Marvel," another responds with "SJWs have attacked them," with SJW standing for social justice warrior. These fans see their medium and the Marvel brand as under attack from liberal, progressive social views, and for them, showing a pregnant superheroine panders to such liberalism. This problematic online discussion of a pregnant superheroine indicates that while norms for the female reproductive body are in the process of being remade, that process is ongoing—after all, comic-industry norms do not change overnight.

Norms are in flux, and as a result, many comics simultaneously uphold and undermine social values regarding female reproductive bodies. Comics are ideologically bound, freighted with the values of the society that produces them. These values, not surprisingly, extend to women's bodies, which comics are notorious for representing in sexually objectified ways. In particular, comics often present the female reproductive body and maternal figures as abject and monstrous, but comics like *Saga* are working to change that norm. By visually illustrating childbirth, breastfeeding, and miscarriage, Staples and Vaughan emphasize and normalize the female reproductive body. In these moments, *Saga* subverts sociocultural norms around pregnant, laboring, lactating, and miscarrying bodies, showing what possibilities yet remain for representing women's bodies in comics.

WORKS CITED

Arya, Rina. 2014. *Abjection and Representation: An Exploration of Abjection in the Visual Arts, Film and Literature.* London: Palgrave Macmillan.

Brown, Jeffrey A. 2011. "Supermoms? Maternity and the Monstrous-Feminine in Superhero Comics." *Journal of Graphic Novels and Comics* 2 (1): 77–87.

Creed, Barbara. 1986. "Horror and the Monstrous-Feminine: An Imaginary Abjection." *Screen* 27 (1): 44–71.

D'Amore, Laura Mattoon. 2012. "The Accidental Supermom: Superheroines and Maternal Performativity, 1963–1980." *Journal of Popular Culture* 45 (6): 1226–33.

Duhaime-Ross, Arielle. 2014. "Listen as Writer Brian K. Vaughan Talks to Us about Comics, Gaming, and *Star Wars.*" The Verge, December 18. https://www.theverge.com/2014/12/18/7415049/saga-comic-brian-k-vaughan-author-comics. Accessed 17 January 2021.

Edgar, Sean. 2014. "*Saga*: Sex, Robots, & Rockets—The Birth of the Sci-Fi Epic." Paste, January 3. https://www.pastemagazine.com/articles/2014/01/saga-sex-robots-rocketsthe-birth-of-a-sci-fi-epic-1.html. Accessed 17 January 2021.

Foss, Katherine A. 2013. " 'That's Not a Bear Bong, It's a Breast Pump!': Representations of Breastfeeding in Prime-Time Fictional Television." *Health Communication* 28 (4): 329–40.

Grosz, Elizabeth. 1990. "The Body of Signification." In *Abjection, Melancholia, and Love: The Work of Julia Kristeva*, edited by John Fletcher and Andrew Benjamin. Abingdon, Oxfordshire: Routledge, 80–104.
The Hawkeye Initiative. 2012. http://thehawkeyeinitiative.com/. Accessed 17 January 2021.
Higgins, Kyle (w), Alec Siegel (w), Phil Hester (p), Eric Gasptur (i), and Craig Rousseau (a). 2014. *Batman Beyond 2.0: Mark of the Phantasm* 28. DC Comics.
Hopeless, Dennis (w), and Javier Rodriguez (a). 2016. *Spider-Woman: Shifting Gears, Volume 1: Baby Talk*. New York: Marvel.
Johnston, Lynn. 1989. *A Look Inside For Better or For Worse: The Tenth Anniversary Collection*. Kansas City, MO: Andrews McMeel.
Johnston, Lynn. 1983. *It Must Be Nice to be Little: A For Better or for Worse Collection*. Kansas City, MO: Andrews McMeel.
Johnston, Lynn. 1981. *I've Got the One-More-Washload Blues*. Kansas City, MO: Andrews McMeel.
Køhlert, Frederik Byrn. 2012. "Female Grotesques: Carnivalesque Subversion in the Comics of Julie Doucet." *Journal of Graphic Novels and Comics* 3 (1): 19–38.
Kristeva, Julia. 1982. *Powers of Horror: An Essay on Abjection*. Translated by Leon S. Roudiez. New York: Columbia University Press.
Lichtenstein, Mitchell, dir. 2007. *Teeth*. Santa Monica, CA: Lionsgate.
Lyvely, Chin, and Joyce Farmer Chevley. 1973. *Abortion Eve*. Laguna Beach, CA: Nanny Goat Productions.
McGregor, Don F. (w), Juan Ortiz (p, i), Candy DeWalt (c), Rene Reynolds (c), and Pete Iro (l). 1985. *Sabre: The Decadence Indoctrination Part 3—Miscellaneous Defenses* 1 (12). Guerneville, CA: Eclipse Comics.
Melrose, Kevin. 2012. "Quote of the Day: Dave Dorman Takes Offense at *Saga* Art." CBR.com, January 9. https://www.cbr.com/quote-of-the-day-dave-dorman-takes-offense-at-saga-art/. Accessed 17 January 2021.
Miller, Frank (w, a), Brian Azzarello (w), Andy Kubert (p), Klaus Jansen (i), Brad Anderson (c), and Clem Robbins (l). 2017. *Batman: Dark Knight III—The Master Race*. Burbank, CA: DC Comics.
O'Brien, Annamarie. 2014. "How Can I Refuse You, Mother Box?!' Abjection and Objectification of Motherhood in Jack Kirby's *Fourth World*." *ImageTexT* 7 (4). http://imagetext.english.ufl.edu/archives/v7_4/obrien/. Accessed 17 January 2021.
"Really Marvel? A Pregnant Superhero?" n.d. ComicVine. Accessed 15 August 2017. https://comicvine.gamespot.com/forums/gen-discussion-1/really-marvel-a-pregnant-superhero-1687665/. Accessed 17 January 2021.
Scott, Suzanne. 2015. "*The Hawkeye Initiative*: Pinning Down Transformative Feminisms in Comic-Book Culture through Superhero Crossplay Fan Art." *Cinema Journal* 55 (2): 150–60.
Staples, Fiona (a), and Brian K. Vaughan (w). 2017a. *Saga* 7 (37–42). Portland, OR: Image Comics.
Staples, Fiona (a), and Brian K. Vaughan (w). 2017b. *Saga* 8 (43, 44, 45). Portland, OR: Image Comics.
Stuller, Jennifer K. 2012. "Feminism: Second-Wave Feminism in the Pages of *Lois Lane*." In *Critical Approaches to Comics: Theories and Methods*, edited by Matthew J. Smith and Randy Duncan, 235–51. New York: Routledge.
Tyler, Imogen. 2009. "Against Abjection." *Feminist Theory* 10 (1): 77–98.
Tyler, Imogen, and Lisa Baraitser. 2013. "Private Views, Public Birth: Making Feminist Sense of the New Visual Culture of Childbirth." *Studies in the Maternal* 5 (1): 1–27. https://www.mamsie.bbk.ac.uk/articles/abstract/10.16995/sim.18/. Accessed 17 January 2021.

Ussher, Jane M. 2006. *Managing the Monstrous Feminine: Regulating the Reproductive Body*. Abingdon, Oxfordshire: Routledge.

Vaughan, Brian K. (w), and Fiona Staples (i). 2013. *Saga* 1 (1–6). Portland, OR: Image Comics.

Wheeler, Andrew. 2012. "Saga Artist Fiona Staples Responds to Dave Dorman Criticism of Breastfeeding Cover." *Comics Alliance*, February 20. https://comicsalliance.com/saga-fiona-staples-dave-dorman-breastfeeding/. Accessed 17 January 2021.

2

THE WOMAN RHETOR AND HER BODY
A Case-Study Analysis of How a Feminist Zinester Constructs Ethos as Corporeal Experiential Authority

Christine Martorana

I am a "Badass Breastfeeding, Babywearing ... Mama," Ashley "Tiyumba" Wright writes on her blog Ms. Wright's Way, and her Instagram page lives up to this self-proclaimed title. On August 7, 2019, for instance, Wright shared two of her breastfeeding photos—her nipples and breasts exposed in both—along with the following caption: "I've never felt more powerful, more present, more grateful . . . more God! For those who doubt themselves, for those who are afraid, allow me to be an example, a testimony, a reason even, for you to nip it out and be proud!"

I have a "quivering belly [and] gelatinous arm fat," Jessamyn Stanley writes, and her 2017 book *Every Body Yoga: Let Go of Fear, Get on the Mat, Love Your Body* keeps this observation central. The cover of the book features Stanley practicing yoga dressed in only a sports bra and underwear, a visual illustration of the book's main claim: any person with any body can do yoga. Throughout the book, Stanley supports this claim through her own firsthand experiences as a "yoga enthusiast and fat femme," the end goal of which is to give her readers "all the tools and supplies that will light up [their] own practice" (7).

Although two different people with two different messages, Wright and Stanley offer examples of what I call *corporeal experiential authority*. As I explain throughout this chapter, corporeal experiential authority is a specific form of ethos in which credibility is cultivated through the strategic presentation of firsthand experiences of the physical body. To help us fully understand corporeal experiential authority, I make three moves. First, I define and situate my use of the terms *ethos* and *corporeal experiential authority*. Second, I present a case-study analysis of the feminist zine *Here. In My Head*, offering specific examples from the zine pages to illustrate corporeal experiential authority in action. Here, I spotlight the potential for corporeal experiential authority to

DOI: 10.7330/9781646420384.c002

stem from two types of physical experiences: past and present. Finally, I consider what this analysis suggests in terms of feminist re-visionings of ethos and our understanding of the rhetorical strategies available to feminist rhetors.

SITUATING TERMS: ETHOS AND CORPOREAL EXPERIENTIAL AUTHORITY

In order to understand my conceptualization of corporeal experiential authority as a specific form of ethos in which credibility is cultivated through the strategic presentation of first-hand experiences of the physical body, it is first necessary to understand my use of the term *ethos*. In line with other feminist scholars, I define ethos as a responsive self-presentation. To acknowledge ethos as self-presentation is to recognize ethos begins with a devoted attention to the self. Feminist scholar Sonia Johnson expresses a similar sentiment: "I want compassion and generosity, first from myself. If I can understand and love myself, I will be merciful and loving to others" (1989, 107). From this perspective, it is only by tending to the self that a rhetor can be responsive to those around her. She must begin with "an awareness about and self-reflection on [her] status and experiences as [a] wom[a]n" (Foss and Foss 1991, 26). In first acknowledging her own situatedness, what Nedra Reynolds describes as "being responsible [with one's own] identities, positions, or locations" (1993, 330), the rhetor can effectively respond to the specific context in which she finds herself. This context includes her audience, their expectations, and their values; thus, when a rhetor's decisions and perspectives align with those of her audience, she can construct for herself a credible ethos. Ethos, then, is not only a self-presentation comprised of "personal rhetorical negotiations" (Harrison 2003, 244). It is also a *responsive* self-presentation, dependent upon a "relationship with one's audience" (Ronald 1990, 38) and the effectiveness with which a rhetor presents herself to that audience.

This is true of ethos writ large; it is also true of ethos within zines specifically. As Brenda Helmbrecht and Meredith Love explain, "Zines develop several different types of ethos, or ethe" (2009, 152), including what they identify as the "Sassy Sexy Ethos" (156), the "Socially Active Ethos" (158), and the "Ethos of Chic Domesticity" (159). While these ethotic constructions are intriguing and valuable for what they suggest about the woman rhetor, none of them specifically focuses upon the potential for the zinester's physical body to explicitly impact ethos formation. Thus, my analysis builds upon the discussion started by Helmbrecht and Love by suggesting an additional ethos produced within zines, one that brings the woman's physicality to the fore. I call this the *ethos of corporeal experiential authority*, a type of ethos cultivated when a rhetor explicitly and strategically references the firsthand experiences of the physical body as a means of connecting and building credibility with her audience. For the woman rhetor navigating a patriarchal culture that regularly degrades and disempowers the woman's physical body, this ethotic construction offers an especially significant source of authority.

HERE. IN MY HEAD

To illustrate this corporeal experiential authority in action, I present a case study analysis of *Here. In My Head*, a feminist zine written by Catherine (Cath) Elms. *Here. In My Head* contains eighteen issues, each approximately twenty-five to forty pages long and focused on Cath's personal experiences with a variety of topics ranging from shyness and sex to misogyny and antifeminism (figure 2.1). Given the ephemeral nature of zines, the first three zines were inaccessible when I discovered *Here. In My Head*; however, I was able to obtain issues 4–13 for my analysis.[1] Thus, my discussion of corporeal experiential authority is based on an in-depth exploration of these zine issues along with the firsthand interview I conducted with Cath.

My decision to focus on zines and this particular zine is purposeful. I agree with Adela Licona's observation that "zines . . . have much to teach us about re-presentations of self" (2005, 110). Whereas more mainstream texts must answer to "the gatekeepers of the traditional publishing marketplace [such as] editors [and] publishers" (Piepmeier 2009, 13), zines exist outside this realm. Zines are self-published texts in which the zinester maintains control over the presentations put forth. Accordingly, when the zinester is a woman, the "re-presentations of self" can lead to especially valuable insights regarding the construction and implementation of women's ethos.

Zine scholars agree that one defining characteristic of the zine medium is its intimate connection to the zinester's physical body. In her discussion of girl zines, for instance, Alison Piepmeier terms this characteristic a "hand-made quality" (2009, 70), describing the ways the handwritten words, scribbles, drawings, and stapled pages "threaten conventional boundaries" (73) that traditionally keep the writer at a distance from her audience. Mary Celeste Kearney agrees, highlighting the ways zines profess an "amateurist spirit" (2006, 163) that makes

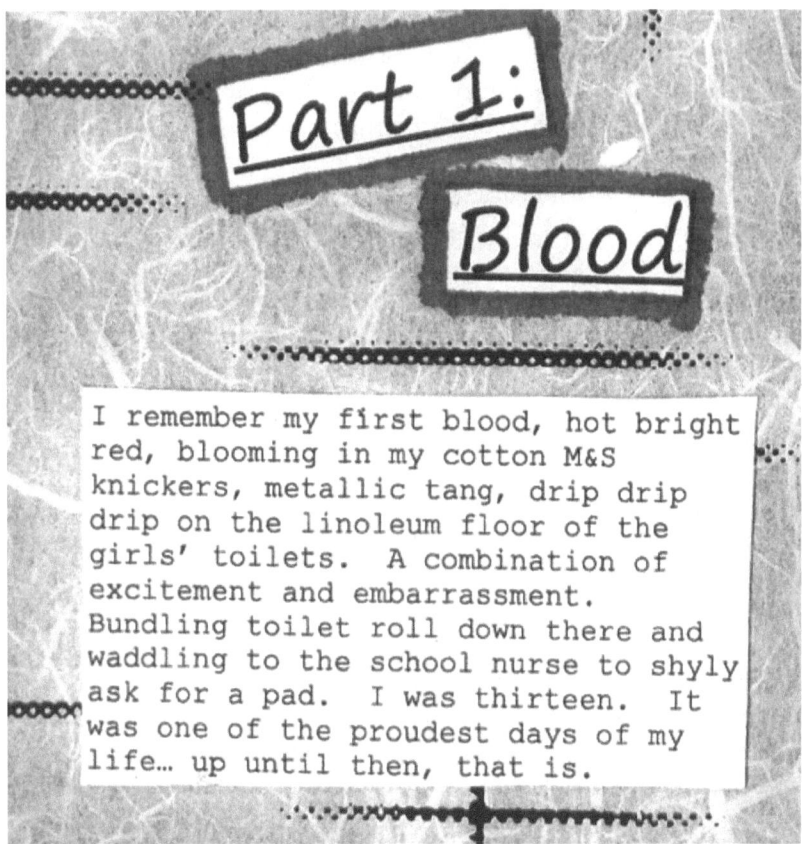

Figure 2.1. In Here. In My Head zine issue 8, Cath describes her early experiences with menstruation. (Permission of and photo by Catherine Elms.)

visible the zinester's physical body, and Anne Hays describes the ways the feminist zine "capture[s] aspects of the self" (2017, 106). Given this unmistakable connection between the zinester's body and her zine, zines offer a prime site for conceptualizing corporeal experiential authority—that is, authority rooted in the firsthand experiences of the rhetor's physical body.

More specifically, and as my analysis shows, one specific subgenre of the zine that allows us to more fully understand corporeal experiential authority is the perzine. The perzine is "a sub-genre of zines, coined by contracting 'personal' and 'zine.'" In perzines, zinesters focus explicitly on "their own personal experiences, opinions, and observations" (ZineWiki). Thus, while most zines do privilege the zinester's physical body in aesthetics, as both Piepmeier and Kearney point out, not all zines do so in content. Perzines, however, are characterized by the personal focus of their content. It is this personal focus on the firsthand experiences of the zinester that turns a zine into a perzine.

Here. In My Head is a feminist perzine: a zine with an explicit dual focus that is both personal and feminist. Cath explains, "My zines are a creative outlet, a free and accessible way . . . to express my thoughts and feelings, and a place to express ideas about being a woman and a feminist that might be new to other people" (Elms 2014). While Cath does use her perzine as an outlet for self-expression, this in and of itself is not the focus of my analysis. Rather, I invite a consideration of the ways Cath makes explicit and observable the experiences of her physical body as a means of discursively presenting herself as a credible and knowledgeable rhetor. This is evidenced within *Here. In My Head* when Cath spotlights the physical experiences of her body and then uses this physicality as justification for the advice she offers her readers. In so doing, she presents the woman's physical body as a legitimate source of authority and knowledge, not just a body on display. In moving from the self outward, first by referencing her own physicality and then by attending to the physicality of her readers, Cath constructs a corporeal experiential authority, a specific type of ethos that takes two distinct forms.

The first form is corporeal experiential authority constructed from past firsthand, physical experiences. For instance, in zine issue 8, Cath goes into explicit detail about her early experiences with menstruation. She writes, "I remember my first blood, hot bright red, blooming in my cotton M&S knickers, metallic tang, drip drip drip on the linoleum floor of the girls' toilets. A combination of excitement and embarrassment. Bundling toilet roll down there and waddling to the school nurse to shyly ask for a pad. I was thirteen. It was one of the proudest days of my life" (figure 2.1). Throughout the following pages of zine issue 8, Cath goes on to describe the intimate experience of approaching the school nurse for a feminine pad. She remembers, "She gave me one without much fuss—no questions, just the business. The thick pad wagging between my legs, I walked down the hallway with a strange combination of shame and defiance—I worried that people would notice that I was bleeding, but was also strangely proud of the fact that they might notice." Here, Cath's firsthand, physical experiences supply the content for her zine. She begins with a devoted attention to the self, her own experiences with dripping blood and feelings of "shame and defiance"—experiences unmistakably rooted in the physicality of her body.

This is not all she does, however. Next, Cath turns her attention outward, to her readers, offering advice regarding how her readers might conceive of their own menstruations. Later in zine issue 8, Cath tells her readers to remember that "menstruation is not bad and it is not dirty. . . . It is not an illness or a disability either." She then speaks directly to her readers and their physical bodies, encouraging them to "love your vagina, and love your period!" In so doing, Cath embraces what I earlier describe as a responsive self-presentation, strategically shifting the focus from her physical body to that of her reader, constructing and acting upon a corporeal experiential authority in two distinct steps. First, she explicitly emphasizes the physicality of her own body—her blood, the pain in her stomach, her vagina—and second, she uses these references to respond to her audience, presenting herself as a credible voice through which she can connect with her audience and offer them advice and ideas regarding their own physical bodies.

A similar example of Cath using the physical experences from her past to construct a corporeal experiential authority emerges in Cath's recollection of a self-esteem workshop she attended. In zine issue 5, she shares, "I recently went to a self-esteem workshop, and one of the exercises we had to do was to introduce ourselves by saying, 'My name is [full name] and I'm awesome/great/fantastic/etc.' I nearly cried while doing that exercise—everyone else was getting into the swing of it and shaking people's hands firmly, declaring proudly 'My name is George, and I'm awesome,' but I couldn't bring myself to say it. I tried it once or twice, but I felt sick and ashamed."

In sharing this memory, Cath spotlights the physicality of her body, the fact that she "nearly cried" and "felt sick and ashamed" during this workshop. This focus continues as she describes her shyness as "a big black ball of yarn knotted in the pit of [her] stomach, tightening around [her] organs, making [her] feel sick and ashamed. I can't relax, I can't breathe, my heartbeat rises, my hands are sweaty, everyone in the room appears to be judging me." Similar to the ways Cath writes about her early experiences with menstruation, she brings her firsthand, physical experiences to the fore. She shares explicit bodily references—feelings deep in her stomach and the specific ways her body physically reacts. This concentrated focus on the physical self marks the beginning of Cath's construction of a corporeal experiential authority within this issue of *Here. In My Head.* That is, as a result of sharing her own firsthand, physical experiences with shyness, Cath's audience is invited to see her as capable of offering credible insights regarding shyness. Shyness is not something about which Cath merely writes; rather, it is an experience she has intimately felt, and her explicit recognition of these feelings constitutes the heart of her discussion.

Following her description of these physical experiences with shyness, Cath then makes a rhetorically savvy move: she shifts from sharing her physical experiences with shyness to offering advice to her readers regarding their shyness. She writes, "I feel I've made a significant amount of progress with my shyness in the last year or so, and I wanted to write a little about the things that I've learned." Here, Cath explicitly presents her personal, physical experiences with shyness as the basis for the specific pieces of advice she will offer. Her tips include being honest about feeling nervous, engaging in conversations nonverbally, and remembering that "you are an interesting and smart person, and deserve to be acknowledged just as much as everyone else in the room." Just as she did when discussing her menstruation, Cath shifts the attention away from the physicality of her body to that of her reader. Since she has shared her personal, embodied experiences with shyness within the pages of zine 5, she is able to credibly offer these pieces of advice to her readers and invite them to reflect on their own experiences. In fact, Cath specifically credits her firsthand, physical experiences for authorizing her to offer advice to her readers. "The advice is all easier said than done," she writes, "but something to bear in mind. I had to experience these things first-hand before I really believed them!"

Similar to sharing her early menstruation experiences, Cath calls upon her experiences with shyness to show the ways firsthand, physical experiences from the past can offer a source of credibility. Put simply, by spotlighting the intimate details of past physical experiences and then using these experiences to establish points of audience connection, the rhetor can construct a corporeal experiential authority. For Cath, these experiences include menstruation and shyness.

However, corporeal experiential authority is not limited to reflections on the past. It can also stem from present-day circumstances within the rhetor's life, experiences the rhetor is in the midst of rather than those she has moved beyond. Thus, the second form of corporeal experiential authority visible within *Here. In My Head* is a corporeal experiential authority based in the present.

For instance, in zine issue 7, Cath shares her personal struggles negotiating social beauty norms and standards. More specifically, she spotlights her internal, physical feelings regarding the expectations attached to her external, physical appearance and the insecurities she feels as a result. Cath writes, "When I lived in a flat full of women in my first year [away at school], beautifying [our]selves was a kind of ritual before a night out—an afternoon nap, followed by a long shower, a little 'fashion show' where [we'd] preview [our] outfits so the rest of us could help choose the best one. Then [we'd] do [our] hair, make-up, and fake tan, all of which would take at least an hour. . . . If I'm honest, I enjoyed it the first few times I got involved. But then again . . . there was something that made me feel quite uncomfortable about it all—the way we all put ourselves down, berating ourselves for not being as thin or as pretty or as well-dressed as the others were." In this reflection, Cath spotlights her physical reaction to this nightly ritual, the fact that this experience with her girlfriends made her "feel quite uncomfortable."

Several pages later, Cath admits this is not just an episode from her past; rather, it is something with which she continues to struggle. She writes, "There is a huge social pressure to be beautiful . . . and there are penalties if we don't adhere. Some women are strong enough to deal with this, but I'm certainly not." No longer is Cath presenting a reflection from her past. Instead, she brings the discussion to the present day, admitting she currently feels weak when it comes to negotiating the physical expectations surrounding her body. In short, this is still a situation that makes her "feel quite uncomfortable." Unlike the previous examples in which Cath uses her physical experiences with menstruation and shyness to reveal the strength and perspective she has gained, this time Cath does not explicitly project a sense of authority. Instead, she admits she still struggles with this situation, ending this section of her zine with a commitment to continue working on this area of her life: "Part of my new commitment to improving my life is to look at things critically and not merely taking them at face value, rationally evaluating what seems like the best way forward. Beauty is one of those difficult issues where I need to keep my wits about me in the face of such pressure, where there doesn't seem to be a straightforward answer." Here, Cath uses the zine space to explicitly encourage *herself* regarding a situation that is in progress rather than offer advice to *her readers* based on a situation from her past.

Yet, Cath does not remain focused on herself. Several pages later within zine 7, Cath presents a coupon targeted directly at her readers. It reads, "This coupon entitles you to an entire day without make-up, hair products, dieting, fancy clothes, and uncomfortable shoes." She goes on to suggest specific activities for her readers, including lounging around the house in knickers, reading magazines about faraway places, and finger painting. Accordingly, this coupon functions as a form of indirect advice from Cath to her readers; it acts as a permission slip, advising her readers to revise their approach to their physical appearance.

This example provides an interesting departure from the previous examples in which Cath uses her physical experiences with menstruation and shyness to construct a corporeal experiential authority and connect with her readers. When Cath shares her experiences with menstruation and shyness, she does so as a result of feeling as if she has made "a significant amount of progress" with these experiences. Her aim is "to write a little about the things that [she has] learned" so her readers might benefit and apply the lessons in their own lives. However, in sharing her experiences with the physical appearance of her body, Cath admits she is still in the midst of these struggles. She calls herself "a woman [still] in chains, [trapped by] norms that are physically and socially limiting." And yet, the current presence of her struggle does not impede her calling upon her physical experiences as a source of credibility. After this devoted attention to the self, she again turns her focus on her readers, suggesting multiple ways they might apply the personal, physical experiences she has shared to their own lives. In short, Cath calls upon her current physical experiences in much the same way she does her past physical experiences: as a source of corporeal experiential authority.

Regardless of whether the construction of this ethos stems from past or present-day happenings, there remains a consistent move from an attention on Cath's physical experiences to those of her reader. Thus, in order to fully appreciate the ways Cath constructs and acts upon a corporeal experiential authority, we must consider her specific readership. Cath identifies her intended audience as "young women, aged between 16 and 25 . . . and/or women who are struggling with mental health issues/low self-esteem/social anxiety" (Elms 2014). From this perspective, we can see that the specific physical experiences Cath shares from her own life are purposeful. Her experiences with menstruation, shyness, and physical insecurities are likely to be familiar to this specific readership. Accordingly, they provide a point of connection between Cath and her readers; they are not only firsthand, physical experiences from Cath's life but also experiences to which her readers can likely relate. Put another way, in choosing to focus on these particular firsthand experiences, Cath presents herself as a credible woman who can offer other women advice on their own similar embodied experiences. The fact that she bases this credibility on her *physical* experiences invites us to recognize the ways Cath constructs and acts upon a form of *corporeal* experiential authority, one especially effective with her specific readership.

FEMINIST RE-VISIONINGS AND RHETORICAL STRATEGIES

My analysis of Cath's use of her physical body to construct and mobilize a corporeal experiential authority has several interesting implications, including two feminist re-visionings of ethos and two specific rhetorical strategies available to feminist rhetors. The two feminist re-visionings of ethos I discuss include ethos rooted in the woman's physical body and ethos constructed from in-progress experiences—two re-visionings that effectively challenge traditional notions of ethos. Additionally, the two rhetorical strategies I spotlight include the public presentation of personal experiences and a strategy I term *selfless introspection.*

According to traditional conceptions, a person's ethos is based on their "credibility, on the speaker's securing the trust and respect of an audience by presenting him or herself . . . as knowledgeable, intelligent, [and] competent" (Cherry 1998, 389). This competence is most often based on what that person has done, past accomplishments that render the rhetor more or less credible. However, as Reynolds points out, feminist re-visionings of ethos consider the ways individuals "establish authority . . . from positions *not traditionally considered authoritative*" (1993, 326; emphasis added).

Thus, I respond to Reynolds's claim by suggesting two such feminist re-visionings. First, my analysis suggests the woman's physical body can offer a source of authoritative knowledge. However, the woman's physical body is not readily seen as a source of authority; rather, "zines contend with the oppressive effects of the social gaze in creative ways" (Licona 2005, 119). As this chapter discusses, by offering her embodied experiences as a source of authority within *Here. In My Head*, Cath presents her body as more than a passive body on display. Instead, her body becomes an active and valuable vessel, one that offers insight and knowledge beneficial to both her and her readers.

This purposeful use of the woman's physical body aligns with what Adrienne Rich calls "a politics of location." According to Rich, a politics of location is integral to "locating the grounds from which to speak with authority as women" (1994, 213). For women, she continues, a politics of location necessarily begins with a reclaiming of the physical body, with an acknowledgement that every thought and instance of speech is rooted in a "particular living human individual, a woman" (213). Thus, enacting a corporeal experiential authority can be an especially effective move for the woman rhetor. That is, through this form of ethos, the woman rhetor can engage in the purposeful reclamation of her physical body and subsequent acknowledgement of the authority that resides there. However, as Aimee Carrillo Rowe points out, it is not enough to only recognize the location of our physical bodies; we must also acknowledge the ways our physical bodies, what Rowe describes as "bod[ies] in motion" (2005, 17), are reciprocally entwined with and inseparable from communities and relations. Rowe calls her framework "a feminist politics of relation," and she explains that her intention in suggesting such an expansion of Rich's discussion is to "make community and belonging central" to our interrogation of feminist rhetorical acts (25). One way of doing so, of "locat[ing] 'location' within community," Rowe explains, is by explicitly exploring and naming the relational conditions that can move the rhetor to embrace a politics of location (19).

Given the fact that one defining characteristic of the zine medium is its creation of "intimate, affectionate connections between [zine] creators and readers" (Piepmeier 2009, 58), Rowe's "feminist politics of relation" is especially applicable to the current analysis. That is, by considering the relational conditions at work in Cath's decision to embrace a corporeal experiential authority—to present her physical body as a source of authoritative knowledge—we can begin to more fully understand the potential for community to facilitate this particular feminist re-visioning of ethos. For Cath, one community that influences *Here. In My Head* includes readers to whom she can personally relate in terms of age and life experiences. Cath envisions a readership of "young women, aged between 16 and 25 . . . and/or women who are struggling with mental health issues/low self-esteem/social anxiety" (Elms 2014). This particular conceptualization of the community within which her zines circulate certainly impacts the experiences she shares and the ways she presents her physical body. In particular, the experiences about which she writes are salient with this readership, and she depends upon this saliency when she offers advice to her readers about their own physical experiences.

As this brief example reveals, Cath's rhetorical decision to spotlight her own physical experience plays an integral role in the construction of corporeal experiential authority, but so do the physical experiences of her readers—their ability and willingness to personally relate to the experiences Cath shares. This suggests we must consider the specific location of the physical body alongside the relational conditions that surround the body if we are to account for the significant ways community can both facilitate and hinder the formation of a corporeal feminist ethos.

The second re-visioning of ethos resulting from my analysis is the recognition that authority need not be based upon past experiences or already-secured knowledge or competencies. Rather, credibility can be established in the midst of experiences still in progress. This observation aligns with that made by Anne Hays in "Reading the Margins: Embedded Narratives in Feminist Personal Zines." In this article, Hays observes that "the zine format seems to provide writers with a works-in-progress platform, in which readers do not expect a final say or final expression" (2017, 106). As Cath's zines show us, this "works-in-progress" perspective can effectively facilitate the zinester's ethotic construction.

To consider in-progress experiences as authoritative is a significant challenge to traditional notions of authority, most of which are rooted in the belief that an experience renders credibility only *after* an individual has fully moved beyond the experience. The assumption undergirding this notion is that by moving beyond an experience, the rhetor can practice "hindsight, reflection, and . . . objectivity," whereas the significance of an in-process experience "has not yet been determined or fully understood" (Foss and Foss 1991, 8). However, Cath's practices broaden our understanding of ethos, inviting us to recognize that present-day experiences offer potential sources of authority. Put simply, women rhetors need not look solely to the past for significant happenings. Rather, they can "engage in self-conscious reflection about their [current] lives as women" (6), drawing upon and sharing in-process experiences and in-progress knowledge.

We can further understand Cath's purposeful presentation of her physical, in-progress experiences through a lens offered by Hannah McGregor's discussion of feminist making. In "Feminism, Fandom, and Maker Pedagogy," McGregor recalls an interaction with a student who created a zine for her class: "When we discussed her project afterwards, she spoke of the satisfaction she experienced in *making something*. . . . She realized that it didn't matter if the zine she made looked good; what mattered was the *process of making it*" (2018). Echoed in this student's recognition is an acknowledgement of the value of the making process. From this perspective, the final appearance of the zine becomes secondary to the act of making the zine because, as McGregor later points out, "zines aren't about marketable skills but about passions."

This is an important distinction and one with direct connection to our understanding of ethos. Zines invite us to move away from the patriarchal perspective of ethos judged from the outside and instead to consider the value a woman places on her own embodied experiences. As a result of her experiences making a zine, for example, McGregor's student came to value her physical experience of creating the zine more than the end product itself. Similarly, Cath's zines present her own embodied and in-process experiences as sources of authority to her zine readers. For both women, zines offer a vehicle to reclaim the physical body.

My analysis not only spotlights two feminist re-visionings of ethos but it also draws our attention to two specific rhetorical strategies available to feminist rhetors. One such strategy is the public presentation of personal experiences. This presentation is evidenced in Cath's decision to give public presence to her experiences with menstruation, shyness, and the physical insecurities regarding her body. By discussing these particular experiences within *Here. In My Head*, Cath refuses to abide by the norms of the "patriarchal unconscious" (Bauer 1990, 392), an entrenched way of thinking that labels experiences such as these inappropriate for public expression. The patriarchal oppression of women greatly depends upon the maintenance of this public/private dichotomy, one that hides and "distort[s] the lived experiences of many people" (Sprague 2005, 14). It is this very fact that makes the public presentation of the personal such an effective strategy for feminist rhetors. That is, a strategy such as this invites the feminist rhetor to work "in direct refutation to the [very dichotomy] that render[s] [her] credibility questionable" (2015, Molloy 145). As a result, the feminist rhetor can challenge this norm while simultaneously revealing its constructedness.

We can more fully understand this rhetorical strategy by considering Aaminah Norris's discussion of hybrid places. In "Make-Her-Spaces as Hybrid Place: Designing and Resisting Self Constructions in Urban Classrooms," Norris describes her experiences working with young women in makerspaces to create handmade artifacts. As she reflects on her experiences with these women, she comes to see the makerspace classroom as a hybrid place. "Hybrid places," Norris describes, "are a fusion of both [real] places and [imagined] spaces where youth learn to develop positive self-concepts" (2014, 73). When a classroom functions as a hybrid place, students are invited to acknowledge the devaluations they experience in their lives while simultaneously making tangible artifacts that work to reframe these degradations. Norris concludes, "Hybrid places allow for marginalized students to develop more positive self-concepts by designing artistic representations of themselves and their lives" (73). Norris conceives of hybrid places as physical locations wherein people create artifacts, and I would like to extend this concept to consider the ways the artifacts themselves can function as hybrid places. More specifically, my suggestion is that the zine can act as a hybrid place—a physical text where real degradations can be reimagined into positive self-constructions. If we return to Cath's public presentation of her personal experiences, we can see the ways *Here. In My Head* functions as a hybrid place. That is, in publicly sharing her personal experiences with topics such as menstruation, shyness, and body insecurities, Cath illustrates one way of engaging with the reality of topics deemed taboo and shameful while at the same time presenting these very experiences as sources of authority. She is, in these moments, imagining herself as "positively constructed" with the pages of her zine.

A second strategy for feminist rhetors suggested by this analysis is what I am calling *selfless introspection*—engaging in self-reflection with the intention of helping others. This strategy contains valuable potential for the feminist rhetor seeking to inspire feminist action in the world around her. As explained, Cath's construction of a corporeal experiential authority begins with an attention to the self. She consciously reflects upon her own physical, embodied experiences, making these reflections manifest within *Here. In My Head*. However, this is not introspection for the sake of introspection; rather, it is what we might consider selfless introspection: self-reflection for the benefit of others.

I am not claiming Cath is completely selfless and does not derive personal benefit through the introspection that takes place within *Here. In My Head*. However, a consistent attention to audience undergirds Cath's acts of introspection, so much so that she evaluates the effectiveness of her zines based upon how much they connect with her audience. Specifically, she says, "[My zines are most effective] when people tell me they enjoyed my work, and that I made them think about a certain topic in a way that they hadn't before, or made them see something in a new light, or when people tell me they're grateful I could put into words a feeling that they previously couldn't name" (Elms 2014). It is significant that the markers Cath uses to evaluate the effectiveness of *Here. In My Head* are all audience centric, focused on the feelings, thoughts, and perspectives of those who read the zine. Accordingly, we can understand Cath's self-reflection as a form of selfless introspection, a practice of looking within in order to extend external offers of support, guidance, and/or resources. Furthermore, given that Cath understands her readership to be comprised of "young women, aged between 16 and 25 . . . and/or women who are struggling with mental health issues/low self-esteem/social anxiety," we can appreciate the ways Cath considers this specific demographic throughout her introspective acts. Put simply, she is careful to reflect upon and share experiences that will be salient with these particular readers. In so doing, she invites her readers to see themselves mirrored in her experiences and therefore capable of engaging in feminist action in their own lives.

Theresa Enos's discussion of writer/reader interaction offers a valuable perspective here regarding Cath's use of selfless introspection. According to Enos, "Writer/audience/text" is the rhetorical counterpart to "author/reader/text" (1990, 341). When a reader identifies with the writer of a text, that reader transforms into an audience—a transformation that occurs as a result of the "connectedness" (341) that forms when "all three elements of writer, audience, text" are tied together (344). Enos maintains a clear distinction between audience and reader. Audience emerges as a result of interaction between writer and reader: the "writer has projected a self [in their text] that invites the reader in, and if readers identify with this self . . . the reader actually becomes the audience" (342). In brief, Enos's analysis presents audience as a joint construct, an offspring produced by the writer and the reader. This perspective invites us to recognize the ways Cath uses her personal corporeal experiences as a means of actively engaging her readers. In turning from her own embodied experiences to those of her readers, in practicing what I am calling *selfless introspection,* Cath creates the opportunity for her readers to connect what they are reading with their own lives, inviting the transition from reader to audience. When this occurs, "both writer and reader come together through the presence of the text" (345); the reader becomes an audience member able to see their own experiences mirrored in those of the writer. They are thus able to see the actions the writer enacts in their own life as realistic options for themself, a feeling of "connectedness" (341) that can move them to act in their own life. Thus, for the feminist rhetor aiming to inspire feminist action in others' lives, selfless introspection can offer a viable rhetorical strategy.

The strategy of selfless introspection invites us to recognize the potential power of introspection, but it also gestures to the ways the feminist rhetor can engage in *responsible* introspection. Specifically, this analysis suggests that the responsible feminist rhetor is one who uses introspection as a means for deep engagement with issues that extend beyond the individual self rather than introspection as a means to indulge the self. Cath illustrates what this can look like in her enactment of a corporeal experiential authority: she first describes her personal, physical experiences with menstruation, shyness, and physical insecurities, and then she uses these descriptions to turn to the embodied experiences of her audience. According to Marilyn Cooper, "Responsible rhetorical agency is a matter of acknowledging and honoring the *responsive* nature of agency" (2011, 422; emphasis added). This definition implies an awareness of others outside the self, and, more specifically, it implies an awareness of others who are capable of responding. Selfless introspection offers one tool the feminist rhetor can use to practice this sort of responsibility: to responsibly consider the ways their own experiences can productively respond to the larger context in which they are embedded.

My intention throughout this chapter is to highlight the potential for the feminist rhetor to make explicit the experiences of their physical body in productive service to ethotic construction. Cath's openness with her physical, embodied experiences reveals the potential for the woman rhetor to do just this. In so doing, she challenges the patriarchal stance that posits the woman's body as a physical form to be subdued, hidden, and/or ignored. Instead, by bringing both completed and in-process experiences of her physical body to the fore, Cath constructs and mobilizes an embodied form of expertise known as *corporeal experiential authority*. The result is a new way of understanding women's ethos and the strategies available to feminist rhetors. As this analysis reveals, the woman rhetor's ethos need not be based on physical appearances or past experiences, and it is not something that must be given or granted. Rather, ethos is something women, in the very act of calling upon and sharing their own physical experiences, can create.

NOTE

1. At the time of my analysis, issues 14–18 had yet to be printed; therefore, these issues are not included in my discussion.

WORKS CITED

Bauer, Dale. 1990. "The Other 'F' Word: The Feminist in the Classroom." *College English* 52 (4): 385–96.

Cherry, Roger. 1998. "Ethos Versus Persona: Self-Representation in Written Discourse." *Written Communication* 15 (3): 384–410.

Elms, Catherine. *Here. In My Head.* Zines #4–#13.

Enos, Theresa. 1990. "Reports of the 'Author's' Death May Be Greatly Exaggerated but the 'Writer' Lives on in the Text." *Rhetoric Society Quarterly* 20 (4): 339–46.

Foss, Karen A., and Sonja K. Foss. 1991. *Women Speak: The Eloquence of Women's Lives.* Long Grove, IL: Waveland.

Harrison, Kimberly. 2003. "Rhetorical Rehearsals: The Construction of Ethos in Confederate Women's Civil War Diaries." *Rhetoric Review* 22 (3): 243–63.

Hays, Anne. 2017. "Reading the Margins: Embedded Narratives in Feminist Personal Zines." *Journal of Popular Culture* 50 (1): 86–108.

Helmbrecht, Brenda, and Meredith Love. 2009. "The BUSTin' and Bitchin' Ethe of Third-Wave Zines." *College Composition and Communication* 61 (1): 150–69.

Johnson, Sonia. 1989. *Wildfire: Igniting the She/volution.* London: Wildfire Books.

Kearney, Mary Celeste. 2006. *Girls Make Media.* Abingdon, Oxfordshire: Routledge.

Licona, Adela C. 2005. "(B)orderlands' Rhetorics and Representations: The Transformative Potential of Feminist Third-Space Scholarship and Zines." *NWSA Journal* 17 (2): 104–29.

McGregor, Hannah. 2018. "Fandom, Feminism, and Maker Pedagogy." *Hybrid Pedagogy*, April 17. https://hybridpedagogy.org/fandom-feminism-maker-pedagogy/. Accessed 17 January 2021.

Molloy, Catherine. 2015. "Recuperative Ethos and Agile Epistemologies: Toward a Vernacular Engagement with Mental Illness Ontologies." *Rhetoric Society Quarterly* 45 (2): 138–63.

Norris, Aaminah. 2014. "Make-Her-Spaces as Hybrid Places: Designing and Resisting Self Constructions in Urban Classrooms." *Equity & Excellence in Education* 47 (1): 63–77.

Piepmeier, Alison. 2009. *Girl Zines: Making Media, Doing Feminism.* New York: New York University Press.

Reynolds, Nedra. 1993. "Ethos as Location: New Sites for Understanding Discursive Authority." *Rhetoric Review* 11 (2): 325–38.

Rich, Adrienne. 1994. *Blood, Bread, and Poetry.* New York: Norton.

Ronald, Kate. 1990. "A Reexamination of Personal and Public Discourse in Classical Rhetoric." *Rhetoric Review* 9 (1): 36–48.

Rowe, Aimee Carrillo. 2005. "Be Longing: Toward a Feminist Politics of Relation." *NWSA Journal* 17 (2): 15–46.

Sprague, Joey. 2005. *Feminist Methodologies for Critical Researchers: Bridging Differences.* Lanham, MD: AltaMira.

Stanley, Jessamyn. 2017. *Every Body Yoga: Let Go of Fear, Get on the Mat, Love Your Body.* New York: Workman.

Wright, Ashley. 2016. Ms. Wrights Way. http://mswrightsway.com/. Accessed 12 August 2019.

Wright, Ashley (@mswrightsway). 2019. "Wright Breastfeeding." Instagram photo, August 7, 2019. https://www.instagram.com/p/B01XNrIgXW9/. Accessed 12 August 2019.

"ZineWiki: The Independent Media Wikipedia." 2012. https://blogs.ucl.ac.uk/library-arts/2012/10/08/zinewiki-the-independent-media-wikipedia/. Accessed 8 January 2014.

3
RIPPED GODDESS
New Ways of Making Women's Fitness

Holly Fulton-Babicke

The performance of identity is a complex dance fundamentally shaped by social practices, texts, and settings. With the advent and proliferation of internet technologies, identities are increasingly enacted in hybrid public/private spaces such as internet forums, supple stages that defy traditional notions of publicity. Communities thrive in these virtual environs, their texts proliferated from any number of online platforms, and their members connected by intangible, electronic threads.

One such collective is the Ripped Goddess online community, a vibrant women's fitness group. The community's web page provides a platform for users to engage in lively discourse on women's fitness and, though emphasized topics include weightlifting and other muscle-building practices, the community also consistently focuses on self-esteem building and exercise as self-care. In this process, members of this community debate, discuss, and share, cocreating multifarious articulations of healthy or fit women's bodies. Overall, the Ripped Goddess community members' ways of making feminine fitness are exceptionally diverse and encourage women to imagine and perform health in pluralistic ways.

In this chapter, I demonstrate how the Ripped Goddess community facilitates both normative and transgressive public performances of femininity in digital and physical milieux—performances enabled by users' texts, practices, and embodied products. To begin, I describe the community's fitness practices and parse topics of interest and modes of intermember discourse. Next, I elucidate the ways the Ripped Goddess community functions as a public, identifying the character of the community's members, texts, and virtual environment. In the three discussion sections that follow, I place the community's practices in context of first, the interplay between virtual and physical worlds; second, the normative gender-based practices that discipline women's bodies in discourses of fitness; and third, the ways Ripped Goddess community members variously accept and resist normative fitness discourses. Ultimately, I demonstrate that Ripped Goddess's distinctive texts and practices facilitate the community members' bodily agency and their rights to diverse performances of femininity in hybrid virtual and physical spaces—enactments of women's contemporary, agentive ways of making their own bodies in networked publics.

In exploring the Ripped Goddess women's online fitness community, I examine *how* the dynamics of this particular virtual environment allow users to perform a wide variety of feminine identities, which fall at all points along the spectrum between traditional and nontraditional gender attributes. My study employs textual analysis and participant/observer methods drawn from ethnography in order to characterize the processes and products cultivated by the Ripped Goddess community members. This work extends cyberfeminist concepts, contributes to scholarship on the performativity of gender, and engages conceptions of networked publics. Ultimately, I argue for the ongoing relevance of elements of early cyberfeminist scholarship (extending the work of notable thinkers such as Donna Haraway and Sadie Plant); in conversation with more contemporary work, these early theorizations prove useful in ongoing efforts to characterize the protean, slippery nature of gender in virtual spaces.

THE RIPPED GODDESS COMMUNITY

Ripped Goddess is an online fitness community run by Connie Itchon, a fitness coach (Itchon 2004). The group has its own web domain, Ripped-Goddess.com (hereafter referred to as "the official site") and a page on Facebook (hereafter referred to as "the Ripped Goddess page"). The official site, managed by Itchon, features interviews with professional female athletes (i.e., body builders and cross-fitness competitors) and a variety of posts on healthy eating, fitness techniques, and so forth; additionally, Ripped-Goddess.com allows users to shop for Ripped Goddess merchandise, such as workout clothing, hats, water bottles, and so forth, which all feature various versions of the Ripped Goddess logo, fitness-themed slogans, and/or original fitness-themed artwork.

The Facebook page, also moderated by Itchon, likewise allows users to shop for Ripped Goddess merchandise and features interviews, photos, and posts similar to those found on the official site but, significantly, prominently features an abundance of user-generated content. Because it allows community members to post regularly, it is much more active—and features more diverse content—than the official site.

The quotidian chaos of an active online community, even one that is moderated, is much more revealing of the texture of its members and the culture in which it participates than is a website designed to speak *to* rather than *with* its audience. So, while the official site is visually appealing, interesting, and easy to navigate, the Facebook page has more of the day-to-day information that allows an observer to identify how community members participate. Given this, I have chosen to focus upon the Ripped Goddess (Facebook) page for this study, as it is a better indicator of the character and activities of the RG community as a whole.

In a charming gesture of identification, the users who post to the site label themselves "RGs," short for Ripped Goddesses. Additionally, Itchon addresses readers as RGs in her posts, indicating her inclusive definition of the term. These related gestures are significant, demonstrating that the concept of a Ripped Goddess is not an abstract ideal that can be striven for but not attained. On the contrary, Itchon invites all members of the community to consider themselves Ripped Goddesses, and the group's participants respond to this in kind, self-identifying as RGs. The identity work engaged in by Itchon and the community members is especially interesting given that popular discourses on fitness—that is, those found in countless "fitness guru" blogs, television shows, magazines, and so forth—elevate paragons of fitness to a distant, superhuman status. In the case of the Ripped Goddess page, Itchon takes a dramatically different approach, pointing out that the page "is a celebration of those who are fit and those still on their journey" and, more important, that "being a Ripped Goddess has less to do with how you look and more to do with how you LIVE!" (Itchon 2004). In short, members of the Ripped Goddess community are *invited* to identify as a Ripped Goddess, to join in the community's activities—and they do, explicitly and enthusiastically.

In order to assess the size and character of the community, I have divided the page's participants into two categories: *members of the community* and *participants*. I define the Ripped Goddess *community* broadly as the users who have Facebook accounts and Liked the page. As of March 2019, the Ripped Goddess page had just over 272,000 Likes. These people are interested enough in the group and its activities to complete the electronic steps that will give them updates on the group's goings-on. Additionally, members of the community are receptive enough to the group's goals to visibly support it, as Liked items are visible to a user's Friends. Unlike the general public, who can read the material posted on the page but cannot contribute to it, these community members are in a position to participate in the group's practices if they so choose.

The group's *participants* constitute a subset of the group's community. Participants are the users who submit content to be posted on the page, or who engage in the conversations taking place in the comments on posted items. Though the Ripped Goddess community includes both women and men, the vast majority of the group's participants are women. As the group is arranged around women's fitness, this makes a certain amount of sense, but it is noteworthy that men do sometimes participate on the group's conversations, and some posted items feature questions from men or images of men pursuing/practicing fitness.

RIPPED GODDESS AS A PUBLIC

It is crucial to consider Michael Warner's work on publics in order to fully understand the types of publicity enacted by an online fitness community. In "Publics and Counterpublics," Warner differentiates between "*the* public" and two senses of "*a* public," pointing out that "*the* public is a kind of social totality. Its most common sense is that of the people in general." He goes on to say that the public in question could include the people of "the nation, the commonwealth, the city, the state, or some other community," that is, Christians, Americans, and so forth (2002, 49). Warner then describes the concept of *a* public, which exists in two senses. In the first sense, *a* public is a group that shares an experience based on some sense of physical bounds, such as a concert or protest; in the second sense, *a* public is a group through which texts circulate, which could include people in temporally and physically disparate locations (50). Crucially, Warner asserts that the divisions between his three concepts of publics are "not always sharp" and can overlap.

Warner's concept of publics bears on the examination of the Ripped Goddess community because the official website is accessible by not only *the* public—any internet user—but also *a* public. Members of the Ripped Goddess community constitute *a* public of users who frequent the page, participating in its discursive events and reading the texts that circulate through the page. So, the public to which the Ripped Goddess page may speak is threefold: *the* public of internet users, *a* public of people who exist within the virtual space of the site (who are within digital "earshot"), and *a* public of people who engage with particular texts (which will be described at length further on).

Ripped Goddess's threefold public nature renders it an eminently productive site of inquiry. By virtue of the public nature of this web page, participants in the official site's dialogue present selves that may be attested to by any number or type of observers. This collective's visibility and potential interaction with the general public allow the community's discourses to bear on larger, related cultural conversations. The status of the site as public renders it a useful artifact to study, as any publicly available text ultimately yields data about not only its subject matter but also about its author, intended audience, and culture(s) in general.

This study builds on prior scholarship that demonstrates the ways social practices migrate and shift between virtual and physical spaces, especially in the context of attitudes and practices surrounding female embodiment. By evaluating the Ripped Goddess community members' ability to engage in both normative and transgressive bodily practices, this work also illustrates the double-edged ways virtual spaces and online communities both reinforce norms *and* foster agency in identity performance. Given the back-and-forth flow of practices and texts between virtual and physical settings, the practices I explicate below have a high potential to bear on femininity in physical locales. The practices observed in this collective may even augur for a "new normal" in women's ways of making femininity and making identities and bodies that reflect these visions.

Although the Ripped Goddess community members are subject to the normalizing forces of society at large—and as such, must cocreate visions of gender and fitness in the context of any number of contemporaneous conversations—these participants also have the freeing benefits of a group that has self-selected due to common interests. Hence, when examining this community, its processes, and its products, one may be able to parse out the push-and-pull of individuals striving to define themselves as individuals in the face of—inevitably—normalizing social trends that occur around them. The mixed processes of yielding to, repurposing, and resisting social practices constitute the materiel individuals use to form and evolve social groups. The individuals who engage with the Ripped Goddess page participate in these processes in order to both function in a culture as it is and redefine it in the interest of individuality.

WOMEN'S FITNESS IN PUBLIC: CYBERFEMINISM, EMBODIMENT, AND TRANSGRESSION

Feminists, sociologists, anthropologists, philosophers, and psychologists, among others, have debated at length the ways the spread of internet technologies has altered humans' social playbook. Among the many considerations within this field of inquiry is the internet's capacity to be deployed by users for social change—a topic researchers have spent substantial time and energy exploring. Scholars have considered the ways the internet can foster the subversion/evolution, as well as replication/reinforcement, of existing social mores. The concept of hybridity—humans and technology, embodiment and disembodiment—is productively deployed in these inquiries, and the resulting "thick understanding," or complex conception, of how humans and technology act upon each other in digital settings provides fruitful ground for continued inquiry.

Cyberfeminist scholars such as Donna Haraway and Sadie Plant theorized that internet technologies could provide a powerful point of entry for subverting power structures, including those of patriarchy and colonialism. Of particular use to my study is Haraway's use of the rhetoric of liminality to highlight the "leaky"-ness of traditional boundaries such as those between human and machine, and physical and virtual (1987, 3). The porousness of these boundaries presents technology users with opportunities to bend social norms such as the social conventions that define femininity and masculinity. This dynamic appears in the Ripped Goddess community, as RGs capitalize on the boundary-pushing potential of online technologies to play with gender norms that have been traditionally cast in strict opposition to one another. Additionally, cyberfeminists' concept of the hybridity of the physical and the virtual bears on the substantial interplay between RGs' online and "real-life" identity constructions.

Despite early cyberfeminists' general optimism regarding the progressive potential of internet-based technology, these scholars also cautioned against the double-edged nature of technologies. Susan Luckman (1999) explains that the empowering possibilities of the internet are considerable, but it is crucial to also consider the institutional and normative practices that "piggyback" into virtual spaces via the expectations and limitations of web users. As Anne Marie Balsamo further cautions, to understand the nature of online dynamics, one must cultivate a "thick perception" of the ways technologies and social practices—the latter rooted in physical practices—interact (1996, 3).

In short, online identities are not independent of the social forces present in the physical world: We cannot simply divide the digital and the physical when seeking to understand the dynamics of online culture(s). Although the internet offers abundant opportunities for users to create new selves, and to selectively disclose elements of their embodied existences, the conventions and hierarchies of the "real world" inevitably hitch a ride into virtual spaces through the expectations, habits, and general preferences of users. Hence, users' social habits, expectations, and overall ways of knowing—developed at length in offline settings—inevitably affect online communities and the identities and practices of these communities' members. Ultimately, the social behaviors of internet users reflect the limitations and potentials of realms both physical and virtual.

In particular, the hierarchical relationships between different types of people—women and men, people of color and white people, LGBTQ+ and straight people, cisgender and transgender people, and so forth—tend to replicate themselves online, despite the ostensibly egalitarian dynamics of virtual environments. So, while online communities may be structured with an eye towards democratic processes, the socialization of the people in these communities may cause the inequalities of physical society to be replicated in their virtual communities. Furthermore, since online communities often vocally assert their prioritization of equality, the incursion of social hierarchies from the "real world" may reify these inequalities even more powerfully than in the physical world since internet technologies purportedly allow users to sidestep the embedded biases and power dynamics inherent to face-to-face social interactions. The invisibility of the physically based power dynamics that inevitably replicate themselves online creates a perilous situation, and cyberfeminist scholars are justified in cautioning against the hegemony-furthering potential of internet technologies. In the context of this study, the dual potential of internet technologies—to both subvert current power inequalities and to reify them—is important to consider, as the RGs often support a fresh, empowered concept of female fitness yet find themselves also supporting normative characteristics of femininity that may undermine a progressive, diversified vision of feminine fitness.

Several normative views affecting women in online settings relate to female embodiment and bodily disciplining. Amanda du Preez (2009), in *Gendered Bodies and New Technologies*, points out that, since the advent of Cartesian dualism and a subsequent grasping towards the transcendence of bodily concerns in Western cultures, women have been portrayed as especially embodied. Between Cartesian thought separating the body and the mind, gnostic obsession with escaping the confines of the body, and Charcot's "hysteric female," a trope emerged: the concept that women were confined by their mysterious, mercurial bodies. The framing of women's bodies as problematic and distracting has persisted, as one can easily parse out by reviewing current women's "health" publications. Magazines and websites such as *Shape*, *Women's Health*, and *Oxygen* promote a vision of women's health founded upon control and negation, hawking techniques to *lose* weight, *manage* eating and appetite, *shrink* body parts, and so forth. As the works of Margaret Carlisle Duncan and Lori A. Klos indicate, one outcome of the rhetoric of constant surveillance and control surrounding women's fitness is that women find themselves in a constant state of bodily disciplining.

As Michel Foucault (1977) observed in *Discipline and Punish*, a disciplined body is a docile body; as such, the vision of women's fitness promoted by popular women's health publications is not so much a way to *create* health as a way to *discipline* undesirable bodily features, to render one's—rebellious, transgressive—body compliant. Normalized visions of women's fitness frame bodily control as empowerment, when really, this rhetoric contributes to a loss of energy or power due to the exhausting, constant investment in bodily control required to achieve "health." As Carlisle Duncan and Klos point out, writers for popular women's health/fitness publications offer "descriptions of what occurs during a diet or exercise program [that] seem like the furthest thing from loving and nurturing one's body. They sound so much more like repugnance, disgust, and self-loathing" (2014, 254). Following du Preez's concept of women as "overly embodied," popular fitness narratives both contribute to the idea that women are trapped in rebellious bodies and endorse the notion that women must spend incalculable quantities of time, energy, and money to overcome the innately problematic nature of their bodily vessels.

POPULAR CONCEPTS OF FEMININE FITNESS VERSUS RIPPED GODDESS: SHRINKING VERSUS BUILDING

One of the noteworthy qualities of Ripped Goddess's approach to women's fitness is its unwillingness to replicate the rhetoric that frames women's bodies as objects to be punished or overcome. Itchon appeals to potential community members by contending that "if you're passionate about sweat, muscles, and you believe in having a little fun now and then—then you'll like this page" (*Health is Wealth* n.d.). Sweat and muscles are both created through the productive use—literally, creating products—of one's body, an endeavor that stands in opposition to the self-flagellation and negation promoted in typical women's health publications.

Overall, the idea that fitness is about *creating* is a distinctive theme in the RG community, pervading posts to the page, RG merchandise, and the site's textual infrastructure (including various logos, photos of Itchon, official explanations of the site's identity, etc.). However, RG's emphasis on creation is not limited to products: Itchon also endorses fitness as a pursuit—a process one may take pleasure in—as opposed to merely a destination to reach at any cost. The prioritization of products *and* process in the RG community provides a rich interplay between the concept of the "journey" of fitness and the ends of fitness, both of which are achieved through the cultivation of women's bodies.

One of the many ways the RG site articulates its processes and products is through the regular, themed texts that appear on the posts section of the site. Itchon names these recurring posts and invites community members to participate by submitting photos of themselves or engaging in discussions in the comments. These playfully named recurring posts include "Flex Friday," "Wicked Wheels Wednesday," "Transformation Tuesday," and "Motivation Monday." These posts feature female—and occasionally male—athletes and fitness aficionados along all imaginable points of the fitness spectrum, demonstrating a wide variety of fitness accomplishments. Original posters and commenters alike often label these photos and videos as *goals*, referring to the desirable outcomes the depicted people have attained. For example, in the case of Flex Friday, the attainment is a set of strong-looking arm muscles; for Wicked Wheels Wednesday, the accomplishment is powerful legs.

The goals RGs strive for are embodied in people who can be placed all along several spectrums in terms of age, abledness, size, profession, class, and ethnicity. Perhaps most critically, the bodily products RGs strive to create are not monolithic: for example, among the themed posts are a video clip of a seemingly out-of-shape woman lifting large weights and a "progress pic" of a woman recovering from an eating disorder by gaining weight. Of course, this site is densely populated with images of often exceptionally physically fit women, but it is important to note that progress and goals are broadly defined and quite inclusive. So, the Ripped Goddess community not only eschews the popular rhetoric of women's health—by emphasizing not the *elimination* or *negation* of particulars of their bodies but the *creation* of tangible products—but also defines desirable products broadly, allowing for an inclusive, pluralistic vision of women's fitness.

The RG community shares qualities with other fitness communities, most notably CrossFit, an organization that develops high-intensity interval training programs and holds fitness competitions ("What Is CrossFit?," n.d.). Ripped Goddess shares several aspects of the CrossFit ethos, particularly a "can-do" attitude, thorough inclusion of women, and an emphasis on fitness-as-process. Too, the RG page frequently features female CrossFit competitors in the community posts as a source of inspiration. There are, however, a few important contrasts between the RG community discourse and CrossFit discourse. First, of course, is RG's explicit focus on *women's* fitness—such a focus allows Ripped Goddess to attend to the factors that particularly impact women (such as exercise after childbirth and weightlifting as a means to combat postmenopause bone-density loss) and to connect RGs to resources and practices explicitly catered to women's needs.

The most critical difference between CrossFit's representations of women's fitness and RG's discourses, however, is that RG not only includes but *elevates* "ordinary" people who participate in comparatively humble fitness practices. While official CrossFit materials invite all to participate ("no matter what your current fitness level is, you can start CrossFit"), official texts such as press releases and promotional materials predominantly emphasize extremely difficult physical activities (including handstand walks and Olympic lifts) and the exceptional athletes who excel at such tasks, especially top CrossFit Games competitors ("What Is CrossFit?," n.d.). In contrast, Ripped Goddess not only invites everyone to be an RG but also consistently *celebrates* fitness as instantiated in "everyday people" at different ages, weights, and abledness; as Itchon puts it in a July 2019 post to the group's Facebook page, "You are already goals . . . own your own brand of excellence." Itchon regularly posts videos and images of overweight women completing workouts modified for feasibility at a high body weight (e.g., substituting step-up movements for jumps), with phrases that salute their hard work and explicitly recognize their belonging in the fitness community (e.g., "Bravo! . . . #womancrushwednesday"). Note that these posts do not identify imperfect bodies as merely something to "overcome"; even if the RGs depicted are making efforts to "transform," such posts affirm the *current* worthiness of these people's bodies and their capabilities. The high frequency of these messages continually reinforces an inclusive definition of RG and furthers Ripped Goddess's message that fitness exists as a process to be celebrated (even enjoyed). Ultimately, RG distinguishes itself from other fitness organizations by—insistently and consistently—positioning itself as a community that highly values the diverse fitness practices of everyday women.

The importance of fitness as a process in RG's vision of female health also contests the popular view of women's fitness as a static phenomenon. Women, even in magazines purportedly highlighting their physical capabilities, are often portrayed as if at rest—static objects to be surveilled, not dynamic subjects performing fitness. Marie Hardin, Susan Lynn, and Kristie Walsdorf make note of this phenomenon, finding that images of female athletes in sports magazines frequently "presented [the women] as motionless, with the focus of the photograph on body aesthetics," reinforcing a patriarchal view of man-as-subject and woman-as-object (2005, 108).

Ripped Goddess sidesteps the concept of women's fitness as a spectacle: the community members promote activities that continually reaffirm the agentive, dynamic qualities of female fitness enthusiasts. In particular, the concept of fitness-as-process is reinforced through a genre of post frequently added to the RG site: videos demonstrating workout routines. Itchon frequently posts video clips—some she created—of women demonstrating fitness activities, some of which are quite impressive and require exceptional strength, but many of which demonstrate actions that are beginner friendly. Videos typically encourage viewers to participate, explain the benefits of completing the depicted activity, and show a woman or several women completing the move(s). Significantly, RGs often comment on their experience of these moves below the posted videos and even post media of their own showing them completing the exercise(s). Through watching posted videos and keeping up with additions, interested RGs can not only complete isolated exercises but can actually build a considerable repertoire of fitness activities, which they can—and do—execute. Hence, RGs are not just consumers or receivers of information circulated by Itchon and other RGs but are active participants in the activities highlighted on the page.

Overall, the practices and products of the RG community bolster the agency of the community members to enact female fitness in the ways each individual might find most engaging or authentic. The Ripped Goddess site's neat sidestepping of popular narratives regarding women and fitness—that women must be small, delicate, and constantly consumed with creating bodily perfection—renders the community a powerful point of entry for women to envision fitness and femininity anew. This community, by offering interventions into ways of making women's fitness, also offers an intervention into the question of what constitutes femaleness in general. In imagining and creating strong and agentic female bodies, the Ripped Goddess community productively disrupts the assumption that a woman is subject to the whims of a chaotic and ineffectual body. Too, the pluralistic, choice-affirming oeuvre in which the RG community functions vexes the traditional assumption that only males may claim bodily agency and creation or successfully apply mind over (bodily) matter. Ultimately, the RG community fundamentally undermines the normative assumption that women's bodies are unruly, ungovernable vehicles, instead casting women as curators and cultivators of their own worthy bodily forms and abilities.

WOMEN'S MUSCLE AS NORMATIVE AND NONNORMATIVE

Countless scholars—hailing from, among others, feminist, sociology, and gender studies backgrounds—have discussed at length the ways female athletes negotiate gender norms by both adhering to and transgressing ideals of feminine aesthetics. Although most scholarship in this vein concentrates explicitly on women bodybuilders, the authors tend to focus on the ways their study participants socially negotiate muscularity in general, which allows their work to bear on any situation in which women produce and/or display muscle. As Sarah Grogan, Ruth Evans, Sam Wright, and Geoff Hunter observe, in Western culture, "Muscularity is generally seen as inappropriate for women," continuing on to assert that "women who aim for a muscular physique are transgressing current Western cultural norms"; such cultural norms persist even as phenomena such as women's CrossFit rise in popularity (2004, 49–50). However, such "transgressions" of gendered cultural norms are often mitigated: as Lex Boyle observes, women bodybuilders, sometimes critically referred to as "muscle Barbies," "can be . . . deeply invested in reproducing normative sex, gender and sexual identities" (2005, 136). Also, Shelley McGrath and Ruth Chananie-Hill found in their interview-based study of female bodybuilders that "[the study] participants [were] all rebels, even as they [were] all conformists" and concluded that these people "assert their right to be women and bodybuilders, to take up space at the gym, and to be nonnormative in various other ways, although they occasionally contradict themselves, thus returning to the realm of normative femininity" (2009, 242).

The members of the Ripped Goddess community, like the female bodybuilders studied by the scholars above, both replicate and transgress traditional concepts of femininity in their practice of female fitness. In celebrating the strength and general athleticism of women, Itchon and the RGs envision femaleness as strong, capable, and worthy of taking up space, all characteristics denied women in traditional concepts of womanhood. Conversely, many RGs also perform normative femininity through details such as manicures, heels, and even surgical enhancement. Overall, the RGs' willingness to integrate and/or reject—based upon individual preference—a variety of normative and nonnormative traits in the public creation and execution of their embodied practices is a definitive characteristic of the community.

Academic discussions of women's muscle-building endeavors indicate both the flouting and replicating of traditional visions of femininity, yielding productively complex, even contradictory, understandings. However, in considerations of the rich conceptual frictions in women's variegated resistances and adherences to norms in fitness practices, a recurrent conclusion nonetheless emerges: muscular women are clearly *active negotiators* of social practices. As the binary of male/female becomes problematic when inspected closely, so too does the dualism of conformity/resistance. Following Judith Butler's (1988) elucidations of gender as performance, the physical traits individuals deploy to signify gender are both fluid and subject to individual enactment. Consequently, women such as the RGs who enact diverse versions of women's fitness are agents who *actively negotiate femininity*, as they variously adhere to established gender norms and/or break these norms; these women allow themselves—whether consciously or not—to choose their own embodied, gendered characteristics, crafting a femininity they find individually authentic. In sum, the RGs enact bodily and gendered agency through their willingness to practice female fitness in a way that may disregard or harness aspects of the dominant culture at the discretion of the individual.

CONCLUSIONS AND IMPLICATIONS: ENVISIONING IDENTITY AND FEMININITIES GOING FORWARD

The Ripped Goddess page offers its community members the opportunity to envision and perform variegated, complex versions of female fitness in a hybrid physical-virtual public. Even more so than other comparatively inclusive fitness communities (e.g., CrossFit), Ripped Goddess's messages celebrate the many affordances and needs of *women's* bodies and affirm the worthiness of all bodies and practices—from competition-prepping professional bodybuilders to grandmothers simply keeping active. This community offers a place for women to create individual, complex visions of femininity(ies) by freely performing traditional femininity, nonnormative femininity, or, more accurately, infinite combinatory variations thereof. The resulting fit female identities are pluralistic, dynamic, and the products of considerable agency, striking public illustrations of the range and depth of embodied femininities.

Maureen Daly Goggin notes that "like grasping a handful of water, identity seeps through the fingers, evaporates, and escapes because it is not a *thing* but an ongoing series of performances that always exceed and are constrained by a given moment" (2009, 19). Indeed, it is important to note that the identity of the community, or of any given member, at one given moment could not accurately encapsulate the complete character of the collective. Consequently, I can offer only a limited interpretation of the group's identity and a limited vision of the RGs' ways of making and practicing—muscles, community, fitness, and identity—through the activities of their community. Even considering this limitation, however, it remains clear that this community offers a place for women to enact agency in their performances of femininity and fitness and the convergences of the two.

The ability of the RGs to practice pluralistic articulations of female fitness bears relevance on several fronts. First, when placed in the context of cyberfeminist scholarship on the flow of physical practices into virtual spaces, and vice versa, Ripped Goddess may act as a clear demonstration of the social dynamics of virtual spaces, especially in terms of how bodily practices may be negotiated anew or replicated—or any combination thereof. This study offers one illustration of the creative gender negotiation made possible through the dynamics of virtual space, as RGs creatively rearrange aspects of gender performance to suit their own philosophies or identities.

Additionally, as a threefold public, the Ripped Goddess community members' practices are not executed in isolation; rather, they perform female fitness upon a stage open to countless observers. As such, the practices of the RGs leak from a virtual platform into physical reality, continuing in a social feedback loop. This possibility is critical to consider at our present technological and cultural juncture: virtual practices and physical practices have considerable interplay, and the practices developed in internet locales almost inevitably transfer into physical environments. Laurie Gries observes that online artifacts are "real thing[s] that spark traceable consequences in the world," a sentiment echoed by countless other scholars of online social interaction (2015, 11). Such virtual-physical interplay means that variegated *online* enactments of female health developed and celebrated by the RGs are a preview of emergent, newly agentive norms for female fitness in *embodied* settings.

Of course, not all social constructions, such as concepts of gender, crafted on the internet—regardless of how much care, originality, and energy is invested therein—may emerge into the "real world" in a recognizable shape. However, given the compelling disruptions and negotiations currently occurring on gender/sexuality fronts, Ripped Goddess's ways of making fit female identity resonate with contemporary values of agency in gender performance. It is a timely, promising moment for collectives such as the RG community to offer pluralistic enactments of femaleness and fitness and for these enactments to find traction by virtue of larger social shifts.

The members of the Ripped Goddess community may demonstrate the next evolutionary stage in gender negotiation: a way of combining normative and nonnormative articulations of femininity that nimbly, organically promote the creators' agency and individuality while allowing for articulation in a pluralistic community. As Jessalyn Marie Keller (2012) and Julia Schuster (2013) observe, the identities internet users create, and the actions they take, in online environs bolster these users' rhetorical agency, helping them craft public selves. Ripped Goddess, more than just providing a playful forum for women to envision fit selves, allows its community members to cultivate and deploy their bodily rhetorical agency, circulating visions of hybrid femininities. Given the ever-porous boundaries between the virtual and the physical, these articulations proliferate into embodied settings, playfully yet firmly advancing our understanding of female embodiment and its myriad potentials.

WORKS CITED

Balsamo, Anne Marie. 1996. *Technologies of the Gendered Body: Reading Cyborg Women*. Durham, NC: Duke University Press.

Boyle, Lex. 2005. "Flexing the Tensions of Female Muscularity: How Female Bodybuilders Negotiate Normative Femininity in Competitive Bodybuilding." *Women's Studies Quarterly* 33 (1): 134–49.

Butler, Judith. 1988. "Performative Acts and Gender Constitution: An Essay in Phenomenology and Feminist Theory." *Theatre Journal* 40 (4): 519–31. doi:10.2307/3207893.

Carlisle Duncan, Margaret, and Lori A. Klos. 2014. "Paradoxes of the Flesh: Emotion and Contradiction in Fitness/Beauty Magazine Discourse." *Journal of Sport and Social Issues* 38 (3): 245–62.

Du Preez, Amanda. 2009. *Gendered Bodies and New Technologies: Rethinking Embodiment in a Cyber-Era*. Newcastle upon Tyne, England: Cambridge Scholars.

Foucault, Michel. 1977. *Discipline and Punish: The Birth of the Prison*. New York: Pantheon.

Goggin, Maureen Daly. 2009. "Fabricating Identity: Janie Terrero's 1912 Embroidered English Suffrage Signature Handkerchief." In *Women and Things, 1750–1950: Gendered Material Strategies*, edited by Maureen Daly Goggin and Beth Tobin, 17–42. Aldershot, Hampshire, UK: Ashgate.

Gries, Laurie. 2015. *Still Life with Rhetoric: A New Materialist Approach for Visual Rhetorics*. Logan: Utah State University Press.

Grogan, Sarah, Ruth Evans, Sam Wright, and Geoff Hunter. 2004. "Femininity and Muscularity: Accounts of Seven Women Body Builders." *Journal of Gender Studies* 13 (1): 49–61.

Haraway, Donna. 1987. "A Manifesto for Cyborgs: Science, Technology, and Socialist Feminism in the 1980s." *Australian Feminist Studies* 2 (4): 1–42.

Hardin, Marie, Susan Lynn, and Kristie Walsdorf. 2005. "Challenge and Conformity on 'Contested Terrain': Images of Women in Four Women's Sport/Fitness Magazines." *Sex Roles* 53 (1–2): 105–17.

Health is Wealth. n.d. https://www.facebook.com/healthiswealth.tsp/. Accessed 17 December 2020.

Itchon, Connie. n.d. Ripped-Goddess. WordPress. http://www.ripped-goddess.com/. Accessed 17 December 2020.

Itchon, Connie. 2004. "Ripped Goddess." Facebook. Facebook, Inc., https://www.facebook.com/rippedgoddess/. Accessed 8 October 2019.

Keller, Jessalynn Marie. 2012. "Virtual Feminisms." *Information, Communication & Society* 15 (3): 429–47.
Luckman, Susan. 1999. "(En)gendering the Digital Body: Feminism and the Internet." *Hecate* 25 (2): 37–47.
McGrath, Shelley A., and Ruth A. Chananie-Hill. 2009. "'Big Freaky-Looking Women': Normalizing Gender Transgression Through Bodybuilding." *Sociology of Sport Journal* 26 (2): 235–54.
Plant, Sadie. "The Future Looms: Weaving Women and Cybernetics." *Body & Society* 1.3-4 (1995): 45-64.
Schuster, Julia. 2013. "Invisible Feminists? Social Media and Young Women's Political Participation." *Political Science* 65 (1): 8–24.
Warner, Michael. 2002. "Publics and Counterpublics (abbreviated Version)." *Quarterly Journal of Speech* 88 (4): 413–25.
"What Is CrossFit?" n.d. CrossFit. https://www.crossfit.com/what-is-crossfit. Accessed 8 October 2019.

4
BUILDING EMBODIED *ĒTHĒ*
Brandi Chastain's Goal Celebration and
the Problem of Situated Ethos

Lorin Shellenberger

Since the passage of Title IX in 1972, women's participation in athletics in the United States has soared. Women are participating in elite athletic performance in ever-increasing numbers, and yet these opportunities have done little to subvert socially constructed gender norms that influence perceptions of women's status in society. For example, while the 2015 Women's World Cup brought some of the highest viewership levels for women's soccer in the United States and one of the most outstanding goal-scoring performances in men's or women's World Cup history, overt sexism lurked behind those record-setting numbers (Brown 2015). The 2015 World Cup was played on artificial turf for the first time in history, a choice that would never have been entertained for a men's World Cup, despite protests from star players such as Abby Wambach, Alex Morgan, Nadine Kessler, and Marta (Fagen 2014).

Although sport has provided women with opportunities to build and transform their physical bodies, thus providing women with a way to challenge gendered expectations about women's appearance, body shape, and size, the very structure of sport simultaneously reinforces gendered expectations for women's behavior and marks them as different from men. Yet because the physical body often serves as a visible marker of racial, cultural, and sexual difference, gendered expectations and cultural values about women's bodies influence how women are perceived by the public and how they may perform ethos. As I argue below, one's ethos may be deflected by racist, sexist, or homophobic perceptions based on one's physical body. Therefore, the relationship between the physical body and ethos is an important consideration for feminist rhetorical scholars because ethos constitutes personal credibility and is typically assumed to be within the speaker's realm of control. However, my analysis suggests that the physical body and the previous cultural

DOI: 10.7330/9781646420384.c004

discourses the body comes to represent may undercut an individual's efforts to construct ethos, meaning certain individuals are limited in their ability to gain ethos, through no fault of their own. Ethos is developed through a variety of factors, including previous cultural narratives, ongoing media discourses, choices about self-presentation, and one's physical body (among others), and rhetoric scholars must attend more specifically to how these various factors might influence the ability to develop ethos rather than relying on a more "fixed" understanding of ethos that emphasizes the rhetor.

Elite female athletes are particularly interesting as a site for feminist research because they represent a tension in feminist scholarship: on the one hand, they subvert gendered expectations by participating in a typically male-dominated sphere. On the other hand, because sport is one of the only social institutions that not only insists on an ontological difference based on sex but actually posits this difference as a moral of fair play, women's very participation in sport also reinforces their difference from men. In addition, dedicated athletic training posits that one can change and master the body, giving female athletes a sense of self-authorship of their bodies, and consequently their ethos. Yet at the same time, the physical body and what it represents symbolically may also limit women's ability to build ethos. The elite female athlete, therefore, provides a particularly interesting illustration of the problems in assuming ethos as completely within the realm of an individual's control because elite female athletes have a different relationship with the physical body. The physical body and the ability to change and shape it through athletic training is a significant part of athletes' ability to develop ethos, and yet there are certain limitations to the malleability of the body. That is, although athletics often assumes and esteems a "mastery" of the body, the athlete cannot always "master" public discourses about their body.

Instead, my analysis of Brandi Chastain's goal celebration in the 1999 World Cup suggests ethos is a specifically embodied concept influenced not only by a rhetor's physical body and the bodily habits and behaviors a rhetor undertakes but also by previous cultural narratives about what that particular body represents. This understanding of ethos is important for rhetorical studies because much of the previous scholarship on ethos assumes ethos is entirely the result of deliberate choices made by the rhetor. However, as I demonstrate, this assumption does not account for how certain factors, such as the rhetor's race or gender or the material conditions and lived realities a rhetor faces, might influence how their ethos is perceived by an audience. In addition, the idea that ethos is shaped entirely by the rhetor also has the unfortunate tendency to oversimplify ethos. Instead, as Kathleen J. Ryan, Nancy Meyers, and Rebecca Jones argue, feminist scholars must "open up new ways of envisioning ethos to acknowledge the multiple, nonlinear relations operating among rhetors, audiences, things, and contexts," suggesting an ecological view of ethos as the plural *ēthe* (2016, 3).[1] In keeping with Ryan, Meyers, and Jones's efforts to open up ethos, I argue we must attend further to how a person's physical, material body affects and is affected by their ethos. By discussing ethos in the context of previous cultural narratives and focusing on the ways the lived, material body influences perceptions of ethos, I aim to provide an alternative model of ethos that might extend understandings of ethos to include how sociocultural factors outside the speaker's realm of control might influence performances of ethos. I offer the term *embodied ēthe* to complement Ryan, Meyers, and Jones's work on expanding feminist understandings of ethos. I specifically emphasize *embodied* because it helps describe how material conditions influence ethos while utilizing Ryan, Meyers, and Jones's plural *ēthe* to convey the multiple, varied ways individuals attempt to build ethos. This understanding is important for rhetoric scholars because it provides a theory of ethos more sensitive to how certain individuals' efforts to build ethos are constrained by factors outside their control, such as the way their physical bodies come to serve as visible markers of difference, and better accounts for how various other influences, such as previous cultural narratives, ongoing media discourses, or choices about the rhetor's self-presentation, might affect an individual's ethos.

My analysis brings together existing sports studies scholarship on the care of the self (Chapman 1997; Johns and Johns 2000; Markula and Kennedy 2012; Markula and Pringle 2006) with rhetorical scholarship on ethos and the body (Hawhee 2004; Pittman 2007; Royster 2000; Ryan, Myers, and Jones 2016) in order to illustrate ethos as a specifically embodied concept influenced not only by one's physical body but by bodily habits and behaviors that come to constitute the self. In my interpretation, these performances might consist of bodily movements, actions, behaviors, and outward adornment, in addition to more traditional understandings that attend to ethos as part of public, linguistically based discourse. Ethos is also related to what I term the *development of the self* or the *care of the self* and also to subjectivity. While the care of the self is commonly associated with Michel Foucault, it has had various iterations throughout history. Foucault discusses the care of the self as a practice or way of life in ancient Greece that valued the ability to care for and train the physical body. For the ancient Greeks, the trained, cared-for body was seen as a sign of a citizen's readiness to participate in civic life. That is, the physical body was symbolic of subjectivity; it signaled the ability to act or take action in a particular context (Foucault 1979; Hawhee 2004). In this way, the self and subjectivity are also closely tied to ethos because ethos amounts to personal credibility and character and thus represents the conception of the self or status as a subject to others.

Important, though, ethos is coconstructed, or negotiated, by the audience and the speaker or performer (Hyde 2004; Smith 2004). We cannot simply "claim" or "earn" ethos; rather, ethos must be granted by an audience. In this way, ethos is both external to and internal to the speaker or performer: ethos may be deliberately styled by the individual for a particular audience and situation, but previous conceptions of that individual's ethos by the audience may also influence how the audience perceives subsequent performances of ethos. Therefore, although the rhetor has a certain amount of agency in each performance of ethos, these performances are always read in the context of the cultural values of the community to which they speak.

Sharon Crowley and Debra Hawhee have attempted to resolve some of the confusion about Aristotelian understandings of ethos as something the speaker controls and other conceptualizations of ethos that position ethos as a negotiation between audience and rhetor by separating ethos into two distinct categories, *invented ethos* and *situated ethos*. In their interpretation, invented ethos refers to the speaker's ability to construct or invent public credibility through the use of linguistic devices, and situated ethos refers to the credibility afforded the speaker prior to discourse, such as the speaker's reputation or the authority of the speaker's social position (1999, 108). In this understanding, a speaker's social position and the power relationships that help establish that social position directly influence how their ethos is received: if a speaker's social status is perceived favorably, it can enhance the speaker's ability in the eyes of the audience, but conversely, a less favorable social status can also compromise communicative ability.

While Crowley and Hawhee's distinction between invented and situated ethos is helpful for understanding the different ways ethos is constructed, the separation between invented and situated ethos assumes these processes are distinct and fails to account for the ways invented and situated ethos may influence each other. For example, Crowley and Hawhee do not explain how social position might limit the ways the individual uses certain linguistic devices and do not account for how a speaker's situated ethos might be always-already compromised by factors outside the speaker's realm of control, such as race or gender. In addition, Crowley and Hawhee's invented ethos focuses more on the speaker's ability to invent the self through linguistic devices and less on how the body—including the ways the body often reveals or is assumed to reveal social position—might factor into how the speaker performs ethos. Therefore, my analysis focuses on the body and bodily practices, in addition to previous discourses that situate and construct the body, considering how a specifically embodied understanding of invented ethos *and* situated ethos work together in order to extend current scholarship that either tends to focus primarily on situated ethos or does not consider the body as part of invented ethos. Embodied ēthe therefore expands the various practices and behaviors that might lead to agency and the different actions women might use to develop ethos.

More recently, Hawhee provides the history and lineage of ethos as a bodily concept by tracing the relationship between rhetoric and athletics in ancient Greece. According to Hawhee, there is a connection between bodily habits and ethos through the idea of *melete*, or repeated practice,[2] in that "*melete* becomes the means through which permanent dispositions develop" (2004, 146). Ethos's connection to the body and to habit suggests that repeated bodily movements, such as those performed by an elite athlete in the course of athletic training, influence both one's own conception of the self and also how others perceive the self. The bodily actions performed in athletic training thus are seen as indications of ethos, which suggests ethos can be developed and trained over time, and that these repeated bodily movements influence how a person's ethos is perceived by others. Building on Hawhee's discussion of bodily ethos, I argue that the repeated bodily movements often performed through athletic training also play a significant role in how the subject is developed, to the extent that these particular movements and behaviors not only reflect someone's ethos to others but come to constitute necessary attributes of the self.

However, while Hawhee's work is important for understanding the relationship of specific bodily movements and habits to the way one may develop ethos, it assumes all bodies have the same opportunities for cultivating these movements and habits that then influence ethos. Likewise, Aristotelian understandings of ethos assume people act from deliberate choice and that we have the means to engage in chosen practices and behaviors that might lead to habit formation. For example, Craig Smith asserts that Aristotle's discussion of virtue in *The Nicomachean Ethics* "reinforces the position that character is derived from deliberate choice" (2004, 9). But this perspective ignores factors that influence ethos and habit formation about which an individual has limited choice: for example, race and the racist stereotypes that may influence certain audience's expectations for that individual, gender and the gendered expectations associated with it, or the material conditions of women's labor and life responsibilities are all aspects over which the rhetor has little control. That is, the repeated practices certain individuals perform (such as feeding children and changing diapers or caring for sick family members) may not necessarily be practices they choose to perform but rather actions they are *compelled* to perform. As Ryan, Meyers, and Jones suggest, it is often "culturally and socially restrictive for women to develop an authoritative ēthe" (2016, 2). In relation to athletics, while an athlete certainly has some agency in the decision to pursue professional athletic training, specific movements and practices, such as regimented diets or maximum timed mile runs, are dictated by coaches and other authority figures, such that certain habits are developed not through the deliberate choice of the individual but because of their subjection to another authority, and these disciplinary practices, whether chosen by the individual or not, contribute to ethos. Reimagining ethos as embodied ēthe offers feminist scholars a means to locate agency *within* subjection (not just in defiance of it), which expands opportunities for ethos to situations where rhetors appear to lack agency or are in marginalized positions. Conceptualizing ethos as embodied ēthe also better describes the various factors rhetors might need to account for in attempting to build ethos, such as previous cultural narratives or media discourses already in circulation about particular bodies or identities.

Though it does not address ethos specifically, feminist scholarship on delivery has also emphasized the importance of considering the social milieu to which a rhetor speaks and how such ideological constraints affect the way audiences perceive the rhetor. For example, Lindal Buchanan's *Regendering Delivery* provides a compelling discussion of the ways antebellum women speakers were "enmeshed within and cognizant of gender ideology in a way that their male counterparts were not" (2005, 129). According to Buchanan, "The woman rhetor was scrutinized for her private performance as well as her public presentation. The audience evaluated her sexuality, gender, body, and ethos for their correspondence to or divergence from an idealized true woman" (129–30). As Buchanan convincingly argues, traditional understandings of delivery often define it in corporeal terms and ignore the social context of the rhetor's delivery, which may pose difficulties for those from marginalized groups (159). Likewise, in her book *The Gendered Pulpit: Preaching in American Protestant Spaces*, Roxanne Mountford claims, "The body is not only an instrument of expression but is also itself expressive of meaning," which suggests that women's bodies may influence their effectiveness as rhetors (2003, 7). Instead, Buchanan suggests scholars consider delivery as "an embodiment of and response to the surrounding social milieu," with the speaker's performance "considered in relation not only to an immediate audience but also to an enveloping context" (2005, 159). In this way, feminist scholarship on delivery supports the argument that ethos is developed through a variety of forces—the social context to which one speaks, circulating cultural narratives, one's physical body, and choices about presentation, among others.

Therefore, discussions of bodily ethos that rely on Aristotelian understandings of ethos do not address the social and political ramifications of ethos as a bodily concept and cannot account for the ways an individual's ethos might be influenced by factors outside their realm of control. That is, because the body often comes to signify identity characteristics such as race and gender, characteristics an individual has little influence over, certain problems arise when ethos is viewed as specifically bodily. Aristotelian ethos is often discussed as an appeal within the rhetor's sphere of control, though work by scholars such as Jacqueline Jones Royster, Coretta Pittman, and, more recently, Ryan, Meyers, and Jones addresses the differences women and other marginalized groups might face in building ethos. For example, some individuals face issues of racism, classism, or sexism that mark them as undesirable or outside an established norm. I want to emphasize, though, that the problem with ethos is not necessarily the deviation from an established norm but that current conceptions of ethos do not discuss ethos relative to the lived, embodied experience of particular individuals. As I demonstrate below, a careful consideration of the relationship between subjectivity and ethos brings us necessarily to the physical body and the need for an embodied understanding of ethos that accounts for how material conditions such as the physical body might influence efforts at establishing ethos. Thus, I argue Ryan, Meyers, and Jones's ecological ēthe points to the need for a specifically embodied understanding of ethos in order to better convey how and why one might utilize (or be compelled to utilize) these other means of gaining ethos. Ultimately, by reimaging ethos to include the perspective of marginalized rhetors and how certain discourses may limit them, feminist scholars can retheorize ethos, opening up further possibilities for feminist analysis and women's agency.

In order to address the complexity of embodied ēthe, it is necessary to consider that subjectivity and one's ability to shape the self is also tied to the body. For Foucault (1979), power operates on the body through disciplinary mechanisms such as ranking and individualization, which work to normalize individuals, and an individual's pursuit of such disciplinary practices in turn reinforces the circulation of power. However, the relationship between athletic training and the body also presents a problem because of the materiality of the body. Elite athletic training posits that the body can be changed, that the tissues and physiological structures of the body can be developed and trained, leading elite athletes to believe they can shape their bodies and thus shape their subjectivities. Yet the understanding of the malleability of the body poses a problem because there are certain aspects of the material body that one simply cannot change, such as race or height, or the types of tissue that can be built or grafted onto the body. This presents elite athletes with the illusion that they are the self-authors of their bodies[3] and the way their bodies are perceived in society, but really their understanding of themselves and the way others perceive them are culturally constructed and situated in discourses shaped by previous cultural narratives, which may limit how they perform ethos and how that ethos is perceived.

In the sections below, I analyze the performance of ethos in Brandi Chastain's goal celebration in the 1999 World Cup, a celebration that has become iconic in women's sports history and an image brought up again and again as representative of women's athletic progress. I argue that Chastain's goal celebration marks a shift in feminist understandings about the body and illustrates the ways the physical body and public discourses about that particular body might influence a person's ethos. In particular, Chastain's celebration illustrates ethos as specifically embodied, which emphasizes ethos as malleable but also situated in previous cultural discourses. Understanding ethos as specifically embodied is important for feminist rhetorical scholarship because it attends to the lived realities of particular individuals and demonstrates the complexity of individuals in performing the self: while ethos can be cultivated by the individual, it is nevertheless subject to previous cultural narratives that might influence audience perceptions of an individual's ethos. More important, and in keeping with Ryan, Meyers, and Jones's vision of expanding feminist understandings of ethos, considering embodied ēthe allows rhetoric scholars to see and understand different capacities for action and to consider how actions and behaviors that may only seem to reinforce societal norms can actually be used to build ethos. Drawing attention to how these cultural narratives might influence ethos will help feminist scholars better discuss the efforts of marginalized individuals in building ethos.

For those unfamiliar with Chastain's goal celebration, here it is in a nutshell: the World Cup final against China was scoreless after

Building Embodied Ethe 81

Figure 4.1. Chastain's goal celebration (photograph by Lacy Atkins [1999]). AP photo. The San Francisco Examiner July 15, 1999.

regulation and two overtime periods, and Chastain's converted penalty kick ensured the win for the United States. Immediately after scoring, Chastain ripped off her jersey and fell to her knees, and this image appeared in countless newspapers and magazines following the match. The moment is especially interesting because the media both criticized Chastain as a flamboyant, exhibitionist sex symbol and exalted her as the triumphant face of Title IX.

The image of Chastain's celebration—shirt removed, biceps flexed triumphantly, abdominals visible, look of sheer joy and elation on her face—was unprecedented and came at a time when some of the first generations of post-Title IX female athletes—that is, women who had always experienced the benefits of Title IX and had access to sporting opportunities from a young age—were earning college athletic scholarships and had established themselves as professional athletes.[4] In contrast to earlier generations of female athletes, Chastain and her teammates, therefore, had a slightly different understanding of how women's bodies were understood in the public sphere. Coupled with women's increased participation in sports, the female body was now not immediately or only objectified. In addition, the more recent body commodification culture of the 80s and 90s resulted in less social stigma for women who displayed their bodies.[5] That is, because Chastain had always had the opportunity to invent and shape her physical body, she saw herself as the author of her own self-image and her body as a marketing asset that was not necessarily gender specific. Chastain's performance of ethos during her goal celebration also represents a critical historical moment within public discourse about women's athletics, and thus it makes sense to revisit this image in order to discuss the relationship between women's bodies and their ethos.

SITUATED ETHOS: THE BODY AS A MARKER OF CULTURAL VALUES

Before discussing Chastain's goal celebration in detail, I want to first explain how the previous cultural narratives already in circulation about the women's soccer team and Chastain in particular influenced public perception of the goal celebration. Chastain's performance of ethos in her goal celebration highlights the importance of understanding how the body serves as a visible marker of cultural values, thus influencing one's ethos. This understanding is important for rhetorical scholarship because in many cases, the body and bodily habits are factors the speaker or performer cannot always utilize in the communicative exchange. That is, while a speaker might temper their argument to appeal to a skeptical audience or an athlete might choose to gain muscle (changing body shape) to intimidate an opponent, the body's materiality poses limits on what can be realistically altered by the rhetor. Consequently, not everyone has the same "available means" of persuasion to draw from, and this disparity often results in certain individuals being granted ethos while others are ignored. For example, as Royster (2000) and Pittman (2007) respectively argue, certain individuals may already face a disadvantage in their ability to construct ethos because their bodies do not reflect the normative values of the community to which they speak, and thus any attempts to establish agency are automatically viewed as deviant. However, Chastain's white, blonde body reflected the cultural values of the middle class and a normative, heterosexual sexuality. In this way, and without any deliberate choice on her part, Chastain inhabited and embodied the social norms of her community.

The players on the US women's soccer team were referred to as someone's sisters, daughters, or "the girls next door" by promoters, organizers, sponsors, the media, and by team members themselves. Donna Lopiano, then the executive director of the Women's Sports Foundation, called the women's national team "a socially acceptable team" with "great appeal to middle America, to corporate America, because this was pretty much an all-white, little-girl-down-the-street, not-too-tough group" (quoted in Longman 2000, 43).[6] Situated in this way, the US women's team "presented a safe-sexy picture of bouncy femininity" that appealed to fans, corporate sponsors, and the media (41). In this framework, the team was encouraged to promote only a certain amount of sexuality, and definitely a certain type of sexuality. Nevertheless, though the media used these discourses, the team seemed to embrace this framing as well, willingly inhabiting these social norms as a means to publicize women's soccer.

Important, while Chastain and the women's soccer team already benefitted from a situated ethos that granted them authority because their (mostly) white, heterosexual, and middle-class bodies happened to reflect certain social norms, their willingness to perpetuate these cultural constructs through commercials and advertising also in turn reinforced those social norms. For example, a Nike commercial promoting the World Cup depicts Chastain, Mia Hamm, Brianna Scurry, Tisha Venturini, and Tiffeny Milbrett on a date. The commercial opens with a man carrying flowers, knocking on a door, and announcing, "I'm here for Tisha [Venturini]." The second man, who answers the door, calls upstairs, "Girls, your date's here!" The players—all wearing their soccer uniforms—file downstairs and are then shown piling into one car while their date goes along, perplexed. The commercial ends with the date promising to call, and the players collectively shrugging their shoulders while Nike's tag line for the World Cup promotion, "We will take on the world as a team," appears over the image (*We Will Take On the World as a Team 2* 2006).

While the end of the commercial does seem to suggest the players are unconcerned with having a man's attention, the commercial strongly situates the players as heterosexual and as perpetuating normative gender roles. And yet again, the players are referred to as girls, rather than women, and their actions are always shown in response to a male figure. In addition, both men in the commercial are white, and their dress and surroundings mark them and the commercial as middle class. For example, both men wear collared shirts, the outside of the players' "home" is well landscaped, and they climb into a red sports car. It seems that *safe, sexy*, and *feminine* are really just code words for *heterosexual, white*, and *middle class*, linking whiteness and straightness and middle-class values with women's ability to gain an audience. Whiteness and middle-class markers such as an expensive car or well-maintained home are circulated (via commercials or other media) into social discourses and become entrenched into cultural memory as indications of "successful" womanhood.

In contrast, the mostly African American 1996 women's Olympic basketball team, although they were just as competitive as the women's soccer team (both teams won gold medals) and garnered the same support from fans (both venues were sold out), were not as endearing to the predominantly white media and were not figured as the "girls next door" (Longman 2000, 43). For example, a Nike commercial that aired prior to the 1996 Olympics featured just Lisa Leslie—no other players on the team—and simply depicts her dribbling and shooting the basketball while a voiceover says, "You don't win silver, you lose gold." The commercial focuses on Leslie's skills as a basketball player, and she is depicted wearing loose-fitting basketball clothing, no jewelry or makeup, and with her hair pulled back tightly into a neat, inconspicuous bun. In contrast to the way the women's soccer team was represented, Leslie's sex appeal and heterosexuality does not seem to be a main focus of the ad, and there are no obvious markers of her femininity. In fact, the commercial opens with and returns several times to a close-up shot of Leslie's face, which cuts out her hair and neck, actually removing markers of her gender and instead presenting a very ambiguous image. At first glance, it is unclear whether the viewer is looking at a man or a woman until the camera pans out and Leslie turns, revealing her hair. Unlike the bouncy ponytails and girlish eagerness of the women's soccer team, Leslie appears serious, focused, and professional, and she is depicted as a skilled athlete, not a potential date.

Other coverage of the 1996 Olympic women's basketball team focused on team members' socioeconomic backgrounds. For example, a minidocumentary also produced by Nike mentions Leslie's mother is a single parent and drives a semi truck, and that teammate Ruthie Bolton grew up playing on a grass basketball court with her eleven sisters and eight brothers. Likewise, *Sports Illustrated*'s Alexander Wolff describes point guard Dawn Staley as "a Philly street kid with a heart of sisterly love" (Wolff 1996). In contrast, the women's soccer team is noted (in the same publication) for their "bright-red toenails," shopping habits, and diaper bags (Reilly 1999).

Because the women's basketball team did not possess the markers deemed desirable and acceptable by the media—that is, because they were not white and were not associated with the markers of the middle class—they received substantially less attention than the women's soccer team at the time and subsequently less opportunity to build and perform ethos. The media's depiction of the women's basketball team, with their working-class, "street-kid" backgrounds and their ambiguous bodies, situated these women as very different from the safety of the white, middle-class, normatively feminine women's soccer team. These narratives about the women's basketball team and the women's soccer team in turn shaped public opinion about the two teams, influencing how their ethos was perceived by their sports-media audiences. This is an important consideration for rhetoric and feminist scholars because it suggests ethos is tied to cultural narratives already in circulation and that such narratives are influenced by one's physical body, which means not everyone has the same opportunity or "available means" of demonstrating ethos.

For example, the attention Chastain garnered was at least in part because she reflected normative femininity, and her white body with its heterosexual markers in many ways helped her build ethos. In the iconic image of her goal celebration, there is the ponytail, which fit with the official World Cup logo, and the faint glimmer of Chastain's wedding ring, a further mark of her normative sexual orientation. Numerous media outlets chose the image of Chastain over one of goalkeeper Briana Scurry, who had made an incredible save in the penalty kicks just a few moments earlier, a no less important moment in the game. The photo of Scurry's save[7]—with her body parallel to the ground, arms completely outstretched—was featured in many newspaper and magazine articles, and there was some debate in several papers about which photo to include, the one of Scurry or the photo of Chastain. But Scurry's black body, larger frame, ambiguous haircut, and intimidating antics—she was known to glare at opponents and yell at herself—"did not fit the wholesome all-American image they were trying to project," according to Harry Edwards, a professor of sociology at UC Berkeley (quoted in Longman 2000, 285). In other words, the all-American image—the ideal reinforced and perpetuated through cultural narratives as articulated in sports magazines, newspapers, and television spots—was not black. That is, because Scurry's black and more sexually ambiguous body was located in discourses that esteemed a very different type of body, Scurry's ethos was less compelling than Chastain's.

Consider also that two other players, Linda Medalen of Norway and Sissi of Brazil, had both celebrated goals by lifting up their jerseys in the same tournament, albeit in less important moments, with very different responses. For example, although Sissi's goal was also a spectacular, game-ending[8] shot that sealed Brazil's quarterfinal victory, her goal celebration was described in a single sentence and without comment about its revealing nature: "[Sissi] sprinted around Jack Kent Cooke Stadium, gesturing for the cameras, pulling her jersey over her head in weary celebration" (Longman, *New York Times*, May 14, 2016). Media coverage of Medalen's celebration was also decidedly different than Chastain's, with a *Sports Illustrated* writer capturing it in this way: "It wasn't exactly what soccer fans had in mind when they talked about more exposure for women" ("What a Rout!" 1999). Was the difference in media coverage simply because they were not American? Or was it partly because their bodies did not display normative femininity and thus their sexual orientation was more questionable? Sissi sported a shaved head, and Medalen had come out as a lesbian in a Norwegian magazine shortly before the World Cup, though it is unclear what the US media knew about her sexual orientation.

Because Chastain's celebration was for the deciding goal of the World Cup, it unquestionably garnered more attention than Medalen's and Sissi's respective goal celebrations. Nevertheless, it would be remiss to ignore the elements of race, class, sexual orientation, and aesthetic appeal Chastain possessed. Chastain's identity as a white, middle-class, heterosexual woman gave her a significant advantage in terms of her ability to construct ethos. Many of the cultural values that her physical body represented and that her bodily actions reinforced were already rewarded by society and perpetuated through dominant cultural narratives, allowing Chastain's performance of ethos to work epideictically. That is, Chastain's racial, class, and gendered identity markers already mirrored the dominant culture's values, making Chastain's performances of ethos more appealing to the public, and Chastain's reinforcement of these values only further inscribes them in cultural memory. Understanding how previous cultural narratives might influence ethos is helpful for rhetoric scholars because it better accounts for how differently located rhetors might develop ethos.

ETHOS AS MALLEABLE: EMBODYING SUBJECT/ OBJECT, PRODUCER/CONSUMER

Chastain's performances of ethos in and leading up to her goal celebration help demonstrate the limitations of viewing ethos as completely within the speaker's realm of control. In the previous section I argue that Chastain's ethos was influenced by media discourses about her body and that Chastain specifically benefitted from the fact that her white, normatively feminine body served as a marker of middle-class, heterosexual cultural values. Yet Chastain also chose to represent herself in a particular way, which capitalized on these identity markers. For example, through advertising deals and photo shoots, Chastain crafted a public image that celebrated her fit, thin body and the aesthetic ideal it represented. Chastain was featured in an ad for a Nike sports bra in which her bare back was visible, and she posed for the men's magazine *Gear*, in which she appeared nude except for her cleats and a strategically placed soccer ball. And when asked by *USA Today*'s Christine Brennan if the team's popularity was due to their physical appearance, Chastain calmly answered, "There are those people who come purely for the soccer. There are those people who come purely for the event. And there are those people who come because they like us, to look at us. Those are three great reasons to come" (Longman 2000, 37–38).[9] In this example, Chastain seems to blur the lines between traditional understandings of producer and consumer, subject and object. She acknowledges her ethos is dependent on her body and the ideals her body represents, but in doing so, she also suggests her own agency in building and shaping that particular body. Chastain's response illustrates the complexity inherent in women's ability to build and shape the self. Traditional feminist critiques about the objectification of the female body, such as that of feminist scholar Mariah Burton Nelson (1994), often focus on normative expectations and the sexualization of the female body. For example, according to Nelson, female athletes may claim they are trying to "show off power" or "redefine beauty," but "there is still a struggle about who's going to define female beauty, who's going to define what women should wear and how they should behave" (quoted in Longman 2000, 40). However, the body Chastain displays and the context of that particular moment complicate the analysis Nelson offers. Instead, I argue that Chastain's celebration demonstrates the fluidity of embodied ēthe in that she blurs the distinctions between active and passive, subject and object. This more fluid understanding of ethos should be of interest to feminist scholars because it questions traditional understandings of ethos as completely within the speaker's control and better accounts for the range of factors that influence how ethos is constructed.

The iconic image of Chastain's celebration highlights a very obviously trained body. The body she displays, though marked as feminine by her sports bra and ponytailed hair, also lacks the obvious curves and breasts that typically symbolize a woman's sex appeal. And in contrast to her *Gear* magazine photos, in which Chastain appears bent over and looking at the viewer, holding the viewer's gaze, in the image of Chastain's goal celebration, her attention is directed away from the viewer. Feminist film studies scholar Laura Mulvey argues that when a woman is displayed as a sexual object and erotic spectacle, she "plays to and signifies male desire" by returning the viewer's gaze (2009, 19). In Chastain's goal celebration, however, her gaze is directed upward; Chastain refuses to return the viewer's gaze. Further, Chastain's body position, with quadricep, abdominal, and bicep muscles all flexed, suggests strength and power, despite the fact that Chastain is shown on her knees. Therefore, while she is pictured in her black sports bra, her body position highlights her physical dominance and ignores the viewer, and because the body she displays is somewhat androgynous, it is difficult to read this image of Chastain as a stereotypically sexualized image of an objectified body. Instead, Chastain occupies both a subjective and objective position: Because she refuses to acknowledge the viewer's gaze, the image figures her as an embodied subject that must be understood through her corporeality, but at the same time, Chastain's status as an elite athlete and the context of the sporting event in particular position her as an object to be consumed by a captive audience. In this way, Chastain's goal celebration extends discussions of women's subjectivity and embodiment and draws attention to the flexibility and mutability of ethos. This insight is valuable for feminist rhetoric scholars because it accounts for the way the physical body and differences in race, sex, class, or gender—which the physical body often comes to represent—may influence the way ethos is performed.

In contrast to Nelson's critique, Leslie Heywood and Shari Dworkin suggest that post-Title IX female athletes "have come to redeem the erasure of individual women that the old *Playboy* model of sexualization performed, rewriting the symbology of the female body from empty signifiers of ready heterosexual access, blank canvases, or holes on which to write one's heteronormative desires, to the active, self-present sexuality of a body that signifies achievement and power and is in that sense 'masculinized' or 'queered' if you follow the traditional equation of masculinity with power and heteronormativity" (2003, 82–83). As they explain, when the body is specifically coded as athletic, it can "redeem female sexuality and make it visible as an assertion of female presence and make that presence amenable to a range of sexualities" (82–83). In this interpretation, the iconic image of Chastain's celebration, while it exposes her body, is a definitive statement of female presence and is clearly an athletic image. As such, her celebration and performance of ethos allow a questioning and queering of traditional understandings of femininity and masculinity. At the same time, however, Chastain's performance of ethos in the particular moment of her goal celebration is also read in the context of other previous performances of ethos, such as her advertising campaigns and the *Gear* photo shoot, which capitalized on a normative standard of femininity and sexuality and had little to do with Chastain's skill as an athlete. As this example illustrates, feminist rhetoric scholars would benefit from considering the range of factors that might affect ethos, such as previous cultural narratives, media discourses, and individual choices regarding self-presentation.

Indeed, Chastain's performances of ethos reveal a definite tension in understanding ethos as completely within the realm of the rhetor's control. For example, in her book, humorously titled *It's Not about the Bra: How to Play Hard, Play Fair, and Put the Fun Back into Competitive Sports* (2004), Chastain seems to both acknowledge and approve of her own use of normative femininity and sexuality to develop ethos *while also* claiming women's sports should not just be about aesthetic appeal. That is, Chastain seems to rely on the fact that her white, heterosexual body inhabits certain social norms, while at the same time she also attempts to resist those social norms. In her book, Chastain claims she was "irritated" when then-president of FIFA Sepp Blatter recommended in January 2004 that women soccer players play in "more feminine clothes like they do in volleyball. They could, for example, have tighter shorts . . . to create a more female aesthetic" (Christenson and Kelso, *Guardian*, January 15, 2014). Chastain claims she was upset because Blatter's comments implied "that it's necessary to add sex to sell our game, and to promote interest, as opposed to selling the game based on the fact that we're good at it" (2004, 172). However, leading up to the World Cup in 1999, Chastain and her teammates *did* add sex to sell the game, capitalizing on the media's attention to their fit, attractive, and mostly white bodies. In this way, Chastain and her teammates represent the paradoxical subject-object: they are both subjects that purposely market their image and ethos, and yet they are commodified as objects whose image is consumed by the public. This analysis demonstrates the complexity of the rhetor's role in developing ethos because it suggests that while ethos may be constructed by an individual, it is always also influenced by previous cultural narratives, of which the rhetor may have little control. Rather, it is a combination of factors that contributes to one's ability to develop ethos, and acknowledging these various facets would help feminist scholars reconsider ethos from the perspective of differently located speakers.

In addition, Chastain admits that when Blatter's comments were made public, her name was tied to them because of her goal celebration,

Nike ad, and *Gear* photo shoot. She defends her own attempts to make soccer sexy by explaining that the *Gear* photo shoot was "pitched to me as a pre-World Cup promotion, so I was caught off guard when I realized that they intended for me to pose nude with a soccer ball" and that the photo shoot "turned out to be a great experience. Nothing critical was revealed, and the photo was tame enough that it was shown on the *Today* show. . . . From that photo shoot, I came to understand that this is who I am, and this is what I'm working with, as the expression goes, and I'm comfortable with myself" (2004, 173–74). Yet Chastain's statements about the *Gear* photos seem to stand at odds with her "irritation" over Blatter's comments. It appears as though Chastain wants to be able to construct her ethos by displaying her body but does not want others to be forced to do so or does not want others to expect her to construct her ethos *only* by displaying her body.

This tension actually reflects a tension within feminist studies between the objectification model and a woman's ability to capitalize on her own sexuality. On the one hand, Chastain opposes wearing the tighter, shorter uniform shorts Blatter suggests because such a choice would objectify her body and reinforce gendered stereotypes that see women's sexuality as at odds with their athleticism. At the same time, however, Chastain's defense of her *Gear* magazine shoot reflects her understanding of her own body as a tool that can be used to gain publicity for her sport. It also illustrates Chastain's assumptions that she is the agent of her own image. That is, Chastain suggests her ethos and her performance of ethos can and should be changeable and that she can control those changes. Like her ability to train and change her body, Chastain expects to be able to change and shape her ethos, but because ethos is negotiated between audience and rhetor, Chastain's ethos is partly shaped by the cultural narratives and epideictic rhetoric that reinforces a particular ideal based on the model of the young, attractive, thin, white woman, which Chastain happens to reflect. Therefore, while Chastain may not experience herself as objectified in images like those in her *Gear* magazine spread, their proliferation in public discourse continues to reify gender norms that highlight women's sexuality instead of their athleticism, further entrenching sport's insistence on an ontological distinction based on sex. Chastain's response thus helps demonstrate that while ethos can be cultivated by the individual, it is nevertheless subject to previous cultural narratives that might influence audience perceptions of an individual's ethos. The cultural narratives already in circulation may have limiting effects, then, on women's and other marginalized groups' ability to establish an authoritative ethos.

All Chastain's performances of ethos leading up to the World Cup—her interviews, ad campaigns, *Gear* photo shoot, and of course her playing—shaped and influenced her response in that moment. Chastain had built her ethos around her ability to shape and transform her body and had capitalized on the media's obsession with an aesthetic ideal that privileged her young, white, fit body. But that moment also called for a specific response. Chastain's celebration was kairotic: it fit the situation and context Chastain found herself in, and it met audience expectations of Chastain's performance and the performance of the team as a whole. Like her World Cup-winning penalty kick, Chastain's celebration was spectacular. The celebration, with its display of her body, also suggested Chastain's ethos consisted of her status as both an elite soccer player—with the fit, athletic body one might expect of a professional athlete—and her status as a white, heterosexual woman who represented the normative cultural values that circulated in public discourses about Chastain and the women's national team as a whole.

In offering embodied ēthe, I seek to reimagine ethos as a specifically embodied concept influenced not only by a rhetor's physical body but also by the bodily habits and behaviors a rhetor undertakes. This understanding of ethos is important for rhetorical studies because much of the previous scholarship on ethos assumes ethos is the result of deliberate choices made by the rhetor. However, as I demonstrate, this assumption does not account for how certain factors such as the rhetor's race or gender or the material conditions and lived realities a rhetor faces might influence how their ethos is perceived by an audience.

An understanding of ethos as specifically embodied better illustrates the ways ethos is influenced by the specific context of the communicative exchange, the cultural values of the community to which one speaks or performs, and the particular body that performs ethos. Chastain's performance of ethos demonstrates ethos as situated in previous cultural narratives that may privilege certain physical bodies over others. Because ethos is specifically embodied, and because the physical body often serves as a visible marker of racial, cultural, or sexual difference, certain individuals already face a disadvantage in their ability to build ethos because of racial and gendered stereotypes. For example, because Chastain's white, thin, conventionally attractive body reflected normative values and ideals, she was able to capitalize on these gendered and stereotyped discourses, redeploying them for her own purposes. Other athletes, such as Scurry, Medalen, and Sissi, however, did not have these opportunities because their physical bodies did not represent these particular cultural values. This is an important consideration for rhetorical scholars interested in body theory, materiality, or ethos because such practices and behaviors are not always chosen by the individual but may be imposed *on* the individual, which suggests the need for an understanding of ethos, such as embodied ēthe, that is more sensitive to the range of factors that might influence ethos and how certain individuals' efforts to build ethos are constrained by factors outside their control.

NOTES

1. Ryan, Meyers, and Jones provide three possible manifestations of ecological ēthe, though they carefully explain that these categories are not exclusive and often overlap: interruption, advocacy, and relation, which expand current understandings of rhetorical ethos to allow a "shift away from an Aristotelian framework toward a conceptualization of women's ethos that accounts in new ways for interrelationality, materiality, and agency" (2016, viii).
2. Jeffrey Walker also links *melete* (or deliberate practice, training) with cultivating ethos in *Rhetorics and Poetics in Antiquity* (2000, 148).
3. While the illusion of self-authorship is not unique to elite athletes (that is, anyone is liable to assume they have personal agency and overlook cultural construction), because athletics posits a "mastery" of the body, elite athletes have a different relationship to the physical body.
4. Although Title IX's influence on athletics has gained the most public visibility, it also applies to every aspect of an educational institution, including financial-aid services, housing, health insurance, and employment and ensures no individual is excluded or discriminated against on the basis of sex.
5. See Leslie Heywood and Shari Dworkin (2003), along with Holly Brubach (2015).
6. Longman argues, "If the American team represented an ideal, it was primarily a white suburban ideal" (2000, 42). Of the twenty players on the World Cup roster, none were Hispanic, and only two—both goalkeepers—were black. The lack of racial diversity was especially glaring on the US women's team because, as Longman points out, "in most places around the world, soccer was a game of the urban poor. But, in the United States it was a suburban sport, played mostly by middle class and upper middle-class whites. . . . The U.S. women reflected, like no other team, the values of mainstream, middle class, middle of the road America" (42–43). However, Longman's and others' assertions that the team reflected "mainstream" America is itself rife with the bias of the white, mostly middle-class media.
7. The photo of Scurry's save, though more athletically exciting than Chastain's, obscured her face, while Chastain's face was clearly visible, perhaps another reason Chastain's photo was chosen over Scurry's.
8. During the 1999 World Cup, overtime periods were played until one team scored, ending the game with a so-called *golden goal*. Sissy's goal was the tournament's first golden goal and gave Brazil the victory over Nigeria.
9. Chastain would later amend this statement in her book, explaining, "I want the reason people come to watch to be because they appreciate hardworking athletes and they enjoy soccer—not because of how we look. To do otherwise would not be fair to the thirty million women worldwide who play this game, and just not the right message to the players and parents reading this book" (2004, 174). Chastain's book, while partly autobiographical, is mostly about sportsmanship in youth sports and targets youth players and their parents.

WORKS CITED

Aristotle. 1955. *The Nicomachean Ethics*. Translated by J.A.K. Thomson. Westminster, London, England: Penguin.
Atkins, Lacy. 1999. *Brandi Chastain's Goal Celebration*. Photograph. *San Francisco Examiner*, July 15.
Brown, Maury. 2015. "GOAAALL! USA-Germany Women's World Cup Match Is the Most-Watched Semi-Finals, Ever." *Forbes, July 1*. https://www.forbes.com/sites/maurybrown/2015/07/01/goaaall-usa-germany-womens-world-cup-match-is-the-most-watched-semi-finals-ever/#6daf49c02883. Accessed 17 January 2021.
Brubach, Holly. 2015. "The Athletic Esthetic." *New York Times Magazine, June 23*. https://www.nytimes.com/1996/07/14/magazine/l-the-athletic-esthetic-082511.html. Accessed 17 January 2021.
Buchanan, Lindal. 2005. *Regendering Delivery: The Fifth Canon and Antebellum Women Rhetors*. Carbondale: IL: Southern Illinois University Press.
Chapman, Gwen E. 1997. "Making Weight: Lightweight Rowing, Technologies of Power, and-Technologies of the Self." *Sociology of Sport Journal* 14 (3): 205–23.
Chastain, Brandi. 2004. *It's Not About the Bra: How to Play Hard, Play Fair, and Put the Fun Back into Competitive Sports*. New York: HarperCollins.
Crowley, Sharon, and Debra Hawhee. 1999. *Ancient Rhetorics for Contemporary Students*. Boston, MA: Allyn and Bacon.
Fagan, Kate. 2014. "OK, Seriously, FIFA—What Are You Thinking?" ESPN, December 30. https://www.espn.com/espnw/news-commentary/story/_/id/11860074/ok-seriously-fifa-thinking. Accessed 17 January 2021.
Foucault, Michel. 1979. *Discipline and Punish*. Translated by Alan Sheridan. New York: Vintage.
Foucault, Michel. 2001. *Hermeneutics of the Subject*. Translated by Graham Burchell. London, UK: Picador.
Hawhee, Debra. 2004. *Bodily Arts*. Austin, TX: University of Texas Press.
Heywood, Leslie, and Shari L. Dworkin. 2003. *Built to Win: The Female Athlete as Cultural Icon*. Minneapolis, MN: University of Minnesota Press.
Hyde, Michael J. 2004. "Rhetorically, We Dwell." In *The Ethos of Rhetoric*, edited by Michael J. Hyde, xiii–xxviii. Columbia, SC: University of South Carolina Press.
Johns, David P., and Jennifer S. Johns. 2000. "Surveillance, Subjectivism, and Technologies of Power: An Analysis of the Discursive Practice of High-Performance Sport." *International Review for the Sociology of Sport* 35 (2): 219–34.
Longman, Jere. 2000. *The Girls of Summer*. New York: HarperCollins.
Markula, Pirkko, and Eileen Kennedy. 2012. *Women and Exercise: The Body, Health, and Consumerism*. Abingdon, Oxfordshire: Routledge.
Markula, Pirkko and Richard Pringle. 2006. Foucault, Sport, and Exercise: Power, Knowledge, and Transforming the Self. Abingdon, Oxfordshire: Routledge.
Mountford, Roxanne. 2003. *The Gendered Pulpit: Preaching in American Protestant Spaces*. Carbondale, IL: Southern Illinois University Press.
Mulvey, Laura. 2009. *Visual and Other Pleasures*. London, England: Palgrave Macmillan.
Nelson, Mariah Burton. 1994. *The Stronger Women Get, the More Men Love Football*. New York: Harcourt, Brace.
Pittman, Coretta. 2007. "Black Women Writers and the Trouble with Ethos: Harriet Jacobs, Billie Holiday, and Sister Souljah." *Rhetoric Society Quarterly* 37 (1): 43–70.
Reilly, Rick. 1999. "The Goal-Goal Girls." *Sports Illustrated, July 5*. https://www.si.com/vault/1999/07/05/263257/the-goal-goal-girls. Accessed 17 January 2021.
Royster, Jacqueline Jones. 2000. *Traces of a Stream: Literacy and Social Change among African American Women*. Pittsburgh, PA: University of Pittsburgh Press.

Ryan, Kathleen J., Nancy Meyers, and Rebecca Jones. 2016. "Introduction: Identifying Feminist Ecological Êthe." In *Rethinking Ethos: A Feminist Ecological Approach to Rhetoric*, edited by Kathleen J. Ryan, Nancy Meyers, and Rebecca Jones, 1–22. Carbondale, IL: Southern Illinois University Press.

Smith, Craig R. 2004. "Ethos Dwells Pervasively: A Hermeneutic Reading of Aristotle on Credibility." In *The Ethos of Rhetoric*, edited by Michael Hyde, 1–19. Columbia, SC: University of South Carolina Press.

Walker, Jeffrey 2000. *Rhetorics and Poetics in Antiquity*. New York: Oxford University Press.

We Will Take On the World as a Team 2. 2006. Nike Commercial. YouTube. https://www.youtube.com/watch?v=kFuPTnJ9ABc. Accessed 17 December 2020.

"What a Rout! Norway Beats Canada 7–1 to Clinch Quarterfinal Berth." 1999. *Sports Illustrated*, June 23. http://sportsillustrated.cnn.com/soccer/world/1999/womens_worldcup/news/1999/06/23/norway_canada/. Accessed 17 January 2021.

Wolff, Alexander. "Steward of the Game: U.S. Guard Dawn Staley Plays with Savvy and Compassion." *Sports Illustrated*. 24 July 1996. http://www.si.com/vault/1996/07/24/216311/steward-of-the-game-us-guard-dawn-staleyplays-with-savvy-and-compassion. Accessed 17 January 2021.

5
POSED TO EMOTE
Making the Emotional-Embodied Work of Rhetorical Training Observable through Yoga Practice

Jacquelyn E. Hoermann-Elliott

In a side room of Fort Worth's Indigo Yoga Studio, Parkinson's disease is shaking the woman writing on the yoga mat next to me; she is the last person to speak about what she wrote. Every participant in class had verbalized a reason for her interest in trying writing and yoga together—disease, alcoholism, body dysmorphic disorder, and infertility, to name only a few—before beginning our sun salutations. Holding onto the reasons we had written, the physical practice lasted about twenty minutes, followed by more writing and more discussion of how physical movement supported new creative and reflective possibilities for our rhetoric-writing practices. My presence in this yoga workshop was predicated on professional development; namely, I was looking to adapt lessons from this workshop for my English 10803: Yoga-Zen Writing class at Texas Christian University (TCU) (see appendix 5.A for course description and outcomes). Instead, I left with a renewed sense of rhetorical-pedagogical energy and a potential dissertation topic.

In this chapter, I explore how, as a feminist rhetoric instructor and a longtime yoga practitioner, I tapped into the potential of embodied movement in my classroom to foster greater personal and rhetorical awareness in my students. Drawing from scholarship on the relationship between physical bodies and rhetorical bodies according to Jennifer Lin LeMesurier, Christy Wenger, and Laura Micciche, I analyze the narratives of three women students enrolled in my Yoga-Zen Writing class in spring 2015 in order to demonstrate the surprising, often-overlooked role emotions play in embodied writing practices. In the case of each student, I analyze reflective writing and offer observations from the course that contextualize the emotions and experiences of embodiment each woman uncovers for herself and to the benefit of her development as a rhetorically effective writer.

DOI: 10.7330/9781646420384.c005

BODIES IN CLASSROOMS

Teaching bodies in the rhetoric classroom is fraught with conflict, just as teaching feminist rhetorics in English departments necessitated scholarly guidance and support for teachers for several years. As an instructor of rhetoric and a certified yoga teacher, I can attest to the fact that teaching bodies to move in proper alignment while also integrating rhetorical instruction or reflection into an embodied writing practice for students requires double the attention I would normally give to a lesson plan. On another level, however, I believe most teachers have grown accustomed to giving extra attention to their bodies and their students' bodies in classrooms, so much so that they no longer notice they are doing it. Most recently, Wendy Ryden's (2017–18) theorizing on corporeal pedagogies found that calling attention to the body invites the public eye to fixate on a private part of ourselves, which in turn makes teacher and student feel uncomfortable. To wit, we are always aware of bodies in the classroom, particularly when those bodies move or emote out of bounds or beyond the parameters of acceptable bodily behavior. Yet, the lack of embodied movement felt in online classes often leaves students and instructors to feel as though "something" is missing despite other affordances of an online environment (Ryden 2017–18, 57).

Likewise, scholars from the field of feminist rhetorics can (and have) testified to the challenges of introducing students and colleagues to women writers for whom the rhetorical canon has provided little space or attention. Take, for instance, how in 2006, the publication of Kate Ronald and Joy Ritchie's collection *Teaching Rhetorica: Theory, Pedagogy, Practice* merited ample attention from feminist scholars and pedagogues. Unwavering and unapologetic, Ronald and Ritchie guided feminist rhetoricians in the teaching of a new canon, for which they argued that "feminist rhetoricians are enjoined without apology to consider the study of the everyday in classrooms" (2006, 126). What is considered "everyday" includes sensory or sensorimotor expressions and movements, such as the physical embodiment of movement or the more sensory practice of meditation, both of which I sought to observe in my teaching of rhetoric students. These everyday experiences, then, become objects of feminist rhetorical study, offering their own "public and personal" histories to each student writer, particularly in terms of the writer's "histor[y] of their use, and the history of personal associations and emotions given to [the object]" (127). The salience of personal history can never be underscored enough in any course centering around a feminist rhetorician's agenda, but the role of emotions in teaching this course can be difficult to anticipate, especially when embodied writing practices are involved.

In the last decade, Sara Ahmed has become a leading authority on the role of emotion in culture and society. Her 2014 book *The Cultural Politics of Emotion* extends the allusion to emotions Ronald and Ritchie mention, offering concrete definitions and claims through which many humanities scholars have come to understand the role of emotions in writing and reading practices. Most significant, Ahmed defines emotions as "feeling[s] of bodily change," reminding us that this word has conceptual and linguistic roots in the Latin word *emovere*, meaning "to move, to move out" (5). In one example she provides, Ahmed describes how fear—as both a feeling and an emotion—makes the body immobile, almost paralyzed (69). I'd argue that fear makes a body mobile too, especially at times when escape is necessary. (Imagine the reluctant or confused writing student who, coincidentally, has the urge to use the restroom as soon as an in-class invention exercise begins.) In the context of a feminist writing classroom that features yoga, I have seen play out what Ahmed calls "feminist attachments," which she describes as the emotional associations with feminism insofar as feminism is "shaped by what it is against, just as women's bodies and lives may be shaped by histories of violence that bring them to a feminist consciousness" (174). I believe that for those better attuned to the role of emotion and embodiment in the writing process, much of their writing is driven by or formed in response to past experiences of emotional or embodied trauma. The Yoga-Zen Writing students I feature in this chapter are no exception.

Long before I became interested in embodied writing practices, the rhetorical nature of the body was being explored more casually by earlier scholars. In 1999 at the Penn State Conference on Rhetoric and Composition, Jack Selzer and Sharon Crowley were positing a claim about the relationship between rhetorical training practices and the role of the body in the rhetoric-writing classroom. Papers presented at that conference were compiled into an edited collection, *Rhetorical Bodies*, in which Selzer discusses the role of nonliterate embodied actions affecting the literate practices of rhetorical training: "Contributors insist that material, nonliterate practices and realities—most notably, the body, flesh, blood, and bones, and how all the material trappings of the physical are fashioned by literate practices—should come under rhetorical scrutiny" to demonstrate "the material circumstances that sustain [literate practices]" (1999, 10). *Rhetorical Bodies* presented the field with research and theory to support the existence of a relationship between physical practices and "literate practices," firmly suggesting that physical practices, such as delivering a speech or reading someone's body language, are shaped by literate practices—as seen in the chapter on working-class women contemplating their bodies through poetry. A few contributors discuss how existing in disabled bodies challenges traditional approaches to composition work or rhetorical creation, but none of the contributors explore the potential benefits of able-bodied physical activity for student rhetoricians.

In 2004, feminist rhetorician Debra Hawhee published *Bodily Arts: Rhetoric and Athletics in Ancient Greece*, which offers our field a thorough historical treatment of rhetorical performance reinforced through physical performance in the gymnasia of ancient Greece. Hawhee's research into ancient wrestling practices found that these practices were held alongside or in conjunction with rhetorical instruction practices (39). The pedagogical belief supporting the combination of these physical and rhetorical training activities was that students would contemplate and enact the metaphors of physical movements that mimicked or mirrored the creation of or fine tuning of rhetorical moves learned in classrooms (147). These findings may be somewhat novel to educators teaching in disembodied contexts, but since Hawhee delved into how ancient rhetoricians connected physical movement to rhetorical performance, a few other scholars have followed suit. Barry Kroll, for one, writes extensively on the martial art of aikido as "provid[ing] a physical, bodily analogue for verbal argument" and giving students "a fresh perspective on verbal conflict" in his 2008 article, "Arguing with Adversaries: Aikido, Rhetoric, and the Art of Peace" (2008, 463–464). In 2012, Kristin L. Arola and Anne Wysocki's *Composing Media, Composing Embodiment* put forth a major claim for all rhetoric and composition instructors: all media are inherently tangled in "feelings of embodiment," so much so that "tensions between those feelings" need to be explored in the rhetoric-writing classroom (2012, 3). Scholars have become increasingly interested in the role of embodiment in the rhetoric and composition classroom, sometimes seeing the role of the body as another instrument of rhetorical creation or a medium through which all rhetorical creation inevitably passes.

In Christy Wenger's 2015 book *Yoga Minds, Writing Bodies: Contemplative Writing Pedagogy*, embodied rhetoric and writing instruction are retheorized and recategorized as "contemplative pedagogy," or a broader, more open-minded approach to teaching rhetoric and composition with "yoga, meditation, and the martial arts" practices (29).[1] In her book, she locates her pedagogical approach at the intersections of feminism, materialism, postmodern/postprocess composition, and contemplative study. In her most poignant definition of her pedagogical approach, she writes, "I will theorize a feminist-minded 'writing yogi' for contemplative pedagogies, a mode of authorship that agentizes student writing and validates students' experiences of embodiment. My notion of writing yogis insists on a level of conscious awareness of our writing bodies; we certainly always write as bodies, but few of us are ready to claim them—especially in academic environments beholden to disembodiment" (25). What I appreciate most about Wenger's definition is how she locates contemplative pedagogy within the role of the rhetor-writer as a physically embodied, feminist-minded pedagogue. She connects her theory back to Kroll's concept of physical analogue, and she acknowledges how doing so is uniquely feminist in approach, particularly in academic rhetoric and writing environments where the body has been dismissed or discounted as an unworthy instrument for rhetorical creation. More recently, Wenger has contended that the practice of yoga gives student writers embodied agency so they might reclaim their senses of purpose for, perspective on, and presence in the writing process (2017–18).

Owing in large part to Selzer, Hawhee, and Wenger, Jennifer Lin LeMesurier is able to offer the field an ethnographic study of dancers to assist in our conceptualizing of bodily movement as a "foundational component of rhetorical awareness" (2016, 292). In her December 2016 *College Composition and Communication* article, she argues that "we need to reconsider how the ways we speak about bodily practices in the composition classroom do or do not support the metacognitive frameworks we also model" (293). She applies two critical adjectives when explaining the relationship between rhetoric-writing activity and embodied movement, "reflexive" and "bidirectional," which both factor into how students deploy knowledge "through bodily memory" (297). Lin LeMesurier interviewed four embodied student writers, all dancers, and describes the connection they see as a process of *bodily uptake*, which she defines as "a process that relies on the ability to shift bodily intention in the moment of reperformance . . . less an instance of situational disguise and more a process of activating latent bodily expertise" (299). More specifically, she goes on to describe bodily uptake as more of a habit or habitual process established by a person's history of movement patterns that results in "strategic bodily iteration" that enables that person "to maneuver through the expectations of other bodies, texts, and affects in a given situation" (313). Among her most notable conclusions, Lin LeMesurier finds that (1) metacognition research is not sufficient for the "unpacking" of what we must "meta-embodiedly attend to" as we write, and (2) scholars must continue "tackl[ing] this conundrum through considering how we accumulate traces of situational knowledge that support rhetorical dexterity in part by the uptakes they condition and secure" (314). Lin LeMesurier's claims, like Wenger's and Kroll's, greatly inform and influence my work as a feminist researcher in the rhetoric and writing classroom. In the next section, I introduce the course I designed to study the role of embodiment in the classroom, and then I introduce the three women whose reflexive work I studied most closely before analyzing and offering conclusions from this study.

THE YOGA-ZEN WRITING CLASSROOM

My course, English 10803T: Yoga-Zen Writing, is a themed section of a required course taken primarily by freshmen at Texas Christian University (TCU). In this course, students are introduced to a range of genres and instructed on how to use rhetorical conventions within those genres. Other learning outcomes for this course include the ability to read, quote, and cite sources with a critical lens, to employ flexible revision and creation strategies, and ultimately to understand how acts of rhetorical creation connected to writing entail a recursive process. As the predecessor to English 20803: Writing as Argument, my course teaches students about rhetorical strategies and practices more generally in preparation for the training in constructing arguments they will receive in English 20803. My class demographics were not reflective of TCU's student body due to the fact that 60 percent of enrolled students were female in 2015 and in 2016, but 84 percent of the students enrolled in my spring 2015 section and 46 percent of the students enrolled in my fall 2016 section were female (TCU: Office of Institutional Research 2016). All the students were traditional-aged college students (eighteen to twenty-two).

In fall of 2014, I submitted a research proposal to TCU's Institutional Review Board to study the effects of integrating contemplative practices—yoga, Zen Buddhism, or mindfulness meditation—into my classroom, hoping to offer students new opportunities to learn with both body and mind engaged at once. Because contemplative practice is not heavily researched in rhetoric, composition, or feminist scholarship, the research questions I began with were rather simple: (1) How might first-year writing students use contemplative learning strategies to improve students' regular writing practice and overall well-being? (2) How might a writing instructor use contemplative learning strategies to support students' learning in and out of the classroom? Students were asked to write in a variety of rhetorically reflexive genres, including in-class journal entries, out-of-class blog asanas, writing challenges (the way

I name complete writing-project submissions), and a final, cumulative project involving the digital remediation of writing texts.

The journal entries were written in class each week, sometimes twice each week, whenever we needed to reflect on a particular meditation, yoga practice, or supplementary reading or reflect on a general question related to our rhetorical development. In the syllabus, I underscored the need to avoid rushing to complete a finished product, asking students to take time to be reflective in journal entries. Likewise, the blog asanas were low-stakes writing opportunities created to support students in each unit of study we entered. Twice for each writing challenge and twice for the final assignment, students produced 350–500-word blog posts. In yoga, an asana is a position or posture that brings about a certain energetic effect within the practitioner. In my students' blog asanas, they explored a proposed issue or idea by posturing their thoughts in relation to that issue or idea, so one can imagine how the use of the term *blog asana* connected to our course and encouraged students to think about rhetorical awareness as a kind of physical activity. Ten asanas were submitted in total, and they were always due before the start of class.

Worth noting is that gender may have influenced the outcomes of this study. I taught this themed course again in fall 2016, and in that section the majority of my students identified as male. While coding data for both the spring 2015 and fall 2016 sections, I was surprised to see that, despite the fact that I used some of the same writing prompts in each section, the more detailed, demonstrative examples of restorative and generative knowing came from women enrolled in my first section, which, again, had an unusually high female-to-male ratio. I found this surprising because the second section of Yoga-Zen Writing I taught featured more in-class yoga and meditation sessions for students and more opportunities to reflect on those sessions in journals and blog asanas. My coding of the work of student writers in the second section of Yoga-Zen Writing uncovered multiple statements regarding the rhetorical-bodily awareness of men enrolled in the course, but none of those statements were long, detailed, or more thought-provoking than the examples of women writers I share in this chapter, the ones who were enrolled in my first section. Candidly, I am inclined to hypothesize that having a higher ratio of males in my second section may have affected this outcome. Based on my observations as teacher-researcher, I noticed that the men enrolled in either sections of my course were less likely to grapple with issues of embodiment or emotion in these assignments. Of course, more time for another semester to reteach this course would yield further findings and allow me to come to a more confident conclusion on whether or not gender impacted the results of this study. However, the student narratives I offer in the next section make for compelling evidence of the possibility that gender may influence rhetorical-bodily awareness in the first-year rhetoric classroom.

POSED TO EMOTE

Of the eighteen students who finished my Yoga-Zen Writing Course, sixteen volunteered to participate in my research study, which was made known to me only after the submission of final grades.[2] One of the most surprising results of teaching this course was how readily and honestly these students shared writing that was personal, emotional, embodied, and rife with physical metaphor. Of course, not every student felt comfortable enough with their own writing to explore embodied positions in journal entries, major assignments, and especially the public blog posts they wrote for evaluation. What surprised me, however, was the willingness of the majority to share such writing with classmates, openly and candidly, and with the academic audience I would write for after our class ended. From the many participants I could choose to feature in this study, I spotlight three. While there were many more than three students who explored their emotions and embodied positions through writing, I chose these three women for how well their work aligned with the emotional and embodied experience of being a "writing yogi," as defined by Wenger. Although these three writers had no knowledge of the term "writing yogi" or how this mode of authorship might "agentize" them or expand their "conscious awareness of [their] writing bodies" (2012, 25), all three women entered into this mode of authorship. Each woman's writing is emotional and embodied.

Sadie

Sadie is an example of a writer who did not feel agentized to speak about her emotional-embodied experiences at the beginning of our course but who quickly became interested in writing from an embodied subject position. In her blog-writing assignments—called *blog asanas* because each post asked students to meditate on and present a personal position on writing-related topics—Sadie quickly cultivated an honest and warmly engaging voice. In her first blog asana, Sadie was asked to relate her "Writing History" position, a literacy narrative of sorts to help students reflect on past experiences with rhetoric and writing. Past experiences with yoga, meditation, or other physical practices were neither mentioned nor solicited. Regardless, Sadie described her love of yoga, along with interests in several sports, and how the course's embodied activities and discussions helped her ease into our coursework.

> Also, I actually took this class the past two semesters, but I didn't pass last spring and this past fall I dropped. I love writing in my journal, and I would love to write in a blog about something I am passionate about; however, I feel so much pressure to write with such correct grammar that I don't feel like I can let my voice come through. For example, this letter. It's informal. I might be making it *too* informal, and I *promise* my grammar skills are *MUCH* better than I'm showing in this letter; however, I feel like I can actually show you my personality. I feel like I can actually let you hear how I speak when I am comfortable.

Sadie and I had many conversations about using personal voice in blog writing as well as academic writing. Oftentimes, our conversations circled around emotional subjects, and I encouraged her to think through ways to express her emotions to unknown readers in a rhetorically effective way so as not prejudice them against her intelligence or dismiss her as being overly emotional. In *Doing Emotion: Rhetoric, Writing, Teaching*, Laura Micciche articulates why so many have "grown weary of the usual depiction of emotion as one of rhetoric's dispossessed offspring" (2007, xiii). In these terms, during our one-to-one conference sessions, we discussed the challenges of using an emotional voice, but what I think is more important to acknowledge is how Sadie writes from an embodied subject position about her previous experiences with yoga before opening up about her emotional challenges as a writer. This entry functioned as a springboard for her, I believe, into the emotional embodied writing she would create in the first unit of our class.

In the first major assignment, the "Mantra Essay" featuring a personal narrative connecting to the writer's beliefs, Sadie felt compelled to write about what had caused her feelings of anxiety and worry. Her piece, titled "Carpe Diem: How I Learned to Seize My Day," began by telling readers, "I have lived my entire life surrounded by worry; worry that I might get sick." She recounts several significant days in her lifetime: the day she was diagnosed with stage 3 neuroblastoma at thirteen months old, the day she had her first seizure at age sixteen while driving her car, and a day one month before writing to her audience, a day she suffered a seizure so grand she admitted to herself she "wasn't normal." She vowed to readers to change the way she was living to take better care of herself and live a life of less worry. Through in-class writing journals, Sadie explored worries that crept up on her on a daily basis. In early April, she wrote candidly about how worries had taken control of her again, reflecting and strategizing ways to take back control of her emotions. In the next journal entry, written on a day when local yoga instructor Brooke Hamblet of Indigo Yoga came to our class to lead us in a guided flow and journal writing, Sadie wrote,

> "I feel blissful. Lately, I've been slightly angry at the world because there are so many things wrong with it, but today reminded me how much I need yoga and how it can clear my head. I feel like I can use the stuff I learned today for future classes just in the sense of when I get stressed. I can just do a couple of sun salutations and then write my paper. Hopefully, clear my mind a lot."

I had hoped this yoga flow and writing reflection activity would support her and other students as they went forward with the end of their semesters. Most of the journal entries seemed to suggest that the workshop supported the students, and Sadie's description of the emotions she was feeling demonstrate how physical practice brought awareness to the mind she had been writing with but not feeling, in an emotional sense and in a way that would support the development of her rhetorical effectiveness, which, again, is one of the primary aims of Lin LeMesurier's theory of bodily uptake. That is, one can benefit from using "latent bodily expertise" to establish a "habit or habitual process" that supports one's rhetorical effectiveness (2016, 299, 313). In her journal entry, Sadie is most certainly referencing the bodily expertise she gains from yoga practice and how that expertise will support her with her writing process in the future—and in a habitual way. We also see her connecting this process to the alleviation of certain emotions she feels. Again, the embodied-emotional connection that filters into her experience takes center stage and is telling of what she may learn by the end of her semester in our course.

During our regularly scheduled final-exam time, Sadie and her classmates shared their final projects, vlogs, or video blogs, rhetorically remixing a past writing project of their choice. Without any consultation, Sadie told me she knew exactly what assignment she wanted to create a vlog on. In her final blog asana, she reflected on this decision, saying, "For the second paper we wrote, I wrote about my struggle with bulimia. So I figured what better topic to make a vlog on than that one? I get to share my story and potentially help other people in the process; that sounds like a win-win to me." When the entire class viewed Sadie's vlog during her final presentation, posted to her public YouTube channel, the support of the embodied classroom space we had worked so hard to make was deeply impressed upon me. Sadie's classmates nodded affirmatively and cheered when in one scene Sadie depicted herself, arms outstretched, dressed in her TCU color-guard uniform, performing confidently before thousands of spectators with her secret written in white block text across the screen: "I've been struggling with bulimia for 3 years." On the next slide, she featured herself again, thumbs up, with text describing the growth that came from her struggle with her body and how it has encouraged her "fight against ideal beauty standards." She titled this piece "The Purge" for obvious reasons, but I suspect the previously reported feelings of worry, anxiety, and Sadie's need for freedom might have also been purged in that moment. Sadie claimed for all to see that her body and her ability to write from an embodied subject position could have a rhetorically powerful effect on her audience, sending a message her classmates applauded loudly. Through bodily uptake, she was able to write from an embodied subject position that was compelling, allowing her to hone her rhetorical effectiveness with her audience and to agentize her own voice in the process.

LeAnna

Seated on the opposite side of the classroom from Sadie was LeAnna, a first-generation college student raised by a single father in San Antonio and committed to many activist issues despite being fairly shy. LeAnna wrote more expressively than most students, writing often about what challenged her emotionally and physically, revealing a bit more each week about the personal hardships she faced. I am of the opinion that LeAnna wrote so eloquently about what troubled her most because she redirected negative emotions into creative energy.

Like Sadie, LeAnna chose to write about challenging embodied experiences, and in her reflective writing she seemed to find the most personal fulfillment when writing from an emotional-embodied subject position. In her first journal entry, she reflected on this with a quote from *Living Your Yoga*, supplementary reading material assigned to help my students grasp ways the physical and meditative practices of yoga might support academic work. LeAnna reflected on this quote: "A crucial and perhaps most powerful aspect of your relationship with yourself is your internal dialogue" (Lasater 1999, 9). To this point, LeAnna shared an emotional position affecting her writing: "This quote really resonates with me. I've struggled with depression for years, and after intense therapy, I've learned that I have the power over my emotions, and to take that power, I had to retrain my thoughts from negative to positive. Now I am a stable and content girl full of optimism." At midterm, I read my students' journal entries for the first time, but I wasn't surprised by LeAnna's entry. A few weeks into the semester, LeAnna came to my office hours to explain a reaction she had in class after receiving a paper scored as a B. She told me then that her anger issues always prompted her intermittent yoga practice and that she was going to therapy on a regular basis. Her anger stemmed from a history of abuse, which she wrote about in her first rhetorical project, the "Mantra Essay." Her last rhetorical assignment, the "Mediated Argument, Essay" argued against public opinion and perpetuation of rape culture. Through using personal voice, LeAnna put herself, her narrative, at the center of her academic writing. Her history of abuse necessarily located her in the text as a body, and her emotional response did not go unnoticed. Many years later, I would come across research on the positive mental health effects of journaling, especially for writers battling depression or struggling with emotional regulation (Suhr, Risch, and Wilz 2017). Knowing this information and feeling awe at the emotional writing work of students like LeAnna, I continue to encourage students to journal from embodied subject positions and to venture into bolder conversations about their emotions in classroom discussions.

With great audacity, LeAnna explored her emotions and embodied subject position as a rhetor continuously throughout the course of the semester. Her more public blog asana posts seemed to prepare her to win over audiences with her rhetorical effectiveness later in the semester. In one of her earlier posts, she reflected on an excerpt from Alex Soojung-Kim Pang's book *The Distraction Addiction (2003)*, which details the chaos of the mind while trying to compose at a computer, sans meditation and contemplation. In one blog post, she wrote,

> My most recent therapist, Scott, gave me a short but extremely effective lesson. He had me stand up and face him as if we were going to spar. I very lazily readied my footing as he told me that he was going to punch my shoulder straight through, and I accepted it. He instructed me to give his fist my complete attention and I hesitantly did as he told. The more his fist reached out (of course, he wasn't actually going to hit me) the more quickly I dodged it. Resilience, he had demonstrated, is synonymous to fluidity. A river's current doesn't push stones out of its way; the water goes over them. . . . Pang has reminded me that I have to be paying very close attention, rather than trying to block everything out, in order to move out of the way of the things that can hurt me.

LeAnna never voiced this or her other blog reflections in class, but they were marled with emotion and embodiment, crafted through the support of yoga movements and contemplative readings. In much the same way, most students related emotions and embodiment in a brave way but without publicly sharing what they wrote. Like that which cannot be made in words only, some of what is explored in loose journaling activity need not be articulated publicly in order to have an effect on one's body. The benefits of such work may not always be understood at first but may be better understood later in some cases. In LeAnna's case, she went on to write poetry relating her struggles with her emotions, and that poetry was published in TCU's creative writing journal, *eleven40seven*, for winning first place in the divinity school's annual Contemplative Poetry Contest (appendix 5.B). LeAnna's rhetorical effectiveness in this competition, I believe, is related to the opportunities she had to engage in bodily uptake and to reflect on her writing from an embodied subject position at multiple points throughout the semester. Thus, having opportunities to move one's body in writing class and to reflect on one's emotions in informal writing assignments seems to be fundamental to any course featuring embodied movement. Future compositionists who want to encourage productive embodied writing sessions ought to be aware of the need for multiple, graduated activities that feature physical movement but build on previous writing sessions in which reflective writing is tied to movement. This part of the process may be easily overlooked. Any instructor can encourage students to write from embodied subject positions with powerful voices, but the act of moving to emote and then write benefits substantially from time spent engaging in reflective writing work.

Vanessa

One final example of student narrative is Vanessa, whose work demonstrated maturity of voice rather early on, albeit without as much rhetorical effectiveness as she was capable of due to her restraint and her hesitation to engage in the emotional work of writing at first. In her first entry, Vanessa explained how her past year of dedicated yoga practice supported her when her "anxiety got to its worst." Several entries later, she brainstormed ideas for a major assignment to research her anxiety and it's "crippling" effects on her creative abilities.

Vanessa loved discussing her yoga practice with the class, so much so that she became the point person in our discussions about yoga's history, varieties of yoga practices, and physical-emotional benefits. Despite her knowledge of yoga as a practice, Vanessa had a harder time allowing herself to break from a traditionally academic, objective voice. In late February, she realized this on her own and wrote about her realization in her journal after the class's second yoga session with a TCU staff member and licensed yoga teacher.

> Today's yoga was much needed—I was surprised to see how strong I was (crow pose, side plank, etc.). I can definitely work on my breathing more; in my practice I tend to forget to link my breath with my body movements. . . . It takes courage for me to write without boundaries—since school has taught me to write within lines, I've been molded into a writer who can only produce work that fits in a specific form (research, rhetorical analysis, etc.). This makes it hard for me to add my own style and creative voice . . . it takes a lot of courage for me to step outside lines and try new things.

Although Vanessa presents two seemingly different points, they relate to one another. Much of what we consider voice in writing is marked by writer's breath. Consider the way we teach students to avoid run-on sentences; we teach them to punctuate by paying attention to where they pause to breathe midsentence. This embodied learning strategy is discussed to an extent in Wenger's scholarship when she claims that "breathing helps us become aware of this need for balance [in writing] and can teach us how to attain it through our bodies and exercise it in our mental and physical abilities" (2012, 28). In other words, the breath is another instrument of the body that brings into focus our writing process. Wenger goes on to recommend being "emotionally flexible" as a writer, meaning that the most rhetorically effective writers pay attention to embodied actions, like breathing, to use emotions to the advantage of their writing processes (28). Doing so supports a writer in the process of agentizing their voice, and one can see how in this passage Vanessa is attempting to link breath to body, to emotional flexibility, to writing process.

Perhaps the greatest testament to Vanessa's development as a more fully agentized rhetor came at the end of the semester. To fully understand how she—an already talented writer and the most experienced yogi in the class—grew as a rhetor, consider an excerpt from her first major writing assignment, her "Mantra Essay," in which Vanessa wrote about her anxiety in less concrete terms.

> I grew up in a blessed family, surrounded by anyone and everything I needed. I had two loving parents, one awesome sister, and an array of friends . . . I respected myself. My pen was furiously scribbling, each and every day, writing my story. But something changed. Towards the end of high school, I began to make choices that were more harmful than helpful to my mind, body, and soul . . . I lost myself in a whirlwind of substance abuse, choosing temporary happiness over the beautiful life I had before me. It wasn't long before my pen slowly stopped writing; I no longer had time to write my story, nor did I want to. I put my pen down and wandered off.

Vanessa finished this first piece with the idea that living with "a healthy mind, body, and soul ha[d] been the most challenging, yet rewarding decision of [her] life." In my feedback to Vanessa, I encouraged her to think about how more detail about her experiences might enrich the rhetoric of the descriptions shared with readers. Doing so may have challenged Vanessa's more anxious, perfectionist tendencies, but over the course of her semester, she wrote on more topics related to her emotional and embodied experiences, like her previously mentioned research report on anxiety and another "Mediated Argument Essay" exploring the psychology of free will. She told her small-group workshopping partners about what challenged her and asked them for their most critical feedback, as shared in her journal. By the end of the semester, I had challenged and brainstormed with Vanessa many times about how to use embodiment to make her rhetoric memorable. Imagine my surprise when, on the day of the class's final vlog presentations, April 23, 2015, Vanessa began her presentation by telling the class she stood before them on that day on her six-month anniversary of being drug and alcohol free. The class applauded and cheered. Vanessa went on to deliver an engaging presentation relating her personal narrative on substance abuse in a new media composition, explaining her design choices thoroughly. She chose bright images of herself when her life was going well and black-and-white renderings of images taken during her heaviest periods of substance abuse, often taken in rave or party environments and flashing more quickly to convey the sense of "numbness" she felt during that time. In this moment and with the click of a mouse, Vanessa shared a powerful rhetorical piece from an indisputably emotional and embodied subject position. More important, she shared what was for her both emotional and embodied, and she did so without shame. Vanessa thoughtfully used embodied practices to claim ownership of her emotions and her embodied subject position as a writer, enabling her to fully explore the depth of her voice and what moves her to write and make meaning of her life after addiction. In this final example, we see how over the course of a semester, Lin LeMesurier's concept of bodily uptake filtered into one writing student's experience, and then how Wenger's concept of the writing yogi played out in a way that agentized the student to be more rhetorically effective. Both scholars give us invaluable terms for naming what the field of rhetoric once leaned on long ago, as Hawhee makes clear in *Bodily Arts*, and what we are seeing more compositionists regain interest in as our field moves toward recovering our history of embodied rhetorical training.

CONCLUSIONS ON EMOTIONAL-EMBODIED RHETORICAL DEVELOPMENT

At the outset of teaching a yoga-inspired movement course, I had hoped and suspected that physically embodied writing might enhance the rhetorical awareness of my students. What I did not anticipate was the significance of emotions in embodied learning. In hindsight, when I reflected on my Yoga-Zen Writing students' narratives, I was most struck by the poignancy of emotions in their embodied writing practices. In much the same way, Micciche writes in *Doing Emotion* that her students' discovery of emotions through writing was distinctively embodied in expression.

> Looking back, I'm surprised that I did not notice at the time that my students' metaphors for writing were nearly exclusively bodily-based. The students' strong connections between embodied experience and writing are instructive to me and certainly go beyond parroting class discussion. After reading Anne Lamott's "Shitty First Drafts" (1999), students posted blog entries in which they crafted metaphors for their writing practices that used as their source material constipation, having a heart attack, and athletic practice, as well as descriptions of bodily activities associated with getting started: walking, smoking, drinking coffee, and drinking beer. (2007, 52–53)

The interplay between emotion and embodiment in our research merits continued research as we learn more about embodied pedagogical practices. Just as I did not expect emotion to infiltrate my course on embodied rhetoric and writing, Micciche did not expect embodiment to filter into her students' emotional composing work. In many ways, I see emotional and embodied practices as enacting a continuous back-and-forth flow of extension and flexion, like a muscle contracting for growth, with a reciprocal effect on the mind that feels and processes the body's movement.

Sadie, LeAnna, and Vanessa are all powerful and surprising examples of students writing from a place of tension and from an embodied subject position in order to discover the agency of their rhetorical voices. This is not to say every student benefiting from an embodied writing practice ought to experience uncomfortable amounts of tension in order to be a successful embodied writer. In several cases, I worked with students who expressed embodied insights about their writing processes with little to no connection to the emotional labor of rhetorical writing. Yet what is most interesting about these three student cases is what is most unexpected, and that is the emotional work of embodied writing practice. The emotional-embodied work of these three women rhetors offers vulnerable, telling accounts of who these writers are as students in unique embodied subject positions, sometimes located within and sometimes located outside the classroom, who are gaining agency and increasing their rhetorical effectiveness through the body. As other scholars take interest in emotional-embodied work, we can only hope rhetoricians pay closer attention to the interconnectedness of physical movement and emotional feeling, seeing the latter not as "rhetoric's dispossessed offspring" (Micciche 2007, xiii) but as a critical component of the feminist writer's rhetorical development.

APPENDIX 5.A

ENGLISH 10803: YOGA-ZEN WRITING
Fall 2016

> There is a yoga to this. An act of connection. A reordering and realigning. Like meditation and yoga asana, writing has the capacity to create and shape the space of our bodies and minds. Writing can heal us. And writing can offer us ourselves."
> —S. Harwood Rubin, *The Huffington Post*

OUR PRACTICE, OUR OUTCOMES

Both yoga and Zen philosophies offer writers profoundly insightful experiences, ones driven by more holistic views of personal development as opposed to striving for unrealistic goals or evaluative benchmarks. In this class, we will explore what these ancient traditions hold for our intentions with writing, especially when we appreciate how awareness of mind, body, and spirit can enhance our writing experience. We'll write individually so that you can better understand your personal practice as well as collaboratively in writing with other writers. Looking at the yoga sutras of Patanjali and other relevant philosophers, we will explore writing in terms of contemplation, discipline, personal power, and realization. With an open mind and commitment to this philosophy, you stand to gain clarity, focus, and the lifelong ability to overcome personal obstacles, letting you channel your intellect into writing that feels powerful to readers, and more importantly, powerful to you. Mastery of your contemplative writing practice will continue to support you in any personal or professional challenges you encounter in the years to come.

This course, like all courses at TCU, has outcomes explaining what students should achieve in the course. The outcomes listed here are the goals we are working toward, and the course was created to best help you meet those ends. By the end of ENGL 10803, students should demonstrate:

- the ability to write in a range of genres, using appropriate rhetorical conventions, such as:
  - Write multiple assignments in several genres, expanding their repertoire beyond predictable forms (e.g. the 5-paragraph essay)
  - Create a text with a focus, thesis, or controlling idea, provide appropriate support for claims, use conventions of format and structure appropriate to the rhetorical situation, and recognize such in others' texts
- competency in reading, quoting and citing sources, as well as competency in balancing their own voices with secondary sources, such as:
  - Find, evaluate, analyze, and synthesize appropriate primary and secondary sources to inform and situate one's own claims.
  - Critically read texts for main ideas and claims, for use of genre conventions, for rhetorical strategy, and for the position of the author.
- the ability to employ flexible strategies for generating and revising their writing, such as:
  - Write multiple revisions that might include substantive changes in ideas, structure, and supporting evidence, enabling students to experience writing as a recursive process.
  - Practice writing assignments as a series of tasks (invention, drafting, revising, editing)

APPENDIX 5.B

CONTEMPLATIVE POETRY CONTEST FIRST-PRIZE WINNER

ELEVEN40SEVEN, TCU JOURNAL OF THE ARTS

Spring 2015, 10th anniversary edition

"Paradox"
centered:
eyes closed, back arched.
neck up, self still.

mind loud, unsettled.
voices rough, self filled.
cringing, struggling,
hesitating, relaxing,
stiffening, softening
click.
i'm floating, body weightless.
i'm fading, self latent.
noise canceled—no plugs.
self silenced, everyone.
all connected, it's mine
it's me, i'm it—
with it, without it,
disconnected, soul in.
inhale, exhale.
back lowered. eyes open.
i'm radiating, i'm reaching
no effort.
i'm here.
(133)

NOTES

1. I also use the term *contemplative pedagogy* when referring to mind-body practices generally.
2. To protect the identities of these students, names have been replaced with pseudonyms.

WORKS CITED

Ahmed, Sara. 2014. *The Cultural Politics of* Emotion. Edinburgh, Scotland: Edinburgh University Press.
Arola, Kristin L., Anne Wysocki. 2012. *Composing Media, Composing Environment.* Logan: Utah State University Press.
Hawhee, Debra. 2004. *Bodily Arts: Rhetoric and Athletics in Ancient Greece.* Austin, TX: University of Texas Press.
Kroll, Barry. 2008. "Arguing with Adversaries: Aikido, Rhetoric, and the Art of Peace." *College Composition and Communication* 59 (3): 451–72.
Lasater, Judith A. 1999. *Living Your Yoga: Finding The Spiritual in Everyday Life.* Rodmell.
Lin LeMesurier, Jennifer. 2016. "Mobile Bodies: Triggering Bodily Uptake through Movement." *College Composition and Communication* 68 (2): 292–316.
Micciche, Laura. 2007. *Doing Emotion: Rhetoric, Writing, Teaching.* Portsmouth, NH: Boynton/Cook.
Pang, Alex Soojung-Kim. 2013. *The Distraction Addiction: Getting the Information You Need and the Communication You Want without Enraging Your Family, Annoying Your Colleagues, and Destroying Your Soul.* New York: Little, Brown.

Ronald, Kate, and Joy Ritchie, eds. 2006. *Teaching Rhetorica: Theory, Pedagogy, Practice*. Portsmouth, NH: Boynton Cook.

Ryden, Wendy. 2017–18. "Corporeal Pedagogies: An Introduction." *Journal of the Assembly for Expanded Perspectives on Learning* 23 (Winter 2017–2018): 56–59.

Selzer, Jack. 1999. "Habeas Corpus: An Introduction." In *Rhetorical Bodies*, edited by Jack Selzer and Sharon Crowley, 3–15. Madison, WI: University of Wisconsin Press.

Selzer, Jack, and Sharon Crowley, eds. 1999. *Rhetorical Bodies*. Madison, WI: University of Wisconsin Press.

Suhr, M., A. K. Risch, and G. Wilz. 2017. "Maintaining Mental Health Through Positive Writing: Effects of a Resource Diary on Depression and Emotion Regulation." *Journal of Clinical Psychology* 73 (2): 1586–98.

TCU: Office of Institutional Research. 2016. "2016 Fact Book: Student Data." http://www.ir.tcu.edu/factbooks/2016/student_data.asp. Accessed 17 January 2021.

Wenger, Christy I. 2012. "Writing Yogis: Breathing Our Way to Mindfulness and Balance in Embodied Writing Pedagogy." *Journal of the Assembly for Expanded Perspectives on Learning* 18 (1): 24–39.

Wenger, Christy I. 2015. *Yoga Minds, Writing Bodies: Contemplative Writing Pedagogy* WAC Clearinghouse. https://wac.colostate.edu/books/perspectives/wenger/. Accessed 17 January 2021.

Wenger, Christy I. 2018. "Embodied Ethos and a Pedagogy of Presence: Reflections from a Writing Yogi." *Journal of the Assembly for Expanded Perspectives on Learning*.23 (Winter 2017-2018): 76–79.

6
YOGA AS FEMINIST TECHNE
Making Space for Administrative Well-Being

Kathleen J. Ryan and Christy I. Wenger

Our *sankalpa*, or intention, in this chapter is to reimagine women's work as writing program administrators (WPAs) through the contemplative practice of yoga. In these pages, we explore the relationship between the processes of making meaning as both yogis and WPAs: together we have twenty years of experience on the mat and fifteen years of experience as university administrators. Over the years, we've found that yoga profoundly shapes how and why we do what we do. To illuminate this observation, we forward the argument that yoga is a *techne*, one that provides us a method of doing and making in feminist administration, based on Kelly Pender's and Janet Atwill's approaches to this term. Techne, which Aristotle defined as knowledge production, is concerned with making, historically an art or craft of making like carpentry or medicine. Pender's composite definitions of techne, traced along epistemological and axiological axes (2011, 14), allow us to consider the multiple, intertwined ways we, as feminist administrators and rhetoricians, understand yoga as techne. Yoga's epistemological and ethical possibilities privileging embodied, contemplative knowing and an orientation toward flourishing for the self and others is intrinsically tied to its instrumentality—the study and practice of poses. This is what teacher Judith Lasater (2015) calls "living your yoga" in her book of the same name. As yogis gain practical experience, they begin to apply contemplative ethical principles to their lives, which ultimately leads them back to their yoga practice to learn more about these new ways of being through their evolving embodiment. As techne, yoga therefore aligns with Atwill's (1998, 2006) definition of *techne* as a contingent and situated process with transformative possibilities—a flexible, situated way for people to intervene in the world, to make something new. Yoga changes us as administrators so we respond differently and more deliberately within our work environments and value the way self-care might inform our administrative

DOI: 10.7330/9781646420384.c006

identities and philosophies. Below, we explore what this looks like in practice and how it transforms our approaches to common tasks such as handling student plagiarism and conducting programmatic assessment.

We understand yoga as a practice of doing but also as a process of (re)making. Conscious and deliberate yoga practice helps us craft new ways of being, of making, and of enacting knowledge. The craft and techne of yoga create, among other benefits,

- new methods of problem solving
- new ways of negotiating and inhabiting spaces
- sustainable relationships
- means of self-care
- a hopeful and holistic mindset
- ecological agency that respects individual integrity

Notable about these benefits is how they are at once personal, collective, and intertwined; they give way to each other. For instance, the WPA who prioritizes self-care must define service to their program differently than one who is wedded to a more corporate model in which individual needs are of secondary priority; they must create new methods of problem solving using different measures of value to judge their administrative actions. Our chapter therefore accounts for both the individual benefits and the professional merits of approaching yoga as techne. This both/and movement honors the holistic philosophy of yoga that disrupts binaries of self/other and body/mind, creating a feminist ecological rhetorical space of potential for our work.

Understanding yoga as techne provides actionable strategies—ones that unsettle the mind/body binary—to employ for working toward our own and our programs' well-being. Bringing yoga to bear on our workplaces reminds us to treat our bodies with kindness, even if that means shortening meetings so we can have a few minutes to breathe or walk before our next obligation, and to similarly respect the materiality of our colleagues. This approach is why we see our project as feminist and ecological: for us, feminism entails both seeking to end all women's oppressions and the broader project of practicing an ethics of flourishing, derived from bringing together feminist rhetorical studies and ecological feminism, which aims for the mutual flourishing of all beings. Flourishing redirects "liberal emphases on atomistic individuals" in favor of living with others as a practice of situated and ethical decision-making (Cuomo 1998, 111). It is oriented towards the vital yet difficult work of being responsible to and respectful of all beings while changing things for the better (72, 76, 109) and has much in common with contemplative ethics. Our work here centers on theorizing yoga as a feminist techne to encourage well-being in the academic workplace, intervene in the status quo at work, and invent different ways of acting/making to create flourishing for ourselves as WPAs and for/with those around us. We answer the following questions: (1) What is a feminist techne? How is yoga a feminist techne? and (2) What are the feminist implications of seeing our professional work through yoga? How does yoga become a motive and means for intervening in the status quo in our departments? Answering these questions helps us illustrate that part of what we "make" in yoga is a reimagined sense of well-being that is both networked and resolutely personal. Moreover, bringing rhetorical thinking to yoga has helped us more consciously recognize the significance of our yoga practices. Yoga philosophy and practice disrupt more hierarchical and less ecological models of the university and helps us open and hold a space for feminist administration.

YOGA AS FEMINIST TECHNE
Productive Knowledge/Process

Yoga is a techne that provides us a method of doing and making in feminist administration that focuses on holistic and humane acts of invention and intervention (Atwill, 1998, 48). We are drawn to Atwill's definition of techne as productive knowledge because of its emphasis on making as a situated and contingent process. As Atwill writes, "Productive knowledge is concerned with the indeterminate and the possible—and that which presents us . . . with alternative possibilities" (195). The transformative possibility of *techne* lies in this indeterminacy; *techne* transforms, in Atwill's words, "'what is' into 'what is possible'" (70). Feminist techne focuses on specific sorts of social critique and transformative action. As feminist WPAs, we resist workplace practices that displace caring for the self and others and undermine the productive promise of enacting writing program administration via an ethics of flourishing. Praising overwork is a common habit in our workspaces, one we actively resist.

Describing yoga as a feminist techne underscores its potential to intervene, first in individual well-being and second in department cultures. Yoga helps us cultivate a more balanced sense of identity and attention to holistic flourishing as persons, not just as academics. Yoga not only makes us less susceptible to illness but also encourages us to focus on what we're doing to be well, practicing mindful self-care rather than participating in the unconscious one-upmanship of hallway conversations about working ourselves into exhaustion. In this way, we draw upon Pender's discussion of techne as a means of inventing new social possibilities by first changing self-identifications (2011, 27). Our individual practices of yoga, centered as they are around increasing our overall well-being, entail identity shifts we and others notice: as we find our understanding of self changing and attentiveness increasing, the ways we connect with others become more open and empathic. Christy, for instance, deepened her study of yoga as a graduate student attempting to survive the high-stress years of advanced doctoral education while teaching and serving as a graduate student WPA. At the time, yoga helped her realize the importance of spiritual and mental health in addition to intellectual health. As Christy developed her awareness through yoga, she was able to focus better on her work and to recognize the need for boundaries around that work, improving the quality time she spent with her spouse—giving up grading at the dinner table, for instance. As WPAs, we actively seek to shift away from academic tendencies towards celebrating a cult of busyness that values ill health; figuring the rational, autonomous, male scholar as the eponymous scholar; and participating in an academic culture that devalues its young women professionals. That Christy discovered these possibilities as a graduate student isn't coincidental according to Atwill, who claims in "Bodies and Art" that techne is often created when novices become socialized into new practices and must "learn by art what those who have long been in those situations have done by habit" (2006, 169).

Like Christy, Kate returned to yoga at a time of need, a couple of years into her second job as an untenured director of composition. Initially, yoga was a means to counter the stressful demands of her heavy workload, one fairly typical for many untenured women WPAs. Ultimately, Kate's yoga practice became even more salient for the way it teaches present centeredness when, just a few weeks before her tenure file was due for review, a department colleague she had previously considered a feminist friend wrote a specious letter against her tenure. Despite her colleague's scant, sexist "evidence" and the illegality of citing collegiality as a reason to deny tenure at the institution, this colleague successfully lobbied Kate's tenured colleagues towards her cause and, as a result, Kate's tenure case was derailed for a year. The ordeal was characterized by verbal attacks by her colleague and the department chair, silence and averted gazes by department colleagues perhaps embarrassed or anxious about the situation and their complicity in it, confidential conversations with tenured colleagues who expressed fear of this woman's bullying, and numerous meetings pertaining to the actual tenure and promotion case—all while Kate continued to direct the composition program.

Yoga was Kate's primary means of self-care during that difficult time, especially the cultivation of nowness as part of a regular yoga practice. Yoga teaches us to dwell in the present moment, which we first learn to do by attending to "the reality of the body" and then extending that learning beyond the yoga mat (MacGregor 2013). Yoga teacher and writer Kino MacGregor writes, "When you surrender your necessity for the present moment to be a certain way you are free to experience it as it is" (para. 4). The ways past and present experiences and future desires recede to focus on the now during asana practice—the current posture, the current physicality of the body, the current breath—is something Kate practiced at work. Each day she went to the office, she imagined physically armoring herself against the negative environment to help her focus on the day's responsibilities moment to moment. Yoga provided a daily respite from wearing this armor, a space to soften and shed her embodied response to the hostility directed at her, even as it taught her to recognize the current usefulness of this act of self-protection at work. Cristyn Elder and Bethany Davila's collection *Defining, Locating and Addressing Bullying in the WPA Workplace* (2019) helpfully names and describes bullying experiences like this one; we understand that by challenging the silences around academic bullying, Elder and Davila are also promoting agentive self-care among WPAs.

Kate's experience highlights the increased attentiveness we've gained through our practices and speaks to how yoga as techne is present-centered, reliant on "nowness," as Atwill suggests of all techne (1998, 57). If the painter produces a painting through the immediacy of their art, the yogi produces a heightened state of awareness through mindfulness. Mindfulness is, as Jon Kabat-Zinn describes, "paying attention in a particular way: on purpose, in the present moment, and nonjudgmentally" (1994, 4). Like other techne, yoga "locates its end outside of the process of making in the use of the thing made" (Pender 2011, 5). While mindfulness as a useable end is less tangible than a painting we might hang on a wall, it is no less transformative or purposeful. Mindfulness as the end and aim of yoga (achieved through the practice of asana) cultivates well-being through acceptance, greater awareness, and connection.

Practicing nowness gave Christy the ability to diagnose her overwork habits and see how those impacted her personal relationships and allowed Kate to give her attention more fully to each moment as it came, regardless of the latest assault on her character or work. For us both, nowness helped us build personal and interpersonal boundaries that allowed us to do our jobs with integrity and foregrounded our feminist values. Today, we find our disciplinary expertise sharpened by our practice of nowness, even when we cultivate present-centeredness in the small, often undocumented moments of interacting with other teachers or students during office hours. These practices have helped establish trust and genuine appreciation in our administrative actions so that we have learned to expect that GTAs, adjuncts, and students are doing their best in their respective roles, even if that "best" doesn't always correlate with grades or other performance indicators. This is an important lesson for the students we teach, too, one Alexandria Peary attempts to impart in her mindfulness pedagogy of writing focused on the nowness of the present rhetorical moment (2018, 24–25). We see this attention to nowness as a feminist practice of recognizing and extending to others the right to their own self-care, of acknowledging to them that they too are whole persons with complex demands on their lives that necessitate different choices, behaviors, and actions. Listening and responding to others' needs is a very deliberate act of care, for ourselves and the people associated with our composition programs.

Ecological/Community Based

WPAs rarely have the luxury of solitary academic pursuits; we're regularly working with others on all sorts of projects and committees, often negotiating difficult power dynamics and claims on our time and programs. Over time, we've come to believe, following bell hooks, that striving to become self-actualized as teachers and administrators is a vital goal to support the mutual flourishing of program leaders, teachers, and students (1994, 15). Like many WPAs, we are regularly positioned to reenvision curricula and teacher development and revise policies and practices. While the prospect of change and transformation is exciting, the reality is often messy and uncomfortable, particularly when we enact feminist administrative practices like decentering authority to invite new perspectives—and even more so when, for instance, we're asked to make curricular or policy changes incompatible with our values.

Practicing yoga as a feminist techne offers an ethical guide to this challenging work. It entails trying to shift to more relational and situated/embodied ways of being in the world, bringing beliefs and practices cultivated on the yoga mat into the university. Kate's yoga teacher, Amy, encourages her class to give a little energy to the group if anyone has extra to share or to take a little if they need it; in doing so, she reminds us of the power of group energy—as surely as we can bring one another down, we can lift one another up. This lesson on the mat reinforces our interest in rhetorical ecological feminist agency, which always locates individuals among others and in particular ecologies.¹ It is particularly important to us when working with adjuncts and lecturers to operate from the perspective that "a community cannot flourish unless a significant number of its members are flourishing. A community's 'flourishing' cannot depend on oppressing or instrumentalizing the members of the community" (Cuomo 1998, 75). Local interventions like making adjunct-hiring processes transparent, creating teacher-development and leadership opportunities, and even appreciating a teacher's daily swimming regimen alter a community's collective sense of well-being. Efforts to foster mutual respect and develop an awareness of others' perspectives and positions help cultivate a community of valuing one another, and they matter tremendously. It was, in fact, the recognition that Kate could no longer flourish, even posttenure, in her department that led her to leave her prior university position. Sometimes possibilities are too tied to factors unlikely to change, and Kate's yoga practice helped her determine that.

Simply, yoga as techne is a means for us to enact ecological thinking within administration and to shape a more responsible feminist ethic of care as administrators. As Christy (Wenger 2014, 125) argues elsewhere, more traditional ethics of care, like Carol Gilligan's "injunction to care" (1982, 159) and Sara Ruddick's "maternal thinking," are implicated in problematic leadership models (1980). These models often subsume individual care to collective care, requiring a kind of selflessness at odds with the ecological sense of flourishing we advocate for here. By examining the uniqueness of a contemplative ethic of care, which locates the individual in relation to others and invites "respect for and attention to embodiment as lived and real" (Wenger 2014, 131), we can see how yoga as techne both invents and disturbs. As invention, yoga allows us to craft new perspectives based on the principles of mindfulness and to imagine new ways of interacting with colleagues and students as we attend to the everyday challenges of WPAing in more humane and holistic ways. As intervention, yoga keeps our efforts focused on personal growth and well-being when the very nature of administration is often driven toward a model of service to others, which tends to negate the needs of the self. In turn, yoga as techne becomes a motive and means for positioning self-care as a necessary complement to the care of and service to others. The care we can give our programs and teachers is first dependent on the care with which we treat ourselves. In learning how to care for ourselves during the busy semester, we better mentor our teachers and students to consider ways to sustain themselves, whether that means encouraging a new teacher to set a timer so they don't spend too much time grading or listening to a student talk through their writer's block to help them strategize ways to move past it. When self-care is present, other care can flourish.

Embodied and Instrumental

At the same time we embrace Atwill's interventionist and inventional prospects of techne, we take from Pender the necessity of thinking about definitions of techne on a continuum and therefore accepting the productive tensions among value, instrumentality, and knowledge making. So, while yoga is valuable in its instrumentality, the making of poses and a flexible body, its value exceeds this physicality to include the (re)making of a life: a value at once instrumental and intrinsic. Yoga is often represented as little more than a series of asanas or poses in popular US culture, a way for trim and flexible bodies to get trimmer and more flexible, yet practitioners soon learn that yoga is more than synchronized movement or glorified stretching. "The body cannot be separated from the mind" says BKS Iyengar. "In India, asana was never considered to be a merely physical practice as it is in the West" (1998, 46). To put it another way, bodyfulness "begins when the embodied self is held in a conscious, contemplative environment" (xxiii). Yoga is holistic, a way of thinking about and perceiving the world—of purposeful being—and not simply a practice that occurs on a sticky mat. Its ethics are rooted in this instrumentality since the practice encourages us to live in harmony with the material world, including other people and the environmental surroundings.

To us, this prospect of embodied change is the promise of potential, a shift toward alternatives, made through our bodies and minds, made through yoga. In particular, we find Pender's composite definition of techne as a "rational ability to effect a useful result" (2018, 16) important for understanding the ways makers learn to make. Pender writes, "At the heart of this definition lies the method, technique, or skill that the artist uses in order to produce" (21). Because techne is situational, "those methods, techniques, and skills must be accompanied by a deeper, more comprehensive understanding of the causes of success and failure if one is to claim possession of a genuine techne according to this definition" (22). In other words, you can learn yoga and you can practice skills or techniques to improve, where improvement may mean doing a pose more deeply and more precisely or achieving a balance of strength and flexibility with calm breath. To enact care for ourselves in practice, we must know our limits to avoid self-harm and must acknowledge negative feelings—both mental and physical—to learn to see yoga practice as a process guided by the intention of uniting body and mind and with the end of creating mindfulness, not perfect poses. That's hard. And it's equally applicable to our work as WPAs.

Kate's practice helped her cultivate new ways of thinking about and responding to negative emotions in program administration to actively disrupt the anger some faculty felt at perceived student transgressions, particularly their responses to student plagiarism and negative comments in their course evaluations. She worked with teachers and students to reframe these situations. Teachers often take student plagiarism or negative commentary too personally and get angry about these activities because they see them as moral transgressions and personal attacks. Yoga helped Kate rethink the emotional work and situational factors tied to these kinds of faculty responses. It helped her shift the conversation on plagiarism from anger and reactivity to inviting compassion and responsiveness to situations as a process of coming to understanding rather than a rush to punishment. A student's plagiarism or negative comment isn't necessarily about the teacher; it's often about the student's choices and beliefs about learning. A student may well plagiarize or criticize a workshop class because of their fears of failure. A more humane approach to "attacks" or "transgressions" is to recognize student agency and to disrupt emotional punishment originating from the teacher's own fears and worries. Inviting teachers to imagine perspectives and responses based on care of self and others shifts the discourse surrounding plagiarism. The equanimity Kate discovered through yoga helped her respond to plagiarism cases and teacher interpretations of course evaluations differently, disentangling facts and consequences from misplaced emotional baggage. It also helped her develop strategies grounded in empathy for encouraging teachers and students to rethink their own actions and responses to these issues.

In Christy's four years as a WPA at her current institution, she has navigated complex relationships between contingent instructors, who regularly teach first-year writing, and fellow tenure-track and tenured colleagues. In an effort to apply mindfulness to her program, she redrafted common syllabi and instituted more professional-development opportunities to increase communication and learning. While her efforts are guided by the intention to create a clear and unified program, some contingent faculty have interpreted these changes as intrusive and as compromising the freedom they once had. Conversely, some tenure-track faculty have taken issue with her mentor program. Not only does this program accelerate communication among all faculty since tenured mentors are required to observe adjunct faculty, but it also opens space for mentees to observe tenure-track faculty's classes as well, which can be interpreted as shifting the power dynamics between these groups. While it would be easy for Christy to dispel tension by framing observations as suggestions and not mandatory initiatives, she has, instead, reiterated her commitment to the collaboration at the heart of feminist administration. This commitment is a way she cares for herself and her program. By cultivating a collaborative environment, not only is she happier an administrator, but she is also relieved of being the *only* source of support for writing instructors.

While "understanding" in Pender's definition of techne focuses on the rational mind, the knowledge making that happens in yoga privileges embodied and situated knowledges often unrecognized in academe. Learning a new pose requires rational knowledge in the sense that learning archer pose, *arkana dhanurasana*, means knowing which toe to grab with which hand and what the grip involves, but it's embodied in that you learn to feel the aim and end of the pose in the strength of the lower spine, the twist in the upper spine, and so on. It's utterly situated in that each practice necessitates being aware of the body at that time on that day to determine how deep in the pose the body can go at that moment. You don't fail at yoga; rather, a student observes and uses cues from their body and teacher to learn more over time, whether better alignment or better breathing technique. Applying this mindset to her mentoring program means Christy is able to approach resistance not as a failure of the program per se but as a means of recognizing suspicion of the shared power of genuine collaboration and using this knowledge to both validate her colleagues' present feelings and work to create more opportunities for meaningful collaboration to slowly normalize within her workplace. All these individual moments of learning, practicing, and understanding combine to create a yoga class, a yoga practice, a yogi practitioner. Seeing yoga as a "useful result" helps us think about how to develop a yoga practice and "inventing new possibilities" helps us see how we are using yoga to change our lives and, further, how we can more deliberately harness it to change typical academic practices and values. In other words, we extend the makings of yoga to writing program administration, although "these strategies will be characterized by 'a certain roughness and imprecision'" (Allen 1993, 88, quoted in Pender 2011, 26). As with yoga, we can learn to be better WPAs and develop ethical methods and abilities to adopt and adapt to different situations.

YOGA AS A MEANS OF FEMINIST INTERVENTION

Book 2 of the *Yoga Sutras of Patanjali*, which focuses on the physical practice, includes this sutra, or aphorism: "Asana is a steady, comfortable posture" (*sthira sukham āsanam*). In his discussion of this sutra, Sri Swami Satchidananda writes, "Unless the body is perfectly healthy and free from all toxins and tensions, a comfortable pose is not easily obtained. Physical and mental toxins create stiffness and tension. Anything that makes us stiff can also break us. Only if we are supple will we never break" (1990, 152). He goes on to tell a story of a "humble" and "supple" weed that bends easily in a flood whereas a great tree is uprooted and carried away by the waters. Yoga creates suppleness through movement linked with breath. We learn over time and practice to control our breathing to be "gentle, slow, and fully controlled, without any agitation." This is the yoga sutra 49: "That [firm posture] being acquired, the movements of inhalation and exhalation should be controlled. This is praṇayama" (158). The union of body and mind comes from practicing asana with controlled breath. This union teaches us how to be calm and flexible in mind and body, that these are utterly entwined states. Mindfulness is bodyfulness. Finding peace on the mat makes it easier (and more desirable) to make peace in your day. In classic hot yoga, learning to be still and have ease of breath despite the distractions of heat and sweat makes it possible to cultivate serenity in the chatter of daily life, quieting the "monkey mind." From yoga we've learned how to better observe when we act out of agitation at work, and we have better tools for calming our minds and bodies through breath and movement, which, in turn, helps us make more deliberate choices and decisions. We do not mean to suggest we are always mindful and never mindless in our professional practice because of our dedication to yoga as techne but that we find we are better able to tap into, understand, and distance ourselves from internal chatter when we find it necessary to increase our focus, productivity, or sensitivity to others. Like Peary's pedagogical method, our approach cycles "between mindfulness and mindlessness and back" to help us "identif[y] recurrent or habitual ways of thinking" (2018, 63).

Yoga consequently helps us approach resilience as a skill that can be learned and applied to WPAing, allowing for the invention of new models and spaces for agency through both action and purposeful nonaction. For us, administrative suppleness translates into what Elizabeth Flynn, Patricia Sotirin, and Ann Brady describe as feminist rhetorical resilience: "not [as] a state of being but [as] a process of rhetorically engaging with material circumstances and situational exigencies . . . not as a quality of the heroic individual but as always relational" (2012, 7). Resilience means attending to the networks within our workspaces to produce lasting, mindful impacts through three key elements: rhetorical agency, which is relational and responsive, "realiz[ing] possibilities and resources by shaping and enacting relationships among selves and others, speakers and audiences, things and dreams, bodies and needs, and so on" (7); metis, or "contextualized intelligence" (8) entailing "innovative resourcefulness" and the ability to find meaning despite change and uncertainty (9); and relationality, or "supported vulnerability" that draws upon an ethic of connection and leads to empowerment (11–12).

A tangible benefit of yoga is the development of rhetorical resilience, particularly evident in the element of *metis*. Metis is responsive and flexible and creates a different kind of power; power *with* as opposed to power *over* others or one's own shortcomings. The introduction of *Rhetorica in Motion* describes metis as "the ability to move side-to-side" (Schell 2010, 28), a nonhierarchical alternative to power in traditional rhetorical structures. Debra Hawhee uncovers how metis is "an encounter with the immediate," a product of the mind and body working together as well as "a mutually constitutive struggle among bodies and surrounding forces" (2002, 150) in classical conceptions of this term. Hawhee argues that learning requires the sustained engagement of habit production, which can only be successful if both mind and body are equally involved in rhetorical training. This idea echoes the contemplative philosophies of yogis like Iyengar, who similarly notes that in the "integrated science" of yoga, "the three levels of being—body, mind and soul—are all involved . . . and can lead man's divided being back to wholeness and health" through mindfulness (*1998*, 85). Metis might be thought of as learning to breathe into a pose despite how it may make you shake and quiver as you engage new spaces in your body or as you recognize the dynamic nature of stability as you sway in a balance pose. It's moving *with* the world and your body as a microcosm of matter. Yoga as techne promotes our development and application of metis, or an embodied and situated intelligence that finds strength in the fluidity of life and through the integration of self by learning to move with it, reshaping what counts as administrative action.

To illustrate, with every passing year at Christy's job, she has faced increased pressure to assess the first-year writing program. This pressure began during her first year on the job—well before she could learn her program. At first, she *reacted* to this pressure and accompanying stress by meeting assessment demands in traditional manners: she grafted a portfolio requirement onto the existing first-semester, first-year writing

(FYW) course within that same year. Once it was in place, she quickly collected a random sample of student portfolios from these classes and requested funding to hold an assessment workshop to train instructors for a comprehensive portfolio review. But to include a representative group of writing instructors, she requested money to fund participation by the contingent faculty who teach 88 percent of FYW at her school—a request she was denied. Christy's initial reaction to assessment pressure was to abandon mindfulness as a guiding factor of her resiliency and strength as an administrator.

The double pressures of assessment and inadequate funding remain a common challenge for WPAs. Many WPAs similarly feel pressure from upper administration, the pressure of power *over*, and we react in turn by issuing top-down changes within our programs. We *react*, whereas mindfulness asks us to *respond* with intention: to create a space between perception and response. In our efforts to please, we may threaten our resilience, well-being, and relationships with colleagues. Alternately, Christy's subsequent response to assessment demands can be understood through our discussion of yoga as techne for feminist administrators. Her responses have been intentional though not measurable by most administrative standards of action. She has embraced the side-to-side movement of *metis* by choosing to read the denial of assessment funds as unjust and as counter to her administrative ethics. She has therefore paused before completing what was expected of her after the denial of funds, creating a secondary assessment measure and implementing a top-down review as WPA. Instead of reacting, Christy has channeled the majority of her energies into power *with* strategies to promote programmatic well-being, refusing the action of assessment for its own sake and using a commitment to portfolios to develop a healthy writing community. To do so, she has worked with writing instructors to study portfolios and to find strategies to better utilize them in order to promote revision and process writing in FYW. In turn, she has built a support network of instructors who have come to see portfolios as essential to their own personal pedagogies and not just necessary for the program's success. As this example illustrates, yoga inspires us to honor "the experiential knowledge of a particular body"—here, Christy's body—while working within the limitations of a particular situation to create new social possibilities and enact cultural critique of university culture (Pender 2011, 29).

The awareness and inner peace we've gained through yoga make us better able to create deliberate interventions as WPAs even as they also make us increasingly unwilling to work in departments that unconsciously foster ill health. This new understanding means we try to change such places for our well-being and for that of our writing students and teachers. In a feminist departure from what is suggested by the victim narratives in WPA literature, we imagine our lives as WPAs can be peaceable and pleasurable; approaching yoga as techne helps us theorize an ethics of flourishing for writing program administration that aligns with our commitment to well-being. The ways we understand our relative success as administrators has shifted as a result of this new ethics. As beginning yogis, we didn't immediately expect to be proficient in a challenging inversion like headstand. Sure, we were amazed by classmates who could defy gravity in this pose, but we knew sustained practice was first necessary. Now, as experienced yogis, we are even more aware of the challenges of a pose like headstand and the importance of keeping the spine and neck safe, so we have even greater patience with our practice. Yet, as beginning WPAs, we often expect (and are often expected to) immediately "fix" writing programs, the equivalent of an inexperienced yogi jumping on a mat and executing headstand perfectly. Seeing our administrative work through yoga means that we must chart progress slowly and that the greatest measure of success is not quick reaction but deliberate, mindful, and situated response. As administrators, this kind of response means we can spend much less time backpedaling from quick actions that don't produce meaningful results, such as Christy's failed first efforts at implementing assessment we detail above, and instead we can carve out time for a healthy personal life that supports our professional responsibilities. It is essential to our overall well-being that we set boundaries around our WPA work so we have not only time but also mental, emotional, and physical energy left for our families and friends and ourselves at the end of the workday. In this way, the self-care necessitated by yoga applied to our administrative ethē helps us be more deliberate about our choices and actions, allowing us to get more accomplished, not less, by channeling our energies into what really matters. Yoga therefore helps us craft meaningful slowness in both our personal and administrative lives.

Yoga as a feminist techne highlights the activist element of a yoga practice in the sense that we're using it to "effect a useful result" in the world; it's a philosophical heuristic for living and administering programs. And for us it has also meant integrating a theme of mindfulness and daily classroom meditations into our classes and shifting hallway conversations towards wellness. We recognize and act on the need to create humane relations and spaces within ourselves and relative to others. Practicing yoga as WPAs helps us develop equanimity to better make difficult program decisions, to discover freedom from injuries and chronic pain in a profession that puts us at a desk a lot and shift our priorities to value self. With increased health in body and mind, we are better able to support others, better able to act on behalf of our programs and teachers.

* * *

We used to think of the Greek god Kairos's balancing act rather than plate twirlers or jugglers to imagine our WPA work (George 1999), but now we think of a yogi, in standing bow, *dandayamana dhanurasana*, simultaneously kicking their right leg back and up towards the sky as they stretch their left arm and fingertips forward toward the horizon. Kicking and stretching must be equal and simultaneous or you fall out of the pose. We call to mind this strong and graceful balancing posture because one of the themes cutting across this chapter is the need to live with opposing forces and ambiguities. These tensions may be caused as much by current circumstances as by the awareness that we can't dramatically change corporate models of higher education but can work to intervene in them locally by opening spaces for self-care and well-being in our programs. Approaching yoga as techne encourages us to start with ourselves by making self-care a priority, but it also pushes us to foster well-being within the community, in relation to others. Our resilience is shaped similarly: it's less about being a hero, able to "deal" or pursue forward action at all costs, and more about learning how to create spaces, moments of self-care, which will then extend to more deliberate choices regarding the care of others.

In the end, yoga as techne gives us a means of framing our work as a process that is flexible, embodied, and teachable. It reminds us that our work as rhetorical ecological feminist administrators is to create spaces where well-being—for everyone and everything—flourishes. If an important implication of seeing our professional work through yoga is both self and other care, then one of the implications of complicating techne through the contemplative is living with the tension between making thoughtful judgments as a WPA—that "reasoned state of capacity to *act*" (Pender 2011, 21)—and cultivating a yogi's nonjudgment, or acceptance of and compassion for ourselves and others. We see feminist writing program administration as significant rhetorical and ethical work that regularly entails trying to make "good" decisions that lead to flourishing. Program decision-making is hard, particularly when we must choose at times between equally "bad" choices or tease apart an issue that entails many people with competing perspectives or priorities.

Seeing WPA work through yoga as techne helps us better address the real, material possibilities of well-being to shape meaning in the lives of untenured women writing program administrators and the programs they direct.

NOTE

1. For a discussion of rhetorical ecological feminist agency, see Kathleen Ryan (2012).

WORKS CITED

Allen, James. 1993. "Failure and Expertise in the Ancient Conception of Art." *Scientific Failure*, edited by Allen Janis and Tamara Horowitz., 83–110. Lanham, MD: Rowman and Littlefield.

Atwill, Janet M. 1998. *Rhetoric Reclaimed: Aristotle and the Liberal Arts Tradition*. Ithaca, NY: Cornell University Press.

Atwill, Janet M. 2006. "Bodies and Art." *Rhetoric Society Quarterly* 36 (2): 165–70.

Cuomo, Chris J. 1998. *Feminism and Ecological Communities: An Ethic of Flourishing*. Abingdon, Oxfordshire: Routledge.

Elder, Cristyn, and Bethany Davila, eds. 2019. *Defining, Locating, and Addressing Bullying in the WPA Workplace*. Logan, UT: Utah State University Press.

Flynn, Elizabeth A., Patricia Sotirin, and Ann Brady. 2012. "Introduction: Feminist Rhetorical Resilience—Possibilities and Impossibilities." In *Feminist Rhetorical Resilience*, edited by Elizabeth A. Flynn, Patricia Sotirin, and Ann Brady, 1–29. Boulder, CO: University Press of Colorado.

George, Diana, ed. 1999. *Kitchen Cooks, Plate Twirlers, and Troubadours: Writing Program Administrators Tell Their Stories*. Portsmouth, NH: Heinemann.

Gilligan, Carol. 1982. *In a Different Voice: Psychological Theory and Women's Development*. Cambridge, MA: Harvard University Press.

Hawhee, Debra. 2002. "Bodily Pedagogies: Rhetoric, Athletics, and the Sophists' Three Rs." *College English* 65 (2): 142–62.

hooks, bell. 1994. *Teaching to Transgress: Education as the Practice of Freedom*. Abingdon, Oxfordshire: Routledge.

Iyengar, B. K. S. 1988. *The Tree of Yoga*. Boulder, CO: Shambhala.

Iyengar, B. K. S. 2005. *Light on Life: The Yoga Journey to Wholeness, Inner Peace and Ultimate Freedom*. Emmaus, PA: Rodale.

Kabat-Zinn, Jon. 1994. *Wherever You Go There You Are: Mindfulness Meditation in Everyday Life*. Westport, CT: Hyperion.

Lasater, Judith Hanson. 2015. *Living your Yoga: Finding the Spiritual in Everyday Life*, 2nd ed. Berkeley, CA: Rodmell Press.

MacGregor, Kino. 2013. "Discover the Power of the Present Moment in Yoga." The Blog, *HuffPost*, June 28, 2013. Updated July 28, 2013. http://www.huffingtonpost.com/kino-macgregor/yoga-being-present_b_3339112.html. Accessed 17 December 2020.

Peary, Alexandria. 2018. *Prolific Moment: Theory and Practice of Mindfulness for Writing*. Abingdon, Oxfordshire: Routledge.

Pender, Kelly. 2011. *Techne, From Neoclassicism to Postmodernism: Understanding Writing as a Useful, Teachable Art*. Anderson, SC: Parlor Press.

Ruddick, Sara. 1980. "Maternal Thinking." *Feminist Studies* 6 (2): 342–67.

Ryan, Kathleen J. 2012. "Thinking Ecologically: Rhetorical Ecological Feminist Agency and Writing Program Administration." *WPA: Writing Program Administration* 36 (1): 74–94.

Satchidananda, Swami. Trans. and commentator. 1990. *The Yoga Sutras of Patanjali*, 3rd ed. Integral Yoga Publications.

Schell, Eileen E. 2010. "Introduction: Researching Feminist Rhetorical Methods and Methodologies." In *Rhetorica in Motion: Feminist Rhetorical Methods and Methodologies*, edited by Eileen E. Schell and K. J. Rawson, 1–22. Pittsburgh, PA: University of Pittsburgh Press.

Wenger, Christy I. 2014. "Feminism, Mindfulness, and the Small University jWPA." *WPA: Writing Program Administration* 37 (2): 117–40.

SECTION 2

Women's Ways of Making Arguments together Using Words and Deeds

7
ELIZABETH I AND THE RHETORIC OF THE MARRIAGE CRISIS
Making Arguments

Jane Donawerth

Two issues dominated public discussion during the reign of Queen Elizabeth I: what shape the state church should take, and who might marry the Queen.[1] From 1558 when Elizabeth ascended the throne until the 1584 death of the duc d'Anjou (Elizabeth's final suitor), a woman was thus at the center of one of the most important public political discussions in sixteenth-century England. The debate over her possible marriage was carried on for over twenty years and across multiple genres: the Houses of Commons and Lords sent the Queen petitions to marry, and Elizabeth replied with orations to Parliament; counselors wrote advisory letters; preachers lauded marriage in the pulpits; plays and entertainments offered guides to her choice and Elizabeth wrote poems; pamphleteers circulated tracts in favor of marriage or against marrying a Catholic, and royal proclamations were issued against such libels. It was a debate that crossed the line between oral, bodily performance (making a speech, performing a play, preaching a sermon) and textual making (writing a letter, a pamphlet, a poem). From examining this debate, we can map the ecology[2] of the marriage-crisis discourse: how arguments migrate across genres; how allusions and other stylistic elements appear and then are repurposed later in the decades-long discussion; how agents change positions and re-vision their strategies from new vantage points; how delivery was difficult to control, as the words of the court debate were seized and redistributed for print delivery; and how Elizabeth's agency and her rhetorical ethos were each a complicated mesh of herself as rhetor, her audiences, the genre, and the shifting political context. While Elizabeth has generally been seen as a master rhetorician who controls the situation and persuades her audience effectively, I am instead arguing that her way of making an argument was a responsive, imitative remaking of previous arguments and a collaboration with the audience at the time—but nonetheless inventive and creative for that method.³

Elizabeth came to the throne after several major changes in religion (from Catholic to Anglican under Henry VIII, to radical Protestantism under Edward VI, back to Catholicism under Mary, and then with her government, back to Protestantism). She followed two monarchs who died without heirs, but their succession had been established with parliamentary approval. After religion, her marriage and her succession were the major political issues of the first two decades of her reign. Her early rule was busy with suitors, both internal and foreign candidates. Internal suitors included Sir William Pickering; Henry Fitzalan, Earl of Arundel; and Robert Dudley, eventually Earl of Leicester. Foreign princes who offered Elizabeth marriage included Emmanuel Philibert, Prince of Piedmont and Duke of Savoy; Adelphus, Duke of Holstein (son of the King of Denmark); Erik XIV of Sweden; Philip II of Spain (her sister Mary's former husband); Charles (younger brother of Maximilian II, Holy Roman Emperor); Henri duc d'Anjou; and François, duc d'Alençon (duc d'Anjou after his brother died). In the first decade and a half of her rule, Elizabeth claimed she preferred the single life but promised marriage, if her choice. After suffering under Mary's foreign consort, Philip II of Spain, the English people and Parliament in general favored an internal candidate, and the most popular with Elizabeth was Robert Dudley, whom she raised to Earl of Leicester. But her council was divided, many fearing Dudley's ambition and his desire for war against Catholics. During the ten years after this first period, Elizabeth leaned toward marriage with the Catholic son of Catherine de Medici, François, duc d'Alençon, later duc d'Anjou, but the English people and most of her Parliament and counselors argued against a Catholic king. Some historians represent Elizabeth as always decisively dedicated to virginity, never intending marriage.⁴ Her decision, however, was the result of a vigorous public debate between Elizabeth and her council and across a broad range of public sites, including Parliament, churches, the reading public, and the theater. As Kevin Sharpe points out, "The rhetorical nature of monarchy . . . in early modern England" (2000, 24) was a major force during the Tudor and Stuart eras.

In this twenty-five-year debate about the Queen's mate, important arguments migrated across genres, even from one side to another.⁵ The public discussion began with the Commons' and Lords' petitions to Elizabeth to marry or to allow Parliament to define succession by law, which were answered by Elizabeth's speeches and interspersed with carefully reasoned letters from counselors. But it was a discussion that spread across numerous genres[6] and multiple media. Drawing on strategies for public discussion and techniques of dissent honed in the Reformation, this debate generated from the marriage crisis was the first multimedia, cross-genre, secular political discussion in England, and the rhetorical resources of humanist learning and the printing press were all invoked. Besides petitions and responses and counselors' letters, there were sermons, plays and dialogues featuring good and bad counselors, sober pamphlets employing biblical examples and dire prophecies, entertainments full of song, dance, spectacle, and minidramas in which the Queen was guided to choose a suitor. While the Queen was the primary audience for the petitions, counselors' letters, and court plays and entertainments, the general public was the audience for the pamphlets, which were aimed to arouse public opinion to influence the Queen. And arguments and examples migrated across all genres, often used by both sides as in the sophistic-influenced school exercises the debaters had participated in in Tudor grammar schools and universities. The Queen herself participated in this debate, often weaving her responses from the arguments of others.

One such topos of argument concerned body politics, the Queen's mortality, and so the need for succession. This topic was especially important because this monarch not only embodied the state but also had the responsibility of producing an heir from her body. In 1562, Queen Elizabeth had smallpox, a disease that was frequently mortal in Elizabethan England, and anxiety about her welfare affected the arguments in favor of marriage in the petitions for the next Parliament. In 1563, both the Commons' and the Lords' petitions pointed to the Queen's mortality and catalogued the dangers to her people that might arise from a ruler's death without an heir, copiously amplifying the risks of foreign invasion without a settled succession. For example, the Commons' petition urged naming successors for "the sure continuance and th'imperial crown thereof in your majesty's person and most honorable issue of your body."[7] Much later, in a very different genre and style, John Stubbs, in the 1579 print pamphlet against Elizabeth marrying the French Catholic d'Alençon, cautions the Queen that bearing children at her age might cause her death.[8] Thus the topos of the Queen's mortal body migrated across genres and was repurposed to account for her aging.

Spinning off from this topos of the Queen's mortality was the related one of the dangers of unkind children, a topic Shakespeare would later treat in *The Tragedy of King Lear*. In a 1559 speech, for example,

Elizabeth argues that her marrying and bearing a child would not necessarily keep England safe, for history shows examples of "issue out of kind"—unnatural children who do not love their parents.[9] In the 1570s, in his letter to the Queen widely circulated at court, Sir Philip Sidney, when Elizabeth is considering marriage to the French duc d'Alençon, turns this argument against her, maintaining that having children with a French Catholic might cause civil war between her heirs (Doran 1996, 68; Sidney 1973, 47).

As we are beginning to see, the discourse of the Elizabethan marriage debate may be seen as an ecology of writing involving readers or audience, accepted methods of argumentation, and the contexts of humanist education, religion, and late sixteenth-century English and continental politics, as well as specific writers or speakers. Writers seem to be aware they are participating in this ongoing conversation: features of the debate migrated from genre to genre, creating a kind of discourse that successive writers referred to, refuted, or refashioned.[10] For example, in her February 10, 1559 speech to Parliament, Elizabeth claims, "[I] chose this kind of life . . . [which] I trust hath been most acceptable to God" (2000, 56), a reference perhaps to Paul's relegation of marriage as secondary to chastity in 1 Corinthians 7:1-9. In 1565, in *The Play of Patient Grissell* put on at court, John Philips assigns this argument to Duke Gualtier when he at first refuses to marry, arguing that "single life preferred is, in sacred scripture true . . . for such as leade a virgins life, and sinfull lust expell / . . . with Christ ther lord shal dwell" (2. 171-75). In Philips's play, however, the duke listens to his people and chooses a wife because of his duty as monarch to provide an heir. In between, Alexander Nowell, Dean of St. Paul's Church, opened the 1563 Parliament with a sermon praising Elizabeth for leading a "holy war" on the side of Protestants (England was not at war), blaming the Queen for her refusal to marry or settle the succession, and warning against evil counselors, such as the biblical Achitophel (1853, 228).[11] In her speech of November 5, 1666, Elizabeth angrily complains about parliamentary petitions and discussion of what should be her private choice and of "two bishops with their long orations" (or sermons), repeating the topos but varying this time in favor of marriage: "I did send them answer by my Council I would marry, although of mine own disposition I was not inclined to" (2000, 95). Here we can see that Elizabeth's agency, her way of making an argument, as Carolyn Miller argues for all agency, is "functional only through interaction" because agency "is the property of a relationship between rhetor and audience" (2007, 149-50). Thus, Elizabeth's rhetoric was a product not only of her classical education and her own invention but also of the complex context she addressed.

Another discourse feature that migrates across genres, to be refuted or repurposed, is praise, not only a convention of addresses to the monarch but also a rhetorical method of persuasion: praising the ruler for virtues the speaker wished she possessed.[12] On August 12, 1572, for example, Warwick town Recorder, Edward Aglionby, made a speech to Elizabeth during a progress, explaining this Renaissance panegyric tactic: "by the pleasant remembrance of [rulers'] known and true virtues made better, being put in mind of their office and government." Elizabeth replied, perhaps acerbically, "And now I thank you for putting me in mind of my duty, and that should be in me."[13] Through this commonplace rhetorical strategy of the function of praise of a monarch, subject and queen acknowledge their rhetorical collaboration. This occasion, then, demonstrates the mesh of epideictic occasion during the queen's travel, public audience response to her rule, and political context: Elizabeth acknowledges occasion and audience in her response but stakes out some agency by reminding her audience that she understands her duty and office as queen.

Allusions and stylistic elements appear and then are repurposed later in this decades-long discussion. Using the figures of antithesis and parison in a petition in 1563, the Lords cite Alexander the Great as a warning: "What but want of a successor known made so short an end of so great an empire as Alexander the Great did leave at his death?"[14] The Commons also deployed the example of Alexander in their 1563 petition.[15] The example of Alexander is used again in Edmund Tilney's 1568 (published again in 1587) *The Flower of Friendship* (1992, 100, 108), an argument for marriage that is also a marriage-advice manual. At the other end of the debate, in 1584, John Lyly (1991) praises Elizabeth's choice NOT to marry the Catholic duc d'Anjou through the example of Alexander: in the play titled *Campaspe*, Lyly portrays Alexander not as unreasonable in his failure to provide an heir but as heroic in his refusal to be ruled by love, reasonably choosing to rule and conquer rather than to marry.[16] Between these disparate uses of Alexander, Elizabeth turns the topos of what Alexander left behind another way: comparing herself to Alexander in a 1564 Latin oration at Cambridge University, Elizabeth cites his "sumptuous edifices" and hopes "[her] age is not yet senile . . . so may [she], before [her] debt to nature . . . , do some famous and noteworthy work" (2000, 87–88). Thus, the example of Alexander, who died without an heir, is introduced, used by both sides in the debate, and repurposed as circumstances change. Elizabeth maintains her agency through acknowledging the arguments of her people but claiming her independence by weaving them into a different pattern, thus making a different argument. In using the example of Alexander, the queen discreetly enters the debate about her marriage, constrained by the language of the parliamentary debate but adapting the example to claim her legacy as building public institutions rather than producing heirs. As Phyllis Mack says of seventeenth-century Quaker women, Elizabeth's agency, her "ability to act according to her own best interests and to resist oppressive power relationships," here is "generated in the context of relationships, of conditions of dependency, or out of the individual's subjection to an external power" (2003, 151). As queen, Elizabeth's agency was constrained not only by her gender but also by her people's expectations for her office.

An ornate humanist style[17] also migrated across genres as persuasive technique, heightening the urgency and seriousness of the issue. The core texts, the petitions by Commons and Lords in the 1560s, for example, were full of alliteration, catalogues, amplification, sententiae, historical examples, balance and parallelism, climactic phrasing, and repetition of sounds—a style that came to be called "Euphuistic" after John Lyly's (2003) use of it in the novella *Euphues*. For instance, in 1563, the Commons petitioned Elizabeth, promising that, if Elizabeth establishes succession, they "shall employ their whole endeavors, wits, and powers, to revive, devise, and establish the most strong and beneficial acts and laws for the preservation and surety of your majesty and your issue . . . and the most penal, sharp, and terrible statutes to all that shall but once practice, attempt, or convey against your safety."[18] The alliteration, the synonyms, the balance and parallelism, the climactic phrasing, the repetition of sounds—all reinforce the argument and heighten the urgency that it is in Elizabeth's own interest to name an heir.[19] The 1563 Lords' petition includes a flattering tone, basing their hope that the Queen will grant their suit on the "bountiful goodness" she has shown already in her reign.[20] Drawing on the solid humanist education she had received under the tutelage of Roger Ascham, Elizabeth replied on April 10, 1563, employing alliteration, climax, repetition of words, and balance and parallelism: "For though I can think [remaining single] best for a private woman, yet do I strive with myself to think it not meet for a prince. And if I can bend my liking to your need I will not resist such a mind" (2000, 79).

As a follow-up to the main argument, good and bad counselors become a theme of many plays aiming to influence Elizabeth's ideas on marriage, and these counselors give their advice in ornate humanist style: in John Norton and Thomas Sackville's 1560/61 *The Tragedy of Gorboduc (1934)*, for example, and in John Philips's 1565 *The Play of Patient Grissell (1919)*. Even the plain-speaking counselor Hephestion in John Lyly's 1584 *Campaspe* uses the ornate style when he advises Alexander against love, drawing on alliteration, balance, parallelism, mythological allusion, and antithesis as he urges that he must "discharge the duty of a subject . . . and the office of a friend": A great warrior must not be conquered by a lowly woman, Mars must remain superior to Venus, women and love are fair but false, and a god-like ruler should not demean himself by bowing to love (1991, 2.2. 33–85). "There is no poison so deadly as love," Hephestion admonishes, because love doesn't listen to counsel (2.2. 86–87).

Over the twenty years of the marriage-crisis discussion, speakers and writers changed positions and re-visioned their strategies from new perspectives. This debate in general moved from the first dozen years or so in which counselors and the populace begged Elizabeth to marry and she resisted, to a second movement of twelve years or so in which discourse and arguments were remixed[21] and Elizabeth seemed bent on marrying a foreign Catholic prince, while most of her public urged her not to.[22] Elizabeth's favorite courtier, Robert Dudley, Earl of Leicester, who of all her suitors, historians agree, came closest to winning Elizabeth's hand,[23] illustrated this kind of change of position and retooling of arguments. When Leicester still had hopes of marrying Elizabeth, in 1575 he sponsored an entertainment at his home at Kenilworth Castle urging the Queen, stopping there on progress, to give up her dedication to virginity and marry: Diana (representing chastity) and Juno (representing marriage) vie for Zabeta's allegiance, and the play climaxes with Iris's speech praising the benefits of marriage.[24] In 1581, however, when Elizabeth was being courted by François, duc d'Anjou, Leicester arranged a masque at court, *The Four Foster Children of Desire*, written by Sir Philip Sidney (Leicester's nephew) and John Lyly, in which four knights besiege the Fortress of Perfect Beauty but are unsuccessful because beauty belongs to the whole world, not just one man, and virtue is stronger than desire (Sidney 1973).

In the early part of her reign, the Lords and Commons, at the beginning of every Parliament, sent a petition to Elizabeth to marry, and she gave a speech or sent a counselor with her speech of polite refusal but acknowledgment of her duty. Twenty years later, when she was considering Anjou, she petitioned her counselors to approve her marriage, which they at first refused, bowing to her wishes only after furious debates. Even seeking her counselors' permission was a result perhaps not of Elizabeth's political diplomacy but of her father's will, in which he suggested that the Privy Council must approve his daughters' marriages. Knowing her people's abhorrence of a foreign king, Elizabeth did not even bring the matter to Parliament. As Susan Hekman points out, agency "is a product of the fluctuating, changing, and often conflictual historical and social influences that impinge on it" (1997, 201). As the political situation changed (England's shifting alliances with foreign powers) and as social circumstances metamorphosed (the decreasing chance with increasing age of Elizabeth's producing an heir), both Elizabeth and her advisors changed their positions. Throughout these changes, Elizabeth's agency was limited by gender and by expectations for her office but at times also by foreign and domestic politics. Her rhetoric, however, reflected her agency as she encountered and responded to these limits.

Throughout the twenty-year debate, Elizabeth sought to control delivery of these arguments—who talked to whom about what—but was generally unsuccessful. She seemed to desire the advice of her favorite courtiers and closest counselors but showed anger when this topic and these arguments were recast and delivered to more public audiences: scolding Parliament in 1566 for discussing the marriage issue,[25] jailing Thomas Wentworth when he and other members of Parliament demanded free speech to discuss her marriage and its effect on England's status as a Protestant country, and cutting off the hand of John Stubbs when he recirculated in a print pamphlet the arguments from Sir Philip Sidney's manuscript letter circulating at court.[26] Her tactics did not prevent this rhetorical debate from extending beyond her inner circle.[27]

In "Rhetorical Agency as Emergent and Enacted," Marilyn Cooper argues that agency for a speaker or writer is the process of creating meaning but also changing structure in response to the consequences of such actions so that persuasion is also "an invitation to listeners as also always agents in persuasion" (1986, 420). I agree with this definition, but also, on the basis of my analysis of the rhetoric of Elizabeth I and the marriage-crisis debate, I want to turn Cooper's definition around and argue that agency is also collaborative, a result not only of the individual speaker's intentions but also of previous speakers' persuasions—effective or not (see Hayden 2017). Elizabeth's initial statements on her marriage were made in response to petitions from Parliament and the Lords and were also answers to letters from counselors urging her to marry; they tread a careful line between claiming her desire to remain a single woman and her acknowledgment of her duty as a monarch to provide an heir. The Queen attempted to circumscribe the debate but finally capitulated to her own desires when she met the duc d'Alençon, desires that at last seemed to align with her people's request of her to marry. However, when her own petition to marry was met with resistance in both the court and the public, she changed again, reestablishing herself as the woman married to her people, mother of her country, unavailable for other marriages (see Elizabeth I, 2000, 347). Elizabeth's agency and the arguments she made were thus a complicated mesh of herself as rhetor, her education in classical rhetoric, her audiences, the genres appropriate to the occasion, other speakers' arguments, and the shifting political context. The Queen's imitation of or responses to argument and the affordances of different genres enabled her to test rhetorical strategies and flex her complicated agency as a female ruler, but the discussion also required that she collaborate in her responses with previous speakers and that she invite her audience to respond. Because of the nature of argument, but also because of her gender, Elizabeth could not make her arguments by herself.

Elizabeth's performances in the marriage debate thus may be used to test feminist theories of argument. Feminists have often turned away from the agonistic side of debate. In *Correct Writing and Speaking* (1904), Mary Augusta Jordan, for example, suggests that the speaker and audience collaborate in an argument: "The audience is not to be dominated, cajoled, or bullied. It is to be interpreted and made to know its own self in terms of something other than prejudice, or passion, or lazy self-indulgence. . . . The successful speaker . . . will use [her] art to enable [her] to discern the signs of the spiritual forces coming into action" (2002, 306). Indeed, Sally Miller Gearhart (1979) viewed all argument as an attempt at dominance and offered as an alternative a method of reaching consensus. Sonja Foss and Cindy Griffin suggest that an "invitational rhetoric" might best serve our purposes, one in which participants share safety from retribution, the value of absolute listening, and freedom (1995, 10–12). These visions of discussion, far from classical argument, do not seem to apply to Queen Elizabeth's deployment of argument: she was trained in classical rhetorical debate strategies, she aimed at dominance (although was frequently prevented from exercising it), and she often threatened the safety and freedom of her opponents. Yet she did listen to her advisors, her people, and those participating in the debate about marriage. Perhaps her way of making argument, reweaving the arguments and rhetorical strategies of others in the debate, is closer to Lindal Buchanan's view of collaboration and women's rhetoric: "a cooperative endeavor involving two or more people that results in a rhetorical product, performance, or event" (2003, 43). But even this view covers mainly sympathetic, supportive collaboration. Elizabeth often worked with more reluctant collaborators who opposed her position. Thus, as Sarah Hallenbeck suggests more generally, Elizabeth's agency rests not in her individual will "but instead is located within a vast and varied network of humans, objects, and discourses that constantly evolves in response to changing linkages among disparate elements" (2012, 19). As Diane Davis might put it, Elizabeth's rhetoric and her agency are not heroic but responsive (2010, 109–13). She makes her arguments in and from a vast political context.

The Elizabethan government, as most governments, was a highly rhetorical institution, and the marriage-crisis debate was conducted in an ecology of argument, relying on persuasion through copia and praise and including writers, audience, previous texts, and political exigencies of the moment. Elizabeth ruled only through an elaborate conversation of texts, voices, and advice—hers perhaps dominating but influenced by the petitions, speeches, letters, pamphlets, sermons, entertainments, and plays directed toward her and her people. Arguments migrated across genres and were often used by both sides, while Elizabeth developed an ethos and an agency that was a fusion of her own intentions and the advice of her counselors and people. Her agency, as Saba Mahmood urges in her argument for expanding feminist methodology to include a broader understanding of agency, may be recognized not so much in her "capacity to realize one's own interests against the weight of custom" (2005, 8) but mainly in "the multiple ways in which one *inhabits* norms" (15)—what Cheryl Geisler and the participants in the Alliance of Rhetoric Societies might call "dispersed" agency (2004, 11). Elizabeth's rhetorical choices were interactions with genre, with commonplace arguments and with styles; her agency sometimes resisting, sometimes disrupting, sometimes ironically and sometimes sincerely accepting. In Elizabeth's speech to the Lords at Hatfield when she assumed the throne, she said, "I mean to direct all my actions by good advice and counsel" (2000, 52). Throughout the twenty-five years of the marriage debate, as her people offered their opinions across a wide range of genres, and while changing her position from choice against marriage but mindful of duty to choice for marriage but mindful of religion, and to choice against marriage again, Elizabeth kept her promise. For Queen Elizabeth, making a good argument at times meant remaking the speaker as well as the audience. Agency for her was thus interactive and responsive, not autonomous.

NOTES

1. On Elizabeth's life, reign, and suitors, see especially Carole Levin, *The Heart and Stomach of a King* (1994); Levin, *The Reign of Elizabeth I* (2002); J. E. Neale (1957); Susan Bassnett (1989); Patrick Collinson (2012); and Susan Doran (1996).
2. Marilyn Cooper, in "The Ecology of Writing," explains that writing must be understood as an ecology, not just an individual's cognitive process, but "language and texts ... [as] social activities"; "Writing is an activity through which a person is continually engaged with a variety of socially constituted systems" (1986, 366–67). Margaret Syverson elaborates in her book on an "ecology of composition": "Writers, readers, and texts, together with their environments, constitute one kind of ecological system," a system characterized by distribution, embodiment, emergence, and enaction (1999, xv).
3. On Elizabeth's rhetoric, see Allison Heisch (1975, 31–55; 1990, 45–56); Leah S. Marcus (1986, 135–53); Mary Thomas Crane (1988, 1–15); Ilona Bell (1995, 57–82); Cheryl Glenn (1997, 158–70); Jane Donawerth (1999); Cristy Beemer (2011, 258–62, 266–73; 2016, 75–82, 85–86); and Giuliana Iannaccaro (2014).
4. See, for example, Theodora Jankowski (2000, 27) on the "queen's perpetual virginity" and Carole Levin (2004, 58). But Levin also argues that Elizabeth was "playing seriously" and considering marriage when Alençon courted her (1994, 60). For an intelligent, skeptical history of the critical concept of the "cult" of Elizabeth as Virgin Queen, see Philippa Berry (1989, 61–165).
5. I take the term *migrate*, by analogy, from Deborah Brandt's discussion of migrating literacy in "Sponsors" (1998). On the Renaissance practice of arguing on both sides of the question, borrowed from classical rhetoric, see Joel Altman on Elizabethan drama (1978).
6. On genre, see Carolyn Miller, "Genre as Social Action": genre is a "category of discourse" based on "social action"; it is a "rhetorical means for mediating private intentions and social exigence" (1984, 163). On the ways ethos is connected to location and genre, see Suzanne Bordelon (2016).
7. See the Commons' petition, read by Thomas Norton on January 26, 1563, in Elizabeth I (2000, 72–77; quotation on 73). For a summary of the petition, see Doran (1996, 62).
8. Laurel Thatcher Ulrich notes that in the early modern world, a maternal death occurred every 150 births (1990, 170).
9. Elizabeth I (2000, 58). There are two versions of this speech (see Elizabeth I, 56–60). Doran (1996, 3) discusses the Privy Council's December 1559 drafting of a petition asking Elizabeth to marry.
10. This argumentative ecology across oral and print genres seems similar to the process of "rhetorical accretion" that Vicki Tolar Collins finds in the histories of some women's texts (1999, 556).
11. For a summary of Nowell's sermon, see Doran (1996, 60–61).
12. On praise or the epideictic kind of rhetoric as a means of persuasion across all kinds of rhetoric, see Quintilian (1920–1922, 3.iv.11); Jeanne Fahnestock (2011, 94, 330, 400); and Susan Wells (2104, 116–18). See also Cynthia Miecznikowski Sheard (1996) and Gerard A. Hauser (1999).
13. Both Algionby's speech and Elizabeth's reply are quoted in Elizabeth I (2000, 110, n5). On Elizabeth's ability in her rhetoric to respond to rapid changes in situation, see Beemer (2011).
14. The Lords' petition of February 1, 1563, is included in Elizabeth I (2000, 81–86, quotation on 83). On antithesis (argument from opposites), see *Rhetorica ad Herennium* (1954, 4.xv.21) and Fahnestock (2011, 231–33); on parison (parallelism), see Fahnestock (225–26).

15. Elizabeth I (2000, 74).
16. This chapter is a companion piece to my essay "Elizabeth I and the Marriage Crisis, John Lyly's *Campaspe*, and the Politics of Court Drama" in a Festschrift for Carole Levin, *Queens Matter in Early Modern Studies*, edited by Anna Riehl Bertolet (Donawerth 2018).
17. Latin humanism, with its Ciceronian style, was a common feature in England from the fourteenth century on, but the vernacular prose and even poetry remained plain through much of the sixteenth century—what C. S. Lewis calls the "Drab Age" (1954, 157–317). However, in the last third of the century, which Lewis terms the "Golden Age" (318–585), humanist rhetoric moved into the vernacular with the periodic sentences and all the figures of Greek and Roman ornate styles, as well as devices of arguing from commonplaces. Lewis, however, posits, instead, that the Golden Age is the result of "native talent" (18), and humanism does not figure in the vernacular until the excesses of the Neoclassical Enlightenment. This seems to me a nonsequitur since almost all the politicians and authors of the Golden Age were humanist educated, as was the Queen. On amplification or copia, see Cicero, *De Oratore* (1942, 3.xxiii.91–92) and Wells (2014, 121).
18. Elizabeth I (2000, 77).
19. On figures as a means of emotional appeal, see Quintilian (1920–1922, 9.i.21) and Fahnestock (2011, 297).
20. Elizabeth I (2000, 86).
21. On remixing, see David Sheridan, Jim Ridolfo, and Tony Michel (2012), especially chapter 4 on remixing and rhetorical velocity.
22. Doran (1996, 181). See also Arthur F. Kinney (1990, 42–43), Katherine Duncan-Jones (1991, 204–10), Susan Frye (1993, 11), and Alan Stewart (2000, 235–38).
23. See, for example, Levin, *The Reign of Elizabeth I* (2002, 15).
24. See George Gascoigne and M. Hunneys, *The Princely Pleasures at Kenilworth Castle* (1575) (1910).
25. See Elizabeth I (2000, 93–98).
26. See Sir Philip Sidney, "A Letter to Queen Elizabeth," in Duncan-Jones and Van Dorsten (1973, 33–57); David Dean (2008) on Peter Wentworth; and John Stubbs (1968). Sidney's letter was circulated at court in manuscript while Stubbs's pamphlet was in print. Also see Daniel Ellis (2012, 30–31) and the letter by counselor William Cecil, Lord Burghley, urging Elizabeth to make a decision, in Elizabeth I (2000, 240–42). Letters did not have a large public audience, but they did have an audience beyond the Queen, through manuscript copies.
27. Ellis argues that the print debate around the French Catholic marriage proposal was part of the developing public sphere in England.

WORKS CITED

Altman, Joel. 1978. *The Tudor Play of Mind: Rhetorical Inquiry and the Development of Elizabethan Drama*. Chicago, IL: University of Chicago Press.

Brandt, Deborah. 1998. "Sponsors of Literacy." *College Composition and Communication* 49 (2): 165–85.

Bassnett, Susan. 1989. *Elizabeth I: A Feminist Perspective*. Berg.

Beemer, Cristy. 2011. "The Female Monarchy: A Rhetorical Strategy of Early Modern Rule." *Rhetoric Review* 30 (3): 258–74.

Beemer, Cristy. 2016. "God Save the Queens: *Kairos* and the Mercy Letters of Elizabeth I and Mary Queen of Scots." *Rhetoric Review* 35 (2): 75–90.

Bell, Ilona. 1995. "Elizabeth I—Always Her Own Free Woman." In *Political Rhetoric, Power, and Renaissance Women*, edited by Carole Levin and Patricia A. Sullivan, 57–84. Albany: SUNY Press.
Berry, Philippa. 1989. *Of Chastity and Power: Elizabethan Literature and the Unmarried Queen.* Routledge.
Bordelon, Suzanne. 2016. "Embodied *Ethos* and Rhetorical Accretion: Genevieve Stebbins and the *Delsarte System of Expression*." *Rhetoric Society Quarterly* 46 (2): 105–30.
Buchanan, Lindal. 2003. "Forging and Firing Thunderbolts: Collaboration and Women's Rhetoric." *Rhetoric Society Quarterly* 33 (4): 43–63.
Cicero, Marcus Tullius. 1942. *De Oratore.* Translated by E. W. Sutton and H. Rackham. 2 vols. Cambridge, MA: Harvard University Press.
Collins, Vicki Tolar. May 1999. "The Speaker Respoken: Material Rhetoric as Feminist Methodology." *College English* 6 (5): 545–73.
Collinson, Patrick. 2012. "Elizabeth I." In *Oxford Dictionary of National Biography.* Cambridge, England: Oxford University Press.
Cooper, Marilyn. 1986. "The Ecology of Writing." *College English* 48 (4): 364–75.
Cooper, Marilyn. 2011. "Rhetorical Agency as Emergent and Enacted." *College Composition and Communication* 62 (3): 420–49.
Crane, Mary Thomas. 1988. " 'Video et Taceo': Elizabeth I and the Rhetoric of Counsel." *Studies in English Literature, 1500–1900* 28 (1): 1–15.
Davis, Diane. 2010. *Inessential Solidarity: Rhetoric and Foreigner Relations.* Pittsburgh: University of Pittsburgh Press.
Dean, David. 2008. "Peter Wentworth (1524–1597)." In *Oxford Dictionary of National Biography.*
Donawerth, Jane. 1999. "Oratory and Rhetoric." Women Writers Project. *Renaissance Women Online: A Final Report*, February 1. https://wwp.northeastern.edu/context/#rEss.rhetoric.xml. Accessed 8 October 2019.
Donawerth, Jane. 2018. "Elizabeth I and the Marriage Crisis, John Lyly's *Campaspe*, and the Politics of Court Drama." In *Queens Matter: Early Modern Studies in Honor of Carole Levin*, edited by Anna Riehl Bertolet, 83–102. London, UK: Palgrave MacMillan.
Doran, Susan. 1996. *Monarchy and Matrimony: The Courtships of Elizabeth I.* Abingdon, England: Routledge.
Duncan-Jones, Katherine. 1991. *Sir Philip Sidney, Courtier Poet.* Yale University Press.
Duncan-Jones, Katherine, and Jan Van Dorsten, eds. 1973. *Miscellaneous Prose of Sir Philip Sidney.* Oxford: Oxford University Press.
Elizabeth I, Queen of England. 2000. *Collected Works.* Edited by Leah S. Marcus, Janel Mueller, and Mary Beth Rose. Chicago: University of Chicago Press.
Ellis, Daniel. 2012. "Arguing the Courtship of Elizabeth and Alençon: An Early Modern Marriage Debate and the Problem of the Historical Public Sphere." *Rhetoric Society Quarterly* 42 (1): 26–43.
Fahnestock, Jeanne. 2011. *Rhetorical Style: The Uses of Language in Persuasion.* Oxford, England: Oxford University Press.
Foss, Sonja K., and Cindy L. Griffin. 1995. "Beyond Persuasion: A Proposal for an Invitational Rhetoric." *Communication Monographs* 62 (1): 2–18.
Frye, Susan. 1993. *Elizabeth I: The Competition for Representation.* Oxford, England: Oxford University Press.
Gascoigne, George, and M. Hunneys. 1910. *The Princely Pleasures at Kenilworth Castle* (1575). In *George Gascoigne, The Glasse of Government . . . and Other Poems and Prose*, edited by John W. Cunliffe, 91–131. Cambridge, England: Cambridge University Press.
Gearhart, Sally Miller. 1979. "The Womanization of Rhetoric." *Women's Studies International Quarterly* 2 (2): 195–201.
Geisler, Cheryl. 2004. "How Ought We to Understand the Concept of Rhetorical Agency? Report from the ARS." *Rhetoric Society Quarterly* 34 (3): 9–17.

Glenn, Cheryl. 1997. *Rhetoric Retold: Regendering the Tradition from Antiquity Through the Renaissance*. Carbondale, IL: Southern Illinois University Press.
Hallenbeck, Sarah. 2012. "Toward a Posthuman Perspective: Feminist Rhetorical Methodologies and Everyday Practices." *Advances in the History of Rhetoric* 15 (1): 9–27.
Hauser, Gerard A. 1999. "Aristotle on Epideictic: The Formation of Public Morality." *Rhetoric Society Quarterly* 29 (1): 5–23.
Hayden, Wendy. 2017. "The Rhetorical Reputation of Forgotten Feminist Lois Waisbrooker." In *Remembering Women Differently: Refiguring Rhetorical Work*, edited by Lynee Lewis Gaillet and Helen Gaillet Bailey, 189–205. Columbia, SC: University of South Carolina Press.
Heisch, Allison. 1975. "Queen Elizabeth I: Parliamentary Rhetoric and the Exercise of Power." *Signs* 1 (1): 31–55.
Heisch, Allison. 1990. "Queen Elizabeth I and the Persistence of Patriarch." *Feminist Review* 4 (1): 45–56.
Hekman, Susan. 1997. "Subjects and Agents: The Question for Feminism." In *Provoking Agents: Gender and Agency in Theory and Practice*, edited by Judith Kegan Gardiner, 194–207. Champaign, IL: University of Illinois Press.
Iannaccaro, Giuliana. 2014. "Elizabeth's Italian Rhetoric: The 'Maximilian Letters.'" In *Elizabeth I's Foreign Correspondence: Letters, Rhetoric, and Politics*, edited by Carlo M. Bajetta, Guillaume Coatalen, and Jonathan Gibson, 167–86. London, UK: Palgrave MacMillan.
Jankowski, Theodora A. 2000. *Pure Resistance: Queer Virginity in Early Modern English Drama*. Philadelphia, PA: University of Pennsylvania Press.
Jordan, Mary Augusta. 2002. Excerpt from *Correct Writing and Speaking* (1904). In *Rhetorical Theory by Women before 1900*, edited by Jane Donawerth, 299–316. Lanham, MD: Rowman & Littlefield.
Kinney, Arthur F. 1990. "Puritans Versus Royalists: Sir Philip Sidney's Rhetoric at the Court of Elizabeth I." In *Sir Philip Sidney's Achievements*, edited by M.J.B. Allen, Dominic Baker-Smith, and Arthur F. Kinney, with Margaret M. Sullivan, 42–56. AMS Studies in the Renaissance 28. New York: AMS.
Levin, Carole. 1994. *The Heart and Stomach of a King: Elizabeth I and the Politics of Sex and Power*. Philadelphia: University of Pennsylvania Press.
Levin, Carole. 2002. *The Reign of Elizabeth I*. London, UK: Palgrave.
Levin, Carole. 2004. "All the Queen's Children: Elizabeth I and the Meanings of Motherhood." *Explorations in Renaissance Culture* 30 (1): 57–76.
Lewis, C. S. 1954. *English Literature in the Sixteenth Century Excluding Drama*. Clarendon.
Lyly, John. 1991. *Campaspe, Sappho and Phao*, edited by George K. Hunter and David M. Bevington. Manchester, England: Manchester University Press.
Lyly, John. 2003 [1578; 1580]. *Euphues: The Anatomy of Wit; and, Euphues and His England*. Edited by Leah Scragg. Manchester, UK: Manchester University Press. https://core.ac.uk/download/pdf/288120335.pdf. Accessed 20 December 2020.
Mack, Phyllis. 2003. "Religion, Feminism, and the Problem of Agency: Reflections on Eighteenth-Century Quakerism." *Signs* 29 (1): 149–77.
Mahmood, Saba. 2005. *Politics of Piety: The Islamic Revival and the Feminine Subject*. Princeton, NJ: Princeton University Press.
Marcus, Leah. 1986. "Shakespeare's Comic Heroines, Elizabeth I, and the Political Uses of Androgyny." *Women in the Middle Ages and the Renaissance*, edited by Mary B. Rose, 135–53. Syracuse, NY: Syracuse University Press.
Miller, Carolyn. 1984. "Genre as Social Action." *Quarterly Journal of Speech* 70 (2): 151–67.
Miller, Carolyn. 2007. "What Can Automation Tell Us about Agency?" *Rhetoric Society Quarterly* 37 (2): 137–57.
Neale, John Ernest. 1957. *Queen Elizabeth: A Biography*. New York: Doubleday. First published by Doubleday in 1934.

Norton, Thomas, and Thomas Sackville. 1934. "The Tragedy of Gorboduc; or of Ferrex and Porrex (1570 ed.)." In *Elizabethan and Stuart Plays*, edited by Charles Read Baskerville, Virgil B. Hetzel, and Arthur H. Nethercot, 79–109. New York: Holt, Rinehart, and Winston.

Nowell, Alexander. 1853. "Mr. Noel's Sermon at the Parliamt. Before the Queen's Matie." In *A Catechism by Alexander Nowell*, edited by G. E. Corrie, 223–29. Parker Society. Cambridge, England: Cambridge University Press.

Philips, John. 1909. *The Play of Patient Grissell*, vol. 1. Edited by Ronald Brunlees McKerrow and W. W. Greg. Malone Society Reprints. London, UK: Chiswick.

Quintilian. 1920–1922. *The Institutio Oratoria*. Translated by Harold Edgeworth Butler. 4 vols. Cambridge, MA: Harvard University Press.

Rhetorica ad Herennium. 1954. Translated by Harry Caplan. Cambridge, MA: Harvard University Press.

Sharpe, Kevin. 2000. *Remapping Early Modern England: The Culture of Seventeenth-Century Politics*. Cambridge, England: Cambridge University Press.

Sheard, Cynthia Miecznikowski. 1996. "The Public Value of Epideictic Rhetoric." *College English* 58 (7): 765–94.

Sheridan, David, Jim Ridolfo, and Tony Michel. 2012. *The Available Means of Persuasion: Mapping a Theory and Pedagogy of Multimodal Public Rhetoric*. Anderson, SC: Parlor.

Sidney, Sir Philip. 1973. *The Miscellaneous Prose of Sir Philip Sidney*. Edited by Katherine Duncan-Jones and Jan van Dorsten. Oxford, UK: Clarendon.

Stewart, Alan. 2000. *Philip Sidney*. New York: St. Martin's.

Stubbs, John. 1968. *John Stubbs's Gaping Gulf with Letters and Other Relevant Documents*. Edited by Lloyd E. Berry, 1–93. Charlottesville, VA: University of Virginia Press.

Syverson, Margaret A. 1999. *The Wealth of Reality: An Ecology of Composition*. Carbondale, IL: Southern Illinois University Press.

Tilney, Edmund. 1992. *The Flower of Friendship: A Renaissance Dialogue Contesting Marriage*. Edited by Valerie Wayne. Ithaca, NY: Cornell University Press.

Ulrich, Laurel Thatcher. 1990. *A Midwife's Tale: The Life of Martha Ballard, Based on Her Diary, 1785–1812*. New York: Random House.

Wells, Susan. 2014. "Genres as Species and Spaces: Literary and Rhetorical Genre in the Anatomy of Melancholy." *Philosophy and Rhetoric* 47 (2): 113–36.

8

FLEUR DE FORCE
Beauty, Creativity, and YouTube

Andrea J. Severson

INTRODUCTION

The beauty community on YouTube consists of thousands of channels, ranging in size from only a handful of subscribers to several million subscribers, but one common connection among these channels and their creators is a love for makeup and fashion. I argue that these women are engaging in a complex set of creative practices in the crafting of their videos that also allows them to negotiate their own way through the messages from the mainstream beauty and fashion industries, making these channels an important rhetorical space worth analyzing. Rather than sitting back and being dictated to by traditional marketing and advertising of the beauty and fashion industries, these young women (and an increasing number of men) are taking control of the dialogue and creating a consumer-driven space within the beauty community on YouTube. Since starting on YouTube in 2009, British YouTuber Fleur de Force has built a highly successful career from her beauty-and-lifestyle-themed channel,[1] with over 1.4 million subscribers.

Using Fleur and her channel as a case study, I show how creators within the beauty community on YouTube are engaging in complex creative ways of making. Going beyond the content of the videos and examining the creative production practices, I argue that creators like Fleur are engaging in a feminist rhetorical act through the construction and marketing of their channels. Unlike the one-sided conversation in mainstream media about beauty, fashion, and women's lives, YouTube, and its beauty community in particular, allows users from a variety of backgrounds to interact and speak in a multiway discussion among creators, subscribers, and commenters about what is important to them and how they define beauty and style and to decide for themselves what their place is within the broader beauty and fashion industries. Where mainstream publishing and advertising create a sense of exclusivity, YouTube

DOI: 10.7330/9781646420384.c008

is the platform for everyone, and within the beauty community, there is room for people of all sizes, genders, sexualities, abilities, races, ethnicities, and socioeconomic backgrounds.

FEMINIST RHETORICAL PRACTICES, IDENTITY, AND THE FEMINIZATION OF THE INTERNET

A great deal of scholarship has been done by third-wave feminist scholars (including Baumgardner and Richards 2000; Dicker and Piepmeier 2003; Findlen 1995; Fishburn 1982; Gillis, Howie, and Munford 2004; and Meyers 1999) looking at the intersections among consumer culture, popular culture, and what it means to be a woman living in those intersections. There has also been an increase in work done on the use of social media for branding and marketing purposes (such as Ashley and Tuten 2015; Labrecque, Markos, and Milne 2011; Shin, Pang, and Kim 2015; Singh and Sonnenburg 2012; and Vernuccio 2014). A growing body of scholarship has begun focusing specifically on YouTube and content creators in general, across all categories (Gauntlett 2011, as well as Snickars and Vonderau 2009, are good examples). As the world of popular culture online has expanded, there has been an almost endless number of directions for the research to follow.

Brook Duffy and Emily Hund (2015) present an interesting case of entrepreneurial femininity and self-branding, and while they focus on fashion bloggers, there are direct implications for the beauty YouTubers who have turned their channels into online businesses and have developed into YouTube/online entrepreneurs. Focusing on YouTube specifically, Rebecca Mardon, Mike Molesworth, and Georgianna Grigore (2018) examine the community aspect of beauty channels and the emotional labor involved in "tribal entrepreneurship,"—the bond, or tribe, that forms between the creator and the subscribers—and the complex balance creators face when creating content, growing their channels, and building their personal brands and online businesses. The role of celebrity is also important in a discussion of the beauty community, as many of the original beauty creators (like Fleur) have gone on to launch business endeavors in the form of book deals and product lines. Alice Marwick's (2013) work on strategic online self-presentation explores the idea of online celebrity and personal branding in general, while other scholars examine the idea of microcelebrity on YouTube. For example, Anne Jerslev (2016) conducted a case study of Zoe Sugg, better known as Zoella, one of the top British beauty YouTubers, with multiple books, product lines, and side businesses under her name since starting her channel in 2007, two years before Fleur de Force started hers. In the early days of their channels, Fleur and Zoe collaborated and appeared on each other's channels, helping each other grow their individual audiences.

In addition, important large-scale research projects like the book *Cupcakes, Pinterest, and Ladyporn: Feminized Popular Culture in the Early Twenty-First Century*, edited by Elana Levine (2015), examine a range of subjects from celebrity gossip blogs to women's television, fashion blogging to chick lit, and Pinterest, and each essay in the collection explores the ways popular culture sites associated with femininity are created and how these cultural products "speak to and about feminine identity, and the ways that audiences, readers, and users engage with and experience this culture" (1). However, among all this research and despite the beauty community becoming a significant portion of the YouTube platform, with some of the most prominent beauty YouTube creators building lucrative careers for themselves with collaborations and sponsorships by many of the top beauty and fashion brands worldwide, there still is not enough scholarship looking specifically at their channels as feminist rhetorical acts or at the creative practices that go into creating, maintaining, and marketing these channels.

At the heart of an analysis of this community, and Fleur's channel in particular, is a discussion of feminism and the beauty/fashion industries, as well as the creative practices these creators are engaging in. Beauty, fashion, and cosmetics have long been subjects of scrutiny by feminist scholars. In Naomi Wolf's landmark work, *The Beauty Myth: How Images of Beauty Are Used Against Women*, published in 1990, Wolf explores the ways images of female beauty and femininity are used politically as a weapon to hinder the advancement of women (11). Wolf explains, "The qualities that a given period calls beautiful in women are merely symbols of the female behavior that period considers desirable: *the beauty myth is always actually prescribing behavior and not appearance*" (13). Wolf and feminist scholars have long argued that traditional media like television ads, women's magazines, celebrity culture, and more have created a distorted view of women's appearances and behaviors, often favoring only one kind of look. YouTube differs from this restricted view in that the beauty community on the platform allows users from all over the world to connect, subscribe, comment, and participate in a range of discussions and conversations about beauty, fashion, and life in general. Each creator is in control of their own channel and their own content because they do not rely on advertisers to fund them. They decide what message they are going to promote, which topics they will address, and which products they will feature. Even when a creator is sent products free in exchange for a review or takes on a sponsored collaboration with a brand, the creator maintains the right to share honest thoughts and opinions and, in most cases, creative control of the final video product. While beauty editors of magazines must negotiate with the beauty and fashion industries they support, beauty YouTube creators can make their own choices about which brands to support and work with, or not, and what messages to promote on their channels. The false ideals and "myths" of beauty are just as prevalent today as they were when Wolf's book was first published in 1990. However, within the beauty community on YouTube, those false ideals are challenged, questioned, and negotiated, implicitly and explicitly, on a regular basis.

CREATIVITY, CRAFTING, AND WOMEN'S WAYS OF MAKING

It is important to also discuss scholarship on creativity, crafting, and gender to better understand the creative practices creators engage in through their channels. In *Making Is Connecting: The Social Meaning of Creativity, from DIY and Knitting to YouTube and Web 2.0*, David Gauntlett explores the ways technology, particularly the internet, has impacted perceptions of creativity. He explains, "Thankfully, the World Wide Web soared in popularity, becoming mainstream in itself, and opened up a world of diversity and imagination where the content itself is created by everyday users" (2011, 3). YouTube allows many You Tube vloggers to explore the diverse and imaginative sides of their personalities to create original content within their community rather than simply consuming content created by the beauty industry. For centuries, women's magazines, from *The Ladies' Mercury* to *Godey's Lady's Book* to *Vogue*, have been a primary way for these kinds of conversations to be brought into the public sphere, so the creation and formation of a community of beauty and fashion-loving women on YouTube is hardly a new concept; YouTube is just a new platform to have these discussions. Similar to the world of women's magazines, YouTube provides a platform for them to share their own views and opinions about products, trends, and issues in their lives and to do so in a creative way, and these beauty channels provide an important rhetorical site for investigation. Each creator finds their own filming and editing style, and while there may be similar aesthetics among groups of creators, no two channels or videos are exactly the same.

For the small YouTuber beauty communities especially, but also for some of the larger channels, YouTube offers a space for creators of all genders, races, ethnicities, classes, and sexualities to create discursive spaces and engage in rhetorical practices. While this paper focuses on Fleur de Force and her channel as an example of a typical beauty channel, it is important to note that compared to several years ago when YouTube first started and early beauty channels like Zoella or Michelle Phan rose in popularity, what is "typical" now is much harder to define and categorize. Fleur and other beauty vloggers are creating content that doesn't naturally translate to or fit into other mediums. The format of YouTube videos, on average ten to fifteen minutes long and with a range of topics, does not lend itself to traditional television formats. They aren't talk shows or makeover shows. Nor do they need high production values or teams of people to produce them. Additionally, one of the key differences between YouTube and network or cable programming is the personal connection between the vlogger and their audience. But it's not just the format that separates YouTube creators from professional television programming, it's the diversity of the creators themselves.

To the outside viewer, being a YouTuber might seem easy, but behind the scenes there are numerous technical and content issues vloggers face on a daily basis, usually handling those issues by themselves. Being the sole writer, director, camera operator, editor, distributor, PR person, and social media manager for a YouTube channel is a lot of work; loving it is key to succeeding at it. While the same could be said of male creators in other YouTube communities, the fact remains that the beauty community is largely dominated by women (with a small, but growing, percentage of beauty creators being men), and for most of these women, the channels they have created on YouTube are the first places they have had full control of the work produced and the ability to fully speak their minds and share their ideas rather than having those ideas dictated to them.

While Gauntlett (2011) ignores gender completely, other scholars are looking specifically at the way gender functions in discussions of creativity (Fennetaux 2009; Goggin 2009; Iskin 2009; MacKnight 2009). These discussions are crucial to my argument for Fleur and beauty vloggers. Looking at scholarship that analyzes crafting and creativity from a gendered perspective makes it easier to see why beauty vloggers are at risk of being dismissed as unimportant. Riane Eisler and Alfonso Monturori (2007), in "Creativity, Society, and the Hidden Subject of Gender: Toward a New Contextualized Approach," discuss how gender has underlying implications in the social construction of creativity. Specifically, they examine the ways women have been excluded from discussions about creativity in scholarship, as well as the exclusion of creative activities typically assigned to women. Making videos about fashion and beauty products might not seem creative to the outside observer, but as I am arguing, for the women within the community, this activity is deeply creative. Eisler and Monturori conclude, "These answers suggest that for men art was perceived as primarily a personal affair, which gave meaning, pleasure, and fulfillment, whereas for the women it was also a process of communication and connection" (486). Gauntlett also makes connections among creativity, communication, and connection. These intersections are important to beauty vloggers because, like artists in more traditional media (painting, sculpture, etc.), they are approaching their videos from a place of meaning, pleasure, communication, and connection, whether it's with their one million subscribers or simply with occasional online passersby.

Eisler and Monturori (2007) also bring up the issue of public versus private and how that distinction impacted the gendering of creativity. They discuss how certain activities that have typically been assigned as "feminine," such as cooking, home decorating, or clothes making, are devalued, but when these activities are performed by men, they are labeled *creative*. They state, "Thus, although women have traditionally performed most of this work on a daily basis in the private sphere of the home, until recently a predominance of male chefs, designers, and interior decorators working in the public sphere have received recognition for 'creativity' in these areas" (489). At first glance, beauty YouTube creators look as if they're operating in the private sphere; many of them film in their bedrooms or other private space. But in reality, the video is then uploaded into the public sphere of the internet.

By ungendering creativity, we open more possibilities for what counts as creative. If we open up creativity in the previously private spheres inhabited by women, we increase what can be considered a creative act. As Eisler and Monturori (2007) state, "It shows, that 'ordinary' people, working in domains that have historically not been deemed to be the locus of creative activities, can in fact, be creative . . . it makes it possible to see that creative activity exists in all domains" (489). This expansion is critical to understanding the work of beauty vloggers. By expanding which domains are considered possibilities for creative practices, we can include an entire community of women sitting in their bedrooms, dorm rooms, and family rooms joined by a common love of beauty and fashion. Eisler and Monturori conclude, "But we believe that as creativity becomes more ungendered and contextualized, we have an opportunity to transform not only creativity, but the social and moral web of human relationships" (496). By expanding our definitions, we can begin to include more people, women in particular, engaging in both high art and in everyday creative practices.

FEMININITY, CREATIVITY, FLEUR DE FORCE, AND THE BEAUTY COMMUNITY

In the several years since starting on YouTube, Fleur's channel has undergone a variety of changes. Starting (as most YouTubers do) by sitting by her bed and talking to the built-in camera on her laptop, Fleur began sharing her thoughts and opinions on beauty products, giving tutorials on how to apply makeup, showing off recent purchases of new makeup or clothing, and addressing other standard video topics within the beauty community, such as "What's in My Bag," or responding to question videos (known as *tag videos*) she'd been "tagged" in by other content creators in the community. Through Fleur's engagement with members of the community and building networks among other creators, her channel grew. As the participants in her channel grew in numbers, and as Fleur gained more experience within the platform, the quality of her videos increased as she began using higher-quality filming and lighting equipment. Even after the birth of her first child in late 2017 and the inclusion of more "mommy" content, her content remained relatively the same, and she is still participating in the same community on YouTube she started in. Her channel has grown and evolved as her life has changed (marriage, moving houses, going through a pregnancy and having a baby, and now life as a wife, mother, and businesswoman), but the heart of her content and the way she approaches her audience has stayed the same. And while new business opportunities have come her way and she is no longer a solo enterprise (Fleur is with a management company that assists in negotiations and partnerships with brands, and she has an assistant or two to help with the administrative side of running a channel), when it comes to the content, Fleur still films and edits all her own content. Rather than hire someone to help with the filming tasks so she could maintain her prebaby uploading schedule, she chose to adjust how many times a week she uploads and continues to do that work herself. Unlike other larger channel creators, who have taken to employing teams of people to help with lighting, sound, photography, videography, and editing for some or all of their videos, Fleur continues to do the bulk of the creative work and audience management herself, responding to comments and engaging with her audience on other platforms (such as Twitter or Instagram).

It's also interesting to note that within the platform, *creator* is the specific term used by YouTube to describe channel operators. All the uploading work is done in the YouTube Creator Studio, so notions of creating and creativity are explicitly laid out by the operators of the YouTube platform itself. And many creators like Fleur use that language when describing themselves, preferring the title *creator* over *influencer*. YouTubers like Fleur still see themselves as engaging in a creative process, sharing the end result each week with their audience, and responding to feedback in the comments.

Additionally, over the last several years, some channels, like Fleur's, have become larger (500k+ subscribers), and with the rise of influencer marketing, creators like Fleur have begun attracting attention from brands and companies within the beauty industry. This growth has led to opportunities ranging from having early access to products to review them on the channel to collaborations between brands and the creator in the form of sponsored videos (featuring the brand in exchange for a financial arrangement). Since starting in 2009, Fleur has released two books featuring advice and tips similar to those offered on her channel, launched a small range of cosmetics through the online beauty retailer Feelunique, and has an ongoing collaboration with the brow and false-eyelash brand Eylure, releasing two separate collections of false lashes, with four styles in each collection, as well as a line of brow products. There have also been numerous collaborations and sponsorships on individual videos, each of which was delicately handled by Fleur to ensure the ad content fit in with her regular style of videos. In a time when subscribers are becoming increasingly aware of brand relationships and being quick to judge if a sponsorship doesn't feel right or seems too gimmicky or too much like a commercial, Fleur has received relatively little criticism in her comments for these sponsorships and has always followed the ever-changing guidelines set by the UK Advertising Standards Agency (ASA), the governing body that regulates disclosure rules for collaborations and brand sponsorships.

Women like Fleur are no longer just amateurs sitting around talking about makeup; they are agents within a larger industry making creative and business choices for their own personal brand. This autonomy is changing the way we view YouTube and these creators, as they now have a power separate from the average consumer yet are not directly employed by or bound to traditional beauty marketing. Caught between consumer and industry insider, hobby and career, they make daily choices and complex negotiations between their identities as creators and their roles as entrepreneurs.

One final thing I'd like to address about the beauty community is that while Fleur, in many ways, is a very average case of a beauty YouTuber, particularly among the group of YouTubers who started in those earlier years between 2007 and 2009, what counts today as "average" or "typical" within the beauty community is changing almost daily. The status of the community has grown to staggering heights, as evidenced by beauty and fashion industries wanting in on the action by way of influencer marketing and collaborations. However, a community that at first might have seemed very white, very straight, very conforming in many ways and shapes has diversified itself greatly.

Creators from all racial and ethnic backgrounds, speaking a wide range of different languages and of varying gender and sexual identities, as well as varying socioeconomic backgrounds, have all found a space on YouTube in general but also within the beauty community specifically. Within the YouTube beauty community alone there has been an increase in creators who don't fit the white, straight, female, thin, and conventionally beautiful mold. There are hijab-wearing Muslim female creators like Dina Tokio and Mona Haydar, black female creators like Jackie Aina, Alissa Ashley, and Nyma Tang, disabled creators like Jordan Bone, and male "beauty gurus" whose channels focus specifically on makeup and disrupt gender binaries, like Patrick Starr, Wayne Goss, Manny MUA, and Jeffree Star. There has also been an increase in content about more traditional men's grooming and fashion, with creators like Robin James and Ali Gordon.

Then there are female creators who create content that disrupts standard definitions of beauty based on size, like the increase in body-positive and fat-positive beauty creators such as Nikki Tutorials and Loey Lane, or creators like Em Ford from My Pale Skin with her viral video *You Look Disgusting* in 2015 and its follow up *Redefine Pretty* in 2018, which at the time of writing this in the summer of 2019 have 31 million and 1.6 million views respectively. Ford tackles the hate and online abuse women face for both wearing makeup or choosing not to wear makeup and has launched an online movement in favor of skin positivity that includes accepting acne and other skin conditions, as well as acknowledging the beauty of all skin colors. Even among more traditional beauty channels like Fleur de Force's, there is a range: from budget beauty channels (usually run by smaller channel creators) that focus on drug-store products, like Alice from Red's Makeup Bag or Shannon from Pages and Polish, to premium and luxury creators like Lydia Elise Millen or Josie from Fashion Mumblr. This list is far from exhaustive, and there are countless other creators who are also doing interesting and disruptive work. The beauty community has grown from a handful of young women making videos in their bedrooms to an ever-expanding and sprawling network of women and men of various ages and racial, gender, sexual, and economic backgrounds, with each of the creators named above worthy of deeper investigation.

It is important to study the rhetorical practices of the beauty community on YouTube to show how it is engaging in creative practices that negotiate daily with traditional notions of beauty and femininity and how many of these channels disrupt those notions on a regular basis. The YouTube beauty community serves as a back channel to the mainstream beauty and fashion industries, a back channel that's becoming increasingly more mainstream. Creators listen to each other and to their subscribers about which products work, which ones don't, which products are or aren't worth the money, and which products are cheaper alternatives (or "dupes"/duplicates) for higher-end products, as well as deciding which trends they like and which are a waste of time or just not for them. These creators also find themselves calling out brands when they've made racist or other insensitive remarks, are not diverse enough in shade ranges for different skin colors, are too exclusive in size ranges for clothing, and other similar concerns and industry controversies; they have become voices and agents of change instead of passive consumers. Rather than unreflectively accepting traditional ideas and ideals of beauty as prescribed by the advertisers and the beauty and fashion industries, creators are deciding for themselves what they consider beautiful or worth spending their money on.

CONCLUSION

This chapter has explored the redefinition and feminization of creativity on YouTube. It is important to remember each channel and vlogger has their own unique identity and microcommunity within their channel. Throughout her channel's evolution, Fleur has engaged in a number of creative practices, both in the creation of the channel's content and in her marketing of the channel on social media. She, like other vloggers, is an active agent who has created an ethos for herself and her channel that promotes a rhetoric of positivity and acceptance for oneself rather than a dependence on the beauty and fashion industries for validation. Though Fleur does not identify specifically as a feminist vlogger, her channel reflects many of the choices and negotiations with the beauty and fashion industries feminist scholars of popular culture call for, and Fleur encourages her viewers to make their own choices and participate in that negotiation process with her rather than buying into traditional notions of beauty and consumerism.

Future analysis should examine the way creators like Fleur interact with their subscribers, both on their channels and through their other social media platforms, and the way they address the variety of issues related to sponsored content while maintaining their credibility as beauty vloggers. While this chapter has focused solely on the creative practices within vlogger channels such as Fleur's, doing a deeper analysis of the creative practices and meaning-making processes Fleur engages in through her other social media platforms and projects would help shine a brighter spotlight on the ways of making evident within the YouTube beauty community and the success of channels like Fleur's. This research would help show how complex these creative practices are and the broader relevance they have beyond the YouTube platform to the ways we view and legitimize the rhetorical acts of beauty vloggers.

NOTE

1. For a sample of her vlog, see Fleur De Force (2015).

WORKS CITED

Ashley, Christy, and Tracy Tuten. 2015. "Creative Strategies in Social Media Marketing: An Exploratory Study of Branded Social Content and Consumer Engagement." *Psychology and Marketing* 3 (1): 15–27.
Baumgardner, Jennifer, and Amy Richards. 2000. *Manifesta: Young Women, Feminism, and the Future*. New York: Straus and Giroux.
Dicker, Rory, and Alison Piepmeier, eds. 2003. *Catching a Wave: Reclaiming Feminism for the 21st Century*. Boston, MA: Northeastern University Press.
Duffy, Brooke Erin, and Emily Hund. 2015. "'Having It All' on Social Media: Entrepreneurial Femininity and Self-Branding Among Fashion Bloggers." *Social Media + Society* 1 (2): 1–11.
Eisler, Riane, and Alfonso Monturori. 2007. "Creativity, Society, and the Hidden Subject of Gender: Toward a New Contextualized Approach." *World Futures: Journal of General Evolution* 63 (7): 479–99.
Fennetaux, Arianne. 2009. "Female Crafts: Women and Bricolage in Late Georgian Britain, 1750–1820." In *Women and Things, 1750–1990: Gendered Material Strategies*, edited by Maureen Daly Goggin and Beth Fowkes Tobin, 91–108. Farnham, UK: Ashgate.
Findlen, Barbara, ed. 1995. *Listen Up: Voices from the Next Feminist Generation*. Berkeley, CA: Seal.
Fishburn, Katherine. 1982. *Women in Popular Culture: A Reference Guide*. Boston, MA: Greenwood.
Fleur De Force. 2015. "Battle of the Birthday Cake! Vlogust 26." YouTube video, 30 August 2015, 8.09. http://wwqw.you2repeat.com/watch/?v=mJoKTFa9mWI. Accessed 28 December 2020.
Gauntlett, David. 2011. *Making Is Connecting: The Social Meaning of Creativity, from DIY and Knitting to YouTube and Web 2.0*. Cambridge, England: Polity.

Gillis, Stacy, Gillian Howe, and Rebecca Munford, eds. 2004. *Third Wave Feminism: A Critical Exploration*. London, England: Palgrave Macmillian.
Goggin, Maureen Daly. 2009. "Stitching a Life in 'Pen of Steele and Silken Ink': Elizabeth Parker's *circa* 1830 Sampler." In *Women and the Material Culture of Needlework and Textiles, 1750–1950*, edited by Maureen Daly Goggin and Beth Fowkes Tobin, 31–49. Farnham, UK: Ashgate.
Iskin, Ruth E. 2009. "Material Women: The Department-Store Fashion Poster in Paris, 1880–1900." In *Material Women, 1750–1950: Consuming Desires and Collecting Practices*, edited by Maureen Daly Goggin and Beth Fowkes Tobin, 33–53. Farnham, UK: Ashgate.
Jerslev, Anne. 2016. "In the Time of the Microcelebrity and the YouTube Zoella." *International Journal of Communication* 10: 5233–51.
Labrecque, Laren I., Ereni Markos, and George R. Milne. 2011. "Online Personal Branding: Processes, Challenges, and Implications." *Journal of Interactive Marketing* 25 (1): 37–50.
Levine, Elana, ed. 2015. *Cupcakes, Pinterest, and Ladyporn: Feminized Popular Culture in the Early Twenty-First Century*. Champaign, IL: University of Illinois Press.
MacKnight, Elizabeth C. 2009. "A Touch of Distinction: Furnishing French Aristocratic Homes in the Nineteenth and Twentieth Centuries." In *Material Women, 1750–1950: Consuming Desires and Collecting Practices*, edited by Maureen Daly Goggin and Beth Fowkes Tobin, 75–91. Farnham, UK: Ashgate.
Mardon, Rebecca, Mike Molesworth, and Georgiana Grigore. 2018. "YouTuber Beauty Gurus and the Emotional Labor of Tribal Entrepreneurship." *Journal of Business Research* 92 (November): 443–54.
Marwick, Alice E. 2013. *Status Update: Celebrity, Publicity, and Branding in the Social Media Age*. New Haven, CT: Yale University Press.
Meyers, Marian, ed. 1999. *Mediated Women: Representations in Popular Culture*. Newburyport, MA: Hampton.
Shin, Wosun, Augustine Pang, and Hyo Jung Kim. 2015. "Building Relationships Through Integrated Online Media: Global Organizations' Use of Brand Web Sites, Facebook, and Twitter." *Journal of Business and Technical Communication* 29 (2): 184–220.
Singh, Sangeeta, and Stephan Sonnenburg. 2012. "Brand Performances in Social Media." *Journal of Interactive Marketing* 26 (4): 189–97.
Snickars, Pelle, and Patrick Vonderau, eds. 2009. *The YouTube Reader*. Stockholm, Sweden: National Library of Sweden.
Vernuccio, Maria. 2014. "Communicating Corporate Brands Through Social Media: An Exploratory Study." *International Journal of Business Communication* 51 (3): 211–33.
Wolf, Naomi. 1990. *The Beauty Myth: How Images of Beauty Are Used Against Women*. London, England: Chatto & Windus.

9
A STUDY OF MAKING-NESS
Texts, Memory, and Art

Kathleen Blake Yancey

On January 12, 2015, just into what promised to be a wonderful new year, the patio door in the bedroom my husband I share was brutally smashed, its solid pane of glass shattered into tiny pieces randomly propelled across and into the carpet, hundreds of tiny sharp shards glistening in the darkness. Bureau drawers, thrown diagonally one atop another, lay on the shards, their contents scattered in and out and across the room—a black bra, a pair of neutral hose I wore to my son's wedding, a brown furrowed sock belonging to my husband, a soft navy sweatshirt recalling a vacation to Seattle taken twenty years before, a tiny red leather box open, crushed white velvet inside, empty.

Not all our belongings could be found, no matter where or how hard we looked. Our passports, mine and my husband's, stamps imprinted at Amsterdam, Paris, and Dublin: gone. My social security cards, pre- and post-marriage: gone. Some British pounds, some American cash: gone. The earrings David gave me the Christmas before, gold with small oval stones dropping from each ear: gone. My mother's wedding band, platinum with discreet diamonds, gone; my father's simple wedding band, gold with beveled edges: gone; my mother's watch, a rectangular face with Gothic letters, tiny diamond chips marking three o'clock and nine o'clock, inscribed on the back to commemorate the day I was born, "To Mommy from Kathy and Jack, July 5, 1950": gone. My grandmother's golden watch, its cover decorated with Victorian filigree surrounding an ornate S for Scott centering it, Scott her maiden name the same as my father-in-law's first name, a watch I opened and closed as a child sitting in her lap, given to me on my eighteenth birthday, when I dedicated my entire small savings to a gold chain worthy of the watch, my costliest piece of jewelry, even if, arms floating free on the face of the watch, it didn't tell time anymore: gone. A pair of simple pearl earrings, each set in a gold flower, that David gave me on the Mother's Day before our daughter was born some thirty years ago: gone.

In talking about the break-in, referring to it impersonally as though it had happened to someone else or was a show one watched on television, I told my son that I would probably write about it, would try to use composing to make sense of it, to remember what was lost, to make peace with it, to somehow make what was lost material, recreated through words.

His reply: *Why not call it Eulogy for a Lost Object?*

DOI: 10.7330/9781646420384.c009

How do we memorialize loss? A eulogy provides one way: a text in which we remember, call up stories of the lost, try to make a coherent whole out of an assembled life—a childhood walk with my father, my tiny four-year-old hand nestled safely in his, my sense of security complete; a father's disappointment and disapproval when I went ever-so-slightly hippie, when I abandoned the Catholic church, when I allowed my children to abandon it with me; the day new wrinkles edging the corner of his left eye warned me that he was finally growing old; his cancer. When he finally died, my sisters and I collaborated on a eulogy for him, but I could not have delivered it, could not have stood and spoken among family and friends. I was glad I had helped craft the eulogy; I was glad one of my sisters had the courage and the resolve and—even in the midst of sorrow—the joy I did not. When my mother-in-law died and I began the draft of her eulogy on behalf of my husband, his siblings, and his father, I had a different problem, an invention problem. I knew and loved my mother-in-law, a high-school teacher of Latin and English, a devoted wife and mother, a mean tennis player and an even meaner bridge player, possibly the most generous person I've met, and certainly the only person who ever brought me breakfast in bed. But in that eulogy, I didn't know what to say, even to myself: How do we sum up, characterize, detail, bring to life a life?

Part of the problem is inherent in the eulogy as a genre; it can serve multiple purposes, among them providing consolation, helping the "bereaved come to terms with death," and "celebrating the deceased's life" (Kent 1997, 176–78). In each of these situations, however, the eulogy functions similarly, according to Karlyn Kohrs Campbell and Kathleen Hall Jamieson's account of how eulogies perform: in acknowledging death, the eulogy "necessitates a juxtaposition of past and present tense which recasts the relationship to the deceased to one of memory" (1978, 20). Others, like Owen Peterson, emphasize rhetorical expectations accompanying a eulogy, most important among them the eulogy speaker's obligation to "heighten the auditors' feeling of regard, love, or appreciation" (1983, 174).

If I am composing a eulogy, it is certainly not of the Peterson type; rather, I take Campbell and Jamieson's point that in eulogizing, we look to "juxtaposition of past and present . . . recast[ing]" a relationship. In the case of the break-in, composing a eulogy for a lost object provides an opportunity to acknowledge what was lost, to move to a future when that loss becomes not the defining event of life but rather and merely an experience integrated into, and a part of, life's social fabric.

The night of the break-in David cut up an old cardboard moving box and, using the last of our packing tape, secured pieces of cardboard to the door frame, covering the hole where the glass had been and shielding pieces of broken glass clinging to what was left of the door. Methodically, I pressed the tips of my fingers on the shiny tape all around the door's circumference, assuring myself that it would keep the cardboard glued tightly, my fingerprints lingering on the tape as though communicating with it, as though asking it to turn the clock back. Lights out, the night dark, I heard every leaf bristle, every owl complain, every insect move out of the way.

Early the next morning, as I get out of bed, I slip my feet into shoes: we cannot walk on the carpet. The doorbell rings. Wesley, who has painted our living room and repaired the gutters over the garage and built us a kitchen pantry, is at the door, used pieces of plywood and an oversized nail gun in hand. We show him the broken door. Silently, he goes outside, moves around the house to the door and covers it with the plywood panels, taking care not to disturb the door's broken glass. The spitting of his nail gun echoes in the neighborhood.

Again, I run the vacuum cleaner across the carpet, again trying to collect all the shards, each one of which announces its arrival in the vacuum bag. My husband says we'll never get them all up; they are too many, too scattered, too embedded into the carpet. Let's get a new rug, he suggests. They even ripped off a pillowcase from the pillow to take our things, I reply; they can't have my carpet, too.

The insurance company wants pictures, photos, images of what's gone, pictures, photos, images I don't have. Would I feel any different now if I did? Would it help to share a photo, to point to the thing that's gone?

On Facebook, our break-in is announced by neighbors I don't know. I live right behind one of the houses that was broken into, says one: I was home with my two kids today too. So scary and upsetting. Interesting, the next person responds; thanks for the info.

Three days later a neighbor three doors down rings our doorbell. What can he do to protect his home, he wants to know. I've never met him before.

In thinking about this eulogy, I also decided the eulogy would take material form, possibly as an artist's book, an object introduced to me by students.

In 2005, as director of the Pearce Center for Professional Communication at Clemson University, I hosted a day-long symposium focusing on the visual. One presentation featured students in a course on early twentieth-century British women's literature, their assignment to create artists' books demonstrating what they had learned. As each student came to the front of the room, shared her book, and explained the rhetorical and design choices, I was fascinated. On the one hand, an artist's book—defined in Wikipedia (2019) as "works of art that utilize the form of the book [and are] often published in small editions, though they are sometimes produced as one-of-a-kind objects"—often relies on a given book as a foundation for the new artist's book, and it can be disconcerting to see how the original book is altered, with pages ripped out, others marked up, in order to make way for the new. We have so fetishized the book that our impulse, my impulse, when seeing a book, even an old one, deliberately damaged in this way was to protest; not to do so seemed like participating in an act of sacrilege. On the other hand, the new book can literally bring the old to life; the books I saw that day, serving and displaying new purposes, were materially rich, with illustrations, ribbons, decorative papers. And often, the concepts of the new book interfaced with those of the old. One student, for instance, used as her foundation a book on Victorian novels, which allowed her to create a context for her focus on the new literature developing from the old, much as the new book developed from the old. Working with individual pages, she highlighted passages in the prior book that she invoked and quoted in her new book; there was, in other words, a kind of material intertextuality making both a new kind of meaning and a new kind of knowledge.

Never did it occur to me that ten years later I'd create my own book to memorize a loss.

> *Friends, they want me to grieve the loss of privacy, the violation of a home we think of as our own. Others want me to grieve the loss of safety: Will I ever feel safe in my own home again? The police, they don't want me to grieve: they want me to plan. The sergeant who comes by the house tells me to buy a gun, to get a dog. Frustrated, I suggest to my husband that we dig a moat, that we fill it with water. He replies that alligators could take up residence, and we'd never leave.*

Artist's books, as Wikipedia suggests, are a genre unto themselves: what's also interesting about them is how they provide for, even invite, transgressions of the conventions defining books. As Andrea Kohashi explains of her own practice:

> During the conceptualization and design stages of producing an artist's book, I am interested in the possibilities inherent in indeterminacies related to ideas of organization and categorization. An artists' book allows me to play with and even subvert the conventions of traditional books. I'm continually questioning the relationship between material, text, image, and structure because text doesn't need to be structured into semantically or syntactically correct sentences, nor do images need to be directly illustrative. Through the seemingly limitless possibilities of the arrangement and placement of text, and the grouping of outwardly disjunctive images, I ask the future reader to find meaning in a new system of organizing and categorizing information. Simultaneously, I'm aware that the further away I move from convention, the greater the possibility of ostracizing my audience. (2015)

Interestingly, this approach to an artist's book engages both aesthetics and rhetoric; through "play[ing] with and even subverting the conventions of traditional books," Kohashi invents and asks the reader to do likewise, "to find meaning in a new system of organizing and categorizing information."

As important, Kohashi, who is an archivist by profession, draws a comparison between her work as an artist's-book creator and her processing of an archival collection, seeing both as "complicated act[s]":

> Just as I question the ways in which my organizing information affects readers when designing an artists' book, when processing an archival collection, I'm constantly evaluating how my organizing and categorizing impact a future researcher's ability to access and process information. Designing an artist's book is never a neutral act, nor is processing a collection. The life of an individual, family, or organization is often a complicated narrative and the items we receive in archives reflect that complexity: papers and artifacts accrue and overlap in chronology and subject matter. (2015)

Kohashi sees differences between these activities as well, but one feature common to both, she says, is their representation of "life and emotions"—in the book, the artist's emotions, and in the archival papers, the life and emotions of those who created the papers being archived.

I begin my book with emotions.

> *This eulogy, like others, intends to say goodbye, to sum up, to make a narrative that consoles, to conclude, but perhaps most of all, to help us, help me, let go.*
>
> *I don't want to let go, don't want to say goodbye, don't want to concede that I'll never see my father's wedding band again, never wear my mother's ring again, never press into my earlobes the pearls I think of as already my daughter's; they will never be hers.*
>
> *How can you let go of that you cannot see, cannot touch, can only remember? If you are only remembering, isn't that a sign that something is gone? Doesn't a letting go presume a prior connecting? If I must let go, couldn't I have been given some warning?*
>
> *I think of other kinds of letting go; much, much worse, not comparable, not in the same universe. The disappeared in South America, mothers and cousins and husbands. A child in New York City suddenly, permanently, gone. Vanished. Their loved ones didn't let go: the missing, they were taken. Then gone—not there; no last hug, no goodbye, no final word of love, no final human touch, no physical memory pressed into, through the skin to the self inside, preserved. I think about what I have lost, also invisible, and am glad and relieved that they are only things—and feel a bit guilty, too, that I'm overreacting, that I'm squandering a sorrow reserved for something important. How can I mourn such trivialities? I console myself with this idea, say that it will be okay, these were, after all, merely things. My daughter, she says that this is what people say only when they really care about the things.*

When the 2015 CFP for the Feminisms and Rhetorics conference was announced, with its attention to "Women's Ways of Making" with the potential of sharing in an exhibition space, I understood I needed not only to write a eulogy, as my son had suggested, but also to share it as a book in the conference exhibition, and more specifically as an artist's book. The theme of the conference endorsed a knowledge making-ness congruent with such a book, I thought, especially in its emphasis on "making[ness]" as an "epistemic endeavor," and in the conference's intention to collapse "several impoverished binaries: mind/body, producer/consumer, passive recipients/active agents, public/private, male/female, and craft/art" (Feminisms and Rhetorics 2014). My intention—in the eulogy, in the artist's book, in this chapter—is in part to collapse the boundary between scholarship as the preeminent way of making knowledge and artful craft as its poor cousin. Working together, they might, I thought, be an especially powerful way of making meaning, of making knowledge.

The process I developed to create the book was interestingly recursive. I began by writing the eulogy, elements of which—phrases, themes—remain in this text; my drafting practice involves close to nine drafts, and the drafting of this text was typical in that regard. Some paragraphs were created, others expanded: the original draft portrayed temporarily repairing the door the night of the break-in in a single sentence I later expanded:

> That night David cut up a moving box and taped it to the door frame to cover the hole where the glass had been; that night I heard every leaf bristle, every insect crawl, every star shine.
>
> The night of the break-in David cut up an old cardboard moving box and, using the last of our packing tape, secured pieces of cardboard to the door frame, covering the hole where the glass had been and what was left of the door. Methodically, I pressed the tips of my fingers on the shiny tape all around the door's circumference, assuring myself that it would keep the cardboard glued tightly, my fingerprints lingering on the tape as though communicating with it, as though asking it to turn the clock back. Lights out, I heard every leaf bristle, every insect crawl, every star shine.

Part of this process was, for me, normal, but given the occasion, it was also unusual in its emotional content; in such a process, I did—and do—understand myself to be making meaning, at first for me, and if the process works, for others as well. And in the larger rhetorical situation of the conference, I knew I would recall a personal experience, expressed in a book of my own making, that I would share with one person at a time. That prospect was intimidating in a way giving a paper, for me, is not. In giving a paper, we stand while the audience sits; in giving a paper, we hold onto the text others cannot see; in giving a paper, we frame it, respond to questions, amend it on the fly. In sharing an artist's book—and it's worth saying I'm not an artist, though I was making an artist's book—I would be able to exercise none of that control: My audience, face to face with me, would make of my book, and my experience, what they would. And more: I would see the making they made.

With a final draft of the text coming into view, I moved into the book-making phase, beginning with a trip to the local Goodwill Bookstore not one mile from my home. There I saw many, many books, most of which, paperbacks addressing topics like Hawaiian vacations and Florida football, weren't appropriate. What I was hoping to find was a slender book with a plain cover that I could repurpose; what I did find was a black-covered hardback book providing a history of Egypt. At over 250 pages, it was too large for my eulogy, so I began tearing pages out, and then bundling pages together, so that a single bit of text from the eulogy would consume more than a single page. I also began drawing on the book pages, sometimes providing a kind of filigree directing the reader to the next page, other times simply crossing out text. As part of this process, I also began literally dividing the eulogy into smaller bits, first printing out the full eulogy, then cutting the text into squares, itself an important part of the process because it required me to think about the text in separated chunks. Ordinarily, I draft texts running on as a single continuous entity from start to finish; the text is only divided into parts through the publishing process, when that continuous entry becomes a set of pages, typically without my participation in the process. But in making this book, I was author, copyeditor, production editor.

In thinking about how to include the verbal text in the book, I never considered simply sizing the text to the pages, which certainly was an option. Rather, I had thought all along that I'd divide the text into parts—into what I began thinking of as episodes—to achieve some rhetorical purpose. One way to do this was to plan it out in advance, identifying episodes and then moving them into the book; another was to cut the text into those episodes, assemble them, plot them into a sequence, and see if they made (felt) sense; if not, cut them again, but differently. I used the latter approach.

> By March, I'm sleeping again; I don't hear the crickets, don't hear the stars shining. The police have come and gone: they won't be returning. The case is open until it's closed, we learn, but they have little hope that any of the jewelry will be found. If it's never solved, it will be open forever? Is there a statute of limitations on open cases? Would that provide closure?
>
> We purchased a new door, nicer and newer than the one it's replaced. We acquired a security system with two signs promoting itself, one by the mailbox on the street, another in front of the house. There's now a pad in the hall with a button I press when I leave home, and with a unique code I key in each time I return.
>
> I completed all the paperwork and had my passport photo taken and explained why I couldn't give them my old passport and answered that, yes, I had called the

theft in, and yes, I'm sure I won't see it again, all so that I could receive a passport empty of an official reminder from Barcelona whose insignia I can still see in my mind's eye, whose outline I can almost trace with my right fingertip.

Initially, I thought I could simply paste each textual bit, each episode, into the book, and I did that for some of them. I had also planned to add a number of images, including photos of the break-in's effects and a map of related robberies in my neighborhood. But working with the pages, I decided on another strategy; I would use other kinds of paper to make other associations, and I would reduce the number of photos so the words carried more of the meaning. In designing the page for the episode when David "cut up an old moving box and taped it to the door," for example, I decided on a two-page layout, placing that descriptive verbal text on the right-hand side, quite simply; placing a large rectangle of unmarked brown-paper-bag paper on the opposite page on the left, making material the description of the moving box-as-door. Likewise, I understood "this eulogy, like others, intends to say goodbye, to sum up, to conclude, but perhaps most of all, to help us, help me, let go" as a turn in the eulogy, so I set this chunk of text off by itself on its own page, and signaling its importance, I framed it several times, the white printed text on a black rectangle, that black rectangle on a large white sheet of paper, that paper pasted onto the page.

Some days,
it's as though it didn't happen,
as though we've heeded the police officer's advice
and simply moved on.
Or moved on.

※ ※ ※

This line also seemed a turning point, and when set apart, reads almost as a poem; I put it on a piece of embossed paper on a page by itself.

※ ※ ※

One Thursday, I'm planning what to wear—a plain black jacket I like to a pair with long sliver dangly earrings ending in pearls caressing my neck. I need a longer neck to look good in them, but I like to think that the earrings make up for my neck. The earrings: gone. Unbidden, I'm reminded.

In April, I visit with my four sisters and apologize for our father's lost wedding band.

In May, I visit with my son and apologize for the small pieces that now are on Craig's List or in a pawn shop or tucked in someone else's ears.

These loved ones, I think, they don't care. I'm grateful for that.

But in writing this eulogy, I understand anew, I still do.

* * *

Three years ago, I served on the doctoral committee for a student in art, Sunny Spillane, who argued that in making art, we make knowledge. She employed a method she called "a/r/tography, an arts-based framework for conducting educational research," relying on "an interrelated process of artmaking and reflective writing" (2013, 3–4). Her project, very different than mine, was to stage different conversations about race with a group of art teachers who would use their art as a way of making meaning of those conversations and of race itself, and I found the project persuasive. Sunny's claim was that the writing and the art worked together, multimodally.

> The integrated methods of inquiry and forms of presentation and communication used in this study are inherently multimodal: meanings are created and communicated in and through multiple, interwoven visual and verbal "modes" (Kress, 2010). Drawing on Barone and Eisner's (1997) work, Sullivan (2006) succinctly summarized their claims for the unique contributions of arts-based research: "What distinguishes this kind of research [from science-based research] is the multiplicity of ways of encountering and representing experience, and the use of forms of expression that can effectively communicate these phenomena" (Sullivan, 2006, pp. 23–24). The design, materials used, images created and presented, and artistic processes engaged in this study and the research text (within the limitations of approved formats for dissertations) evidence this multimodality. (9)

Nithikul Nimkulrat, another artist, makes something of the same point but in the context of drawing distinctions between practice-*based* research and practice-*led* research. She claims that the first is oriented to art, the second to making knowledge from artistic work based on "conscious exploration."

> First, the difference is drawn on the nature of art/design practice. Practice in practice-based research can be carried out freely for its own sake in order to produce artifacts. This is fairly similar to the general conception of art/design practice. On the contrary, practice in practice-led research is conscious exploration with the knowledge involved in the making of artifacts. Second, the difference is in the roles of practitioner and researcher. In practice-based research, the practitioner's role may be more dominant than the researcher's role. The emphasis seems to be on practice, since a practitioner-researcher carries out her research solely based on her own practice. In practice-led research, the two roles appear to be equally important, because research becomes an intertwined part of practice. (2007)

My experience, of course, was different than Nimkulrat's, but through my amateur artistic practice, I did make a kind of meaning and perhaps a kind of knowledge, the latter conceptualized as a set of lessons. Six of those lessons seem especially important.

First, the process of writing this text—which is now taking a third form: first, the text-as-eulogy; then the eulogy-as-made-book; then the text-as-(this)-chapter—involved materials I don't usually use in composing: paper and markers and highlighters. With the addition of those materials, I could make a new kind of meaning, one both aesthetic and rhetorical. We are often more inclined to work materially on the web, but that materiality is different than paper materiality; what we learn from working with each is a good area for additional research.

Second, because of the nature of book as a genre, I needed to decide how to produce the eulogy: we academic writers, as much as we write, don't usually (aren't allowed to?) think in those terms. I could have sized the text to fit the page(s) but would have lost the affordances the page could offer were it not seen as merely the transporter of text. Taking a cue from the book-as-genre, I could have thought in terms of chapters, but that elaboration seemed at odds with the nature of the experience. In other words, desiring to keep the text as a eulogy but producing it in a book required me to develop another alternative: the idea of episodes.

Third, episodes as a means of arrangement also functioned as a means of invention (Yancey 2004). This lesson was made especially salient to me when I began literally working with the text by cutting it into pieces. That process of cutting up text into bits and chunks, and temporarily putting one next to another, invited consideration of how the experience had played out, of what patterns I could see in retrospect. The size of the pages that would host the bits of text no doubt played a role in this: pages of this size can host a smaller rather than larger text; an episodic approach is thus convenient. But my improvisational play with the text also led me to think in terms of episodes. Hence, the experience as episodic, which is the way I think of the break-in and its aftermath now.

Fourth, I'm also much more aware and appreciative of the relationship between form and content. A book, like a eulogy, rewards closure: I felt myself working against that imperative in both the text and in the book, but that convention also prompted me to think about why I was resisting closure, why I still resent and mourn.

Fifth, I did share the book at the conference. I was gratified when someone would come by; one kind colleague read the book and remarked that I write well. At lunch later in the day, a group of younger scholars wanted to see the book, and I shared it with them. At home, a student wanted to read it, and I lent it to him; he observed that it made him sad. Although I don't want anyone to feel sad, that is the emotion I sought to evoke; the book mourns with me.

Sixth, this chapter I have appreciated writing because it allows me to think yet again about our lives, about writing, about the various ways we make meaning. But in taking up these questions here, I have moved outside the experience itself: different genres host different kinds of meaning making.

* * *

My husband suggests that we replace the jewelry; he wants to buy me a pair of earrings, a ring, a watch for every stolen one. Such an impossibly sweet gesture. What's gone was multifold, each item carrying the DNA of treasured others, each item imbued with memory real and created, each item speaking to a past now doubly gone, a past we cannot restore.

* * *

This process has been epistemic, as the conference suggested. My earlier title, for example, doesn't deliver on its promise: this isn't, I'm afraid, *A Eulogy for a Lost Object*, as much as I've resonated to the title and its idea, as much as I appreciated that title as a gift from my son. I've changed the title because . . . well, for one thing, there's not an object to eulogize, exactly. Oh, there are objects, of course, several of them, some of them identified here. I loved that watch of my grandmother's, and I do feel robbed—not of her, nor of her memory, but of the reminder of her, the physical token that I could touch, turn over in my hand, wear around my neck, that I could think of as a kind of talisman speaking to our shared heritage, to our relationship, *and* to a future I had assumed was secure, embodied in a watch that didn't tell time any longer, providing a through line from my grandmother, Nana, to my father, to me, to my daughter or son, to mothers and children I will never meet, to a great-grandchild who might have turned it over, its filigree fading, in her small hand. I loved the pearl earrings David gave me for that first Mother's Day, when Genevieve was with me but had not yet joined the world, those small earrings a dear gift in a graduate-school time of few material gifts, a gift that also evoked memories, in this case of my moving into motherhood but not quite yet arriving, a tender time, hopeful and precious. My new memory, of the break-in, comes unbidden; it does not need a physical reminder. The memories I want to recall can no longer be prompted by physical objects no longer with me. I can still remember each object, can describe them verbally, can see them in my mind's eye. Will that always be so? And is this writing, and the book commemorating these objects and their loss, a way of creating a surrogate material object testifying both to their existence, their once belonging to me, and to what has been lost? If I hold this text and my book-eulogy in hand, will they evoke my grandmother's memory? Could they deliver a future I thought the break-in had erased?

Commemorating what was and what will not be: that perhaps is the purpose of this eulogy. Clearly, it is not a eulogy of a given object, as my son's title suggests; several of the objects were dear to me, and choosing among them, much as in William Styron's *Sophie's Choice*, is an impossible task. My mother's wedding band, or my father's? My grandmother's watch, or my small pearl earrings? And just as clearly, it's not a eulogy of a set of objects, either; in the set, we lose the particulars that gave each definition, the memories that made them dear. And it's not, as my friends would have had it, a loss of security. My neighbor needn't have worried about her children: the person or people who broke in, who created a storm in my home and left with my treasures, didn't want to hurt anyone physically, which is one reason the theft occurred when we were away; another is that they didn't want to see people; they wanted to take people's treasures precisely without anyone seeing them. In my neighbor's sense, the loss of the break-in wasn't human. In mine, it was. What I still mourn, however, even now, long after the event, is that when they took that jewelry, they took a connection—in some cases, my one remaining physical connection—to people I loved, disappointed, annoyed, cherished, and brought into this world.

That loss is worth both commemorating and eulogizing.

* * *

I share this eulogy with my beloveds. My daughter, the girl, says that she's learned from it, that she hadn't realized that my dad had given the watch to my mother when I was born. So sweet, she says; it makes her think of them more like my in-laws, more like marriage partners who cared about each other, though she phrases it more tactfully than this. The girl likes thinking about my parents that way, too, she says.

I ask about the ending. The story itself, the boy says, seems to wrap up well, even if the story in my life hasn't.

I nod.

* * *

This text is reflective, epistemologically oriented, autobiographical; it is rhetorically feminist.

Reflection, I have argued elsewhere, is itself rhetorical, a "process we use to make meaning and make knowledge, a kind of meaning and knowledge unique to reflection given its intersectionality, its insistence that only through bringing the human and the world together to theorize can a reflective knowledge and meaning be made. Such knowledge and meaning making is contingent, subject to change in a world also changing, a knowledge that, in philosopher Thomas Pfau's (2004) formation, requires, even demands, attention" (Yancey 2016, 304). Attention: in some ways, this attending, this was the most difficult part of this project. Refusing to attend, or failing to attend, provides an escape, a means for denying that which has happened. Attending, reflectively attending, requires one to acknowledge experience and articulate it, acknowledgement witnessed in articulation, articulation a confirmation of acknowledgement, the both providing a means for making sense of experience, and—here, in my eulogy-that-isn't—a process for beginning to let go. If there is need to let go, there is an exigence prompting that, and attending . . . well, attending brings the exigence into painful relief.

The Western, Cartesian world located in divides, between mind and body, object and process, is at odds with a text like this. The makers of knowledge in science, according to Celeste Condit, in breaching the Cartesian divide point to another approach more in line with feminist epistemology:

> In philosophical language about human discourse, Westerners have operated with an object/idea distinction. In contrast, good natural scientists employ an object/process dichotomy. One can examine the physiological objects of the body (thymine, cytosine, guanine, and so forth) in a context of understanding the process with its functions (goals or purposes) and outcomes. On [sic] this model, both object and process are seen as material, and meaning is viewed as deriving from the object/process combination. Meaning literally could not come into being, could not exist, without the object, because the process is embodied in the object. (quoted in Clary-Lemon 2014)

My eulogy-that-isn't is an object-based inquiry. With objects stolen, other objects out of place, so too is life, part of it missing, much of it out of place. When textually expressed, my reflective processes—making a record of objects and experiences, making sense of both, making smaller and larger meanings of both—called for an object, here an artist's book incorporating a good deal of those meaning-making processes, which motivated yet another account, this text teasing out meaning made in the book object itself, meaning made through attending to the book in an after-the-fact reflective exercise. Sometimes described separately, these processes, objects, and experiences are most meaningful when made whole.

This eulogy-that-isn't, also autobiographical and feminist, is located in the material of the everyday as a prime source of knowledge. Explaining such an approach to feminist epistemology, Liz Stanley starts by resisting more conventional feminist critiques of a materialist autobiographical method: "I consider that feminist postmodernist writing about 'the self' and autobiography is insufficient on a number of grounds, in particular because narrative is the key to the complexities of the self and not something to be excised, as this approach suggests, from the feminist analysis of lives" (1994, 133). Stanley points to the excised and to the role including it plays in providing richer accounts, ones that do not hide the self but that, rather, understand it as a contextualized complex source of knowledge.

> "The self" is immensely complex and feminist conceptualizing of it, within as well as across conventional discipline boundaries, needs to be correspondingly complex. Biography and autobiography are not only intertextually referential of each other, but also "self" does not exist in isolation from interrelationship with other selves and other lives; it is grounded in the material reality of everyday life, and a key part of the constitution of this material reality is formed by the narrations of selves and others that figure so importantly in everyday talk as well as being a "hidden" component of much academic writing. (133)

This chapter focuses on an event in my life, one raising questions for me and foregrounding larger questions, I hope, for all of us. It does so in many ways: by including the very personal, what Stanley calls the ordinarily "excised" and the " 'hidden' component of much academic writing," a personal always in reference to an/other/s—my husband, a daughter and son, friends and neighbors, police and a handyman, each an important node on a larger social network; by employing materials, like embossed paper and pieces of paper bags that are, as ordinarily construed, nonacademic; by devising a new arrangement inside a given form tending to closure, a book, and in doing so, reinventing the event and pushing against the form; and by working and reworking the narrative, by making and remaking it so as to know, to represent, and to reflect meaning that is always contingent, always a process of coming to terms.

* * *

Eulogies, lives: different stories we seek to connect, this one still at odds with itself.

WORKS CITED

Campbell, Karlyn Kohrs, and Kathleen Jamieson. 1978. *Form and Genre: Shaping Rhetorical Action*. Falls Church, VA: Speech Communication Association.

Condit, Celeste. 1999. "The Materiality of Coding: Rhetoric, Genetics, and the Matter of Life." In *Rhetorical Bodies*, edited by Jack Selzer and Sharon Crowley, 326–56. Madison: WI: University of Wisconsin Press.

Clary-Lemon, Jennifer. 2014. "Archival Research Processes: A Case for Material Methods." *Rhetoric Review* 33 (4): 381–402.

Feminisms and Rhetorics 2015, 10th Biennial Conference: "Women's Ways of Making." 2014. Call For Proposals. http://media.wix.com/ugd/8b3b57_609015fa847c48 38948d0ce498995bc5.pdf. Accessed 18 January 2021.

Kohashi, Andrea. 2015. "The Book Artist and the Archivist: A Shared Perspective." *Archive Journal* 5. http://www.archivejournal.net/issue/5/notes-queries/the-book-artist-and -the-archivist-a-shared-perspective/. Accessed 18 December 2020.

Kent, Michael. 1997. *The Rhetoric of Eulogies: A Generic Critique of Classic and Contemporary Funeral Oratory*. PhD diss., Purdue University.

Nimkulrat, Nithikul. 2007. "The Role of Documentation in Practice-Led Research." *Journal of Research Practice* 3 (1). http://jrp.icaap.org/index.php/jrp/article/view/58/83. Accessed 18 January 2021.

Peterson, Owen, ed. 1983. Introduction to *Representative American Speeches 1982–83*. New York: H. W. Wilson.

Stanley, Liz. 1994. "The Knowing Because Experiencing Subject: Narratives, Lives, and Autobiography." In *Feminist Perspectives in Epistemology*, edited by Kathleen Lennon and Margaret Whitford, 132–48. Abingdon, Oxfordshire: Routledge.

Spillane, Sunny. 2013. "Creative Counter-Narratives by Arts Educators in Urban Schools: A Participatory, A/r/tographic Inquiry." PhD diss., Florida State University.

Wikipedia, s.v. "Artist's Books." 2019. Last updated October 2, 2020. https://en.wikipedia .org/wiki/Artist%27s_book. Accessed 18 January 2021.

Yancey, Kathleen Blake. 2004. "Postmodernism, Palimpsest, and Portfolios: Theoretical Issues in the Representation of Student Work." *College Composition and Communication* 5 (3): 738–62.

Yancey, Kathleen Blake. 2016. "Defining Reflection: The Rhetorical Nature and Qualities of Reflection." In *A Rhetoric of Reflection*, edited by Kathleen Blake Yancey, 303–21. Logan: Utah State University Press.

10
RED TENT
Creating Art and Our Lives in Jail through Feminist Rhetorics

Jill McCracken, Amanda Ellis,
Melissa Greene, and Charlese Trower[1]

I blame Red Tent for the love I have for women and the motivation to find my passion and go for it. At one point in my life women were the enemy, and now they empower me and are my inspiration and the love I've been looking for.
  —Melissa Greene, Red Tent Participant

The needle is an appropriate material representation of women who are balancing both their anger over oppression and pride in their gender. The needle stabs as it creates, forcing thread or yarn into the act of creation. From a violent action comes the birth of a new whole. Women are channeling their rage, frustration, guilt, and other difficult emotions into a powerfully productive activity.
  —Ricia A. Chansky

We all continually create and remake our lives. We experience strengths and weaknesses—often simultaneously—and work to get our needs met. We continually need and offer support, and we build knowledge that helps us solve problems, share successes, and better understand how to negotiate and cocreate families, organizations, policies, and institutional structures. We are Red Tent.

INTRODUCTION: WHAT IS RED TENT?
The Red Tent Women's Initiative (Red Tent) provides a weekly support group for nonviolent female offenders within the Pinellas County Jail (PCJ) in Clearwater, Florida. Grounded in an initiative that provides life skills and creative art classes within the county jail, Red Tent has served

over fifteen hundred women since its inception in 2012. The group meets three times per week for four hours each session and consists of fifteen female participants and two group facilitators. Red Tent is first and foremost a support and empowerment group—a place where women can come together to feel complete acceptance, safety, support, and love while being simultaneously guided to form bonds with one another, build self-esteem and respect for themselves, and become more connected as women, mothers, sisters, and members of society. Because many women who are incarcerated have experienced trauma and violence, Red Tent strives to create a space for women to offer and seek support to help them understand and process trauma, addiction, and stress management. Red Tent also offers education about parenting, financial empowerment, and mindfulness. While in this supportive environment, the women sew and embroider crafts that symbolize their life experiences, personal goals, and successes. In addition to the group that meets inside the jail, Red Tent also holds a variety of group meetings outside the jail to offer ongoing support to anyone who identifies as a woman, whether formerly incarcerated or not. The organization serves as an active advocate for each participant, connecting women with resources that meet their unique needs.

Housed within intersectional frames of oppression and matrices of domination (Collins 2000), incarceration has been increasingly used as a punishment for women. In the last three decades, the number of women incarcerated has increased by 786 percent, surpassing the male population in all fifty states and making it the largest growing segment of the US prison population (Conly 1998). The numbers quickly become staggering and hard to imagine. As authors Elizabeth Swavola, Kristine Riley, and Ram Subramaniam outline in their report *Overlooked: Women and Jails in an Era of Reform,* "Since 1970, the number of women in jail nationwide has increased 14-fold—from under 8,000 to nearly 110,000—and now accounts for approximately half of all women behind bars in the United States" (2016, 6). Eighty percent of the women in jail are mothers, and by and large, unlike their male counterparts, are single parents, solely responsible for their children (7). The number of women in prison with minor children has grown 131 percent since 1991, and again nearly doubled that of fathers, which increased by 76 percent in the same amount of time (Glaze and Maruschak 2008, 1).[2]

It is within this context that Red Tent enacts feminist rhetorics: spaces are created and held where participants actively generate knowledge and make meaning for themselves that drives their own healing and growth. In this chapter we document how Red Tent and its participants engage in feminist rhetorical practices that can positively impact and improve their lives. Red Tent works actively to disrupt the helpless victim or criminal roles often associated with people who are or were formerly incarcerated. Rather than viewing participants as victims waiting to be helped and aided, they disrupt this concept to reveal participants' complex identities as active agents. Red Tent would not *be* Red Tent without former participants as leaders.[3] In line with that practice, the authors of this piece include two individuals who have no direct experience with incarceration and two individuals who were formerly incarcerated. We are all current or former leaders in Red Tent, and together, we weave our perspectives and voices to demonstrate how shared wisdom emerges and lifts all of us up as we teach, learn, mentor, question, and create art together within Red Tent.

We draw on Karlyn Kohrs Campbell's encyclopedic definition of feminist rhetoric: "first, as the battle to be allowed a voice in public affairs; second, as the effort to appear credible; third, as discourse sometimes based on equality and sometimes on sexual difference; and, finally, as an analysis of patriarchy in which consciousness-raising is a political process, a rhetorical style, and a way of knowing" (2011, 262). Red Tent is a mechanism through which feminist rhetoric occurs. For example, it is within the Red Tent circle that women explore and better understand their experiences leading up to incarceration and incarceration itself. The women have a voice, and many become leaders in Red Tent, bringing their voices to the larger community. Perhaps most significant, Red Tent creates spaces where consciousness-raising can happen. Understanding consciousness-raising as a way of knowing helps explain Red Tent's impact. Campbell explains:

> As a process, consciousness-raising is not entirely personal and experiential. The winnowing that distinguishes the idiosyncratic from the systemic incorporates research and critical analysis. In addition, it requires a relatively homogeneous, leaderless group in which all participate. Thus, as a style of communicating and learning, consciousness-raising is personal, experiential, participatory, and, hence, emotional and egalitarian. It proceeds inductively, moving from personal experiences toward generalizations that reflect the systemically shaped conditions of women generally. (264–65)

This inductive movement from the personal to more generalizable occurs within the collaborative Red Tent space that literally constitutes active knowledge and meaning makers. Combining active teaching and learning, community building, and participatory and community arts, Red Tent participants create art and grow our lives. Red Tent participants come together to tell our stories, share our lives, and learn from one another. We weave new knowledge about and a greater understanding of ourselves and our roles in society by paying attention to our voices, perspectives, and experiences—personal, professional, painful, and joyful. Red Tent demonstrates how feminist rhetorics can impact the world and is a model for applied feminist rhetoric. Because we articulate Red Tent and our practices *as* feminist rhetorics, they can then be applied to other communicative and physical spaces, impacting the material conditions of all stakeholders' lives.

Red Tent founder Barbara Rhode is a licensed marriage and family therapist. Based on her experience working with women prisoners, Rhode created Red Tent and incorporates theory from *The Tending Instinct* by Dr. Shelley Taylor. In this book, Taylor describes a pattern of behavior in women that "from an evolutionary standpoint . . . is a plausible account of female responses to stress" (2002, 22). Taylor explains that as social animals, women produce increased levels of oxytocin, a brain chemical that helps them feel safe and secure, after spending time in the company of other women. Her concepts of "tending and befriending" include coming together to share stories and to help, empathize with, and mentor each other. Later, Rhode happened upon the book *The Red Tent*, in which author Anita Diamant (2010) describes the red tent of biblical times as a place where women could go and stay when they were ill, depressed, alone, grieving, or afraid; a place where young and old women and children could share stories, wisdom, and compassion. Rhode asked herself, "Where is our red tent now, and what happened to this tradition that benefitted men, women, and children and brought about this sense of community and togetherness?" As an answer to her question, she founded the Red Tent Women's Initiative. Her goal was to establish a space inside the jail where women could come together to learn new skills, create art, benefit from guest speakers who share their wisdom, and, most important, "tend and befriend" each other.

In some studies, crafting has been shown to increase dopamine levels, which reduces depression and anxiety, improves self-efficacy, regulates overwhelming emotions, and prevents irrational thoughts, all of which can then strengthen one's ability to overcome challenges and setbacks (Gutman and Schindler 2007). Creating crafts can reduce stress and inflammation and produce effects similar to meditation and mindfulness, allowing the brain to relax (Geda et al. 2011). Red Tent draws on these theories and works to create an environment that facilitates emotional openness within the Red Tent circle and the ideas presented there. It is through participants' work on their projects that they engage in mentoring, shared teaching and learning, laughter, and friendships that would not exist under other circumstances—most especially inside a jail.

The group is facilitated as a support group where everyone sits in a circle and shares together while working on a variety of art projects. This process occurs through social interaction among group members, mediation by the facilitators, and guidance from external experts and guest speakers. The facilitators also provide instruction and guidance on the creation of marketable handmade items (Toseland and Rivas 2012). The lessons do not have a specific structure or schedule, which allows the groups and topics to be participant driven. The group settings also incorporate elements of mindfulness from Thich Nhat Hanh (1999) to "resist and transform the speed and violence of our modern society." Facilitators also include lessons from Lisa Najavitz's evidence-based intervention for posttraumatic stress disorder (PTSD) and substance abuse, *Seeking Safety* (2002).

It is important to note the theories at the foundation of Red Tent are not necessarily categorized as feminist rhetorics. Taylor's argument about "tending and befriending" draws from biologically gendered ideas about women and how they work together to protect themselves (Pitman 2003; Sherman et al. 2017), and Diamant's *Red Tent* is based on historical accounts of women's physical separation from the rest of society when they were menstruating or in pain.[4] Although in Diamant's account the Red Tent construct allowed the women to create community together, it starkly contrasts with Campbell's definition of feminist rhetoric wherein battles are waged to gain a public voice and establish credibility, patriarchy is explored, and consciousness-raising is developed as a political process. And yet, within Red Tent, these rhetorics are created, which require us to consider how separatist and feminist rhetorics are complex and can and do coexist.[5]

WHO ARE WE?

We, the authors, are Amanda Ellis, Melissa Greene, Jill McCracken, and Charlese Trower, and our perspectives reflect our own positions in the world. Amanda is a thirty-year-old white female who was born in Florida and began her work with Red Tent as a student while finishing her master's degree in social work at the University of South Florida. When we began writing this chapter, Amanda served as program director. She now lives in Tennessee with her partner, raising their son, Logan. Melissa is a thirty-four-year-old white female who has lived in St. Petersburg, Florida, all her life. She was incarcerated at PCJ and participated in Red Tent

Figure 10.1. Coauthors after Feminisms and Rhetorics conference presentation in Phoenix, Arizona. From left to right: Charlese Trower, Amanda Ellis, Melissa Greene, and Jill McCracken. (Permission of and photo by Amanda Ellis.)

gatherings for approximately sixty days. She is now raising her daughter Riley and son Damian, and she stays active in her daughter Destiny's life, who is now an adult. Melissa is a volunteer with Red Tent and participates in fundraisers and community events. Jill is a forty-eight-year-old white woman who was born in New Mexico and has lived all over the country. She is a professor of rhetoric, writing, and gender and sexuality studies. She began volunteering with Red Tent in 2014, and she has conducted community-based participatory research projects with women both inside and outside the jail. She is a single mom to her son, Nathaniel. Charlese is a forty-four-year-old Black female who was born in North Carolina and grew up all over the East Coast. She was incarcerated at PCJ and participated in Red Tent gatherings for three months. She is married and has two children, Saundra and Jordan, and she volunteers with Red Tent. Together, we presented at the Feminisms and Rhetorics conference, wrote this article, stay in touch on Facebook, and continue to share our lives.

WHO IS SERVED?

Federal and state prisons and local jails house an estimated 655 adults per 100,000 US citizens. While the United States' incarceration rate is staggering compared to the rest of the world, this rate is the lowest the United States has seen since 2008, the year incarceration rates began trending downward for the first time in thirty years (Kaeble and Cowhig 2018). Despite the downward trend of incarceration rates, the number of women being incarcerated in the United States has failed to decrease; rather, the proportion of women to men has steadily increased, making women a greater percentage of the adults filling US prisons and jails (World Prison Brief n.d.).

Aleks Kajstura (2018) reports in "States of Women's Incarceration: The Global Context 2018," "Only 4% of the world's female population lives in the U.S., but the U.S. accounts for nearly 30% of the world's incarcerated women." Because most of the numbers account for men, women's incarceration rates are often overshadowed. Of the 655 people incarcerated per 100,000 residents, women's incarceration rate is 133—the highest incarceration rate for women in the world. Recent reforms have reduced the total number of people in state prisons since 2009, and yet the number of women incarcerated has increased dramatically (Sawyer 2018). Kajstura (2018) draws attention to the numbers by comparing the women's incarceration rates in every state in the United States to countries around the world. As the "World Women's Incarceration Rates if Every U.S. State Were a Country" visual in Kajstura's article makes abundantly clear, twenty-six US states have higher incarceration rates than Thailand (130 people per 100,000), the country that incarcerates the highest number per capita after the United States (133 people per 100,000). Florida is number twenty-two on this list, having an incarceration rate of 1 in 159. Of the reported 700,000 women incarcerated globally, more than 200,000 (211,870) are in the United States (Walmsley 2017). Rather than comparing per capita, as Kajstura does, Roy Walmsley looks at overall numbers of girls and women who are incarcerated, including pretrial detainees.

Walmsley finds the next highest total number of incarcerated women and girls occurs in China (107,131), plus an unknown number of women and girls in pretrial and "administrative" detention. Females made up 7 percent of the total US prison population by the end of 2016 (Florida Department of Corrections 2018). The female population in jail has increased 44 percent between 2000 and 2013 (National Resource Center on Justice Involved Women, n.d.).

The vast majority of women involved in the criminal legal system have a high-school education or less, are poor, and have a history of physical and sexual abuse. Nearly half report having lost custody of their children (Ferraro and Moe 2003), and an estimated 40 percent of incarcerated women have been diagnosed with a mental illness but lacked sufficient mental health services before incarceration. Many of the circumstances affecting the lives and actions of women are ignored; couple that with the ongoing war on drugs, longer sentencing, and lack of support, and more and more women are finding themselves incarcerated and alone (Kraft-Stolar 2015). Research also suggests the cycle of incarceration is difficult to break and being a child of parents who have been incarcerated is a significant risk factor associated with later criminal activity (Johnson 2005; Kakar, Friedemann, and Peck 2002; McGee et al. 2014; Mullings, Hartley, and Marquart 2004).

Once incarcerated, an individual can find it difficult to break the cycle of engaging in illegal behavior, resulting in further arrests and subsequent incarceration. As recidivism continues, escaping these cycles becomes exceedingly more difficult (Benda, Corwyn, and Toombs 2001; Reisig, Holtfreter, and Morash 2006). Shanhe Jiang and L. Thomas Winfree (2006) report anecdotal evidence indicating the increased need for social support for incarcerated women. They further suggest that additional institutional support may lead to a reduction in perceived stress levels and overall infraction violations. Red Tent helps interrupt these self-perpetuating cycles of incarceration and depression.

Nonviolent female offenders who have completed sentencing and are serving less than a year are eligible for Red Tent. The majority of participants report they suffer from co-occurring disorders, PTSD, and intimate-partner violence. Red Tent participation is subject to change daily, depending upon scheduling, location, and participants' release from jail. The participants may encounter barriers to attending class due to institutional policies such as lockdowns,[6] available staff to transport participants, new work assignments that can interfere with class, or their release from PCJ. Program staff work closely with the Pinellas County Sheriff's Office Program Services to advocate that new participants have a minimum of thirty days prerelease to enter into Red Tent. Guest speakers cover topics such as emotional intelligence, career-readiness training, recovery, conflict resolution, anger management, and other issues the women experience when reintegrating into society from jail. Once participants are released, they are provided with a list of community resources for ex-offenders and potential employment sites. The women are encouraged to apply for a program-funded thirty-day bus pass, which they receive upon release at Red Tent's community sites. These community sites offer safe spaces where participants can spend time with other women to reconnect, share, mentor, and access services. These gatherings are open to all women who feel Red Tent would be useful for them.

WHERE IS THE RHETORIC?

At its most simplistic level, Red Tent creates space whereby community is formed. Drawing on Barry Brummett's concept of quotidian rhetoric, or the "rhetoric of the everyday" (1991), we define rhetoric as a communicative or symbolic interaction and understand this rhetoric to reveal and cocreate values. At its most basic, quotidian rhetoric is rhetoric that manages public and personal meanings: those that "affect everyday, even minute-to-minute decisions. This level of rhetoric is where decisions are guided that do not take the form of peak crises . . . but do involve long-term concerns as well as the momentary choices that people must make to get through the day. . . . People are constantly surrounded by signs that influence them, or signs that they use to influence others, in ongoing, mundane, and nonexigent yet important ways" (41).

Brummett argues quotidian rhetoric is carried out through appropriational manifestations of rhetoric, or what is most appropriate in a given situation. In other words, people appropriate phrases, actions, and nonverbal signs, among others, already available in the given society or community. Individuals then present to others—through dress, facial expressions, terms, and a myriad of other communicative acts—the texts of everyday life. Brummett argues that because these texts and acts are immersed within and emerge from the culture, people, in general, are relatively "less consciously aware that the management of shared meanings is underway," which means they are "less likely to take or assign responsibility for a rhetorical effort" (42). Because appropriational rhetoric is *participation in* as much as it is *production of* meaning, individual responsibility for both is less defined. As coauthors who inhabit different spaces within Red Tent, we draw on Brummett's definition and explore how the foundations of Red Tent—to create art, connect women in the community, provide support for one's self and others, embrace acceptance and healing, share wisdom and compassion, and experience empowerment—are rhetorics, and, in particular, feminist rhetorics.

WOMEN IN COMMUNITY

Like any community in which we live or participate, there are rules or expectations for participants in Red Tent. These are outlined in the form of a Participant Agreement (see appendix 10.A) and in general include that participants maintain confidentiality in terms of what is discussed in the group, accept each person exactly as and where she is, withhold judgment, use "I" statements, refrain from giving advice, use respectful language (please and thank you, no curse words), and refrain from cross-talk (only one person speaks at a time). These quotidian differences are articulated in the group agreements, but they are also realized in the "feel" of the group. As Jill explains,

> Upon entering, we all greet each other with hugs, laughter, and brief "catching up" about our lives. We go to the tables and begin looking at material for our projects or locate projects we have already begun. Two of us offer to make coffee and tea for the others and begin taking orders. The room is brightly lit from windows and natural lighting. There is art, positive statements on the boards and walls around the room, and the many projects created by Red Tent participants. The plants next to the window are green and full, and one of us takes responsibility for watering them on a weekly basis.

The beginning moments feel like a gathering of old friends who are comfortable together. The atmosphere is much like a party where we talk, share ideas, contradict, sew, and drink coffee. And most important, we laugh, get angry, and feel pain. This space contrasts the jail's sterile environment where the women walk single file, are searched upon entering and leaving the Red Tent room, and are told not to talk to each other while walking from one place to another. The differences are palpable and staggering, and there is a feeling of lightness and joy—an air of being one's self and accepted—as we all walk into the room.

Melissa describes her experience of the Red Tent community:

> While in PCJ for about two months, I remember seeing girls that were sentenced getting all dolled up and excited. I asked one of them, "Do you have a visit today?" She said, "No, I'm going to Red Tent." I asked, "What's Red Tent?" She said, "It's a women's group where we get to sew and make some pillows, purses, blankets, all kinds of stuff, eat cookies, and drink tea and coffee while women talk about their struggles and get support from each other." Another girl exclaimed, "We get to go walk outside to get to

Figure 10.2. Red Tent setup in PCJ. (Permission of and photo by Amanda Ellis.)

the group too!" Being able to walk outside while in county jail is a privilege and something we look forward to. The girl told me there was a waiting list and I should sign up so that by the time I was sentenced, I would be able to join the group. The first thing I noticed about the Red Tent girls was that they stuck together, and they tried to hold a standard for all the girls that went to Red Tent, unlike most of the other inmates. I figured I was going to be there [in jail] for another month and a half and some coffee and cookies besides the ones on commissary would be nice. And being able to feel the grass and the outside air would help pass the time, so I decided to see where I was on the waiting list. Luckily, I went to Red Tent the very next week.

When they first called my name for Red Tent, I was nervous and excited. . . . My first day in Red Tent I interviewed with a Red Tent facilitator. I remember her asking me a few questions I can't recall, and I remember I broke down and started to cry. I explained how I just wanted a new life. I wanted to be happy. I wanted to find freedom from active addiction, and I wanted help. I knew if I didn't change now, I would be going to prison for a long time, or I'd be dead soon. . . .

During my first time [in the group], I got some help from one of my girlfriends from my old pod [housing unit]. She helped me pick out fabric and showed me how to thread a needle, which I had never done before. I was adamant about not making anything because I didn't want to embarrass myself by comparing my art with the artwork I had seen displayed. The girls all worked together helping each other. Later, as I approached my release date, I made two pillows—one for each of my children.

I was released March 26, 2015, to my halfway house. In my new surroundings, I had to live in close quarters with strange girls. The only place I felt at home was in Red Tent. My very first Tuesday out, I attended Red

Tent, and the women there welcomed me with open arms as if we were best friends. There were some familiar faces, but even the ones I didn't know, I felt like we had a bond, a closeness, because of Red Tent. Still to this day, I attend Red Tent weekly meetings, and I'm a big part of it. I blame Red Tent for the love I have for women and the motivation to find my passion and go for it. At one point in my life women were the enemy and now they empower me and are my inspiration and the love I've been looking for. Being part of a woman community is the high I've been searching for, the comfort and compassion I've needed since I was a little girl. Recently my mom has also been involved and volunteers for Red Tent, and the bond we have formed with each other getting involved is something I've searched for since I was a little girl. There's so much I can say about Red Tent and what it's done in my life. I love Red Tent and what it stands for.

TWO WORLDS

Although perhaps apparent to both "insiders" and "outsiders" that there are cultural differences between women's experiences in jail and in Red Tent gatherings, articulating these differences reveals how quotidian rhetoric operates. We offer a snapshot of the differences to demonstrate how culture is created and supported through both quotidian and institutional rhetoric. As Charlese explains, "A typical pod is an open, cold-cemented box that never had a quiet moment. You feel lost, and you feel like you don't matter. But as soon as I step into Red Tent, I feel like I have a purpose." Melissa expands on this contrast and offers the reader a glimpse into the visual, physical, and sensual environment in which they live.

> The pods are set up dormitory style in central division. When you walk down the hallway of the floor, there are four pods, two on each side of the hallway. The first door is to a vestibule which is about fifteen feet in length, and there is a door that leads to one of the rooms they put you if you get into trouble. These rooms are called *solitary confinement*, otherwise known as "the cage." The central command station in the center of each hallway is in charge of opening and closing the electric doors. Only one door can open at a time, and when it locks shut they can then open the entrance door to the pod. All day long you hear the buzzing that occurs when a door is opened, along with the loud heavy metal doors opening and slamming shut. The deputy stands at a podium next to the door with a computer and a phone in front of her. Only women deputies are allowed in the women's pods. We get the privilege of having a microwave and hot-water spout, but if your pod is on lockdown or in trouble, the whole pod gets punished, and our privileges are revoked.
>
> On the back wall there are two flights of cells—eight on the top and eight on the bottom—with between three and five beds in each cell. The bed chart is an example; cell #4 lower left, with your last name. You are not

allowed to choose your bed or your roommates, so you're lucky if you get somebody that doesn't smell, snore, or steal. There is also a TV room off to the side with super uncomfortable chairs that are welded together in three rows of about five. Each room number is assigned a cleaning date, so cell #7 upper and lower would clean after each meal, spray and wipe, sweep and mop. Those rooms usually get to choose the TV channel selection for that day.

On the side of the pod towards the edge of that floor there is a door that leads to the basketball court. This court is the only outside space you get. It only occurs at selected times, and if the deputy does not feel like allowing you to go outside, she doesn't have to. The court is surrounded by huge slabs of concrete with about a four-inch opening on the bottom and a few feet on the top with chain-link fencing. There is just enough space to smell and see a small part of the outside air. I didn't go out there that much because it was depressing to me. The rules on the court were you had to have sneakers on, no sandals. So, if you didn't buy any sneakers at the commissary or borrow some, you were not allowed to go out. You were not allowed to sit out there in big groups unless permitted for a Narcotics Anonymous (NA) meeting or something like that because otherwise it caused suspicion of gang activity or organizing a crime. Some deputies were cool and would let us get a good basketball game going. You could be on the court with a plain white t-shirt and your commissary shorts, and some deputies would allow us to lay on the court around 6 p.m. to let us catch the forty-five minutes of sun we can feel through the top opening of the court.

Every thirty minutes the deputy has to walk around the entire pod for a head count, and they kept track with a stick that they run across a security badge that beeps in sections of the pod. Most of the inmates were just trying to survive until their release date, while others created drama, started fights, or just did whatever to get attention. Some girls were in competition with how much commissary they would get from people on the outside, only to be used or beat up or robbed for it. Some girls were known as snitches, and to lessen their sentences would give information to the police or prosecutors. If you were in jail long enough, people found out, and the rest of your stay might be torturous or spent in solitary confinement, which is even worse. Although I always had commissary, visitors, pictures, and letters from loved ones, it was sad to see more than half the women had nothing and no one. . . .

On the inside of jail there's always an intense feeling, whether it's a girl being sent to prison for a long time or someone leaving a visit or phone call from a loved one that left them upset or extremely excited to be released. Never any happy medium feelings, just intense from either wanting to leave and can't or to excitement that it's one more day closer to release date.

In contrast to the Red Tent space, the jail is designed—rhetorically, physically, sensually, and through discipline—to abolish intimacy and privacy. The lights and sounds are continually jarring, and it is difficult to find peace or calm. There is very little space to cultivate reflection, thought, and connection between women.

SENSING THE DIFFERENCES: TOUCH, TASTE, AND SMELL

One's senses also clearly delineate the differences in the two worlds. Melissa explains the transition that occurs when the women make their way to the Red Tent room in the jail.

> While walking from the pod, you are called out by name. Even if you have been attending Red Tent, if they don't call your name, you can't go. You walk in a single-file line in the hallway outside your pod for a pat-down search and then wait for an elevator. You must always stay in a single-file line, and when you get to the outside area, the girls walk on the right side so as to not look at or talk to the boys. Some of the guards are lenient and will let you talk to the other girls. If there's a pregnant woman or someone who walks slowly whether because of age or health status, she is to be in the front of the line so nobody lags behind. The same routine is repeated on the way back. The guards confirm the count by name, and then a more thorough pat search occurs, assuming inmates are more likely to sneak things from Red Tent than to it. Most girls get away with sneaking some Sweet 'n Low packets for their coffee or tea, and you used to be able to sign out and return a magazine or book from Red Tent, but I don't think they allow that anymore....
>
> Each evening I would make a commissary recipe dinner and dessert and share it with some of my friends that didn't have anything. Food from commissary was like gold—it was the drug in jail. Women would hustle, barter, or do whatever they could to have it. Women would steal, fight and have sex, risking a new charge or harsher sentences for it. Some of the women braided hair, yarned eyebrows, drew pictures, and made holiday cards for food or things they needed. These activities are not allowed, but it is the one thing jail will never be able to control or fully stop.
>
> Body odor is also prevalent because they don't give you any decent hygiene products and most of the women don't have any money for commissary. The bathrooms are fully exposed, so if someone had bad bowels or gas, everyone had to endure the aroma. Meals came on trays stacked on carts. Breakfast is at 4 a.m.; lunch at 10 a.m.; and dinner at 4 p.m. I hated getting up early for breakfast, but by 6 a.m. you would be starving. The tray food was horrible, but it was expensive to eat only commissary food, and therefore, to save money and not starve, after a while most girls got used to it and ate all their tray food.
>
> There are three to five trustees in each pod. The trustees are in charge of handing out new uniforms two times weekly, handing out food trays, and anything extra the deputies ask of them. Some would kiss ass, and we would give them nicknames like "okay deputy no badge!" Everything is on a set schedule, so it feels like *Groundhog Day* every week. Two days a week our commissary orders would arrive, and we would get locked down until

our name was called. We could then come with a pillowcase and our IDs and a pen to check our orders. The whole pod could see your entire order, which sucked because at some point being nice and sharing left me without, and I couldn't say I didn't have it if they saw my order. Some women would beg or even make up sob stories to get food or candy, and with an average of seventy women and more than half who don't have anything, it started to make me stay in my cell, guard my food, and not share anything.

Melissa reveals how the sterile jail environment and the Red Tent space physically affect her senses.

> One of the most distinctive things to me about being in jail is the smell. Everything you eat and every hygiene product on the commissary is bland—no smells or taste. The only good smell we get is the whiff of the deputies' perfume when they walk by to do a count. The first time I walked in the Red Tent room, I remember a strong smell of coffee being made—real coffee. It reminded me of my mom's house, and it gave me a warm and cozy feeling inside. That first breath took me completely from the jail to my home.

The contrast in smells reveals how the material space directly influences *how* one is programmed or allowed to act, communicate, and even feel. Creating a space where feelings and being oneself are not only allowed but also encouraged is pivotal to Red Tent. As Melissa explains, "Jail is a place where one's self must be monitored and controlled. One's guard must be up, and the feelings are frequently intense. Red Tent creates an opportunity for individuals to be themselves, to feel what she feels, and to take a 'break' from the emotional confines of jail." And yet even the space created to hold the women's responses to the multiple oppressions in their lives is constrained: Red Tent facilitators are warned not to allow the women to experience or uncover too much sadness or anger because if a participant returns to the pod unable to "control" herself due to what was discussed or experienced during Red Tent, she may no longer be allowed to attend. And if this problem continues to occur, the Red Tent program could be ended.

Melissa explains the contrast between the Red Tent room and the rest of the jail.

> The biggest difference to me between jail and Red Tent was how I could truly express my feelings and share my shame and guilt without being criticized or judged. In jail you had to put up a front and not let your guard down; it was the only way to protect myself from being bullied or taken advantage of. Being nice in jail wasn't always the right way to be, where Red Tent let me be myself and not have to act so tough. It allowed me to be vulnerable, to just be, and to feel loved. It was the stepping stone I needed to not just get released from jail and start all over but to start the

healing process needed to recover and show me there is another way to live, and I was not only qualified, but I could help other women see they were too.

We learn we can take care of ourselves and trust the decisions we make toward empowered action. We trust and rely on other women in the group, which is an inherent challenge for most participants, and we establish a sisterhood—a community of women—which many of us have never known before. And then we pass that knowledge, love, and experience on to others. Bridges are made between those who have experienced incarceration and those who have not through shared life experiences that have nothing to do with jail.

Red Tent is a space that has been consciously, rhetorically, and physically created so that these conversations can exist and occur—through initial interviews and in the continued discussions that occur weekly inside and outside of jail. These rhetorics are then demonstrated in the commitments participants make to each other to heed confidentiality, as well as the camaraderie developed when participants cocreate projects and share their lives with each other.

FINDING OUR VOICES

All our voices and experiences were central to our Feminisms and Rhetorics presentation and discussion. As Melissa explains,

> In October of 2015, I was chosen to be a participant in the Feminisms and Rhetorics conference held in Phoenix, Arizona. This not only assured me as long as I kept doing the next right thing, anything was possible, but my self-esteem and self-worth grew enormously. Trying not to make the other Red Tent girls jealous, I quietly bragged to my sponsor, my family, and friends. Red Tent even came to court with me to represent Red Tent and ask permission for me to leave the state to attend this conference.[7] It was a success, and the trip was amazing. I have yet to find it necessary to pick up a drink or drug. Some of the women and volunteers of Red Tent are also in recovery, and although this is not a recovery-related program or group, that is another connection that I have found with Red Tent that is like no other.

Amanda explains her experience of bringing Red Tent to the mountains surrounding Phoenix.

> I had one of the most rewarding and enlightening experiences while hiking the Pima Canyon in Phoenix, Arizona. Melissa, Charlese, and I decided we were going to hike to the top. It was no easy task, but through encouragement, support, and laughter, we were able to reach the summit, pushing one another to overcome doubt and exhaustion. Once we

Figure 10.3. Coauthors at the top of Mt. Pima, Phoenix, Arizona. (Permission of and photo by Amanda Ellis.)

reached the top and took in the breathtaking views, I led us in a brief meditation, reciting the script we often use when leading meditation with the group in jail. As I began to say, "Now open your eyes to the room," I was overwhelmed with emotion because I realized when I had last led a meditation with these two women, they were in jail, and now they can open their eyes to the *world*. We literally have the world at our fingertips, which is what Red Tent is all about.

Charlese agrees: "It was definitely a time of cleansing. We are on top of the world."

RED TENT'S IMPACT ON INDIVIDUALS AND THE COMMUNITY

Although Red Tent is a relatively young organization (founded in 2012), it has already impacted the

Figure 10.4. On top of the world, Phoenix, Arizona. (Permission of and photo by Amanda Ellis.)

community and demonstrated positive results for participants and volunteers alike. As Amanda explains, "Not only do we strive to make a difference in every person's life, I have never been involved in a more supportive, loving, accepting, and innovative initiative. It has the same impact on its staff as it does its participants." According to jail deputies, Red Tent has the highest program participation rate in the PCJ, and it has an ongoing extensive wait list for new participants. Unlike other programs, judges do not mandate Red Tent participation; it is entirely voluntary. Preliminary assessment of the program outcomes suggests the recidivism rate for participants is 20 percent, compared to 54 percent of the general inmate population (Barbara Rhode, pers. comm., October 10, 2015).[8] Last, the program has retained several postprogram participants who serve as its biggest advocates (L. Nokko, pers. comm., February 7, 2014). The women's social connection and subsequent support serve as the most cited benefits. For example, Joyce, a former Red Tent participant, said the following about the program and her participation in it:

> It changed my life. It gave me something to be accountable for again. I lost everyone I cared about. I didn't want to be here anymore, but I wasn't going to kill myself either. I became very self-destructive. I got a case of the F-its, and it landed me in jail. Red Tent showed me how to live again when everything else I tried didn't. It helped me to heal. It gave me resources to start over, glasses so I could see, dentists so I could keep a tooth that would otherwise be pulled, medical help. But most of all, my dignity. They really care. Receiving all of this from women who genuinely want to see other women succeed—how could I let them down? Why would I ever want to do that?

Red Tent has changed all of us. Participants, facilitators, and volunteers are all accepted for where they are currently and encouraged to grow together. As Amanda explains, "Red Tent is dedicated to providing ongoing support and engagement with its participants and community members. Our long-term goal is to create a community movement of engaged women who come together to share wisdom, compassion, and encouragement."

Red Tent has also physically changed the spaces where the community lives. For example, Red Tent was awarded a community grant to restore a courtyard and garden in an impoverished area of South St. Petersburg. Participants and volunteers led the efforts, dedicating time, tools, and hard work to improve the community. The garden serves as a peaceful and restorative space for the community to participate in yoga classes, group meditations, and community events. Moreover, the vegetables planted during the day of service are given to the local community as

Figure 10.5. Display of Red Tent participants' artwork at December 2015 Community Fundraiser, St. Petersburg, Florida. (Permission of and photo by Amanda Ellis.)

a means of improving access to healthy foods in an area largely considered to be a food desert.

This example is one in which consciousness-raising becomes personal, experiential, and participatory. It brought attention to Red Tent and its goals, but it also allowed Red Tent to physically manifest its goals in the community, which, in turn, impacts the "systemically shaped conditions of women generally" (Campbell 2011, 265).

RED TENT AS FEMINIST RHETORIC CREATES COMMUNITY AND CHANGE

Red Tent combines feminisms *and* rhetorics to create communicative and material spaces that encourage women to create and remake their lives. We live feminist rhetorics as we work together building community, creating arts-based projects, and contributing to society. Red Tent fully engages and embraces feminist rhetoric both inside and outside the jail, constituting active meaning makers and contributing knowledge—through art and community—to the way we live our lives.

> Red Tent
> Ms. Barbara wanted a safe place where women could go and vent.
> She started an amazing women's group called Red Tent.
> Red Tent helps women who are in jail
> They also provide us with resources so we won't fail.
> Red Tent allows us to make beautiful art
> While we are working on our brand-new start
> I thank God every day for Red Tent
> It was without a doubt Heaven sent.
> Charlese Trower
> June 2014

APPENDIX 10.A

PARTICIPANT AGREEMENT

Welcome to Red Tent Women's Initiative, Inc.

Please read the following rules carefully before you sign this contract. Your participation depends on your complete understanding & compliance with these rules. Classes meet Thursdays & Fridays from 11:30–3:30 PM.

This voluntary program depends on your participation & adherence to the following rules.

1. You must leave every class with only the items you brought in with you. All materials will be counted according to Pinellas County Sheriff Dept. rules & class can end only after all supplies have been collected & accounted for. Any materials taken out of this room will be treated as contraband & dealt with by jail staff.

2. All materials need to be respected & used only as directed by staff/volunteers.

3. Red Tent staff & volunteers are committed to treating you with respect; assisting you & this program in creating a successful experience. Your participation requires that you do the same.

4. Staff/volunteers are not permitted to give participants items such as candy, gum, sewing materials, supplies . . . Please respect this rule by not requesting anything other than use of the program supplies.

5. Books can be borrowed & returned to class by signing it out on the Red Tent Borrowers List. If you leave the jail before you are able to bring it back to class, please turn it over to the jail staff so it can be returned to our book shelf. You are also permitted to take 1 magazine from class for your use. It is not necessary to return it. Please share!

6. Class will be held in a quiet, peaceful atmosphere. Yelling, cursing, or threatening behavior will not be tolerated & will be a violation of program participation.

7. Class space is limited. If you decide to end your participation in class or know that you will be leaving jail in the next week, please inform the class instructor so your space can be filled. Missing 2 consecutive classes will remove you from our attendance list so please do not schedule visits or other commitments on Thursdays or Fridays. *Participation is a commitment on your part & your seat will be held for you as long as you are interested & responsible.*

8. The items you create will be held for you by the jail, to be placed in property for you to take upon release. It is your responsibility to give your completed items to Polly or Noko at least 5 days before your release date to ensure safe delivery to property. If you cannot do that, you can pick up your completed crafts from Barbara Rhode, Director, by calling her to arrange a meeting.

Name _____

Date _____

NOTES

1. We want to thank research assistant Nicole Locklear for her research contributions to this chapter and to research assistant Amber Nicol for her research and organizational contributions in the revision of this chapter.
2. To provide additional clarification, many sources reference jail or prison, and some combine both, and therefore it can be even more difficult to understand how the numbers have changed and increased. Jail is used to house people who have not yet been sentenced or when the individual is sentenced to less than one year. Prisons are used for individuals whose sentences are longer than one year and a day. Within this paper we specify whether the sources are referencing jail, prison, or both.
3. Of course, all is not perfect in Red Tent, and we do not wish to make it appear so. There is always work to be done to increase awareness of privilege and dismantle oppression. There are aspects of Red Tent that can be improved, and writing this chapter has created an opportunity for us to detail how we are effective, as well as where we can improve. As a new and growing organization, Red Tent continues to refine its project outcomes and has developed program assessments with coauthor Jill McCracken, which further enables Red Tent to locate and address concerns with the program.

4. In contrast to historical accounts, Vladamir Tumanov argues "that the paganism of Rachel, Leah, as well as other women in Jacob's family, is a humane and natural form of spirituality in contrast to the bloodthirsty Yahwism of Jacob and his sons" (2007, 1).
5. See McCracken (2019) for a more in-depth analysis of Red Tent values and how they impact the project and participants.
6. A lockdown requires all prisoners to go to and remain on their bunks until further notice. Lockdowns are implemented during head count and shift changes if a deputy deems there is misbehavior in the pod and wants to provide greater regulation and quiet. Once a lockdown is initiated, the prisoner must stay on her bed above the covers. No talking or eating is allowed, and she must raise her hand to be allowed to go to the bathroom.
7. As part of Red Tent's ongoing support and advocacy efforts, former program director, Amanda Ellis, Red Tent interns, and the executive director of the Pinellas Ex-Offender Re-Entry Coalition attended Melissa Greene's probation hearing to provide support and highlight Melissa's success in rebuilding her life. The supporters detailed her continued sobriety and dedication in her recovery efforts, noting that her selection to attend the conference was well considered and spoke to the trust and faith she had stirred in all of us.
8. This rate has not been evaluated for statistical rigor and is based on personal feedback and monitoring of 130 program participants.

WORKS CITED

Benda, Brent B., Robert Flynn Corwyn, and Nancy J. Toombs. 2001. "Recidivism Among Adolescent Serious Offenders: Prediction of Entry into the Correctional System for Adults." *Criminal Justice and Behavior* 28 (5): 588–613.

Brummett, Barry. 1991. *Rhetorical Dimensions of Popular Culture.* Tuscaloosa, AL: Alabama University Press.

Campbell, Karlyn Kohrs. 2011. "Feminist Rhetoric." *Encyclopedia of Rhetoric and Composition: Communication from Ancient Times to the Information Age*, edited by Theresa Enos, 262–65. Abingdon, England: Routledge.

Chansky, Ricia A. 2010. "A Stitch in Time: Third-Wave Feminist Reclamation of Needled Imagery." *Journal of Popular Culture* 43 (4): 681–700.

Collins, Patricia Hill. 2000. *Black Feminist Thought: Knowledge, Consciousness, and the Politics of Empowerment.* Abingdon, England: Routledge.

Conly, Catherine. 1998. *The Women's Prison Association: Supporting Women Offenders and Their Families.* Washington, DC: National Institute of Justice.

Diamant, Anita. 2010. *The Red Tent: A Novel.* New York: St. Martin's.

Ferraro, Kathleen J., and Angela M. Moe. 2003. "Mothering, Crime, and Incarceration." *Journal of Contemporary Ethnography* 32 (1): 9–40.

Florida Department of Corrections Bureau of Data Analysis. 2018. "Florida County Detention Facilities Average Inmate Population." December. http://www.dc.state.fl.us/pub/jails/2018/jails-2018-12.pdf. Accessed 18 January 2021.

Geda, Yonas E., Hillary M. Topazian, Robert A. Lewis, Rosebud O. Roberts, David S. Knopman, V. Shane Pankratz, Teresa J. H. Christianson, Bradley F. Boeve, Eric George Tangalos, Robert J. Ivnik, and Ronald Carl Petersen. 2011. "Engaging in Cognitive Activities, Aging, and Mild Cognitive Impairment: A Population-Based Study." *Journal of Neuropsychiatry and Clinical Neurosciences* 23 (2): 149–54.

Glaze, Lauren E., and Laura M. Maruschak. 2008. *Parents in Prison and Their Minor Children.* Washington, DC: US Department of Justice, Office of Justice Programs. http://www.bjs.gov/content/pub/pdf/pptmc.pdf. Accessed 18 January 2021.

Gutman, Sharon A., and Victoria P. Schindler. 2007. "The Neurological Basis of Occupation." *Occupational Therapy International* 14 (2): 71–85.

Hanh, Thich Nhat. 1999. *The Heart of the Buddha's Teaching: Transforming Suffering into Peace, Joy & Liberation: The Four Noble Truths, the Noble Eightfold Path, and Other Basic Buddhist Teachings.* New York: Random House.

Jiang, Shanhe, and L. Thomas Winfree. 2006. "Social Support, Gender, and Inmate Adjustment to Prison Life: Insights from a National Sample." *Prison Journal* 86 (1): 32–55.

Johnson, Toni Kay. 2005. *Hidden Voices: The Life Experiences of African American Adolescent Girls with Mothers in Prison.* PhD diss., University of Texas.

Kaeble, D., and Cowhig, M. 2018. "Correctional Populations in the United States, 2016." Washington, DC: US Department of Justice, Office of Justice Programs, Bureau of Justice Statistics. https://www.bjs.gov/content/pub/pdf/cpus16.pdf. Accessed 18 December 2020.

Kajstura, Aleks. 2018. "States of Women's Incarceration: The Global Context 2018." Prison Policy Initiative, June. https://www.prisonpolicy.org/global/women/2018.html. Accessed 18 January 2021.

Kakar, Suman, Marie-Luise Friedemann, and Linda Peck. 2002. "Girls in Detention: The Results of Focus Group Discussion Interviews and Official Records Review." *Journal of Contemporary Criminal Justice* 18 (1): 57–73.

Kraft-Stolar, Tamar. 2015. *Reproductive Injustice: The State of Reproductive Health Care for Women in New York State Prisons.* A report of the Women in Prison Project of the Correctional Association of New York. New York: Correctional Association of New York.

McCracken, Jill. 2019. *Learning with Women in Jail: Creating Community Based Participatory Research.* Springerbriefs Anthropology and Ethics Series. New York: Springer.

McGee, Zina T., Spencer R Baker, Bertha L. Davis, Douglas J. Muller, and Alfreada B. Kelly. 2014. "Examining Risk Factors for Recidivism and Disparities in Treatment among Female Probationers." *Journal of Sociology* 2 (2): 219–32.

Mullings, Janet L., Deborah J. Hartley, and James W. Marquart. 2004. "Exploring the Relationship Between Alcohol Use, Childhood Maltreatment, and Treatment Needs Among Female Prisoners." *Substance Use & Misuse* 39 (2): 277–305.

Najavits, Lisa M. 2002. *Seeking Safety: A Treatment Manual for PTSD and Substance Abuse.* New York: Guilford Press.

National Resource Center on Justice Involved Women. n.d. "Fact Sheet on Justice Involved Women in 2016." https://cjinvolvedwomen.org/wp-content/uploads/2016/06/Fact-Sheet.pdf. Accessed 21 February 2019.

Pitman, Gayle E. 2003. "Evolution, but No Revolution: The 'Tend and Befriend' Theory of Stress and Coping." Review. Review of *The Tending Instinct: How Nurturing Is Essential to Who We Are and How We Live*, by Shelley E. Taylor. *Psychology of Women Quarterly* 27 (2): 194–95.

Reisig, Michael D., Kristy Holtfreter, and Merry Morash. 2006. "Assessing Recidivism Risk across Female Pathways to Crime." *Justice Quarterly* 23 (3): 384–405.

Sawyer, Wendy. 2018. "The Gender Divide: Tracking Women's State Prison Growth." Prison Policy Initiative, March. https://www.prisonpolicy.org/reports/women_overtime.html. Accessed 18 January 2021.

Sherman, Gary D., Leslie K. Rice, Ellie Shou Jin, Amanda C. Jones, and Robert A. Josephs. 2017. "Sex Differences in Cortisol's Regulation of Affiliative Behavior." *Hormones and Behavior* 92 (June): 20–28.

Swavola, Elizabeth, Kristine Riley, and Ram Subramanian. 2016. *Overlooked: Women and Jails in an Era of Reform.* New York: Vera Institute of Justice.

Taylor, Shelley E. 2002. *The Tending Instinct: How Nurturing Is Essential to Who We are and How We Live.* New York: Macmillan.

Toseland, Ronald W., and Robert F. Rivas. 2012. "Historical and Theoretical Developments." In *An Introduction to Group Work Practice*, 7th ed., 45–66. Boston: Allyn and Bacon.

Tumanov, Vladamir. 2007. "Yahweh vs. the Teraphim: Jacob's Pagan Wives in Thomas Mann's *Joseph and His Brothers* and in Anita Diamant's *The Red Tent*." *Nebula* 4 (2): 395–407.

Wacquant, Loïc. 2002. "The Curious Eclipse of Prison Ethnography in the Age of Mass Incarceration." *Ethnography* 3 (4): 371–97.

Walmsley, Roy. 2017. "World Female Imprisonment List: Women and Girls in Penal Institutions, Including Pre-Trial Detainees/Remand Prisoners," 4th ed. London, England: Institute for Criminal Policy Research. http://www.prisonstudies.org/sites/default/files/resources/downloads/world_female_prison_4th_edn_v4_web.pdf. Accessed 1 March 2019.

World Prison Brief. n.d. "Highest to Lowest—Prison Population Rate." World Prison Brief. https://www.prisonstudies.org/highest-to-lowest/prison_population_rate?field_region_taxonomy_tid=All. Accessed 13 November 2018.

SECTION 3

Women's Ways of Making the Academy

11
RENEWING FEMINIST PERSPECTIVES ON WOMEN WPAS' SERVICE AND LEADERSHIP

Hui Wu and Emily Standridge

Twenty-first century US higher education is faced with challenges similar to those in the postwar era in the second half of the nineteenth century when a rising middle class's demand for a college education as a path to upward mobility exploded. Universities are again flooded with students who need to learn to write professionally and academically. Professional preparation again dominates student choices of majors. Professional and preprofessional programs are now witnessing increases in student enrollment. However, English majors have declined by 25 to 30 percent at many universities.[1] Many English departments at Research 1 universities rely on their rhetoric and composition doctoral programs, and of course required composition, for survival and revenue. As for the curriculum, thanks to women's participation in higher education and their advocacy for over 170 years, rhetoric, originally an exclusively male field from which composition has evolved, gradually shifted from the rhetoric of persuasion to one of written discourse (Connors 1997, 24; Gold, Hobbs, and Berlin 2012), finally embracing writing for multiple purposes—first-year composition, creative writing, WAC, WID, technical/professional writing, and others, as we witness today (Connors 54–55, 64–67; Gold, Hobbs, and Berlin 2012; Mendenhall 2014; Ritter 2012, 8–10; Russell 2002, 3–14, 286–87). This change has led to the eventual placing of women trained in rhetoric and composition as writing program administrators. We are, however, faced with a series of new challenges. How do compositionists meet the new challenges in this new era? What political and ethical issues may the challenges entail in our discipline and in the university? What shall we do to avoid repeating the problems, especially the gender-related problems, of the past? How can we use this new era to increase WPA leadership in the wider university, as we have not been able to do very successfully in the past?

To answer these questions, it is necessary to analyze compositionists' concerns about the service status of compositionists through a renewed feminist approach in order to reveal patriarchal ideologies that determine values of academic work and administration, and to reconceptualize student service as public service. Using transnational rhetorical feminist theories, this study points out that feminist critiques on women's work in writing program administration have yet to move beyond male-dominated values and gender binaries within the traditional academic setting. It further argues that only by liberating our feminist conceptualization of labor, service, and women's work from the influence of traditional academic thinking models can women WPAs be recognized as leaders, not merely as service providers. This study also conveys a belief that women WPAs are uniquely ready for upper-university leadership, for they have transcended traditionally defined gender traits and labor divisions through handling work traditionally marked men's and women's in administration, scholarship, teaching, and faculty training.

CURRENT STATUS OF WPAS AND PERCEPTIONS ON SERVICE

PhDs in rhetoric and composition have had a robust job market since the 1990s, with options to teach and to direct first-year composition, writing programs, writing centers, and writing-across-the-curriculum (WAC) or writing-in-the-disciplines (WID) programs. Shane Borrowman's optimistic statement is not an exaggeration—"We have a job market that reflects not only the vibrancy of rhetoric and composition as a field but also its diversity—with hundreds of jobs listed annually in MLA's *JIL*, many of them tenure-track positions" (2009, 359). Better still, "a growing number of WPAs are now serving as chairs of departments, directors of programs, deans of colleges, provosts of campuses" (McLeod 2002, 113). Further, Richard Bullock argues that "WPAs are experts and scholars testing and refining their knowledge in the practice arena of application. The administration of writing program . . . advances our knowledge of the teaching of writing" (1987, 14). Recognizing the skills and scholarship potential of WPAs against the political backdrop of literature-dominated English departments was crucial, and this political battle eventually led to recognition of writing program administration work as comparable to the research, teaching, service, and theorizing work done by all faculty.

Despite prolific scholarship, tenure-track positions, tenured positions, and even WPAs' relatively high pay scales within the male-dominated institutional structures of English departments, writing administration, along with composition, is still largely feminized. A case in point is the gender distribution of writing program and composition directorships. In the 1980s, 71 percent of WPAs were men (Hartzog 1986; Holbrook 1991, 211). In the first half of the 1990s, the majority of WPAs were still men (Enos 1996, 7). Under them, the majority of composition instructors were women. By 2008, 68 percent of WPAs were women (Skeffington, Borrowman, and Enos 2008). In 2013, women constituted over 73 percent of the WPAs and composition directors who participated in a survey conducted by Shirley K Rose, Lisa Mastrangelo, and Barbara L'Eplattenier (2013, 49).[2] The movement of women into tenure-track "mid-level managerial" positions has been celebrated and has led to a belief that women have been elevated to more equitable work conditions and gender structure. However, a comparison of these survey reports reveals that the administrative structure of programs that include writing/composition sustains a gender hierarchy in which men are still above women. In 2013, most female WPAs worked for male department chairs (Rose, Mastrangelo, and L'Eplattenier 2013, 49). Indeed, "no matter how feminist the administrator, she still has to meet the demands of a masculinist academy" (Glenn 2018, 179), which not only continues to perpetuate the underclass status of composition within English departments but also limits women's leadership roles. For example, comparing their findings about WPAs' authority with that in Gary Olson and Joseph Moxley's 1989 study, Rose, Mastrangelo, and L'Eplattenier conclude that "some conditions that were present in 1989 still persist and continue to hold writing program directors back from being able to garner sufficient authority to do their work effectively" (2013, 45). Even though more and more WPAs are women, their work is still not valued as it should be nor are they as free from patriarchal structures, as mere numbers suggest.

Part of this undervaluing of WPA work can be seen in the problem of "service" in composition. For over three decades, composition scholars have been fighting the label of *service* in the hope that composition would be recognized as an independent discipline. We have tried to disrupt the "historic displacement of composition within the university as a service course" (Crowley 1998, 28) because literature faculty tend to see composition instructors mainly in a "service role" (Hairston 1985, 276). They see the work of composition as less intellectual because it is not a "higher art" like literature and because there are so many students taking the course to be better prepared for later courses; thus, composition courses "serve" the university. "When we accept their [literature faculty's] definition of writing courses as service courses," Maxine Hairston warned in 1985, "we ourselves denigrate what we do and buy into their value system" (276). To her, "writing courses are not service courses, but courses in the exercise of a primary intellectual activity" (278).

The term *service* in composition has become loaded with negative connotations, but it does not exclusively have those meanings in broader usages. There are two kinds of service implied in public-service jobs, such as those held by elected and local government officials. When someone performs public service, this person has a desirable, ranked, higher position whose service involves making decisions, negotiating policies, and speaking for constituents. However, people in these positions tend to have assistants, most of whom are likely women, to provide quiet behind-the-scenes service through daily, detailed organization and coordination activities that involve making coffee, collating documents for signatures, typing and copying, planning meals, scheduling appointments and meetings, processing paperwork, handling public relations, and so on. In terms of labor, the former position is commonly perceived as dignified, grand, creditable, and respectable, and the latter as undignified, trivial, tedious, and contemptible, oftentimes with implicit, yet "natural," associations with servitude. A person in the former position is called a *public servant*, in the latter, a *servant*, or a *maid*. Historically, social hierarchy has been set up to make public service exclusively accessible to men while determinedly inaccessible to women. What this scenario reveals is that a word can have different, even opposite, meanings when gender is involved, and the meaning is largely controlled by the established social hierarchy. With changed connotations of the word that signifies the nature of an occupation, the perception of that word is changed. As Enos says, "The marking of work as 'women's' or 'men's' is based on social concepts of gender" (1996, 4).

This complicated understanding of service and the linking of service and servant with gendered implications also affects the way compositionists perceive their work and labor. For example, Sue Ellen Holbrook seemingly moves from "service" to "servant" naturally, when discussing WPA work. She says "we serve generously and energetically to fulfil the needs of students. . . . But dedicated servants that we are, . . . whose servants are we?" (1991, 211). Although *service* and *servant* share the same semantic root, her seamless lexical move from "service" to "servant," whether conscious or unconscious, indicates academics' general, and confused, perception of *service*. The evolution of writing program administration from a male-dominated area to one involving more and more women provides further evidence for Enos's argument, building on claims in Holbrook's 1991 study (202), that "'Women's work' is characterized by a disproportionate number of women workers (as in academe's writing programs); it is service-oriented (like classroom teaching); it pays less than 'men's work' (traditional forms of scholarship); it is devalued (females get fewer promotions and less pay)" (1996, 4).

The above analysis reveals that for decades, until recently, the undertone of scholarship on writing program administration indicates our rejection of composition as a service course, our anger at being treated as servants, and our fear of labeling WPA work as *service*. Our intentional dissociation with service has derived from historical lessons. Those who engaged in writing administration scholarship to address labor, equality, and quality issues without complying with the established publication criteria struggled with resource constraints and work overload. Take, for example, Edwin Hopkins at the University of Kansas (1889–1937) and Regina Crandall at Bryn Mawr College (1902–1923). Hopkins was "best known for his publications associated with his crusade to improve the plight of the labor of composition teachers at college, secondary, and elementary levels" (Popken 2004, 6). His most influential monograph at the time, *The Labor and Cost of the Teaching of English in College and Secondary Schools with Especial Reference to English Composition*, went through sixteen editions and sold one hundred and thirty thousand copies throughout the country (Popken 2004, 7). Despite his long publication list, public recognition, and federal research funding, he struggled "to coordinate his own workload with his research goals" (11), having to teach six writing and literature courses a semester and serving as a program director at the same time. For twelve years, he negotiated with his dean, chancellor, and secretary of the University Board for reassigned time and clerical support with little avail due to their disdain for his nontraditional project (17). Hopkins had to endure this rejection of his work while witnessing his colleagues publishing literary research and enjoying rewards and status (16).

At Bryn Mawr College, the battle of Regina Crandall, director of the Essay Department, "reminds us how lack of a secure, well-defined professional status can suffocate even the most dedicated writing teachers" (George 2004, 23). President M. Carey Thomas, a turn-of-the-century feminist, created graduate fellowships and recruited world-class research faculty to enable women to learn classical literature, history, and languages but "refused to admit that teaching writing or directing a writing program were [*sic*] legitimate academic work" (24–25). Within the male-dominated academic culture that marked Crandall's work as "drudge work, unintellectual work, and therefore women's work" (25), Thomas denied Crandall "a seat on the faculty and a salary equal to that of other department heads," while some of Crandall's subordinates who published literary research were appointed faculty in the Literature Department (27–29). Crandall's expression of grievances about oversized classes and overworked writing instructors led to her removal from the department-head position. If the supporting alumnae and public had not pressured President Thomas, she would not have regained her position (30–32). While Hopkins's case argues for recognition of WPA work as critical scholarship for professionalizing the English discipline, Crandall's reveals the profound degree to which patriarchal academic values are at odds with teaching and student service.

Despite this rejection of service, from its outset, composition required rhetoric professors to gear their hearts and minds toward students. Composition professors placed student service and success before or parallel to their own academic pursuit and pleasure. Our history shows that most professors of rhetoric at Harvard and other universities were, in fact, willing to devote their expertise to teaching students. John Brereton's study of instructional manuals and writing textbooks from 1875 to 1920 shows that putting student service before faculty's personal interests is our disciplinary tradition (1995). Newer historical studies of local colleges other than northeastern elite ones and early big public universities provide more evidence that all writing/composition directors, regardless of gendered identity, made student academic progress the heart of the curriculum and their passion. In addition to the examples of Edwin Hopkins at the University of Kansas and Regina Crandall at Bryn Mawr College, women WPAs at Mount Holyoke, Wellesley, Vassar, and Smith Colleges, and those in HBCUs, all saw service to students as the main part of their academic work (L'Eplattenier and Mastrangelo 2004). Dispersed across the country, the writing/composition programs were "concerted efforts at teaching and administering composition programs" (138).

Indeed, if we were not to accept that composition is considered a "service," we would reject teaching as the core component of our discipline. "The culture of composition," says Peter Elbow, "carries a concern not just for teaching but also for students: attention, interest, and care for them, their lives, and what's on their minds. The core activity in teaching composition is the act of reading what's on students' minds; the core activity in teaching literature is reading the literary text" (2002, 537). In contrast to "the comfort and pleasure of planning a whole class around a literary text" in his preparation for a literature course, Elbow's preparation for a composition class is "a richer process" in which he plans and devises workshop activities through student group work, peer reading, and writing exercises (535). All these activities are student oriented. As he recalls, "Class planning feels more like trying to manage complex activities than quiet immersion in an amazing text. This approach to teaching that I learned as a teacher of writing tends to result in classes that are livelier and more active than my old literature classes: fewer dead spells, less tooth pulling, less talk from me, more learning" (535). Our denial of the service role of composition denies the very fact "that these are precisely what are involved in the 'capacity of the academic profession to review itself and pass on' its distinctive forms of expertise" (Report of ADE, 4, quoted in Miller 2010, 5).

That we are unable to escape the service role of composition for even the more traditionally "academic" research and writing in the field leads us back to the importance of service. Recent publications have enriched and renewed our understanding of the history of writing administration, past and present problematics of program building and work environment, college writing curricula, and future directions of writing program administration work, as well as helped us see how WPAs put students first. Take, for example, Shirley K Rose and Irwin Weiser's *The Writing Program Administrator as Theorist* (2012), L'Eplattenier and Mastrangelo's *Historical Studies of Writing Program Administration* (2004), Stuart Brown and Theresa Enos's *The Writing Program Administrator's Resource* (2002), Linda Adler-Kassner's *The Activist WPA* (2008), Rose and Weiser's *Going Public: What Writing Programs Learn from Engagement* (2010), Skeffington, Enos and Borrowman's *The Promise and Perils of Writing Program Administration* (2008), Donna Strickland's *The Managerial Unconscious in the History of Composition Studies* (2011), Susan McLeod's *Writing Program Administration* (2007), and Colin Charlton, Jonikka Charton, Tarez Samra Graban, Kathleen J. Ryan, and Amy Ferdinandt Stolley's *GenAdmin: Theorizing WPA Identities in the Twenty-First Century* (2011), just to name a few. As a matter of fact, writing program administration, WAC, WID, the writing center, and composition instruction demand that we focus more and more on teaching and student service. The booming job market for PhDs in rhetoric and composition demonstrates that our service counts. For this reason, we are unable to, nor should we, escape the service roles of teaching and training our PhDs to be great composition teachers, composition directors, and WPAs who can provide public service through the university. We should recognize that the nature of our discipline is largely service.

A CRITIQUE OF FEMINIST STUDIES OF WPAS

Despite having a better gender distribution of WPAs and an enhanced position for WPAs within English departments, writing program directors triple their "service"—teaching writing, training instructors, and administering "a slice of bureaucracy" (Bullock's 1987, 14). However, arguments still exist that writing program administrative work is not seen in local relation to universal paradigms and that scholarship in writing program administration is more important than the work itself; Bullock believes that "WPAs are experts and scholars resting and refining their knowledge in the practice arena of application. The administration of writing programs . . . advances our knowledge of the teaching of writing" (14). In other words, Bullock argues that WPAs are doing intellectual work, not "just" teaching work or "just" women's work. Furthermore, Enos suggests, "Writing program administration should be recognized not as service, but as a separate and special category of administration or intellectual work worthy of tenure and promotion" (1996, 84). For this reason, she does not think WPAs should accept the characterization of their work as "service" (2002, 59). Hairston would like to treat WPAs as scholars and administrative figures to professionalize the field and to reposition writing instructors (1998). But these scholars look at WPAs' work within the traditionally masculine framework already in place in the university. This reliance on old frameworks does little to advance the status of WPAs' work.

Recent feminist studies of WPAs have incorporated ethics, and gender theories have started to transform these conceptions. Carrie Leverenz argues for a feminist ethic in writing administration to associate it with the public good in higher education (2010, 3–18). Her research reaffirms that faculty's traditional aversion to service has much to do with patriarchal values of the university, illustrating the need to move beyond patriarchal structures; in an effort to theorize service, Julie Marie Jung contrasts a male professor's "just say 'no' approach" to student requests and committee work with her own sense of responsibility for students' academic development (2009, 168–69), concretizing the usefulness of Leverenz's standpoint. Other concepts derived from feminist sociology and literary criticism, for example, include "emotional labor of service" and "affective relationship" (Jung 2009; Snyder 2009), as well as *"ecriture feminine"* and *"erotics"* for "might desire" (Gunner 2010).

However, the current feminist scholarship on writing program administration and women's labor has yet to transcend the mainstream academic feminist analytical model that separates women's work from men's, a binary interpretive framework already challenged by transnational feminist rhetorical theories. Two issues challenge these feminist interpretive models. First, Leverenz's application of extant feminist theories on ethics to call for women WPAs to move beyond the patriarchal structure is effective, but her study has yet to develop a new feminist theoretical framework for the interpretation of service to uplift women WPAs' status. Jung's perception on women's acceptance of service, as well, has yet to offer a liberating model for women WPAs. We often hear male colleagues say, "Women excel at 'service' work." Male chairs and professors often use this rhetoric to "value" women's administrative work and to get themselves out of the "tedious" details and complicated tasks that require time and patience. In many cases, this praise for women's service makes male academics and administrators comfortable with accepting women in the academy because they can assign service, which is gendered female, to them. This male comfort, in turn, assigns more labor to women and entrenches them in mental and physical exploitation. Contrasting men and women in analyzing the feminization of writing program administration may risk the ethical danger of repeating the traditional predisposition to ascribe different virtues to men and women and re-essentialize women simply because of the same differences that a gendered society already uses in gender oppression. Second, the borrowed concepts that emphasize emotion, affection, feminine writing, and feminine desire warrant reexamination because using women's emotions and bodies as analytical lenses may further deepen the gendered mark of service and jeopardize women WPAs' work and careers. The feminized terms may sustain traditionally perceived gender dichotomies—male/female, culture/nurture, rational/emotional, logic/care—which are recognized to have distinct roots in Euro-American tradition (Hall and Ames 1998, 83–84). As Hui Wu has pointed out, "Insofar as the feminist binaries have also developed in the Euro-American intellectual context, they, too, have grown out of Western historical and cultural influences, as exemplified by the very pattern of using binaries" (2005, 172). From this viewpoint, feminist "body talk" about desire, language use, and meaning, in fact, continues to put the female body under the male gaze as a sexual object instead of liberating it from sexual oppression (2001, 414–417). These feminized terms must be disrupted in order to transform the gendered perceptions of service and WPAs' work.

Our renewed feminist perspective informs that scholarship on feminization of writing administration based on might desire, power and authority; for example, the work of Gunner (2010) and Rose, Mastrangelo, and L'Eplattenier (2013, 50–51) must be regendered to shift the style of thinking of traditional academia and to eliminate any desire to imitate men's behavior based on what makes men successful in male-dominated academic culture. The established style of thinking follows supposedly gender-neutral, but actually male, standards to encourage women to imitate men and entrench women in the "men-and-women-are-the-same" trap, which Mao's regime used to measure Chinese women against male standards (Wu 2001, 2010). Although the women's-liberation movement encouraged women to be like men and to resist essentialization, such encouragement only subordinates women to men because it naturally makes men's behaviors the standard. The talk of women's might desire, power, and authority in writing administration implicitly confines women in a behavioral framework traditionally built by men and for men, which Adrienne Rich calls a "suicidal obsession" (1979, 130).

Moreover, the feminized terms based on gender dichotomies may stop feminist studies of writing program administration from being accepted as "real" scholarship by the mainstream patriarchal academic culture, again, simply because of its difference as judged by patriarchal criteria, virtues, and principles. Therefore, feminist studies built on gender dualism may, instead, further entrench women in exploitation without offering solutions. It may also limit women WPAs' potentials for academic leadership beyond the writing program. Finally, it is evident women WPAs have transcended traditionally defined gender binaries. They have made achievements in areas conventionally occupied by men—scholarship and academic administration—and in those traditionally for women—teaching and student service. Embodying culture, nurture, rationality, care, logic, and affection, they have strategically distinguished themselves from, rather than imitated, male-gendered behavior in and attitude toward service. Based on her own experience, Cheryl Glenn recommends feminist strategies for WPA work, including "the ability and willingness to reach out, collaborate, negotiate (use listening, silence, and dialogue), strive for mutual understanding (rather than persuasion), and work strategically—and with hope—toward a vision" (2018, 186). Her feminist wisdom has transformed the established administrative framework based on gender binaries, proving that "women's work" in writing administration constitutes critical values, particularly in this new era of higher education.

On a daily basis, women WPAs perform what has been marked as men's work. Similar to male WPAs, they must address various issues through cross-institutional communication to maintain quality teaching, thus developing overall desirable qualities of a leader. For example, convinced that teaching writing to first-year students is educating citizens and training future world leaders, they have a passion for curriculum development and innovative instruction with regard to critical thinking, reading, and writing, the fundamental areas in higher education. Thanks to their research and leadership on each campus, women WPAs, along with their male counterparts, are continuing the Cooperative Writing Movement that began at the turn of the twentieth century (Lindblom and Dunn 2004; Russell 2002) to implement WAC and WID and develop courses in writing studies at both undergraduate and graduate levels. As part of public administration, they focus on their responsibility to serve and empower citizens by enhancing their literacy through writing administration.

In addition, almost all women WPAs are familiar with and practice feminist principles in teaching and administration to advocate equity and fairness as part of democratic values and civic discourse. The feminine traits of women WPAs—care, affection, and nurturance—are now considered core qualities of leadership (Eisler 2012; Simola, Barling and Turner 2012; Turkel 2014). These traits, rather than being suppressed, make women WPAs sensitive, caring leaders in the traditional gendered hierarchy. In facilitating their leadership role, their feminist practice makes them fulfill "a moral obligation" to assure "processes are fully consistent with norms of justice and fairness" (Denhardt and Denhardt 2000, 554), norms women WPAs regender to address inequality among sexes and among teaching staff of different ranks (Gunner 1994; Reid 2010, 137–39). Since they are aware of their differences but do not let their differences be the reasons for oppression, they tend to be innovative in creating an employee-friendly culture to increase morale for strong performance and productivity. Under their supervision, composition instructors develop a sense of ownership of the program, are trained well in composition theory and practice, and teach well in the classroom. By upholding feminist principles, women WPAs transform the nature of power and authority instead of fighting for them and hold integrity and ethics at the heart of their leadership (Gunner 1994, 2010; Leverenz 2010). In doing so, women WPAs have created a new goal for higher education that coincides with a new notion of public service— "shared interests and shared responsibility" (Denhardt and Denhardt 2000, 554). The new goal is "not to find quick solutions by individual choices" but to develop "a collective, shared notion of the public interest" in providing public service (554).

REDEFINING WOMEN WPAS AS UNIVERSITY LEADERS

Our examination of scholarship on service and feminist studies of WPAs urges us to renew our feminist language in order to redefine WPA work as public service and WPAs as leaders at the university, or public servants, as respected as male ones in the public domain. The university at large has shifted from a culture of faculty-student hierarchy to one of faculty-student equity, paying increasing attention to teaching and learning outcomes and, at the same time, increasing faculty's service work. Gone are the "good old days" when academics thought "they [were] doing good work when they advance[d] their own careers and the knowledge base and status of their disciplines" without thought of student success (Leverenz 2010, 4). Change is happening to traditional academic culture, "that happy realm of exactness where pure thought can disport itself in freedom" (Bertrand Russell quoted in Hairston 1985, 276). The increased workload cannot rest mainly on women faculty, and they themselves should not take all the workload simply because they "cannot say no" in a patriarchal academic culture that marks their gender traits as well suited for teaching and service. Meanwhile, a booming writing economy inside and outside the university increases academic positions for compositionists and WPAs. The demands of service by the university and students, apparently, are higher and cannot be fulfilled with "women's work" alone. Women WPAs must be aware that "the gender equity issue does not lie with the lack of women's skills or aspirations, but with the changing nature of the university" (Blackmore 2014, 95). In this sense, women WPAs bear the responsibility of being change agents, bringing all faculty to transform the patriarchal nature of the university to an authentic culture of gender equality that a progressive, democratic society holds.

It is particularly critical now, when women dominate WPA positions and more GenAdmins are academically prepared as specialists in higher education administration, to reconceptualize service, to eliminate any possibility of repeating the contempt composition has experienced (Charlton et al. 2011). Using the concept of public service to change the context of teaching and writing program administration, we can redefine writing program administration as part of the public service provided by higher education for the public good and redefine the professoriate as a position dedicated to students' success, not one mainly for faculty's self-advancement. Even intellectual work in the form of scholarship contributes to public knowledge and student learning, as in undergraduate research, and not to professors' own rewards as in the traditional understanding of research. Once the term *service* is placed in *public service*, we can equate writing program administration with public administration, an academic field for the study and preparation of public leaders.[3] All these terms tie writing administration to public leadership traditionally marked as "men's work," respectable and noble, as discussed previously.

Unfortunately, writing program directors are often named *administrators* but not *leaders*. Current studies limit them primarily to "lower managers," "mid-level managers," "activists," and "agents" (Alder-Kassner 2008; Bousquet 2008, 160–66; Rose and Weiser 2012; Snyder 2009; Strickland 2011). In fact, to be successful, a WPA must be both a manager and a leader (McLeod 2002, 113). Providing service does not require leadership, but providing leadership requires administrative service. WPAs should be called *academic leaders*. First, but with a slightly different scope, the responsibilities of a WPA are interestingly similar to those of a chair or a dean, who is identified as a *leader*. Most job advertisements for deans' or chairs' positions show that academic leadership requires organizational and management skills, including such responsibilities as personnel hiring and evaluation, student success, academic and research-program development, professional accreditations (in WPAs' case, assessment of writing courses and programs), strategic planning, interdisciplinary collaborations, and fiscal management and efficiency. All WPAs can check off each of the required qualifications and then some because they also teach in the classroom and publish scholarship. As Louise Wetherbee Phelps points out, "The teaching mission of composition is programmatic. It requires leaders with the skills to build and administer imaginative, conceptually sound, pedagogically and politically effective programs in complex cross-institutional designs involving multiple constituencies, collaborative partnerships, in nontraditional formats" (2002, 14).

More important, many of today's WPAs are trained academically and formally to be university administrators through coursework, administrative graduate assistantships, and dissertations or other academic scholarship on the issue. In comparison to academics and administrators in other disciplines, their training gives them advantages and uniqueness—they are prepared for academic leadership even before they complete their PhDs. With their training and ever-growing conviction in their role of service for public interest, WPAs exhibit marketable professional flexibility as published scholars, teachers, and academic leaders. For these reasons, we are not surprised that many ex-WPAs have moved on to higher academic positions. Theirs are not individual incidental success stories but represent a group identity, an identity GenAdmins are seeking and trying to define—What is next after writing program administration? (Charlton et al. 2011, 66–67). Without intent to overlook other ex-WPAs who now serve as presidents, provosts, vice provosts/presidents, deans, and chairs, we are using Elaine Maimon, president of Governors State University, as an inspirational model for women WPAs. She received the American Council for Education (ACE) Donna Shavlik Award for women's leadership and the 2014 Chicagoland Athena Award (Maimon, pers. comm., March 28, 2014). Her journey to the university presidency reflects the labor history of our field. Like other senior WPAs, after getting a PhD in literature, she started directing composition as an adjunct and then became one of the founders of the Council of Writing Program Administrators and WAC. In her keynote speech at the American Council of Education State Coordinators' Conference, she says, "Many women presidents have followed unusual career paths and developed special skills and perspectives through jobs on the periphery of institutions. . . . I know that men are much more likely to follow a linear, focused career path to the presidency: from assistant to associate to full professor, to department chair, dean, provost, and then president" (2014, 6). Her career as a university administrator is rooted in her passion for teaching writing, because "student writing [is] the signature of the institution" (Maimon 2018, 15). She still leads the faculty at her university to CCCC to present their WAC program design. Even today, she holds deep gratitude to her mentors—Mina Shaughnessy, Harriet Sheridan, and Win Horner (Maimon, pers. comm., March 28, 2014). Looking back at her experience as chief executive at three universities where she has led many strategic planning processes, Maimon concludes, "I learned most of these presidential skills very early in my career when I was a writing program administrator" (2018, 15). Maimon's story tells us that women WPAs are well suited for upper academic leadership.

In conclusion, as a result of our reconceptualizing service as the core value of university leadership, we now realize why we are so passionate about teaching writing and directing writing programs. We are leading a field critical to the development of the citizenry. For this reason, women WPAs bear the major responsibility of transforming the structure of academia. Only after the structure is changed can the academic culture, style of thinking, and labor division change. As Rich says,

> Women in the university therefore need . . . to change the center of gravity of the institution as far as possible; to work toward a women-centered university . . . because only if that center of gravity can be shifted will women really be free to learn, to teach, to share strength, to explore, to criticize, and to convert knowledge to power (1979, 128).

To women WPAs, power should not hold its traditional masculine glory and value. Nan Johnson suggests that our field's historic attachment of "power" to the status of rhetoric as "the critical and pedagogical arbiter" is problematic in that it is "a prestige rationalization" (2011, 242). To break with the patriarchal perception of service in the professoriate, a prestige itself, we must reinvent ourselves to influence and educate all scholars to shift the priorities of the professoriate. This may be what Johnson calls the "ordinary forms" of rhetoric and "the true scope of the rhetorical" (243). In this transformational moment of higher education, propelled by an ever-thriving economy of writing, GenAdmins will likely move to upper central administration. Women WPAs' leadership roles then are likely to change the landscape of the university and the paradigm of English studies in the near future.

NOTES

1. The information was shared on the ADE English Chairs-Listserv in 2014.
2. Among the two hundred writing directors surveyed by Rose, Mastrangelo, and L'Eplattenier, 58 of 79 directors of composition, or approximately 73.4 percent, were women, and 78 of 102 WPAs, or approximately 76.5 percent, were women (2013, 49).
3. See Mark Rutgers's "Beyond Woodrow Wilson" (1997) for a historical view on the identity of public administration as an academic discipline.

WORKS CITED

Adler-Kassner, Linda. 2008. *The Activist WPA: Changing Stories about Writing and Writers.* Logan: Utah State University Press.
ADE (Association of the Departments of English) Ad Hoc Committee on Staffing. 1999. "Report of the ADE Ad Hoc Committee on Staffing." *ADE Bulletin* 122 (Spring): 7–26.
Berlin, James. 1996. *Rhetorics, Poetics, and Cultures: Refiguring College English Studies.* West Lafayette, IN: Parlor.
Blackmore, Jill. 2014. "'Wasting Talent'? Gender and the Problematics of Academic Disenchantment and Disengagement with Leadership." *Higher Education Research & Development* 33 (1): 86–99.
Borrowman, Shane. 2009. "Star Struck but Unfazed: An Interview with Theresa J. Enos." In *Renewing Rhetoric's Relation to Composition: Essays in Honor of Theresa Jarnagin Enos*, edited by Shane Borrowman, Stuart C. Brown, and Thomas Miller, 346–59. Abingdon, England: Routledge.
Bousquet, Marc. 2008. *How the University Works: Higher Education and the Low-Wage Nation.* New York: New York University Press.
Brown, Stuart, and Theresa Enos. 2002. *The Writing Program Administrator's Resource: A Guide to Reflective Institutional Practice.* Lawrence Erlbaum.
Brereton, John. 1995. *The Origin of Composition Studies in the American College, 1875–1925: A Documentary History.* Pittsburgh, PA: University of Pittsburgh Press.
Bullock, Richard H. 1987. "When Writing Administration Becomes Scholarship: The Future of Writing Program Administration." *WPA: Writing Program Administration* 11 (1–2): 13–18.
Charlton, Colin, Jonikka Charlton, Tarez Samra Graban, Kathleen J. Ryan, and Amy Ferdinandt Stolley. 2011. *GenAdmin: Theorizing WPA Identities in the Twenty-First Century.* Anderson, SC: Parlor.

Connors, Robert. 1997. *Composition-Rhetoric: Backgrounds, Theory, and Pedagogy.* Pittsburgh, PA: University of Pittsburgh Press.

Crowley, Sharon. 1998. *Composition in the University: Historical and Problematic Essays.* Pittsburgh, PA: University of Pittsburgh Press.

Denhardt, Robert, and Janet Vinzant Denhardt. 2000. "The New Public Service: Serving Rather Than Steering." *Public Administration Review* 60 (6): 549–59.

Eisler, Raine. 2012. "Transforming Economics: Caring Economy Leadership." *Integral Leadership Review* 12 (2): 1–5.

Elbow, Peter. May 2002. "The Culture of Literature and Composition: What Could Each Learn from the Other?" *College English* 64 (5): 533–46.

Enos, Theresa. 1996. *Gender Roles and Faculty Lives in Rhetoric and Composition.* Carbondale, IL: Southern Illinois University Press.

Enos, Theresa. 2002. "Reflexive Professional Development: Getting Disciplined in Writing Program Administration." In *The Writing Program Administrator's Resource: A Guide to Reflective Institutional Practice,* edited by Theresa Enos and Stuart C. Brown, 59–70. Hillsdale, NJ: Lawrence Erlbaum.

George, D'Ann. 2004. "Replacing Nice, Thin Bryn Mawr Miss Crandall with Fat, Harvard Savage: WPA at Bryn Mawr College, 1902–1923." *Historical Studies of Writing Program Administration,* edited by Barbara L'Eplattenier and Lisa Mastrangelo, 23–36. Anderson, SC: Parlor.

Glenn, Cheryl. 2018. *Rhetorical Feminism and This Thing Called Hope.* Carbondale, IL: Southern Illinois University Press.

Gold, David, Catherine Hobbs, and James Berlin. 2012. "Writing in School and College English." In *A Short History of Writing Instruction,* edited by James J. Murphy, 232–72. Abingdon, England: Routledge.

Gunner, Jeanne. 1994. "Decentering the WPA." *WPA: Writing Program Administration* 18 (1/2): 8–15.

Gunner, Jeanne. 2010. "Checking the Source(book): Supplemental Voices in the Administrative Genre." *Performing Feminism and Administration in Rhetoric and Composition Studies,* edited by Krista Ratcliffe and Rebecca Rickly, 19–30. New York: Hampton.

Hall, David, and Roger Ames. 1998. *Thinking from the Han.* New York: University of New York Press.

Hairston, Maxine. 1985. "Breaking Our Bonds and Reaffirming Our Connections." *College Composition and Communication* 36 (3): 272–82.

Hairston, Maxine. 1988. "Some Speculations About the Future of Writing Programs." *WPA: Writing Program Administration* 11 (3): 9–16.

Hartzog, Carol P. 1986. "Composition and the Academy: A Preliminary Report on AAU Writing Programs" *ADE Bulletin* 83 (Spring): 49–52.

Holbrook, Sue Ellen. 1991. "Women's Work: The Feminizing of Composition" *Rhetoric Review* 9 (2): 201–29.

Johnson, Nan. 2011. "Take Back the Ordinary." In "Rhetorical Historiography and the Octalogs," by Lois Agnew, James Murphy, Cheryl Glenn, Nan Johnson, Jan Swearingen, Richard Leo Enos, Jasper Neal, Linda Ferriera-Buckley, Janice Lauer Rice, Janet M. Atwill, Kathleen Ethel Welch, Roxanne Mountford, Thomas Miller, and Victor J. Vitanza. Special issue, *Rhetoric Review* 3 (3): 241–42.

Jung, Julie Marie. 2009. "Theorizing Service, Servicing Theory." In *Renewing Rhetoric's Relation to Composition: Essays in Honor of Theresa Jarnagin Enos,* edited by Shane Borrowman, Stuart C. Brown, and Thomas Miller, 168–81. Abingdon, England: Routledge.

Leverenz, Carrie. 2010. "What's Ethics Got to Do with It? Feminist Ethics and Administrative Work in Rhetoric and Composition." In *Performing Feminism and Administration in Rhetoric and Composition Studies,* edited by Krista Ratcliffe and Rebecca Rickly, 3–18. New York: Hampton.

L'Eplattenier, Barbara, and Lisa Mastrangelo, eds. 2004. *Historical Studies of Writing Program Administration*. Anderson, SC: Parlor.

Lindblom, Kenneth, and Patricia A. Dunn. 2004. "Cooperative Writing 'Program' Administration at Illinois State Normal U: The Committee on English of 1904–05 and the Influence of Professor J. Rose Colby." In *Historical Studies of Writing Program Administration*, edited by Barbara L'Eplattenier and Lisa Mastrangelo, 37–70. Anderson, SC: Parlor.

Maimon, Elaine. 2014. Keynote Address presented at the American Council of Education Coordinators' Conference, March 9. Email. March 28, 2014.

Maimon, Elaine. 2018. *Learning Academic Change: Vision, Strategy, Transformation*. Sterling, VA: Stylus.

Mastrangelo, Lisa, and Barbara L'Eplattenier. 2004. "'Is It the Pleasure of This Conference to Have Another?' Women's Colleges Meeting and Talking about Writing in the Progressive Era." In *Historical Studies of Writing Program Administration*, edited by Barbara L'Eplattenier and Lisa Mastrangelo, 117–44. Anderson, SC: Parlor.

Mendenhall, Annie. 2014. "The Composition Specialist as Flexible Expert: Identity and Labor in the History of Composition." *College English* 77 (1): 11–31.

McLeod, Susan. 2002. "Moving Up the Administrative Ladder." In *The Writing Program Administrator's Resource: A Guide to Reflective Institutional Practice*, edited by Stuart Brown and Theresa Enos, 113–24. Mahwah, NJ: Lawrence Erlbaum.

McLeod, Susan. 2007. *Writing Program Administration*. Anderson, SC: Parlor.

Miller, Thomas. 2010. *The Evolution of College English: Literacy Studies from the Puritans and the Postmoderns*. Pittsburgh, PA: University of Pittsburgh Press.

Olson, Gary A., and Joseph M. Moxley. 1989. "Directing Freshman Composition: The Limits of Authority." *College Composition and Communication* 40 (1): 51–60.

Phelps, Louise W. 2002. "Turtles All the Way Down: Educating Academic Leaders." In *The Writing Program Administrator's Resource: A Guide to Reflective Institutional Practice*, edited by Stuart Brown and Theresa Enos, 3–40. Mahwah, NJ: Lawrence Erlbaum.

Popken, Randall. 2004. "The WPA as Publishing Scholar: Edwin Hopkins and the Labor and Cost of the Teaching of English." In *Historical Studies of Writing Program Administration*, edited by Barbara L'Eplattenier and Lisa Mastrangelo, 5–22. West Lafayette, IN: Parlor.

Rich, Adrienne. 1979. *On Lies, Secrets, and Silence: Selected Prose 1966–1978*. New York: Norton.

Reid, E. Shelley 2010. "Managed Care: All-Terrain Mentoring and the 'Good Enough' Feminist WPA." In *Performing Feminism and Administration in Rhetoric and Composition Studies*, edited by Krista Ratcliffe and Rebecca Rickly, 125–41. New York: Hampton.

Ritter, Kelly. 2012. *To Know Her Own History: Writing at the Woman's College, 1943–1963*. Pittsburgh, PA: University of Pittsburgh Press.

Rose, Shirley, and Irwin Weiser, eds. 2010. *Going Public: What Writing Programs Learn from Engagement*. Logan: Utah State University Press.

Rose, Shirley, and Irwin Weiser, eds. 2012. *The Writing Program Administrator as Theorist: Making Knowledge Work*. Portsmouth, NH: Heinemann.

Rose, Shirley, Lisa Mastrangelo, and Barbara L'Eplattenier. 2013. "Directing First-Year Writing: The New Limits of Authority." *College Composition and Communication* 65 (1): 43–66.

Russell, David. 2002. *Writing in the Academic Disciplines: A Curricular History*, 2nd ed. Carbondale, IL: Southern Illinois University Press.

Rutgers, Mark. 1997. "Beyond Woodrow Wilson: The Identity of the Study of Public Administration in Historical Perspective." *Administration & Society* 29 (3): 276–300.

Simola, Sheldene, Julian Barling, and Nick Turner. 2012. "Transformational Leadership and Leaders' Mode of Care Reasoning." *Journal of Business Ethics* 108 (2): 229–37.

Skeffington, Julian, Shane Borrowman, and Theresa Enos. 2008. "Living in the Spaces Between: Profiling the Writing Program Administrator." In *The Promise and Perils of Writing Program Administration*, edited by Theresa Enos and Shane Borrowman, 5–20. Anderson, SC: Parlor.

Snyder, Laura Bartlett. 2009. "Feminism and the Problem of Complicity in Writing Program Administrator Work." In *The Writing Program Interrupted: Making Space for Critical Discourse*, edited by Donna Strickland and Jeanne Gunner, 28–40. Portsmouth, NH: Boynton/Cook.

Strickland, Donna. 2011. *The Managerial Unconscious in the History of Composition Studies*. Carbondale: Southern Illinois University Press.

Turkel, Marian C. 2014. "Leading from the Heart: Caring, Love, Peace, and Values Guiding Leadership." *Nursing Science Quarterly* 27 (2): 172–77.

Wu, Hui. 2001. "The Alternative Feminist Discourse of Post-Mao Chinese Writers: A Perspective from the Rhetorical Situation." In *Alternative Rhetorics: Challenges to the Rhetorical Tradition*, edited by Laura Gray-Rosendale and Sibylle Gruber, 219–34. Albany, NY: SUNY Press.

Wu, Hei. 2005. "The Paradigm of Margaret Cavendish: Reading Women's Alternative Rhetorics in a Global Context." In *Calling Cards: Theory and Practice in Studies of Race, Gender, and Culture*, edited by Jacqueline Jones Royster and Ann Marie Mann Simpkins, 171–85. Albany, NY: SUNY Press.

Wu, Hei. 2010. "Post-Mao Chinese Literary Women's Rhetoric Revisited: A Case for an Enlightened Feminist Rhetorical Theory." *College English* 72 (4): 406–23.

12
OTHER WAYS OF MAKING IT
Transcending Traditional Academic Trajectories

Theresa M. Evans, Linda Hanson,
Karen S. Neubauer, and Daneryl Weber

During a conversation at the Conference on College Composition and Communication in 2014, three of us who had been among the same cohort of doctoral students in a rhetoric and composition program began noticing similarities in the stories we were sharing, especially regarding our experiences while seeking degrees and in our subsequent professional lives. We had faced (and continue to face) similar challenges, not only as women but especially as women of "nontraditional" age for being a student. Although we were employed full time, with busy lives and multiple obligations, we had begun interrogating our choices, career paths, and levels of success, and at least one of us was questioning her self-efficacy in the workplace. Striking was not the fact of reflection so much as the similarity in the kinds of questions each woman was asking herself about having "made it"—a subtext of wondering whether she'd gotten where she had hoped to go and whether, indeed, she would ever get there. For perspective, we turned to one of our faculty mentors—a woman we assumed had made it as a "traditional" scholar but who, it turns out, had followed her own meandering path. This article, and the initial research it presents, grew out of that conversation at CCCCs, and was further fueled by our presentations at the 2015 and 2017 Feminisms and Rhetorics conferences and at the 2017 CCCC.[1]

PERCEPTIONS OF NONTRADITIONAL SCHOLARS

In *Women's Ways of Making It in Rhetoric and Composition*, Michelle Ballif, Dianne Davis, and Roxanne Mountford define successful women in the field using the following checklist: PhD, full professors at academic institutions, tenured, well published, cited regularly, contributors of significant work in field, frequent keynote speakers at national conferences, mentors of women in field, achievers of life/work balance (2008, 7). The book is directed to women who aspire to careers in research-oriented institutions, where tenure is the goal and writing a book is the minimum qualification for achieving it. Although Ballif, Davis, and Mountford focus on the unique challenges of women in tenure-track positions in rhetoric and composition, they use traditional, male standards of success in defining "making it."

In a review of the book, Halina Adams and Melissa Ianetta note the narrow focus of that definition.

> Accordingly, the research-related advice focuses on achieving the standard of the single-authored monograph, rather than the challenges facing women faculty at teaching-intensive colleges and universities where the support for conference and research travel can be negligible. Just as a more expansive definition of "making it" may have been desirable, so too the titular category of women might have been opened further. (2008, 146)

Ballif, Davis, and Mountford do acknowledge in their book's introduction that it does not include the experiences of about 80 percent of women in rhetoric and composition—those in non-tenure-track and contingent positions—further noting that "the entire path to a tenure-track position is designed for young men (not middle-aged women—or perhaps any women)" (2008, 3). Our work seeks to examine how one segment of that 80 percent is interrogating male standards and redefining success to work around the rigid expectations of the traditional academic career trajectory. For us, gender also intersects with age, a late start in academia intersects with career expectations, and all are crosscut by economics, family responsibilities, and personal and professional support.

In 2013, Kristin Bivens, Martha McKay Canter, Kirsti Cole, Violet Dutcher, Morgan Gresham, Luisa Rodriguez-Connal, and Eileen Schell argued in "Sisyphus Rolls On: Reframing Women's Ways of 'Making It' in Rhetoric and Composition" that most women *cannot* "make it" as defined by Ballif, Davis, and Mountford, and they question the usefulness of a book focused on traditional tenure-track career paths in rhetoric and composition. In 2018, on the tenth anniversary of their book, Ballif, Davis, and Mountford responded directly to that question, contending that "the current state of the market makes our book more necessary than ever for those who do aspire to that traditional path, where the available positions are few and extraordinarily competitive" (203). They acknowledged that they would revise their book for the current job market and were more open to the idea that "graduate students and junior faculty in the field obviously need to learn and practice strategies for other sorts of successes as well, and they need to be open to other types of rewarding positions, inside and outside of the academy" (203). Yet the state of the market has not motivated departments to reduce or eliminate doctoral programs or to fully respect the work of those outside tenure-line appointments, much less beyond the academy.

In her 1996 study *Gender Roles and Faculty Lives in Rhetoric and Composition*, Theresa Enos tied the perception of rhetoric and composition as "women's work" to its devaluation (2); more than two decades later, not much has changed, especially for women on nontraditional career paths. With shrinking tenure lines, even women pursuing traditional academic career paths have found themselves caught in a job market that resembles a ruthless game of musical chairs, in which the "losers" must settle for contingent or non-tenure-track jobs—or leave academia altogether. In fact, Ballif, Davis, and Mountford—and some of the women they profile—admit in *Women's Ways of Making It* that today's ramped-up publishing expectations required to land that first tenure-track job would have prevented some of our field's stars from getting their first foothold in the field. If defined only by number of tenure-line appointments, that field is shrinking. According to a study conducted in 2011 by the American Association of University Professors, 76.4 percent of instructional staff are contingent faculty, non-tenure-track faculty, or graduate student employees (Barnshaw and Dunietz 2015, 2), with approximately 50.8 percent of those female (18). A survey conducted in 2010 by the Coalition on the Academic Workforce found that 82.9 percent of faculty are contingent (CAW 2012, 5), with 40.9 percent identifying themselves as part-time workers (6). Of part-time workers who identified their gender, 61.9 percent identified as women (7).

In some ways, the three of us occasionally felt our own experiences as nontraditional women in academia substantiated the argument in Susan Miller's essay "The Sad Women in the Basement: Images of Composition Teaching" (1991). Her discussion about the stigma of such feminized jobs—most contingent or non-tenure-track—brings to mind for us images of worn-out cooks and maids who do the tedious, detailed "dirty work" (of teaching multiple undergraduate sections) that keeps the upper-floor inhabitants (tenured faculty and top administrators) comfortable and the overall system functioning more smoothly. The sad women are nameless, shapeless, faceless, and, decidedly, often not young. The "sad women's" expertise is valued only for its role in maintaining the system; it does not justify entry to the upper floors or more respectful framings of the legitimate and necessary work of these invisible spaces. In today's context of reduced state funding, institutions rely more heavily than ever on tuition dollars to fund operating costs; that is, the delivery of undergraduate instruction is now what keeps the lights on. Yet instead of raising the status of instruction, colleges and universities may tend to divert tuition income away from instruction and treat instructors as interchangeable commodities. Further, tenure-line faculty may not be fully aware that service courses taught by graduate students and contingent faculty are often a primary source of funding for their own appointments.

Stephen North's term "teacher lore" describes a similar attitude towards the work of those with practical experience but no official sanctioning of their knowledge making and no official voice within their departments and institutions—a situation further complicated by composition's emerging professionalization and turf wars with related disciplines, which continue to challenge its status at some institutions (1987, 21, 23). Further, if they see themselves as toiling away alone, these workers lose the power of collaboration and visibility. Although they may range from newly minted scholars to those winding down careers, their perspectives, voices, and research are important and valid. As the largest and fastest-growing segment of the postsecondary workforce, contingent faculty represent the academy at the classroom level and, therefore wield powerful influence over millions of undergraduates (Coalition 2012, 6), but sheer numbers do not translate into institutional power.

Given an arduous journey to a seemingly inauspicious fate, we were curious about the reasons other women had for choosing to pursue graduate study later in life, what kinds of support they received, what obstacles they faced, and whether they would do it all again. We wondered whether the risks of graduate study paid off for them and how they defined success. We were curious about how nontraditional academic women find ways of making a space for themselves in the field of higher education and whether they can find ways of making their voices heard. We wanted to learn how nontraditional academics find ways of making it in the academy—on their own terms and as active agents—rather than passively hoping the system will change or resigning themselves to the way things are.

PILOT SURVEY: WHO IS NONTRADITIONAL?

In order to explore women's ways of making it on nontraditional paths—off the tenure track, in midlife, and/or after they've been successful in other careers—we designed a pilot survey. Immediately, however, we ran into the questions of how exactly to define nontraditional.

Arguably, all women in academia are—historically, at least—nontraditional (Archbald 2011, 14); ultimately, we came to define nontraditional women in academia broadly as those who spent time outside academia between receiving their undergraduate degree and pursuing an advanced degree. Defining an age threshold is also problematic given that degrees such as clinical and professional doctorates are traditionally begun after significant work experience (16); however, we noted that the National Science Foundation's Survey of Earned Doctorates (SED) for 2014 puts the median age of doctorate recipients at 31.4 for males and 31.9 for women. The 2014 SED reports that 41.5 percent of women earning doctorates in 2014 were age thirty or younger and 29.9 percent were thirty-one to thirty-five. After age thirty-five the numbers drop significantly: 11.5 percent were ages thirty-six to forty, 6.2 percent were ages forty-one to forty-five, and 10.2 percent were over forty-five (National Science Foundation 2015).

For our study, based on a time to completion of five to nine years,[2] we set the cutoff for nontraditional student as women who entered doctoral programs in their thirties and beyond. Of those responding to our survey question about what decade of life they decided to go back to school for an advanced degree, 55 percent were in their thirties, 33 percent in their forties, 11 percent in their fifties, and two responders made the choice in their sixties or beyond. Although early doctoral students studied full time, today's graduate students often hold jobs and attend class part time (Offerman 2011, 23); 76 percent of respondents to our survey said they were or had been full-time students. At first, we also leaned toward the assumption that most nontraditional academic women would be in non-tenure-track positions; however, the survey revealed that the terms *nontraditional* and *non-tenure-track* are not interchangeable, even though a considerable segment of nontraditional academic women are employed in non-tenure-track jobs.

The survey included fourteen questions (see appendix 12.A) and was disseminated through a range of channels in October 2015, including the listserv of the Coalition of Women Scholars in the History of Rhetoric and Composition, the listserv of writing program administrators, and the Writing Center Mailing List. Each researcher also shared the survey with members of her own institution and with friends and colleagues who then passed it on. Within those parameters, respondents were self-selected and anonymous. We received a total of 270 responses at the beginning of the survey and a consistent 207 responses by the end (December 2015). Sixty percent of responders identified as nontraditional female students pursuing a doctorate; 48 percent identified as master's students (more than one response was possible for each person). A vast majority of respondents (63 percent)[3] had pursued or were pursuing degrees in English, rhetoric and composition, writing, or literature, with the balance in counseling, education, communication, and miscellaneous degrees such as nursing and history.[4]

Several aspects of the responses seemed striking, particularly the overall positive evaluation women assigned to their experiences. About 96 percent had finished or planned to finish their degrees, 68 percent had been motivated to go back to school to find a more satisfying career, and 49 percent had desired better employment. Although nearly 20 percent had incurred debts of more than $60,000, most respondents, a full 88 percent, stated they would do it again if they had the chance. Not surprisingly, financial challenges were the number one obstacle for women trying to finish their degree. Lack of time, which we had considered a given in designing the barrier question, was raised as an issue in many of the comments.

In this article, we examine a few of the survey responses after we first define and interrogate the label of *nontraditional* in higher education. Next, we discuss the risks economics and ageism pose as nontraditional faculty try to make their way within the academy. Finally, we consider women's own voices in discipline knowledge making and their importance in shaping the academy as a space where multiple perspectives are heard and truly valued. Recognition already exists that such perspectives have received little attention to date. For example, a September 2014 article published in *Inside Higher Ed* reports, "Kiernan Mathews, director and principal investigator at the Collaborative on Academic Careers in Higher Education, said there's scant data on this corner of the professoriate: older adjuncts" (Flaherty 2014). We conclude with a plan to go beyond anecdotal evidence and the initial survey responses to conduct further research that makes way for the voices of nontraditional women throughout academia to be acknowledged.

DEFINING "NONTRADITONAL"

According to Douglas Archbald, the term *traditional doctorate* has "two meanings: one fixed and one relative" (2011, 16). The fixed term, emerging from long-standing European traditions, particularly the German model of "scholarly inquiry and research" (9), referred to a doctoral degree in traditional academic (as opposed to professional) disciplines. Studies took place in traditional structures: in an on-campus residence with subsidized housing; in brick-and-mortar classrooms, laboratories, libraries, and offices; and in student centers. Coursework for the degree often took two to three years, plus several more to write the dissertation, often in conjunction with a teaching assistantship. The traditional student was a young adult early in his career, typically a white male who continued on to graduate school directly or shortly after obtaining his bachelor's degree (a term the *Oxford Dictionary of the Middle Ages* traces to vernaculars signifying a single male) (2010).

The term *nontraditional*, therefore, can apply to the degree itself—with the wider range of possible fields of study opened up over the course of the last century—and also to the student in pursuit of that degree. As Archbald points out, "As the number and variety of degrees, programs, pedagogies, and institutions has grown, the distinction between the traditional and nontraditional doctorate has become more blurry and multi-dimensional" (2011, 15–16). With broad societal changes over the last century, the demographics of higher education, too, have shifted. In the 1920s, roughly 12 percent of advanced-degree seekers were female; in 2009, approximately 46 percent were female, according to the National Science Foundation (National Science Foundation 2009, quoted in Archbald 2011). In rhetoric and composition, those numbers are significantly higher; the Survey of Earned Doctorates for 2017 reports that 67 percent of rhetoric and composition doctorates were awarded to women, even as total doctorates received by women rose only slightly to 46.6 percent (National Science Foundation 2015, table 16).

We question whether the term *nontraditional* even provides a useful distinction, not only in terms of gender and age but also in terms of characteristics such as race, areas of study, and path to completion. We also question how many career paths follow a traditional, linear model. *Nontraditional* may be more descriptive of many new scholars today—continuums of young and old, male and female, white and "not white"—as opposed to what retiring tenured scholars are not. Meanwhile, the path to tenure has not only remained linear, but it has also become relentlessly narrow, with fewer points of entry. Under these conditions, we argue that validating nontraditional paths also requires us to redefine what success means in rhetoric and composition. In a review of the edited collection *Rewriting Success in Rhetoric and Composition Careers* by Amy Goodburn, Donna LeCourt, and Carrie Leverenz, Beth L. Hewitt suggests that efforts to legitimize non-tenure-track and nonacademic paths within rhetoric and composition often "trip over an implicit core assumption that those alternative choices are *not* legitimate and therefore require traditional academics to legitimize them" (2015, 232).

Further, she suggests that the editors' term *"alternative paths"* signals that such work is still perceived as illegitimate, as functioning outside the discipline (233). Likewise, we wonder whether the term *nontraditional student* also functions as a mark of illegitimacy.

A more recent edited collection, *Women's Professional Lives in Rhetoric and Composition*, does resist linear trajectories to focus on "the circuitous ways professional and personal commitments have evolved and on the intersectionality of identities regardless of position on a continuum from greater to lesser privilege or marginalization" (Flynn and Bourelle 2018, 3). Yet despite their circuitous routes, most of the authors in the collection are scholars who have achieved positions closer to the center than to what the editors term the "periphery of the profession" (2).

Certainly, the meandering paths of women who decide, at whatever point in their life journey, to return to school for an advanced degree are worth exploring, whether they remain on the periphery or find their way to the center of the profession. As we dug deeper into this inquiry, we began to realize that nontraditional female students not only demonstrate a focus on internal rewards and emotional over financial satisfaction—a tendency, we note, that can lend itself to exploitation—but also great courage in taking risks and pursuing dreams that may pay great personal dividends, whether or not those dividends are recognized and validated by the external world, including in their own academic institutions and disciplines. We are encouraged that many of the respondents stated a love for what they were doing, as well as a deep emotional satisfaction with the paths they were on; however, we do acknowledge this response may in part be due to the self-selective process of the survey.

RISKS AND REWARDS

Some women go back to graduate school to gain skills that will help them get higher-paying jobs outside academia; for those whose goal is to become part of academia, money is not the primary reward, but it poses a considerable risk/reward consideration. Not everyone who completes a doctoral degree finds a tenure-track job, and that risk may be compounded by graduating long past the traditional age for academic job seekers or by taking out student loans.

It's an established mythology that those who work in academia accept reduced wages to do the work they love, but left unacknowledged is that most tenure-line faculty earn a relatively stable living compared to faculty who must wait each year to find out whether their contracts are being renewed or who must scramble each semester to cobble together teaching assignments from several institutions at subpar rates. The myth that tenured faculty are overpaid persists, even though 2014–2015 report data published by the American Association of University Professors (AAUP) show professors make less on average than most equivalent nonacademics (Barnshaw and Dunietz 2015, 12).[5] Still, the same report shows a mean full-professor salary of more than $116,000, plus benefits (11), while comparable wage/benefit data for full-time non-tenure-track and part-time faculty are difficult to come by, especially for the latter, for whom pay is per course rather than per person.

The Coalition on the Academic Workforce reports a median income of $22,400 for adjunct instructors with a doctorate, annualized with a load of eight classes over an academic year (CAW 2012, 31). Meanwhile, a full-time, year-round worker with a doctorate earns a median income of $91,900 (31). This disparity is further exacerbated for faculty on contingent appointments because many pay their own professional, office, and healthcare expenses (14) and are not reimbursed for class preparation and administrative time, which the Internal Revenue Service estimates at an additional 1.25 hours for every hour of teaching (17). Clearly, although tenure is under attack,[6] it still does, for the most part, protect faculty who have obtained it from the vagaries of the typical job market experienced by workers who are not protected by a union. Perhaps this security is why "desire for better employment" and "more satisfying career" were the top-rated reasons for pursuing graduate study selected by respondents to our survey. As one woman added, "[I] recognized the only way to have a tenure track job was with [a] terminal degree." Today, however, a doctorate is no guarantee of a tenure-track job. With a glutted and gutted job market, non-tenure-track positions that used to require an MA are now stating preferences for a PhD.

Low wages for non-tenure-track faculty cannot be explained away by recent hard economic times—they are a long tradition for women and for fields highly represented by women, such as rhetoric and composition. In "The Lure of 'Easy' Psychic Income," Katherine V. Wills contends that "psychic income" is used as an excuse for paying contingent workers low wages (2004, 205), and a long-time assumption is that respect for the work—as perceived by those outside academia—is psychic compensation for the lack of livable wages. Another long-time assumption is that contingent faculty, especially those with part-time assignments, get—or should get—their basic economic needs met elsewhere, either from a full-time job with another employer or from a partner. Eileen Schell argues, "In fact, many institutions feel it is acceptable to hire large numbers of women at the contingent ranks because it is still assumed that they have male partners who are supporting them financially, a dubious claim in a society where half of all marriages end in divorce and where many adult women are single" (2017, xv).

This is not to say the only path to job satisfaction is a tenure-track position. In her 2011 study, "Non-Tenure Track Women Faculty: Opening the Door," Jeni Hart contends, "Satisfaction is not a proxy for fair treatment, and to systematically treat one category of faculty (and in this case, one that is highly feminized) as marginal is unethical, and possibly even illegal" (2001, 118). A 2001 study of non-tenure-track faculty at one research university found that non-tenure-track faculty see their status as a class issue rather than a gender issue (Harper et al. 2001). On the face of it, that seems plausible; however, another study published that same year by Laura W. Perna focused on the relationship between family responsibilities and status as a faculty employee. Perna found that women hold a higher percentage of part-time non-tenure-track faculty positions, not necessarily out of preference but because full-time positions are unavailable to them (2001, 604). Her findings suggest that the economics of academia are issues of both class and gender. In any case, comments in our survey bear out such assertions and demonstrate that little has changed in the intervening years. One respondent lamented, "Faculty looked down on me as an adjunct and were verbal about it." Another put it more bluntly: "Part-time contingent faculty status sucks."

How does being a nontraditional female student factor into the economics of academia? Our survey produced two results in particular that surprised us: tenure-track jobs are in the realm of possibility for nontraditional academics, and most of the nontraditional academic women we surveyed would choose to pursue their degrees again, if given a second chance. Approximately 29 percent of respondents indicated they currently held or had in the past held tenure-track positions; 17 percent were fully tenured. While less than one-third of nontraditional academic women surveyed had held a position on the tenure track, 88 percent of respondents said that if they had to do it again, they would still pursue their graduate studies. This result may be partially due to the fact that some respondents hadn't yet completed their degree or had not yet given up hope of finding tenure-track work. Based on the comments explaining why they would repeat their graduate training, which for some was a "hellish experience," it seems apparent that these women were motivated by intellectual challenge, personal growth, and a desire to make a difference. A few indicated that they landed jobs that paid well, and a few others said they were financially worse off than before; however, most seemed to indicate that their academic jobs neither improved nor harmed their financial situation but greatly improved their work life and intellectual life.

More troubling was the financial cost of getting the degree. Approximately 54 percent of respondents graduated either debt free or with less than $20,000 of debt; however, 43 percent of nontraditional academic women reported debts between $20,000 and $60,000, with 18 percent owing $60,000 or more. The National Science Foundation (NSF) reveals that fellowships and research and teaching assistantships continue to be the most significant source of funds (2015, table 35). Fewer doctoral students rely on loans or personal earnings and savings than in past years, while fellowships or grants have remained stable since 2004 (5). NSF figures from 2017 are similar, indicating that 78.9 percent of doctoral recipients had funding from assistantships and fellowships (2018, table 35). However, older graduate students are more likely to be financially responsible for themselves *and* supporting dependent children who may be pursuing their own degrees. Although some parents may have saved to fund their children's undergraduate studies, few likely had the foresight to set aside funds for their own graduate studies. Kiplingers reports that most financial aid programs have no age restrictions but cautions older students to consider how their shorter career life, compared to those who graduate in their twenties and thirties, will affect their ability to pay back loans before they retire (Block 2013).

The costs of pursuing graduate work as a nontraditional student can be high if the student does not have both the emotional and financial support of a partner: One respondent said flatly, "It ruined things. My kids, my finances, and my job chances." Another respondent expressed ambivalence, explaining both why she would and would not want to go through the process again: "I would do it again for the intellectual stimulation and rewards of working in academia. I wouldn't do it again because of the burden of student loans and because I am missing years of being able to be with my husband during his retirement." Another respondent acknowledged the financial challenges, but she found the option of not pursuing graduate work even riskier: "The conflict and emotional, economic and health-related consequences of the PhD process are nothing to the loss of my own identity as a thinking person and a writer if I accept the constraints placed on me by age, gender, and class-related expectations." One comment in particular emphasized both the risks and rewards nontraditional academic women face: "Returning to school later in life has significantly impacted my retirement options, and the difficulty of finding employment has severely limited my options. On the other hand, I truly love teaching and I am lucky to work with amazing colleagues."

Constraints of time were mentioned multiple times as a risk factor of pursuing graduate study. We had not overtly included it in survey question 13 (appendix 12.A) as a category among obstacles to degree completion, but it was frequently added to the other/comments category. We had assumed that time constraints were a given with graduate work and that the idea of time constraints was satisfactorily embedded within the available responses. Comments related to time were frequent enough that we recognized it should have had its own category; these comments ranged from simply the word "time" to those about the stress of balancing demands of school, work, and family. One respondent referred to the opportunity cost of graduate work, which emphasizes the risk of the time lost to the undertaking at a point in life when recovery from failure is more difficult. Another said, "Time would have passed anyway," indicating that the potential for reward and the risk of missing a last-chance opportunity outweighed any other opportunity costs.

Overall, the nontraditional academic women in our study seemed to be motivated primarily by the intellectual stimulation of academic work, and most of them entered the process with their eyes wide open about the financial risk, given that so many of those surveyed said they would do it all again. On the other hand, the risk for some was likely mitigated either by a lower dependence on their jobs as the primary source of monetary income or a willingness to accept a possibly lower standard of living to do the work they love. For those who depended on academic work as their sole income, especially those who borrowed heavily to pay for their education, lower wages could not be offset by love of the work.

AMBIGUITIES OF AGEISM

Universities usually have mission statements that promote goals of diversity and inclusion, so nontraditional students often assume, perhaps incorrectly, that pursuing a career in academia will help them avoid age discrimination in the workplace. Ageism is a raw fact of life in the private sector, but in academia it may take a different twist because the tenure system tends to protect older scholars: the ageism issue is often cited by younger women, who may sometimes feel they are condescended to because of their youth, irrespective of their position on the tenure track. Ageism in academia is often defined as the young untenured scholar versus the old tenured scholar, where age is equated with respect and stability. Young, in academia terms, is defined in a much "older" sense than in the private sector, as those with PhDs in the early stages of their academic careers and on the traditional trajectory are often in their thirties rather than their twenties. Marc Bousquet notes, "Taking all academic fields together, doctoral degrees are awarded around age thirty-three, but the average age of those winning tenure-stream jobs is thirty-nine" (2004, 1). In academia then, age (at least when accompanied by tenure) is protected and respected.

Perhaps existing law explains why conversations about diversity in academia seldom pertain to variations in age. The Amendment of the Age Discrimination in Employment Act of 1967, signed by President Reagan in 1986, extended protection to tenured faculty over seventy as of 1994. With the removal of a mandated retirement age for tenured faculty, universities tend not to view age as a category of discrimination or an area where additional diversity is desired. That protection from ageism does not extend to nontenured faculty or to older workers trying to obtain a tenure-track position. There are legal, if questionable, ways to keep older workers (and, increasingly, a majority of workers altogether) out of the tenured realms of academia: eliminate positions or make them nontenure track; request that applicants have narrow and trendy research specialties older academics are less likely to possess; screen CVs based on evidence of graduation dates and work experience outside academia. As only one example, Stephen Winzenburg argues in the *Chronicle of Higher Education* that the use of the word "energy" in job posts is "actually code for 'younger' or at least 'not older'" (2012). The rationales for such coded language often betray discriminatory practices, such as claims that young scholars are a better long-term investment, have more in common with students, can "grow" into their roles, and do not further skew the age distribution of faculty towards middle age and older.

Nontraditional women in academia add a further complication to the binary of protected age versus vulnerable youth. Karen Kelsky, a former tenured professor and now career consultant to academic job seekers, points out that "for those who are just finishing their Ph.D.'s [*sic*] or who are struggling on the job market, or enduring year after year of adjuncting, at an age beyond the 'approved' trajectory, ageism and the pressures of age are real and urgent indeed" (2012). Their age, life experience, and work experience outside academia make them less attractive to academia, and their experience may grant them little respect. For example, during a workshop on writing curriculum vitae, one of us was advised to remove all nonacademic work experience from her curriculum vitae, despite two decades as a professional writer and editor in corporate contexts.

The "youth" of nontraditional students, in terms of being in the early stages of an academic career, becomes a liability because their chronological age matches neither the youthful inexperience of their cohorts nor the expectations of what scholars their age should already know and have accomplished. They are neither the rising generation nor the respected scholars of the field. In "Profile of the Nontraditional Doctoral Degree Student," Michael Offerman notes that nontraditional students are more likely to want to take advantage of their professional experience and more likely to be interested in applied, rather than theoretical, research (2011, 27). They may see faculty advisors as colleagues and mentors rather than as instructors (24). One respondent to our survey, who was in her midforties, commented on the disconnect between her age and her status as student: "The dynamic between me and my professors is odd. I'm older than some of them and I actually have more teaching experience than many of them." Another respondent said, "It was hard to fit in with my peers who were younger. My instructors were about my age, and while I would say I got along with them, I still did not quite fit in." Nontraditional students and faculty who do not fit the prescribed career trajectory or match the perceived disciplinary expertise expected of their age group are often vulnerable, not respected. Because most nontraditional students and faculty are women, this becomes an issue of both age and gender.

Interestingly enough, the topic of age discrimination did not come up often in our survey, perhaps because respondents accepted it as a possibility when they embarked on their course of study. More often, such discrimination may be muddled in with attitudes about gender, as well as about academic insiders and outsiders. For example, discrimination against older students and non-tenure-track faculty is sometimes based on the resistance those women may express toward accepted mantras of their academic discipline. Kelsky describes academia as a cult with rigid expectations: "What I have observed in my work with clients is that older students are more resistant to the indoctrination process than younger students. Their identities are more fully formed, and they have more years of previous values and habits that have to be displaced to make room for the new ones" (2012).

Another possibility is that students with practical experience may discover their contributions to the academic conversation are not welcome, and their attempts to interrogate academic theories may be dismissed. Women who persist and complete their doctoral work still face challenges because their mode of critical thinking is not always in line with expectations. Kelsky states, "The process of indoctrination of older students is more likely to be incomplete and tentative. And that has serious consequences for the older PhD as end product of the system" (2012). Whether or not particular disciplines, programs, or professors are willing to entertain the unique perspectives of nontraditional students, as they encourage those students to also consider multiple perspectives, challenges to academic ways of thinking are not always welcomed, even though such challenges may represent badly needed fresh perspectives. One respondent to our survey noted such emotional and intellectual challenges as one of her greatest obstacles to completing her PhD: "I did not realize that a doctoral program would require us all to think alike and spout the same rhetoric—I thought, idealistically, that we were supposed to think for ourselves—as an older, independent woman, I found this nonsense to be most difficult." A nontraditional academic woman may not fit the traditional career pattern or thinking pattern of academia: she makes her way speaking academia as a second language, and she may never lose her accent.

On the other hand, the nontraditional academic woman is intellectually curious, and, having fought through the obstacles, is ready to pay it forward to the next generation. A respondent who says she would make the journey all over again stated, "I learned to respect my own intellectual abilities. I have found that many undergraduate women that I teach likewise doubt their own intellectual abilities and I am glad that I am now in a position to nurture them—for whatever they choose to do." As a field, rhetoric and composition should consider itself fortunate that such women bring new energy, emotional depth and maturity, and fresh perspectives not in spite of their age. but because of it.

DECISION-MAKING VERSUS KNOWLEDGE-MAKING

Unfortunately, what is impressive on a resume may count for little on a CV, especially in an academic hierarchy built on the foundation of tenure and in which some disciplines hold higher institutional status than others. In our survey, several respondents self-identified in their comments as writing center directors/coordinators or writing program administrators. On the surface, positions like these that require deep disciplinary knowledge and significant management skills might seem especially appropriate for women who can build on skills honed outside academia. But as Carrie Leverenz points out in her discussion of feminist ethics and rhetoric and composition administrative work, the academic interest in advancing the knowledge base and status of the discipline, promoting social justice, and improving the institution often do not jibe with institutional goals of staying on budget, managing personnel, and maintaining the status quo (2010, 4). Nontraditional academics may seem to possess the skills to efficiently meet the latter expectations, leaving them more time to pursue research; however, academic hierarchy often demands such an administrative position be tenure line. Depending on the institution, scholarship related to writing center or writing program management may not be weighted as heavily in promotion and tenure as other research, meaning a tenure-track faculty member who takes on the additional administrative responsibilities does so at the peril of their career.

There is also an issue of administrative status at the institutional level, especially in a field of study like rhetoric and composition, which reached academic and scholarly maturity only in the last few decades and is still considered a service discipline, even within some English departments (North 2011, 12). Writing center and writing program administrators spend most of their time working with those who have the least institutional power: instructors and students. Meanwhile, control over the larger decisions about a center or program's future, and guiding assumptions about how the job should be done, are located higher up the chain of academic command (Leverenz 2010, 14). Gender differences may influence expectations as much here as they do in the business world, where the traditional masculine archetype of a firm, tough, independent leader can be seen as more efficient than the image of the caring, service-oriented negotiator often associated with female administrators. The latter can take time away from teaching and research and "attract responsibility, not rewards" (Barr-Ebest 1995, 66, quoted in Leverenz 2010, 15). Efforts to be more inclusive and give voice to those who have little institutional status, such as teaching assistants and contingent faculty, can be met with resistance by those who see such invitations as unpaid service work (16). Competing understandings and expectations are evident in comments from our survey, where one respondent wrote, "I love my job directing a writing center," and another bemoaned, "Working for a for-profit in a smaller writing center absolutely sucks. I have to get out of here."

One respondent described her role as writing center administrator as a staff position and added that she was a contingent faculty member at another university. This combination is an example of nontraditional opportunities for academic careers that take advantage of the decision- and knowledge-making skills older scholars have built over time, which include other staff opportunities for those with advanced degrees, such as leadership roles in faculty-development centers. While small institutions often rely on faculty members to provide their own development opportunities, 65–70 percent of doctoral and research universities support larger departments that conduct scholarship of teaching and learning, which assist faculty in developing their teaching expertise (Cook and Marincovich 2010, 277). One of us found her way onto this off-tenure-track path, and while it may not provide the stability of tenure, it affords many of the rewards shared by respondents to our survey.

CONCLUSION

As stated above, the generally positive responses to the survey leave us with hope. Research shows emotional connection is crucial to student success, not to mention to one's own personal fulfillment, and a number of women who responded to this survey spoke in terms of a strong emotional connection to the work they were doing: "I like my job"; "[Going to graduate school] was very rewarding on both an intellectual and emotional level. It gave me, not only confidence in what I can accomplish, but also security that I will be doing something that I love in my future"; "It was hard. The hardest thing I have ever done. But, I LOVE my job. I cannot imagine having to try making a satisfying future on the path I was on before going back to school"; "I love what I'm doing. I hated what I was doing before. The tradeoff is worth it"; and simply, "I love this work." In other words, what our respondents valued most—more than money, more than recognition or success—was the emotional and intellectual satisfaction that comes from doing fulfilling work one loves. By that measure, nearly 90 percent of respondents were "making it" in ways that have yet to be fully validated, recognized, and rewarded, challenging a system that must go beyond valuing traditional ways of measuring success.

In their landmark book, *Women's Ways of Knowing*, Mary Belenky, Blythe McVicker Clinchy, Nancy Rule Goldberger, and Jill Mattuck Tarule emphasize the importance of women making sense of their experiences outside patriarchal conceptual schemes that marginalize or erase them as outside the accepted way of knowing (1986, 203), such as a fixed-term traditional doctorate. Resistance to preconceived notions of the "right" path to a doctorate or the "right" path for a career seems especially strong among women who return to college years after earning an undergraduate degree. These older graduate students already see themselves as "knowers" rather than "potential knowers" awaiting confirmation of their knowledge at graduation (195).

Jeni Hart notes the limited research on non-tenure-track faculty, and she calls for further research, especially of women in such positions:

"Given the clustering of women in these positions and the degree to which they have become a significant portion of the instructional workforce in academe, it is critical that the work life experiences of these women are better understood in order to create and/or maintain a climate for academic success" (2001, 97). Scholarship on the experiences of nontraditional female faculty—both on and off the tenure track—also still must be written. Our goal in pursuing this research is to focus on the experiences of nontraditional academic women in rhetoric and composition in order to get a fuller picture of their life experiences, how they see themselves, and how they perceive their work, whether or not their work is externally validated.

APPENDIX 12.A

COVER MESSAGE

Dear colleagues,
I am writing to ask that you share this survey with female students and faculty at your institutions. We would like to collect responses from women who attended or who are attending graduate school in their 30s, 40s, and beyond. Please forgive any duplicate postings with other listservs.

The survey explores the life circumstances, conditions, and challenges of women who are or were graduate students of nontraditional age. The survey consists of 12 questions and should not take more than 5–10 minutes to complete. Survey responses are completely anonymous.

Survey results will be presented at the upcoming Feminist Rhetorics Conference 2015 and may also serve as the basis for further publication.

Here is the survey link: https://purdue.qualtrics.com/SE/?SID=SV_0NRKNekmA5Qxl5P

If you have any questions, please contact us: Tess Evans (evanstm3@miamioh.edu), Karen Neubauer (neubauer@purdue.edu), or Dani Weber (dweber@sunysullivan.edu).
Thanks for your time.

Greetings!
We are group of nontraditional academic women gathering information to construct a more accurate picture of the life situations of nontraditional women in higher education.

All information will be kept confidential and used as research data. The entire survey should not take longer than 5–10 minutes.

In order to help us, please answer the questions below. Provide as much detail as you like in the comment boxes, and choose or type "No

Response" for any question you do not wish to answer. You will have the opportunity to provide your email address for follow-up at the end of the survey, but all responses will remain anonymous.

The first question asks if you consent to participate in the survey; please answer it, even if you decline, because this answer is also data.

If you have any questions, or need assistance completing the survey, contact Tess Evans (evanstm3@miamioh.edu), Karen Neubauer (neubauer@purdue.edu), or Dani Weber (dweber@sunysullivan.edu) to assist you.

Thank you for participating in our survey, and please feel free to share this link with anyone else who might be interested in taking part. https://purdue.qualtrics.com/SE/?SID=SV_0NRKNekmA5Qxl5P

CONSENT FORM:

Do you consent to participate in the survey? Y/N [N skips to thank you at end of survey]

SURVEY QUESTIONS:

1. I am / was a nontraditional female student in pursuit of the following degree (check all that apply):
   - ❏ MA
   - ❏ PhD
   - ❏ No response

2. I am / was (check all that apply):
   - ❏ a full-time student
   - ❏ a part-time student
   - ❏ No response

3. In what field of study is your advanced degree? (Or type "No response.")

4. I have finished my degree: [No skips to #5]
   - ❏ Yes
   - ❏ No
   - ❏ No response

5. I plan on finishing my degree.
   - ❏ Yes
   - ❏ No
   - ❏ No response

6. In what decade of your life did you decide to go back to school for an advanced degree?
   - ❏ 30s
   - ❏ 40s
   - ❏ 50s
   - ❏ 60s or beyond
   - ❏ No response

7. I have served in the following positions (check all that apply):
   - ❏ Graduate assistant
   - ❏ Part-time contingent faculty
   - ❏ Full-time contingent faculty (contract faculty)
   - ❏ Non-tenure-track faculty
   - ❏ Tenure-track faculty
   - ❏ Tenured faculty
   - ❏ Other (administrative, staff, etc.)
   - ❏ No response
   - ❏ Comments

8. Why did you decide to go back to school? Check all that apply. Please feel free to comment on your reasons for seeking an advanced degree.
   - ❏ desire for better employment
   - ❏ job loss
   - ❏ more satisfying career
   - ❏ long-term dream
   - ❏ lifetime learning
   - ❏ age of children
   - ❏ change in marital status
   - ❏ No response
   - ❏ Other/comments

9. What is/was your perceived level of support (emotional, financial, etc.) during the pursuit of your degree from family members, peers, colleagues and friends? [Drop-down scale]
   - ❏ None 1
   - ❏ Little 2
   - ❏ Some 3
   - ❏ High 4
   - ❏ Very high 5
   - ❏ No response

10. What is/was your perceived level of professional support (job-search advice, preparing for interviews, publishing, etc.) during the pursuit of your degree from your degree-granting institution? [Drop-down scale]
    - ❏ None 1
    - ❏ Little 2
    - ❏ Some 3
    - ❏ High 4
    - ❏ Very high 5
    - ❏ No response

11. How much total debt did/will you incur to obtain your degree?
    - ❏ None
    - ❏ Under $20,000
    - ❏ Under $40,000
    - ❏ Under $60,000
    - ❏ $60,000 or more
    - ❏ No response

12. What are/were the greatest obstacles for you to the completion of your degree (check all that apply, and discuss as you wish)?
    - ❏ Intellectual challenges
    - ❏ Emotional health
    - ❏ Financial challenges
    - ❏ Physical health
    - ❏ Childcare
    - ❏ Family relationships
    - ❏ Relationships with cohorts
    - ❏ Relationships with professors, advisors, mentors, etc.
    - ❏ No response
    - ❏ Other/comments

13. If you had to do it again, would you? Why or why not?
    - ❏ Yes
    - ❏ No
    - ❏ No response
    - ❏ Comments

14. If you would be willing to participate in a follow-up interview, please email your contact information to: nontradstudy@gmail.com

END-OF-SURVEY MESSAGE:
Thank you. Please share the following survey link with anyone you think might be interested in participating: https://purdue.qualtrics.com/SE /?SID=SV_0NRKNekmA5Qxl5P

NOTES

1. Our knowledge-making efforts to this point are focused through, but not exclusive to, the lens of composition and related English studies.
2. Chris Golde and George Walker put the average time to degree for an English PhD at nine years (2006, 352).
3. The number of responses to individual survey questions varied because responders were always given the option to not answer a question. For example, there were 234 responses to the question, "In what field of study is your advanced degree?"
4. The question about field of study for the advanced degree was open-ended, and some respondents identified more than one discipline.
5. These numbers are based on occupations that are full-time, require a doctorate or other advanced degree, do not require prior work experience in a related occupation or on-the-job training, and offer historically stable, long-term employment (Barnshaw and Dunietz 2015, 11).
6. For example, legislation has been introduced in Wisconsin (Flaherty 2015, "Wisconsin"), Iowa, and Missouri demanding the elimination of tenure in publicly funded institutions (Flaherty 2017).

WORKS CITED

Adams, Halina, and Melissa Ianetta. 2008. Review of *Women's Ways of Making It in Rhetoric and Composition*, by Michelle Ballif, Diane Davis, and Roxanne Mountford. *Composition Studies* 36 (2):144–47.

AAUP: American Association of University Professors. 2018. "The Annual Report on the Economic Status of the Profession, 2017–2018." *Academe* 104 (2). Washington, DC: AAUP.

Archbald, Douglas. 2011. "The Emergence of The Nontraditional Doctorate: A Historical Overview." *New Directions for Adult & Continuing Education* 129: 7–19. Education Source. doi.org/10.1002/ace.396.

Ballif, Michelle, Dianne Davis, and Roxanne Mountford. 2008. *Women's Ways of Making It in Rhetoric and Composition*. Abingdon, England: Routledge.

Ballif, Michelle, Diane Davis, and Roxanne Mountford. 2018. "Here We Go Again: More Ways of 'Making It,' Circa 2018." Review of *Women's Professional Lives in Rhetoric and Composition: Choice, Chance, and Serendipity*, edited by Elizabeth A. Flynn and Tiffany Bourelle. *Composition Studies* 46 (2): 203–11.

Barnshaw, John, and Samuel Dunietz. 2015. "Busting the Myths: The Annual Report on the Economic Status of the Profession, 2014–15." *Academe* 101 (2). www.aaup.org/sites /default/files/files/2015salarysurvey/zreport.pdf. Accessed 18 January 2021.

Barr-Ebest, Sally. 1995. "Gender Differences in Writing Program Administration." *WPA: Writing Program Administration* 18 (3): 53–73.

Belenky, Mary, Blythe McVicker Clinchy, Nancy Rule Goldberger, and Jill Mattuck Tarule. 1997. *Women's Ways of Knowing: The Development of Self, Voice, and Mind*. New York: Basic Books.

Bivens, Kristin, Martha McKay Canter, Kirsti Cole, Violet Dutcher, Morgan Gresham, Luisa Rodriguez-Connal, and Eileen Schell. 2013. "Sisyphus Rolls On: Reframing Women's Ways of 'Making It' in Rhetoric and Composition." *Harlot: A Revealing Look at the Arts of Persuasion*, 10. harlotofthearts.org/index.php/harlot/article/view/119/141. Accessed 18 January 2021.

Block, Sandra. 2013. "Financial Aid for Older Adults Going Back to School." *Kiplinger*, May 31. www.kiplinger.com/article/college/T042-C000-S002-game-plan-financial-aid-older-adults-back-school.html. Accessed 18 January 2021.

Bousquet, Marc. 2004. "Introduction." *Tenured Bosses and Disposable Teachers: Writing Instruction in the Managed University*, edited by Marc Bousquet, Tony Scott, and Leo Parascondola, 1–10. Carbondale: IL: Southern Illinois University Press.

CAW: Coalition on the Academic Workforce. June 2012. *A Portrait of Part-Time Faculty Members: A Summary of Findings on Part-Time Respondents to the Coalition on the Academic Workforce Survey of Contingent Faculty Members and Instructors*. CAW. http://www.academicworkforce.org/CAW_portrait_2012.pdf. Accessed 19 December 2020.

Cook, Constance Ewing, and Michele Marincovich. 2010. "Effective Practices at Research Universities: The Productive Pairing of Research and Teaching." In *A Guide to Faculty Development*, edited by Kay J. Gillespie and Douglas L. Robertson, 288–92. Hoboken, NJ: Wiley.

Enos, Theresa. 1996. *Gender Roles and Faculty Lives in Rhetoric and Composition*. Carbondale, IL: Southern Illinois University Press.

Flaherty, Colleen. 2014. "No Country for Old Adjuncts." Inside Higher Ed, September 24. https://www.insidehighered.com/news/2014/09/24/recent-legal-cases-point-link-between-anti-adjunct-bias-and-age-bias. Accessed 19 December 2020.

Flaherty, Colleen. 2015. "Wisconsin Faculty Incensed by Motion to Eliminate Tenure from State Statute." *Inside Higher Ed*, June 1. www.insidehighered.com/news/2015/06/01/wisconsin-faculty-incensed-motion-eliminate-tenure-state-statute.

Flaherty, Colleen. 2017. "Legislation in Two States Seeks to Eliminate Tenure in Public Higher Education." *Inside Higher Ed*, January 13. www.insidehighered.com/news/2017/01/13/legislation-two-states-seeks-eliminate-tenure-public-higher-education.

Flynn, Elizabeth, and Tiffany Bourelle, eds. 2018. *Women's Professional Lives in Rhetoric and Composition: Choice, Chance, and Serendipity*. Columbus, OH: The Ohio State University Press.

Golde, Chris M., and George Walker. 2006. *Envisioning the Future of Doctoral Education: Preparing Stewards of the Discipline. Carnegie Essays on the Doctorate*. Jossey-Bass.

Harper, Elizabeth P., Roger G. Baldwin, Bruce G. Gansneder, and Jay L. Chronister. 2001. "Full-time Women Faculty off the Tenure Track: Profile and Practice." *Review of Higher Education* 24 (3): 237–57. Project MUSE. doi:10.1353/rhe.2001.0003.

Hart, Jeni. 2001. "Non-Tenure Track Women Faculty: Opening the Door." *Journal of the Professoriate* 4 (1): 96–124.

Hewitt, Beth L. 2015. Review of *Rewriting Success in Rhetoric and Composition Careers*, edited by Amy Goodburn, Donna LeCourt, and Carrie Leverenz. *Composition Studies* 43 (2): 229–33.

Kelsky, Karen. 2012. "Ageism and the Academy: My Thoughts and a Request for Yours." *The Professor Is In, April 24*. theprofessorisin.com/2012/04/24/ageism-and-the-academy-my-thoughts-and-a-request-for-yours/. Accessed 18 January 2021.

Leverenz, Carrie. 2010. "What's Ethics Got to Do with It? Feminist Ethics and Administrative Work in Rhetoric and Composition." In *Performing Feminism and Administration in Rhetoric and Composition Studies*, edited by Krista Ratcliffe and Rebecca Rickly, 3–18. New York: Hampton.

Miller, Susan. 1991. "Sad Women in the Basement: Images of Composition Teaching." In *Textual Carnivals: The Politics of Composition*, 121–41. Carbondale, IL: Southern Illinois University Press.

National Science Foundation, National Center for Science and Engineering Statistics. 2018. "Doctorate Recipients from U.S. Universities: 2017." Special Report NSF 19-301. Arlington, VA: Division of Science Resources Statistics, National Science Foundation. ncses.nsf.gov/pubs/nsf19301/report. Accessed 18 January 2021.

National Science Foundation, Science and Engineering Doctorates. 2015. "Doctorate Recipients from U.S. Universities: 2014." Special Report NSF 16-300. Arlington, VA: Division of Science Resources Statistics, National Science Foundation. https://www.nsf.gov/statistics/2016/nsf16300/. Accessed 18 January 2021.

National Science Foundation, Division of Science Resources Statistics. 2009. "Doctorate Recipients from U.S. Universities: Summary Report 2007–08." Special Report NSF 10-309. Arlington, VA: Division of Science Resources Statistics, National Science Foundation. https://wayback.archive-it.org/5902/20160210152216/http://www.nsf.gov/statistics/nsf10309/. Accessed 18 January 2021.

North, Stephen M. 1987. "The Practitioners." In *The Making of Knowledge in Composition: The Portrait of an Emerging Field*, 21–55. Portsmouth, NY: Boyton/Cook.

North, Stephen M. 2011. "Notes on the Origins of *The Making of Knowledge in Composition*." In *The Changing of Knowledge in Composition: Contemporary Perspectives*, edited by Lance Massey and Richard C. Gebhardt, 11–14. Logan: Utah State University Press.

Offerman, Michael. 2011. "Profile of the Nontraditional Doctoral Degree Student." *New Directions for Adult and Continuing Education* 2011 (129): 21–30.

Oxford Dictionary of the Middle Ages, s.v. "Baccalarius." 2010. Oxford: Oxford University Press.

Perna, Laura W. 2001. "The Relationship between Family Responsibilities and Employment Status among College and University Faculty." *Journal of Higher Education* 72 (5): 584–611.

Schell, Eileen E. 2017. "The New Faculty Majority in Writing Programs: Organizing for Change." Forward to *Contingency, Exploitation, and Solidarity: Labor and Action in English Composition*, edited by Seth Kahn, William B. Lalicker, and Amy Lynch-Biniek, ix–xx. Fort Collins, CO: WAC Clearinghouse.

Wills, Katherine V. 2004. "The Lure of 'Easy' Psychic Income." In *Tenured Bosses and Disposable Teachers: Writing Instruction in the Managed University*, edited by Marc Bousquet, Tony Scott, and Leo Parascondola, 201–8. Carbondale, IL: Southern Illinois University Press.

Winzenburg, Stephen. 2012. "A Discriminatory Word in Academic Job Descriptions." *Chronicle of Higher Education*, September 11. https://www.chronicle.com/article/a-discriminatory-word-in-academic-job-descriptions/. Accessed 18 January 2021.

13
MAKING IT AS A FEMALE WRITING PROGRAM ADMINISTRATOR
Using Collective Action and Feminist Mentoring Practices to Transgress Gendered Boundaries

Angela Clark-Oates, Bre Garrett,
Magdelyn Hammond Helwig, Aurora Matzke,
Sherry Rankins-Robertson, and Carey Smitherman Clark

> Survival can thus be what we do for others, with others. We need each other to survive; we need to be part of each other's survival. To be committed to a feminist life means we cannot not do this work; we cannot not fight for this cause, whatever it causes, so we have to find a way of sharing the costs of that work. Survival thus becomes a shared feminist project. . . . Feminism needs feminists to survive. . . . Feminists need feminism to survive.
> —Sara Ahmed

SARA AHMED, LIVING A FEMINIST LIFE

In *Rhetorical Feminism and This Thing Called Hope,* Cheryl Glenn reminds us that in the Western tradition of academia, mentorship, like leadership, has been characterized as white, masculine, individualistic, and hierarchical (2018, 149–50). This tradition is one way, then, that the academic world, as progressive as it may espouse to be, continues to marginalize women, people of color, and LGBTQ+ communities in and outside academe. These traditional mentoring practices contribute to documented trends of women in academia taking longer to achieve the rank of full professor, receiving lower salaries than men, and being critically underrepresented in upper administrative roles. These trends become more egregious when you make visible the overlapping identities of gender and race, revealing that higher education has failed abysmally to construct pathways for hiring, mentoring, retaining, and promoting women of color (Mercado-Lopez 2018).

In "Gender and Leadership: Reflection of Women in Higher Education Administration," Dana Dunn, Jeanne Gerlach, and Adrienne

DOI: 10.7330/9781646420384.c013

Hyle discuss the impact of the underrepresentation of women on the future of higher education. They write, "[Underrepresentation is a] waste of administrative talent at a time when higher education faces serious challenges that will be met only with strong, effective leadership. . . . Women possess great potential to be transformative leaders in the academy at a time when their talents are much needed" (2014, 9). Even in a field like rhetoric and composition, where females have historically secured leadership positions as writing program administrators (albeit contested positions viewed more as service roles than leadership ones) and have researched and theorized their administrative practices through a feminist lens for decades (Enos 1996; Micciche 2002; Miller 1996), transformative leaders continue to experience stifling working conditions under masculine ideologies that devalue and obscure feminist mentoring models. How we come to this work with one another is best described in "On Mentoring"; Win Horner writes, "The relationship is built on common interests, common goals, and most of all, respect for the other. In the end those mentoring relationships develop into deep and long-lasting friendships" (2008, 17), and like Lisa Costello in "Standing Up and Standing Together: Feminist Teaching and Collaborative Mentoring," our experiences as female administrators and teachers speak to the need of "broadening the idea of 'mentoring' to encompass collaborative and group relationships at a variety of institutions" (2015, 8). This is especially relevant when, as female administrators, we confront institutional walls of whiteness, masculinity, and heteronormativity; decenter marginalizing practices and habits; work to transform the institution; and commit to constructing more equitable and inclusive spaces. To understand writing program administration as a feminist project, to embody the work as a feminist, requires a network, a cadre of feminists—mentors and friends. In the epigraph to this chapter, taken from *Living a Feminist Life*, Sara Ahmed (2018) reminds us there is a cost to engaging in the intellectual, creative, administrative work of an institution as a feminist, one that requires an intersectional army. Consequently, this article, and our continued work together as authors, administrators, and collaborators, serves to underscore the necessity of intra- and interinstitutional, micro-co-mentoring to promote feminist leaders, structures, and community well-being.

LITERATURE REVIEW

Hildy Miller writes about feminist leaders struggling as writing program administrators within "masculine academic structures." She states, "At every turn, established authoritarian forms of leadership threaten to destroy nascent programmatic philosophies that would cooperatively guide such concerns as teacher training, mentoring, and curriculum development" (1996, 49). Although Miller identified this contact zone over twenty-five years ago, female leaders continue to face a lack of representation in higher education and marginalization of their work and accomplishments, which further constrict opportunities to benefit from or enact feminist mentorship practices, particularly in writing program administrator positions.

More recently, in "The Power of Dialogue and Meaningful Connectedness: Conversations between Two Female Scholars," Christine Nganga and Nakini Beck argue for a feminist co-mentoring praxis, writing, "The hierarchical nature of traditional mentoring models offers some limitations for women and faculty from underrepresented populations. . . . Men typically have more senior positions than women, [and] traditional mentoring sometimes reifies the masculine notions of power that limit definitions of scholarship and intellectual contributions by women" (2017, 554). Unlike these traditional frameworks of mentoring, Glenn reminds us, "Feminist mentoring in academia strives toward greater nimbleness, variety, and interactions. It calls for collaboration, reciprocity, and connection" (2018, 151). Thus, as collaborators, we have found that traditional mentoring structures rely on locality in ways that are problematic for most of the authors. While knowledge of the local landscape may be an invaluable asset a mentor provides a mentee, leadership at our institutions is predominantly masculinist and does not proceed from a feminist leadership paradigm. Consequently, as Collin Craig and Staci Perryman-Clark assert, "Looking at WPA work from both a gendered and racial perspective extends the implicative roles of identity politics in navigating administrative work within the context of university writing programs" (2011, 38). Of course, these masculinist through lines of power are even more problematic for women of color, as Anna Ribero and Sonia Arellano note: "A mentoring model for Women of Color in the discipline must account for the obstacles along intersecting lines of race and gender that we face in white dominant academia" (2019, 338).

Moreover, as the #metoo movement has strikingly highlighted, the difficulties women face in career recognition and advancement are both a product and reinforcement of gender-based harassment and inequality. The latest report on gender equity from the American Council on Education, prepared by Heather L. Johnson, director of the Center for Gender and Sexuality at the University of Michigan–Flint, shows that since 2006, women have earned more than 50 percent of all doctoral degrees granted, yet as of 2015, women held only 32 percent of full professor positions, and as of 2016, women held only 27 to 33 percent of all presidencies, depending on institution type (2016, 3, 5, 21). When we juxtapose the dearth of female leadership in higher education with the material conditions in which female leaders are expected to thrive, innovate, and transform, we uncover an exigence for examining women's ways of making themselves (and being made) into leaders. In particular, it compels us to investigate how we as coauthors navigate our own identities as developing leaders across our institutions—especially as we work to diversify the ways community, mentorship, and collaboration are enacted (or not) to support decision-making.

Because higher education lacks diversity in top administrative positions, it also has failed to embrace diverse leadership styles. When women secure administrative positions in higher education, whether at the departmental, college, or university level, they face the expectation that they will exhibit certain masculinist attributes (such as being tough, assertive, decisive, and independent). At the same time, women are often condemned or belittled when they act in ways perceived as (too) masculinist—often labeled as *aggressive*. To combat this contradiction, women in positions of power within academia must make new spaces where feminist attributes are not only accepted but celebrated, spaces where women's ways of leading are valued and encouraged. Such intra-, inter-, and extrainstitutional spaces provide overlapping contact zones, where we can work to build new models of female leadership that highlight connection, where, as Pamela VanHaitsma and Steph Ceraso remind us, "Feminist discussions of 'making it' leave room for a multiplicity of located experiences while encouraging flexible, adaptive strategies" (2017, 212).

As Dunn, Gerlach, and Hyle report, because women have not been "socialized in accordance with the male-centric leadership model, they are relative outsiders who must forge new ways of leading" (2014, 9), which can be difficult without mentorship. As Janet Giele's research confirms, a woman's past experiences serve as "the most powerful influences on a [her] career pattern" (2008, 389). So it was crucial for us, as we constructed new ways of leading on our campuses, to rely on micro-co-mentoring strategies to construct critical dialogues with one another that could address our sociohistorical contexts while aligning with the research from feminist scholars, teachers, and administrators in the field of rhetoric and composition who continue to research and write about the imperative to "reframe the portraiture" of female leadership. For it is here where successful leadership is recognized and valued as "a collaborative enterprise that values and engages all stakeholders, including students, TT faculty, NTT faculty, and partners in the community" (Detweiler, LaWare, and Wojahn 2017, 463). We hope the lived experiences we share in this chapter serve to underscore the necessity of examining co-mentoring roles as a means of promoting feminist leaders and structures.

WAYS OF MAKING ARGUMENTS: RESPONDING AS FEMALE ADMINISTRATORS

In this chapter, the six authors offer vignettes of experiences, provided within text boxes, that we have encountered and shared with one another during our time as WPAs. Our experiences are rooted in similar positionalities: all the authors present as cisgender, white, and predominantly first-generation scholars; however, the material conditions under which we work are incredibly varied, including land-grant, private, and liberal arts colleges and open-access institutions with a focus on minority populations. In naming our identities, we acknowledge the limitations of our positionalities, but our hope is to offer "partial perspectives" to illustrate how feminist leadership can be employed across locations (Haraway 1988). The vignettes intentionally interrupt our scholarly text in order to evoke in the reader the same abrupt and disruptive experiences we have lived. This structure also mirrors our attempt to disrupt traditional gendered boundaries by pushing against generic expectations for academic essays while also reflecting a feminist leadership model that values disparate voices, encourages conversation, and seeks to understand how we might find points of contact—opportunities to employ feminist mentoring practices—despite our seeming isolation. In addition, we transition from these seemingly jarring moments to micro-co-mentoring in order to (1) acknowledge, as Glenn notes, that "no matter how feminist the practices of an individual WPA, she still has to meet the demands of a masculinist academy" (2018, 179), (2) provide narratives of how women in leadership roles in academia are being treated today to disrupt the myth that discrimination and misogyny exist in the past, and (3) provide potential moments of micro-co-mentoring in the body of the article with examples of how we have moved the conversations at our home institutions. We then synthesize the vignettes to show how, as a collective, the experiences have helped us situate our local environments, make meaning toward a pedagogy of administration, and construct a future with other female administrators.

> A few months into my role as the writing program director, I was pulled aside by an older female colleague who, after critiquing several recent decisions I had made, said to me, "Honey, you've got balls." Her tone was part pitying, part chiding—I was being put in my place. "Honey" was not a term of endearment, but rather a word choice seeking to belittle and shame me for being a woman who behaved like a man. I had transgressed. I had exceeded the boundaries of proper female behavior in the workplace, specifically in higher education, and yet, I had been doing my job.

Over twenty years ago, Sally Barr-Ebest's "Gender Differences in Writing Program Administration" reported that male WPAs "fare far better" than female WPAs, despite having "common training, background, duties, and responsibilities" (1995, 53). Barr-Ebest recorded one female WPA as stating, "Since WPAs of either gender are not taken seriously, female WPAs get a double whammy: they're scorned as women and as WPAs" (65–66). Another female WPA in Barr-Ebest's study summarized well the distinction between perceptions of women and men in leadership roles: "Women take responsibility; men take authority" (65). While Barr-Ebest's research is more than two decades old, the vignette above demonstrates that academia is still not so far away from infantilizing ("honey") and reifying ("you've got balls") if a feminist leader transgresses in her role as WPA.

> At a university function with a high-ranking administrator, my partner and I were asked several questions about the length and structure of our relationship. The questions became increasingly pointed regarding my feminist work and beliefs about gender roles before the administrator finally asked, "So who wears the pants in your family?"

Feminist leaders also must consider what to do when positionality overshadows performance in administrative circles defined by masculinist hierarchies of power. Yvonne Benschop and Margo Brouns report female academics' achievements receive lower evaluations than comparable achievements of male academics, leading them to conclude, "The idea of excellence fits better with representations of masculinity than of femininity, especially in an academic context" (2003, 205). This effect is even more pronounced in administrative positions, where women administrators are evaluated against patriarchy-based norms of leadership in addition to patriarchy-based norms of academic achievement and norms about work/home balance—particularly when called out with comments like "Who wears the pants in your family?" According to Louise Kloot, "Societal norms define the expected roles of behaviours of men and women, and managerial characteristics are often assigned to men (Marongiu and Ekehammer 1999). The same behaviour in men and women is judged differently" (2004, 472). This is the insidious nature of metaphors of masculinity and leadership—they suggest women's behavior does not count as leadership, and they also compel women to behave in masculinist ways that work to perpetuate gender hierarchies and bar too many women from acquiring positions of power. Frankly, they also promote stress, burnout, and cognitive dissonance on the part of the feminist administrator—consequences all the authors of this chapter have experienced. Of course, this burnout can be exacerbated through paternalistic patterns within the leadership structure.

> In my first year as WPA, my male department chair insisted that he take on some of my more formal duties in order to protect me since I didn't have tenure. He made sure his vision for the program stayed firmly in place instead of incorporating my vision. As a result, faculty in my department and those I had partnered with on campus went around me and straight to him for all programmatic questions since it was clear to everyone that he was "in charge."

Women are critically underrepresented at almost all levels of academia, though this is most evident at the levels of highest rank and in administration. According to "AAUP Faculty Gender Equity Indicators 2006," 40 percent of all full-time faculty in US higher education are women, but only one in four full professors is a woman (West and Curtis 2006). In 2012, the American Council on Education reported in "The American College President Study" that only 26 percent of institutional leaders were women (Cook 2012). As the authors of this piece, we see direct examples of these statistics in our universities. At the time of our writing, one of our home institutions had a male president and female provost; but below these two top ranks, men far outnumbered women in administrative appointments. At the same institution, four of the six associate provosts and academic vice presidents were men; eight of thirteen deans and directors were men. At another of our home institutions, an author has a female dean with two male associate deans, while fourteen of seventeen chair positions are held by men. In terms of faculty, the institution has 139 male full professors and 61 female; that's 71 percent of (full) professors who are men. In addition, 60 percent of associate professors are men, and just over 50 percent of assistant professors are men. Of non-tenure-track faculty, 71 percent are women. It is clear that women are underrepresented at all levels, except at the lowest, often least respected, and least remunerated level. According to Laura Meyers, "Even after controlling for several factors related to human capital, demographics, and structural characteristics, female faculty members earn *approximately 2.8% to 4.5% less than male faculty*" (2011, 7; emphasis added). Consequently, it's not just representation; it's also compensation.

> A male upper administrator threatened to remove me from my administrative position because he said I didn't "support him enough" while in a department meeting. He said he didn't think I was able to "straddle the fence." We met again three days later, and he "took it back," claiming he had been upset but was "over it" now. He never apologized or recognized the imbalanced infrastructure of power.

Similar issues are described in "Gender Equality in Academia: Bad News from the Trenches, and Some Possible Solutions" by Kristen Monroe, Saba Ozyurt, Ted Wrigley, and Amy Alexander. The authors surveyed 220 female faculty members at the University of California at Irvine (UCI), and then they interviewed 92 of the surveyed faculty members. Through this research, Monroe et al. found gender inequality was still prevalent at their institution of higher education, and a widespread perception existed that the university did not have a sincere commitment to changing this issue. Any motivation shown by the university seemed to stem more from "the desire to protect itself legally [than from] a genuine concern to improve the situation for women on campus" (2008, 226). While this study was not focused on female administrators specifically, the results show findings that illustrate the continued imbalance of women in positions of protected classes or administration.

> After seeking out a high-ranking female administrator regarding my removal from a committee, I was told by the administrator that some members of the committee found me to be "abrasive." After several committee members approached me at different intervals following this conversation, upset that I was no longer included, it became clear the female administrator had lied—no committee members found me abrasive; she wanted me off of the committee for reasons unknown to anyone.

In Sungjoo Choi's article "Breaking Through the Glass Ceiling: Social Capital Matters for Women's Career Success?," she discusses the potential of social capital for women's upward mobility in the workforce. While there may be positive connections between mentors and supervisors of the same gender for female administrators looking to work in more critical positions within the institution, the results of Choi's study show social capital is only more beneficial to women than to men in assignment of *temporary* promotions (2018, 16–18). Therefore, social networking doesn't seem to play an overly positive role in female administrators' advancement or increased respect in the positions they hold. Arguably, we see that being promoted temporarily could further deprofessionalize these women administrators by implying they are not worthy of permanent promotions.

Perhaps a surprising factor all the authors of this piece have in common is that we each have experienced varying degrees of difficulty at the hands of senior females in positions of power across our campuses. As our senior female colleagues have likely suffered from even more pronounced gendered expectations, the authors entered their leadership positions believing most senior female faculty would be allies, working against such gendered expectations rather than perpetuating them. As more and more women enter positions of power in academia, we must remember to make spaces that are welcoming to the next generation of female administrators.

As women in administrative positions, the six of us have experienced firsthand the institutionalized sexism represented by the gender pay gap, the disproportionate percentage of men who make up the higher ranks of academia, and the gendered performance expectations that affect women at all levels of academia. Half of us have discussed issues of sexism in academia elsewhere (see Garrett, Rankins-Robertson, and Matzke 2017). We believe, as Kloot asserts, that "the gender imbalance problem lies not with women, but with the way leadership is defined and conceptualized" and that "masculinity is an implicit construct in the perception of leadership, and what women do is rarely defined as leadership" (2004, 472). Specifically, we have found "embodied leadership is about knowing how to enter and access particularly rhetorical moves," and we call for "feminist leadership collaboration" (Garrett, Rankins-Robertson, and Matzke 2017, 278, 285). In the remainder of this article, we explore alternate models of leadership, drawing on feminist theories as well as our own experiences.

WAYS OF MAKING KNOWLEDGE: APPLYING FEMINIST ADMINISTRATION

> In working on a new curricular design project, I sought out two adjunct faculty with whom to collaborate on program research and assessment. We presented our research at two different conferences and have a chapter forthcoming in a book collection. Collaboration on curricular projects is a way to share the responsibility of administration. But, also, part-time faculty find a more permanent place in the program—as teachers and as researchers—through publication options. In addition, as a teacher of teachers, I find myself explaining curriculum and subject matter in con-

texts and to audiences beyond the students enrolled in my classes. Aligning other faculty as codesigners of program materials allows me to delegate the role of teaching teachers to fellow colleagues.

Our pedagogies of writing program administration emerge from a confluence of histories, theories, and practices, reflections and refractions of the embodied identities of the authors and the participants in the vignettes. Like Jonikka Charlton and Shirly Rose, we believe "WPA is not just a job title, but a way of being" (2009, 114). And as Katherine Sang argues, "Being a feminist intersect[s] with other social identities in ways which [confer] both advantage and disadvantage for women academics" (2016, 202). Working from this point, then, the personal is pedagogical.

In "Thinking Ecologically: Rhetorical Ecological Feminist Agency and Writing Program Administration," Kathleen J. Ryan advocates for WPAs to develop an ecological habit of knowing, one that will allow us to define ourselves as "situated, embodied, interconnected persons whose recognition of the limits of perspectives positions them to be accountable for what they know and do because they are cognizant of politics of location and relation" (2012, 77–78). Working from this idea, we openly discuss and attempt to challenge historically masculinist definitions of power, position, and influence in our day-to-day—we work to respond instead of react; we individually and collectively recount, name, and problem solve with one another to practice micro-co-mentoring across institutional boundaries; we remind one another that there are others doing good work and that this work is often small and repetitive. Together, these practices coalesce into a pedagogy of writing program administration uniquely practiced by women in localized spaces.

> My counterpart at another university and I developed a composition conference to bring in national scholars so our contingent faculty would have the opportunity and experience of presenting at a conference, building their vitae for application to full-time jobs and graduate programs, and bringing together collective voices at the local level for a common conversation on composition.

Women WPAs often find themselves trying to show attentiveness to their programs and trying to remain open to the kinds of changes that will result in more thoughtful, focused, and successful programs. However, these WPAs must navigate bureaucratic power struggles in order to make any significant moves. In *Developing Successful College Writing Programs,* Edward White (1998) asserts that writing program administration should be deliberate and attentive—and open to change. This builds on his earlier discussion of negotiating ideas of power in "Use It or Lose It: Power and the WPA," where he argues,

> Power is in some ways like money or sex; it is only of pressing importance if you have none. But those with official power wield it so naturally and, often, so skillfully, that those on the receiving end never know what hit them. Administrators, including WPAs, cannot afford the luxury of powerlessness. The only way to do the job of a WPA is to be aware of the power relationships we necessarily conduct, and to use the considerable power we have for the good of our program. (1991, 12)

White's scholarship helps us understand that WPAs must constantly, and consistently, work to evaluate the localized power structures within which they operate. And, in many ways, this evaluation can be more deliberate with a micro-co-mentor who is not a part of your localized landscape. When a WPA works to describe the power dynamics with and under which they operate, it can help promote positive and impactful differentiation, cutting down on stress and cognitive dissonance in the naming and defining of such moments. Thus, theory guides us in the performance of these positions while we maintain ongoing conversations about the considerations of female WPAs—including priorities, issues of power, and program situatedness. Consequently, as Sarah Burton reminds us, "Feminist positions work in paradoxical and contradictory ways—as supportive, generative, and creative, but also demanding of onerous and time-consuming emotional labour, thus arguably disadvantaging the feminist academic" (2018, 115). Thus, feminist perspectives and attention to identity and difference also become major strands in talking about our pedagogy of administration.

In "Breaking Our Bonds and Reaffirming Our Connections," Maxine Hairston discusses the state of writing programs and administrators of those programs within larger English departments in the mid-1980s.

> Our experience is much like that of the women's movement. One can look at how far we have come and rejoice at our progress, or one can look at the barriers that still exist and become discouraged. I believe, however—and once more the situation is analogous to that of many women—that a major reason we get discouraged is that our worst problems originate close to home: in our own departments and within the discipline of English studies itself. And we are having trouble solving those problems precisely because they are so immediate and daily, and because we have complex psychological bonds to the people who so frequently are our adversaries in our efforts to make the writing programs in our departments as good as they should be and can be. (1985, 273)

Hairston's assertions are still very true today for women WPAs who coexist in institutional contexts that merge languages and communications into one department or program. But we have seen progress in the last two decades—more women serving in WPA positions and leading both writing programs and departments. Women administrators continue to struggle against the stereotype of what it means to be an administrator and to expand on that definition (Burton 2018; Sang 2016), but this struggle must continue in order for WPAs to best represent their programs, and more broadly writing as a discipline, within their universities, communities, and the larger field. To disrupt these stereotypes, we construct our pedagogy of administration from the personal, local, and dialogic, promoting reciprocity in our teaching and mentoring and recognizing that both our strengths and our vulnerabilities emerge from the historicized, theorized, and practiced identities of female WPAs.

In *Teaching to Transgress*, bell hooks argues, "Teaching is a performative act. And it is that aspect of our work that offers the space for change, invention, spontaneous shifts, that can serve as a catalyst . . . [to] create new ways of knowing, different strategies for the sharing of knowledge" (1994, 8–9). One of the primary responsibilities of WPA work involves the mentoring of new teachers, teaching of teachers, and developing ongoing professional development. It is within these pedagogical spaces we can most overtly bring the critical conversations of feminist administrative models to bear on our choices as leaders.

WAYS OF MAKING SENSE: MENTORING AS WRITING PROGRAM ADMINISTRATORS

> To professionalize and mentor faculty, I ask the composition faculty to reflect on their own needs and goals. For example, in faculty annual reviews, I ask instructors to set scholarly/creative goals for themselves; we then create plans for how I can support them to achieve those goals. In one case two years ago, I supported a small pilot study in our second-semester first-year writing course for two instructors to implement meditative exercises in the guided practice students participated in to develop and reflect on the habits of mind. After a year, the instructors applied to present at CCCC, and I advocated for them to receive travel grants from the college. Finally, I mentored them through the IRB process, so they will continue to study our curriculum through a meditative framework, which has been a mutually beneficial project.

While it is true that finding local female mentors is difficult, we reach toward our cross-institutional foremothers, our dissertation directors, our feminist colleagues who have paved the way for us as female WPAs, and to women who have worked their way up the male hegemonic ladder of higher education to help bridge this felt gap. We call out in thanks to some of those women here: Linda Adler-Kassner, Kathleen

Blake Yancey, Lisa Ede, Maureen Daly Goggin, Cheryl Glenn, Gail Hawisher, Erika Lindemann, Brenda Helmbrecht, Andrea Lunsford, Cynthia Lewiecki-Wilson, Staci Perryman-Clark, Georgia Rhoades, Kate Ronald, Jacqueline Jones Royster, Shirley K Rose, and Cynthia Selfe. As more women move into administrative roles, female administrators who are partnered and/or parents have more access to mentors who can relate to navigating those roles while working as a female administrator in a male-dominated professional environment. This access to women in these roles is something that has changed dramatically for women only in the last few decades.

What also complicates our roles as female WPAs is that frequently we are in mentorship positions for graduate students, junior faculty, and (at times) senior faculty new to the teaching of writing. Christine Hult, in "Politics Redux: The Organization and Administration of Writing Programs," joins this conversation by asking us to rethink our power relationships within the university. She contrasts higher education with democracy, asserting that higher education works in a hierarchy, whereas an ideal democracy would "[include] reciprocal controls with no one person or group dominating" (1995, 48). Hult cautions WPAs against continuing to operate in this hierarchy without examining other more democratic alternatives.

Like Hult, Miller questions the ways WPAs can work within the masculinist hierarchy in higher education. In "Postmasculinist Directions in Writing Program Administration," she discusses issues of WPAs struggling to establish and wield power (as well as feelings of powerlessness) within this typical hierarchical administrative structure. According to Miller, a feminist theory of administration provides a way for WPAs to rethink ideas of power in that the focus shifts from personal power to relational leadership, relational mentorship. Advocacy and activism are critical for an area, writing administration, with such widespread and complicated institutional responsibilities and ramifications. Many times, advocacy and activism involve a complex struggle for power and recognition—in particular for many of our contingently employed teachers. Power is not only a lived, felt sense of something we experience in relation to those higher than us but also a responsibility we carry to speak for others who cannot speak for themselves. As three of us have explored in "'Nevertheless She Persisted': Strategies to Counteract the Time, Place, and Culture for Academic Bullying of WPAs," academic bullying is oftentimes normalized, with strong ties to academic hazing. It should not be tolerated, and infrastructures for reporting it are needed (Matzke, Rankins-Robertson, and Garrett 2019).

When I encountered a bully in the academic workplace during the first week I arrived on campus, I found solace in the women with whom I coauthor this article but also with women who held senior leadership positions within my discipline. These women made themselves available to me and offered advice, but as important as their interactions with me, they offered a clear perspective on the ways women should support one another throughout our lifetimes within this profession. My sisters in the discipline provided a listening ear and commiserated with me, but my academic mentors encouraged me to vocalize to my administration that the bullying was occurring. Ultimately, these conversations gave me the courage to let the tenured professor in my department know that I would not sit quietly while she moved from one target to another. I know I cannot stop what she does, but rather than participate in the vicious cycle that seems to be part of the culture on my campus, I can advocate for a different community for women on my campus.

Miller suggests that the feminist administrative model can be placed within the larger hierarchical structure of the university, decentering the position of WPA and advocating for a community that shares ideas and concerns. Miller illustrates this model:

> In general, the concept of community in which leadership is shared can be substituted for the notion of hierarchy. With the self seen as interrelational and personal power enhanced by empowering others, such a community is marked by collaboration and cooperation. Rather than striving to develop uniform and universalized rules, feminist communities tend to produce flexible decisions arising from experiential contexts. Ideas are tentative, and thus subject to alteration as contextual needs change. While not all members of a community need to agree on all details, there is generally basic consensus on important points. (1996, 55)

The idea of decentering WPA work is indicative of the kind of work that happens in many writing programs that value the contributions of their members in shaping and growing them. Writing programs have historically embraced a collaborative approach, often stemming from the ways the classroom in our discipline is often facilitated, with an understanding that shared ownership is likely to create more long-term, substantive gains across the diversified teaching and student bodies with which we work.

At the center of our pedagogy of administration—our micro-co-mentorship mantras—is the idea that all faculty, part or full time and graduate student teachers, need opportunities to use their expertise, pursue creative and professional endeavors, and influence the evolution of the program they teach in, based on their lived experiences as practitioners. Taking a line from Gloria Steinem's playbook, then, our mentorship strategies begin with one guiding principle: *ask the turtle* (Gagliano and Newman 2015). When Steinem was a young student on a geology field trip, she rescued a mud turtle she had found on the riverbank near the asphalt road. She carried the turtle back to the river, but no sooner had she released it into the river than her professor questioned her, "Did you ask the turtle before you moved it?" And then the professor told her the turtle had been purposefully making its way to dry land to lay its eggs; Steinem, with all her altruistic intentions, had made a crucial decision for the turtle without understanding the motivation and purpose of the turtle's needs.

Putting these concepts into practice—asking instead of mandating, dialoguing instead of telling, and constructing cultures of shared expertise instead of claiming ownership over the expertise—is challenging for all administrators, especially as women advocating for professionalism for contingent faculty within an institutional structure that does not understand (or value) collaborative teaching as intellectual work. In corporatized higher education, the turtle is not viewed as an agent. The turtle is thought of and treated as an assembly-line worker. Women may construct administrative pedagogies, but to become an advocate, you must first ask the turtle—and perhaps remember what it is or was like to be the turtle.

WAYS OF MAKING THE FUTURE: LEADING WITH FEMINIST MENTORING PRACTICES

As we work to navigate the landscapes of our respective institutions, we often find ourselves reaching out to one another. These check-ins continue to ground and expand our repertoire of available responses. Without relationships with each other, we're not sure we would have sustained momentum in the various places we remain. At the very least, we would have lacked the persistence we often found essential as female administrators. We urge our readers to seek out cross-institutional micro-co-relationships not only with other women who share like positions but also with an academic mentor or coach who has traveled the path you desire. Establish sustainable relationships that enable reflective talk unavailable in explicitly local contexts. This recommendation is also consistent with the themes that emerged from the narratives collected in the Dunn, Gerlach, and Hyle study (2014), particularly building a network.

Through the narratives, Dunn, Gerlach, and Hyle's study participants acknowledged the importance of building a network. One participant wrote, "I had so many colleagues both internally within the university and externally at other academic institutions who were willing to help me get my work done" (2014, 13). This, too, has been foundational to our successes. By checking behavior and actions across institutions, we are able to better understand the patterns of power that emerge across our differing landscapes. The issues become less about us and more about the systems we find ourselves in. We've found this open acknowledgement of gendered problems that reach beyond individual circumstance to be powerfully motivating and settling. Yes, understanding that the problems are far reaching can be overwhelming. At the same time, we reinforce for one another, time and again, that we are not alone. We discuss with each other the advantages provided by foremothers who have fought for us to hold these positions.

Great gains in our discipline have been made through feminist, collaborative structures. We do not proceed in a vacuum. Collective organization has led to bargaining power in feminist subgroups at CCCC—including the feminist workshop, the Feminisms and Rhetorics conference, the journal *Peitho*, the creation and maintenance of the Women's Coalition of Scholars, and the newly approved CWPA Position Statement on Bullying in the Workplace, to name just a few. We urge our readers to become involved in disciplinary organizations that are explicitly feminist so they might experience groups committed to distributed power models and reciprocal leadership. With this experience, WPAs might more easily translate feminist distributed power models to their home institutions, as well as foster relationships with like minds that may provide rest and resources as the years roll.

We also recommend that all WPAs, new or seasoned, make use of the Writing Program Administrators Workshop that occurs each year at the Council of Writing Program Administrators Conference. A number of us met during this preconference workshop. As a postgraduate space of collaboration and learning, the workshop fosters connections across institutional, pedagogical, and geographic boundaries that otherwise would make some collaborations nigh on impossible. As WPAs, we have found we don't have the time to wander around conference sessions, cross our fingers, and hope to bump into women in similar circumstances with similar administrative interests. The workshop does this initial guesswork for participants, in addition to providing all participants with built-in WPA mentors.

WPA work can be isolating, and many WPAs function as the sole writing expert in their departments and universities. Sole writing advocate. Sole writing expert. Sole woman in the room. It can be overwhelming and disheartening, as we are often asked to serve on committees as the female junior faculty or the female administrator. So, here we offer a last call to those who have entered the ranks of the female (junior faculty) administrator:

Contact us.
Become collaborators with us.
Reach out to the authors in this collection.

We will help you. We will commiserate with you. At the very least, we'll have drinks or coffee with you, as we do with each other, through web conferencing platforms or in person at conferences. It's the micro moments in community with female administrators, as we work together to solve and respond to these isolating issues, that elevate us—to thrive, innovate, and transform women's ways of making themselves into leaders.

WORKS CITED

Ahmed, Sara. 2018. *Living a Feminist Life*. Durham, NC: Duke University Press.
Barr-Ebest, Sally. 1995. "Gender Differences in Writing Program Administration." *WPA: Writing Program Administration* 18 (3): 53–73.
Benschop, Yvonne, and Margo Brouns. 2003. "Crumbling Ivory Towers: Academic Organizing and Its Gender Effects." *Gender, Work and Organization* 10 (2): 194–212.
Burton, Sarah. 2018. "Writing Yourself In? The Price of Playing the (Feminist) Game in the Neoliberal University." In *Feeling Academic in the Neoliberal University: Feminist Flights, Fights, and Failures*, edited by Yvette Taylor and Kinneret Lahad, 115–36. Palgrave Studies in Gender and Education. London, England: Palgrave Macmillan.
Charlton, Jonikka, and Shirley K Rose. 2009. "Twenty More Years in the WPA's Progress." *WPA: Writing Program Administration* 33 (1/2): 114–45.
Choi, Sungjoo. 2018. "Breaking Through the Glass Ceiling: Social Capital Matters for Women's Career Success?" *International Public Management Journal* 22 (2): 295–320.
Cook, Bryan. 2012. "The American College President Study: Key Findings and Takeaways." *The Presidency*. Washington, DC: American Council on Education.
Costello, Lisa A. 2015. "Standing Up and Standing Together: Feminist Teaching and Collaborative Mentoring." *Feminist Teacher* 26 (1): 1–28.
Craig, Collin Lamont, and Staci Maree Perryman-Clark. 2011. "Troubling the Boundaries: (De)Constructing WPA Identities at the Intersections of Race and Gender?" *WPA: Writing Program Administration* 34 (2): 37–58.
Detweiler, Jane, Margaret LaWare, and Patti Wojahn. 2017. "Academic Leadership and Advocacy: On Not Leaning In." *College English* 79 (5): 451–65.
Dunn, Dana, Jeanne Gerlach, and Adrienne Hyle. 2014. "Gender and Leadership: Reflections of Women in Higher Education Administration." *International Journal of Leadership and Change* 2 (1): 9–18.
Enos, Theresa. 1996. *Gender Roles and Faculty Lives*. Carbondale, IL: Southern Illinois University Press.
Gagliano, Rico, and Brendan Francis Newman. 2015. "Gloria Steinem's Guide to Maneuvering Around Misogyny." *The Dinner Party Download*. National Public Radio, November 6. https://www.dinnerpartydownload.org/gloria-steinem/. Accessed 18 January 2021.
Garrett, Bre, Sherry Rankins-Robertson, and Aurora Matzke. 2017. "Renegotiating the Positionality of MiddleMAN Administrators in Higher Education." In *Surviving Sexism*

in Academia: Strategies for Feminist Leadership, edited by Kirstie Cole and Holly Hassel, 277–86. Abingdon, England: Routledge.

Giele, Janet Zollinger. 2008. "Homemaker or Career Woman: Life Course Factors and Racial Influences among Middle Class Americans." *Journal of Comparative Family Studies* 39 (3): 393–411.

Glenn, Cheryl. 2018. *Rhetorical Feminism and This Thing Called Hope.* Carbondale, IL: Southern Illinois University Press.

Hairston, Maxine. 1985. "Breaking Our Bonds and Reaffirming Our Connections." *College Composition and Communication* 36 (3): 272–82.

Haraway, Donna. 1988. "Situated Knowledges: The Science Question in Feminism and the Privilege of Partial Perspectives." *Feminist Studies* 14 (3): 575–99.

hooks, bell. 1994. *Teaching to Transgress.* Abingdon, England: Routledge.

Horning, Win. 2008. "On Mentoring." In *Stories on Mentoring: Theory & Praxis*, edited by Michelle F. Eble and Lynee Lewis Gaillet, 14–17. Anderson, SC: Parlor.

Hult, Christine. 1995. "Politics Redux: The Organization and Administration of Writing Programs." *WPA: Writing Program Administration* 18 (3): 44–52.

Johnson, Heather L. 2016. *Pipelines, Pathways, and Institutional Leadership: An Update on the Status of Women in Higher Education.* Washington, DC: American Council on Education. https://www.acenet.edu/Documents/Higher-Ed-Spotlight-Pipelines-Pathways-and-Institutional-Leadership-Status-of-Women.pdf. Accessed 18 January 2021.

Kloot, Louise. 2004. "Women and Leadership in Universities: A Case Study of Women Academic Managers." *International Journal of Public Sector Management* 17 (6): 470–85.

Marongiu, Sophia, and Bo Ekehammar. 1999. "Internal and External Influences on Women's and Men's Entry into Management." *Journal of Managerial Psychology* 14 (5): 421–33.

Matzke, Aurora, Sherry Rankins-Robertson, and Bre Garrett. 2019. "'Nevertheless She Persisted': Strategies to Counteract the Time, Place, and Culture for Academic Bullying of WPAs." In *Defining, Locating, and Addressing Bullying in the WPA Workplace*, edited by Cristyn Elder and Beth Davila, 49–68. Logan: Utah State University Press.

Mercado-Lopez, Larissa. 2018. "Want to Retain Faculty of Color? Support Them as Faculty of Color." National Center for Institutional Diversity, May 18. https://medium.com/national-center-for-institutional-diversity/want-to-retain-faculty-of-color-support-them-as-faculty-of-color-9e7154ed618f. Accessed 18 January 2021.

Meyers, Laura E. 2011. "Gender Pay Equity in Higher Education: Salary Differentials and Predictors of Base Faculty Income." Order No. 3485499, University of Washington, 2011. https://eric.ed.gov/?id=ED534486. Accessed 18 January 2021.

Micciche, Laura R. 2002. "More Than a Feeling of Disappointment and WPA Work." *College English* 64 (4): 432–58.

Miller, Hildy. 1996. "Postmasculinist Directions in Writing Program Administration." *WPA: Writing Program Administration* 20 (1/2): 49–61.

Monroe, Kristen, Saba Ozyurt, Ted Wrigley, and Amy Alexander. 2008. "Gender Equality in Academia: Bad News from the Trenches, and Some Possible Solutions." *Perspectives on Politics* 6 (2): 215–33.

Nganga, Christine W., and Makini Beck. 2017. "The Power of Dialogue and Meaningful Connectedness: Conversations between Two Female Scholars." *Urban Review* 49 (4): 551–67.

Ribero, Ana M., and Sonia C. Arellano. 2019. "Advocating *Comadrismo*: A Feminist Mentoring Approach for Latinas in Rhetoric and Composition." *Peitho Journal* 21 (2): 334–56.

Ryan, Kathleen J. 2012. "Thinking Ecologically: Rhetorical Ecological Feminist Agency and Writing Program Administration." *WPA: Writing Program Administration* 36 (1): 74–94.

Sang, Katherine. 2016. "Gender, Ethnicity, and Feminism: An Intersectional Analysis of the Lived Experiences Feminist Academic Women in UK Higher Education." *Journal of Gender Studies* 27. (2): 192–206.

VanHaitsma, Pamela, and Steph Ceraso. 2017. "Making It" in the Academy through Horizontal Mentoring *Peitho Journal* 19 (2): 210–33.

West, Martha, and John W. Curtis. 2006. *AAUP Faculty Gender Equity Indicators 2006*. Washington, DC: AAUP: American Association of University Professors. https://www.aaup.org/reports-publications/publications/see-all/aaup-faculty-gender-equity-indicators-2006. Accessed 20 December 2020.

White, Edward M. 1991. "Use It or Lose It: Power and the WPA." *WPA: Writing Program Administration* 15 (1–2): 3–12.

White, Edward M. 1998. *Developing Successful College Writing Programs*. Portland, ME: Calendar Islands.

ABOUT THE AUTHORS

Carey Smitherman Clark is the director of the UCA Center for Writing and Communication. She is also associate professor of writing at the University of Central Arkansas, where she teaches undergraduate and graduate courses in nonprofit writing, first-year writing, composition theory and pedagogy, and professional writing. Her research is focused on writing program administration and writing center pedagogy. Previously, she served as director of the first-year writing program and interim department chair.

Angela Clark-Oates is an assistant professor of composition and rhetoric and the writing program coordinator in the English Department at California State University, Sacramento. Her research interests include multimodal literacy, high school–to-college transition, feminist theory and critical pedagogies, and writing program administration. Her scholarship has been published in the journals *Communication Design Quarterly* and *the Journal of Writing Assessment*. She has also published in the anthologies *The Framework for Success in Postsecondary Writing: Scholarship and Applications*, *A Fresh Approach to the Common Core State Standards in Research and Writing*, *Working with Faculty Writers*, and the *Rhetorics of Names and Naming*.

Jane Donawerth, professor emerita of English and affiliate in women's studies, is a distinguished scholar-teacher and former director of academic writing at the University of Maryland. She has published nine books, including *Conversational Rhetoric: The Rise and Fall of a Women's Tradition, 1600 to 1900* with Southern Illinois University Press, *Rhetorical Theory by Women before 1900: An Anthology*; *Selected Letters, Orations, and Rhetorical Dialogues by Madeleine de Scudéry* (translated with Julie Strongson); *Women's Speaking Justified and Other Pamphlets* by Margaret Fell (edited with Rebecca Lush); and *Shakespeare and the Sixteenth-Century Study of Language*. She has won seven teaching awards, two NEH fellowships, and career awards for her work on early modern women's writings (from the Society for the Study of Early Modern Women) and for gender and science fiction (from the International Association for the Fantastic in the Arts).

Amanda Ellis, MSW, MPH, CPH, was the program director for the Red Tent Women's Initiative. She discovered Red Tent in her final semester of her MSW from the University of Southern Florida. She has a passion for justice and social change. Her involvement with the justice system, nonprofit development and management, and grant writing provides a positive outlet for her to effect social change. She is also a certified Reiki Master and applies the principles from her personal and professional lives to positively impact Red Tent, women, families, and the broader community. She currently lives in Tennessee with her partner and son.

Theresa M. Evans is an assistant teaching professor in the Department of English at Miami University of Ohio. She teaches online and face-to-face courses in professional and technical writing and works on assessment and curriculum development. After graduating with a BSJ from Ohio University and working for two decades in advertising and marketing communications, she earned an MA in English composition and rhetoric from Wright State University, followed by a PhD in English with a concentration in rhetoric and composition from Ball State University. Her interest in the intersections of feminism, capitalism, and academic labor issues led her to examine contingency through the rhetoric of self-sacrifice; the resulting essay was published in *Rhetoric Review*.

Holly Fulton-Babicke is a lecturer at Stanford University and holds a PhD in writing, rhetorics, and literacies from Arizona State University. Her research centers upon intersectional rhetorics and consensus building in networked publics, and she particularly inspects the ways speakers/writers offer new perspectives in public settings in ways that "crack open" existing social expectations and hierarchies. These productive rhetorics, which she terms *knowledge-building interventions*, are often blocked by *bad-faith rhetorics* (her dissertation research). In settings such as TED Talk comments and international trade policy documents, she explores the frictions between productive and bad-faith rhetorics and identifies how these frictions impact consensus on public issues. She has received several recognitions for her research and teaching, including the 2018 Theresa J. Enos Anniversary Award for Best Essay for her *Rhetoric Review* article "'I Can't Breathe': Eric Garner and In/Out-Group Rhetorics."

Bre Garrett is an associate professor of English and director of the composition program at the University of West Florida. She teaches undergraduate and graduate courses in writing and rhetorical theory, digital writing, women's rhetorics, and composition pedagogy. Her research intersects the areas of embodiment and writing studies. She has published articles and book chapters on embodied composing and invention, on delivery and multimodal composing, on writing studio curricular design, and on leadership in writing program administration. Bre is currently at the beginning stages of a new project, composing a manuscript on the rhetorical and pedagogical practices of Maria Montessori.

Maureen Daly Goggin is professor of rhetoric in and former chair of the Department of English at Arizona State University. She is the author and editor of eleven scholarly books and several editions of a textbook and a pedagogical book. Her latest work includes *Serendipity in Rhetoric, Writing, and Literacy Research* (2018), coedited with Peter N. Goggin, and *Meditating and Mediating Change: State, Society, and Religion* (2020), coedited with a graduate student. In both journals and edited collections, she has written widely about the history of rhetoric, writing pedagogy, gender, visual rhetoric, and women and material culture.

Melissa Greene is a stay-at-home mom and has three children. She is in recovery from addiction, and she volunteers and is active in her church during the week. Melissa has been involved with the Red Tent Women's Initiative since her incarceration in Pinellas County Jail in January 2015 and continued her participation upon her release. Melissa was chosen to copresent on behalf of the Red Tent Women's Initiative at the Feminisms and Rhetorics conference in October 2015. She continues to be an active volunteer and participant with Red Tent. Melissa is honored to be part of the Red Tent Women's Initiative, as it has been a huge part of her growth and recovery process. Red Tent women have not only helped her to grow in the right direction but also have provided the connections and resources to do so.

Linda Hanson is professor emeritus at Ball State University, Muncie, Indiana. As a member of the rhetoric and composition area from its inception in the Department of English, Hanson served as the coordinator of basic writing (1985–92), assistant department chair (1989–92), department chair (1992–95), and site director for the Indiana Writing Project (1995–2011), as well as the Indiana Network director for the five National Writing Project sites in Indiana (1998–2011). Hanson began her academic life, though, with degrees in literature (MA and PhD, University of Pennsylvania). Her publications, conference presentations, and administrative work reveal a consistent pragmatic approach over thirty years, whether focused on using assessment data to improve instruction and curriculum (beginning with those basic writers who changed her trajectory), building collaborative networks to improve teaching and learning, or seeking the reflexive links between theory and practice in British Romanticism, rhetoric, and writing.

Magdelyn Hammond Helwig is director of writing programs and associate professor of English at Western Illinois University where she teaches first-year composition, pedagogy, advanced composition and rhetoric, and poetry. Her research focuses on collaborative writing, visual rhetoric and multimodal composition, verbal-visual collaboration, modern and postmodern transatlantic poetry, and textual culture. Her poetry and essays can be found in the *Journal of the Midwest Modern Language Association*, *Kairos*, the *Ekphrastic Review*, the *Walt Whitman Quarterly Review*, and *Plainsongs*.

Jacquelyn E. Hoermann-Elliott is a doctoral candidate at Texas Christian University (TCU), where she researches the relationship between physical activity and writing activity in advanced writers. She serves as an assistant director for TCU's New Media Writing Studio, where she continues to teach Yoga-Zen Writing courses and pursue professional certification in the teaching of yoga.

Christine Martorana is an instructor in the writing and rhetoric program at Florida International University where she teachers first-year writing and upper-level writing and rhetoric courses. After growing up near Dayton, Ohio, Christine received a master's degree from the University of Dayton in 2009 and a PhD from Florida State University in 2015. Her current research circulates around discourse and agency, feminist zines, and composition pedagogy.

Aurora Matzke is an associate professor of English and codirector of the English writing program at Biola University. She teaches undergraduate courses in feminist rhetoric(s), writing, and style. With recent book chapters and articles on feminist, inclusive, and digital pedagogies, her research interests most closely align with her administrative work and her desire to be a strong advocate for all students. Her current work elucidates the ways by which a bricolage approach to core curricular reform can encourage broad faculty buy-in and participation.

Jill McCracken, PhD, is an associate professor of rhetoric and gender and sexuality studies at the University of South Florida St. Petersburg and cofounder/codirector of the sex workers outreach program (SWOP) Behind Bars, an organization that provides direct support for incarcerated sex workers and victims of trafficking in US prisons and jails and connects them to the sex-worker rights movement. Her research focuses on sex work and trafficking in the sex industry, women and incarceration, and the impact of sexuality education on marginalized communities. Her current book, *Learning with Women in Jail: Creating Community Based Participatory Research* (SpringerBriefs in Anthropology and Ethics, forthcoming 2019), documents the research process she and her coresearchers (women who are and were incarcerated in the Pinellas County Jail) created and conducted to better understand incarceration and recidivism. She is currently working on the Adolescent Sexual Health Education and Research (ASHER) Project with youth in high-risk situations to better understand and prevent exploitation and violence.

Karen S. Neubauer, assistant director of special projects for the Center for Instructional Excellence at Purdue University, spends her time in other people's classrooms, working with faculty members, continuing lecturers, and graduate teaching assistants who seek to transform lecture-based classrooms into learning-centered environments. A former newspaper editor and public-relations specialist, Karen entered academia as a community college adjunct teaching journalism, speech, writing, and research courses. Twenty-seven years after earning her bachelor's in journalism from Iowa State University, she earned a master's in liberal studies at Indiana University South Bend. She studied rhetoric and composition at Ball State, where she completed her second master's before pursuing a PhD in educational psychology at Purdue. Karen's research focuses on the use of reflection in graduate teacher development—a topic of numerous conference presentations.

Sherry Rankins-Robertson is an associate professor of rhetoric and writing at the University of Arkansas at Little Rock, where she teaches courses in first-year composition, nonfiction, and composition theory. Her scholarship has appeared in *Kairos, Computers and Composition*, and *the Journal of Writing Assessment*, along with diverse edited collections. She served as coeditor of the *WPA* journal. With Nicholas Behm and Duane Roen, she edited *The Framework for Success in Postsecondary Writing: Scholarship and Applications* (Parlor Press, 2017). Her recent publication is an edited collection with Joe Lockard titled *Prison Pedagogies: Learning and Teaching with Imprisoned Writers* (Syracuse University Press, 2018).

Shirley K Rose is professor of writing, rhetorics, and literacies and former director of writing programs in the Department of English on the Tempe campus of Arizona State University. She has published essays on writing program administrators as archivists and the rhetorical work of professional archivists and has coedited several collections on studies of writing program administration with Irwin Weiser, including *Going Public: What Writing Programs Learn from Engagement* and *The Internationalization of US Writing Programs*. Professor Rose is a past president of the Council of Writing Program Administrators and currently serves as the director of the WPA Consultant-Evaluator Service.

Kathleen J. Ryan is an associate professor of rhetoric and writing at Montana State University. She is a coeditor of *Rethinking Ethos: A Feminist Ecological Approach to Rhetoric*, a coauthor of *GenAdmin: Theorizing WPA Identities in the Twenty-First Century*, and coeditor of *Walking and Talking Feminist Rhetorics: Landmark Essays and Controversies*. In addition, she has published articles in a range of writing and rhetoric journals. Along with her coauthors, she is a past recipient of the CWPA Best Book Award, the Kathleen E. Welch Outstanding Article Award, and the Elizabeth A. Flynn Award. Kate has been a yoga practitioner for about twenty years, has taught yoga in the Bishnu Ghosh lineage, and practices Neelakantha meditation.

Rachael A. Ryerson earned her PhD in rhetoric and composition from Ohio University and is currently a lecturer there as well as the director of composition. Her first-year writing courses center around a cultural competencies curriculum, but she also researches, writes, and teaches multimodal composition, comics, and feminist and queer theories of rhetoric and composition. Her article "Multimodal Composition in *Kairos*: A Rhizomatic Retrospective" catalogues the myriad ways authors have discussed multimodal composition in *Kairos* over the last ten years, and her forthcoming article in the *Journal of Multimodal Rhetorics* analyzes queer multimodal rhetoric in queer comics. Also forthcoming is a coedited collection of essays speaking and storytelling at the intersection of queerness and Appalachia.

Andrea J. Severson holds a PhD in writing, rhetorics, and literacies with a focus on fashion rhetoric and material culture from Arizona State University and two masters of arts degrees, one in media arts from the University of Arizona (2007) and the other in English rhetoric and composition from ASU (2013). She has been teaching at Arizona State University and the Maricopa County Community Colleges since 2010. For the past ten years, she has also worked as a freelance costume designer on various theatrical and film projects. She has been a member of the Arizona Costume Institute since 2010 and served on its board of directors from 2011 to 2014. Her work has been featured in *For His Eyes Only: The Women of James Bond* (2015).

Lorin Shellenberger earned her PhD in rhetoric and writing from Virginia Tech, where she taught first-year composition and served as the editorial assistant for *the Minnesota Review*. Her research interests include embodied rhetorics, sports studies, feminist theory, classical rhetoric, and Kenneth Burke, and her work is featured in *Keywords in Writing Studies* and *Textual Overtures*. She currently teaches first-year writing at the University of Lynchburg.

Emily Standridge is assistant professor of English and writing center director at the University of Texas at Tyler. Her research focuses on writing pedagogies, especially in first-year composition, and one-on-one writing tutorials. She has written for *Peer Review* and coauthored with Hui Wu *Reading and Writing about the Disciplines: A Rhetorical Approach*.

Charlese Trower was born in North Carolina and grew up all over the East Coast. She has been involved with Red Tent for three years. Char was chosen to copresent on behalf of the Red Tent Women's Initiative at the Feminisms and Rhetorics conference in October 2015. She is married, has two children, and works at Chick-Fil-A, a job she loves.

Daneryl Weber, an associate professor of English, lives in the Catskills and teaches writing and literature at SUNY Sullivan Community College. After teaching ESL in Germany for thirteen years, Dani earned her PhD in English with a concentration in rhetoric and composition from Ball State University and now teaches a wide variety of literature, composition, and writing classes. Dani has served as writing center director at several institutions and also teaches writing and literature in the local maximum-security correctional facility. Recent publications include an analysis of George W. Bush's speech to a joint session of Congress after 9/11, a chapter on contingent faculty working in writing centers, and a coauthored chapter on online instructional design.

Christy I. Wenger is an assistant professor of rhetoric and composition and English at Shepherd University in Shepherdstown, West Virginia, where she serves as the director of writing and rhetoric. She is the author of *Yoga Minds, Writing Bodies: Contemplative Writing Pedagogy*, and her articles appear in *English Teaching: Practice and Critique, JAEPL*, and *WPA: Writing Program Administration*. She has also published several chapters in collections such as *Rethinking Ethos: A Feminist Ecological Approach to Rhetoric*. Christy serves as the treasurer and membership chair for the Assembly of Expanded Perspectives on Teaching and edits the organization's professional blog. Her research considers the intersections of contemplative mindfulness, feminism, and writing for students, teachers, and administrators. Christy has practiced yoga for over ten years, using her practice as a wellspring for her professional leadership and pedagogical methods.

Hui Wu is professor of English and chair of the Department of Literature and Languages at the University of Texas at Tyler. Her research encompasses the history of rhetoric and composition, comparative rhetoric, and global feminist rhetorics. One of her articles, "Lost and Found in Transnation: Modern Conceptualization of Chinese Rhetoric," won the 2009 Best Article Award from the journal *Rhetoric Review*. She is the editor and translator of *Once Iron Girls: Essays on Gender by Post-Mao Literary Women*. Her translation into Chinese of C. Jan Swearingen's *Rhetoric and Irony: Western Literacy and Western Lies* was published in China in 2004. She also translated and coedited *Guiguzi, China's First Treatise on Rhetoric* and coauthored with Emily Standridge *Reading and Writing about the Disciplines: A Rhetorical Approach*.

ABOUT THE AUTHORS

Kathleen Blake Yancey, Kellogg W. Hunt professor of English and distinguished research professor at Florida State University, has served in several elected leadership positions, among them president of the Council of Writing Program Administrators (CWPA); president of the National Council of Teachers of English (NCTE); and chair of the Conference on College Composition and Communication (CCCC). Immediate past editor of *College Composition and Communication*, she serves on several boards, among them the Association for Authentic, Experiential and Evidence-Based Learning (AAEEBL). Author/coauthor of over one hundred articles and chapters and author/coeditor of sixteen scholarly books—including *Assessing Writing across the Curriculum; Delivering College Composition: The Fifth Canon; Writing across Contexts: Transfer, Composition, and Sites of Writing; A Rhetoric of Reflection;* and *Assembling Composition*—she is the recipient of several awards, including the Purdue Distinguished Woman Scholar Award, the FSU Graduate Mentor Award, and the CCCC Exemplar Award.

INDEX

AAUP. *See* American Association of University Professors
abjection: in *Abortion Eve,* 21; in *For Better or For Worse,* 21; comics scholarship on, 21–22; and criticism, 18–19; of female reproductive bodies in mainstream comics, 20–22; in *Fourth World,* 20; in *Justice League International,* 21; in *Zero Hour: Crisis in Time,* 21
Abortion Eve (Lyvely and Chevely), 21
academics, nontraditional: academic women, 232, 233; ageism, ambiguities of, 232–35; decision-making vs. knowledge-making, 235–37; definition of, 226–28; and non-tenure-track, 225; pilot survey to identify, 224–26; scholars, perceptions of, 221–24; "youth" of nontraditional students, 234
ACE. *See* American Council for Education
actively negotiating femininity, 69
Adams, Halina, 222
Adler-Kassner, Linda, 209, 256
Advertising Standards Agency (ASA), 157
ageism, in academia, 232–35
Aglionby, Edward, 139
Ahmed, Sara, 97, 245–46
Aina, Jackie, 158
Alexander, Amy, 252
Alliance of Rhetoric Societies, 144
"alternative paths," 228
"amateurist spirit," 42
American Association of University Professors (AAUP), 223, 229
American Council on Education (ACE), 216, 247, 251
Archbald, Douglas, 226, 227
Arellano, Sonia, 247
Aristotle, 77; *The Nicomachean Ethics,* 3; types of wisdom, 12n1, understandings of ethos, 76, 79
arkana dhanurasana, 124
Arola, Kristin L., 98
artist's book, 10, 164–68; Kohashi's views, 165–66; process of making, 167–69
Arya, Rina, 18, 29
Ascham, Roger, 140

Ashley, Alissa, 158
Atwill, Janet, 115, 122
authoritative ethos, 90

Ballif, Michelle, 221, 222, 223
Balsamo, Anne Marie, 62
Baraitser, Lisa, 23, 25, 26
Barr-Ebest, Sally, 250
Bassnett, Susan, 145n1
Batman Beyond 2.0, 34
Batman: Dark Knight III: The Master Race, 29
beauty community: creativity and, 156–59; femininity and, 156–59; Fleur de Force, 156–59; role of celebrity, 151; on YouTube, 150–60
Beauty Myth, The (Wolf), 152
Beck, Nakini, 247
Beemer, Cristy, 145(n3)
Belenky, Mary Field, 3, 237
Bell, Ilona, 145n3
Benschop, Yvonne, 250
Berry, Philippa, 145n4
Bertolet, Anna Riehl, 146n16
Birth Rites collection, 25
Bivens, Kristin, 222
Blake Yancey, Kathleen. *See* Yancey, Kathleen Blake
Blatter, Sepp, 89–90
blog asana, 101, 102
Bodily Arts (Hawhee), 12n3, 98, 109
bodily ethos, 77, 79
bodily uptake, 99
body/bodies: in classrooms, 96–100; as marker of cultural values, 82–86
bodyfulness, 122, 125
Bolton, Ruthie, 84
Bone, Jordan, 158
book creation, 163–75; commemorating, 173; eulogy and, 163–64; include verbal text, 168–69; lessons for, 171–72; process of, 167–69; reflection, 174
Borrowman, Shane, 204
Bousquet, Marc, 233
Boyle, Lex, 68
Brady, Ann, 125

Brandt, Deborah, 145n4
breastfeeding: in *Batman: Dark Knight III: The Master Race*, 29; in *Sabre*, 28–29; in *Saga*, 27–33
Brennan, Christine, 87
Brereton, John, 208
Brouns, Margo, 250
Brown, Jeffrey, 27
Brown, Stuart, 209
Brubach, Holly, 92n5
Brummett, Barry, 185
Buchanan, Lindal, 78, 79
Bullock, Richard, 204
Butler, Judith, 69

Campaspe (Lyly), 139, 141, 146n16
Campbell, Karlyn Kohrs, 163, 179
Canter, Martha McKay, 222
Chananie-Hill, Ruth, 68
Chansky, Ricia A., 177
Charlton, Colin, 209
Charlton, Jonikka, 209, 254
Chastain, Brandi, 8, 74, 85–91; *Gear* photo shoot, 89, 90–91; goal celebration, 80–82, 87–88; identity of, 86; *It's Not about the Bra*, 89; performance of ethos, 82, 88–89, 91; and situated ethos, 83
Chevely, Joyce Farmer, 21
childbirth, taboos of, 22–27
Choi, Sungjoo, 252
Chronicle of Higher Education (Winzenburg), 233
Clark-Oates, Angela, 5, 11
Clinchy, Blythe McVicker, 3, 237
Coalition of Women Scholars in the History of Rhetoric and Composition, 225
Coalition on the Academic Workforce (CAW), 223, 229
Cole, Kirsti, 222
Collaborative on Academic Careers in Higher Education, 226
Collinson, Patrick, 145n1
ComicVine, 36
Composing Media, Composing Embodiment (Arola and Wysocki), 98
Condit, Celeste, 174
Conference on College Composition and Communication, 221, 260
Cooper, Marilyn, 54, 142, 145n2
Cooperative Writing Movement, 213. *See also* writing program administrators
corporeal experiential authority, 40, 41–42; embodied form of expertise, 55; *Here. In My Head*, 42–48
Correct Writing and Speaking (Jordan), 143

Council of Writing Program Administrators, 216
Council of Writing Program Administrators Conference, 260
crafting: creative practices in, 150; and women's ways of making, 153–56
Craig, Collin, 247
Crandall, Regina, 207–8
Crane, Mary Thomas, 145n3
creativity: and beauty community, 156–59; and women's ways of making, 153–56
Creed, Barbara, 23
CrossFit, 66–67, 68
Crowley, Sharon, 12n3, 76–77, 97
Cultural Politics of Emotion, The (Ahmed), 97
Cupcakes, Pinterest, and Ladyporn (Levine), 152
cyberfeminism, 61–64

D'Amore, Laura Mattoon, 20
dandayamana dhanurasana, 129
Davis, Diane, 221, 222, 223
Developing Successful College Writing Programs (White), 254
Dewey, John, 4
Diamant, Anita, 180, 181
Discipline and Punish (Foucault), 12n3, 64
Distraction Addiction, The (Pang), 106
Doing Emotion: Rhetoric, Writing, Teaching (Micciche), 103, 110
Donawerth, Jane, 5, 9, 12, 145n3
Donna Shavlik Award, 216
Doran, Susan, 145n1
Dorman, Dave, 29, 30, 31
Doucet, Julie, 17, 22, 23, 24
Driver, Felix, 12n3
Dudley, Robert, 136, 141
Duffy, Brook, 151
Duncan, Margaret Carlisle, 64
Dunn, Dana, 245, 248, 259
du Preez, Amanda, 63, 64
Dutcher, Violet, 222
Dworkin, Shari, 88, 92n5

Ede, Lisa, 257
Edwards, Harry, 85
Eisler, Riane, 154, 155
Elbow, Peter, 208
eleven40seven, 107, 112–13
elite female athletes, 74; training, 80
Elizabeth I (Queen), 5, 9; agency, 138–40, 143, 144; on marriage of, 135–38; deployment of argument, 143–44; initial statements on marriage, 142–43; Lords and Commons sent petition for

marriage, 141–43; plays to influence ideas on marriage, 140–41; princes offered marriage, 136; Queen's mortality, 127–28; Renaissance panegyric tactic, 139; and rhetoric of the marriage crisis, 135–44; speech to Lords at Hatfield, 144; speech to Parliament (February 10, 1559), 138
Ellis, Amanda, 5, 10, 181–82, 192, 194, 197n7
Elms, Catherine, 42, 44–55; rhetorical decision, 50; self-reflection, 53; zines, 51
embodiment, 61–64
embodying subject/object, 86–92
emotional-embodied rhetorical development, 110–11
emovere, 97
Enlightenment, 4
Enos, Theresa, 53–54, 206, 209, 223
episteme, 3, 4
ethe, embodied, 75, 77, 91; complexity of, 79–80; ethos as, 78
ethos, 40, 41–42, 73–92; Aristotelian understandings of, 76, 79; authoritative, 90; Chastain's goal celebration, 80–82; of corporeal experiential authority, 42; and development of self, 75–76; elite female athletes and, 74–75; factors in development of, 74; invented, 76–77; as malleable, 86–92; physical bodies and, 73–74; revisionings of, 49–51; situated, 76–77
eulogy, 163–64, 173; inherent problem in, 163
Eulogy for a Lost Object, A, 172
Euphues (Lyly), 140
Evans, Ruth, 68
Evans, Tess, 11
Every Body Yoga (Stanley), 40

Fashion Mumblr, 158
femininity, 69, 71; actively negotiate, 69; and beauty community, 156–59; culture sites associated with, 152; entrepreneurial, 151; markers of, 84; nonnormative, 69; normative, 63, 68, 85, 86, 89; performances of, 57–58; physical fitness, 8; social conventions and, 62; traditional visions of, 68–69
Feminisms and Rhetorics Conference, 3, 6, 10, 12
"feminist attachments," 97
feminist rhetorical practices, 151–53
feminist techne, yoga as, 117–24; activist element of yoga, 128–29; ecological or community based, 120–22; embodied and instrumental, 122–24; productive knowledge/process, 117–20
feminization of internet, 151–53
Fitzalan, Henry, 136
Fleur de Force vlog, 9–10, 150, 152, 154, 156–60
Flower of Friendship, The (Tilney), 139
Flynn, Elizabeth, 125
For Better or For Worse (Johnston), 21
Ford, Em, 158
Foss, Katherine, 32
Foucault, Michel, 12n3, 64, 75, 79
Four Foster Children of Desire, The (Sidney), 141
Fourth World (Kirby), 20
Frank, Arthur, 12n3
Fulton-Babicke, Holly, 8

Garrett, Bre, 5, 11
Gauntlett, David, 153, 154, 155
Gear (magazine), 87, 89, 90–91
Gearhart, Sally Miller, 143
Geisler, Cheryl, 144
GenAdmins, 214, 215, 217
gender dichotomies, 212
Gendered Bodies and New Technologies (du Preez), 63
Gendered Pulpit: Preaching in American Protestant Spaces, The (Mountford), 78–79
Gender Roles and Faculty Lives in Rhetoric and Composition (Enos), 223
Gerlach, Jeanne, 245, 248, 259
Giele, Janet, 248
Gilligan, Carol, 121
Glenn, Cheryl, 145n3, 212, 245, 249, 257
Godey's Lady's Book, 153
Goggin, Maureen Daly, 69, 257
Goldberger, Nancy Rule, 3, 237
Golde, Chris, 242n2
Goodburn, Amy, 227
Gordon, Ali, 158
Goss, Wayne, 158
Graban, Tarez Samra, 209
Greene, Melissa, 5, 10, 177, 181–82, 186, 188, 191, 192
Gresham, Morgan, 222
Gries, Laurie, 70
Grigore, Georgianna, 151
Grogan, Sarah, 68
Gualtier, Duke, 138
Gunner, Jeanne, 211

Hairston, Maxine, 205–6, 210, 255
Hallenbeck, Sarah, 144
Hamblet, Brooke, 104

Hamm, Mia, 83
Hanh, Thich Nhat, 181
Hanson, Linda, 11
Haraway, Donna, 62
Hardin, Marie, 66
Hart, Jeni, 230, 237
Hawhee, Debra, 12n3, 76–77, 98, 99, 126
Hawisher, Gail, 257
Hawkeye Initiative, 17
Haydar, Mona, 158
Hays, Anne, 43, 50
Heart and Stomach of a King, The (Levin), 145n1
Heavy Flow (comic), 17
Heisch, Allison, 145n3
Hekman, Susan, 142
Helmbrecht, Brenda, 41, 42, 257
Helwig, Magdelyn Hammond, 5, 11
Here. In My Head (feminist zine), 40, 52, 53; corporeal experiential authority in, 42–48; menstruation experiences, 43; source of authority within, 49
Hewitt, Beth L., 227
Heywood, Leslie, 88, 92n5
History of Sexuality, The (Foucault), 12n3
Hoermann-Elliott, Jackie, 8
Holbrook, Ellen, 206
Hopeless, Dennis, 36
Hopkins, Edwin, 207, 208
Horner, Win[ifred Bryan], 216, 246
Hult, Christine, 257
Hund, Emily, 151
Hunter, Geoff, 68
hybrid places, 52
Hyle, Adrienne, 245–46, 248, 259
"hysteric female," 63

Ianetta, Melissa, 222
Iannaccaro, Giuliana, 145n3
identity, 58, 59; envisioning, 69–71; and feminization of internet, 151–53; internet technologies and, 57; online, 62–63
invented ethos, 76–77
Itchon, Connie, 58, 64–68
It's Not about the Bra (Chastain), 89
Iyengar, BKS, 122

James, Robin, 158
Jamieson, Kathleen Hall, 163
Jankowski, Theodora, 145n4
Jaws (film), 27
Jerslev, Anne, 151
Jiang, Shanhe, 184
Johnson, Maureen, 4
Johnson, Nan, 216–17

Johnson, Sonia, 41
Johnston, Lynn, 21
Jones, Mark, 5
Jones, Rebecca, 75, 78, 79, 80, 92n1
Jordan, Mary Augusta, 143
Jung, Julie Marie, 210, 211

Kajstura, Aleks, 183
Kearney, Mary Celeste, 42, 43
Keller, Jessalyn Marie, 71
Kelsky, Karen, 233, 234
Kessler, Nadine, 73
King Lear (Shakespeare), 137
Kirby, Jack, 20
Kloot, Louise, 250
Klos, Lori A., 64
Kohashi, Andrea, 165–66
Køhlert, Frederik Byrn, 22
Kristeva, Julia, 18–19, 35
Kroll, Barry, 98, 99, 100

Ladies' Mercury, The, 153
Lamott, Anne, 110
Lasater, Judith, 115
LeCourt, Donna, 227
L'Eplattenier, Barbara, 205, 209, 211
Leslie, Lisa, 84
Leverenz, Carrie, 210, 227, 235
Levin, Carole, 145n1, 146n16
Levine, Elana, 152
Levy, Daisy, 4
Lewiecki-Wilson, Cynthia, 257
Lewis, C. S., 146n17
Licona, Adela, 42
Lindemann, Erika, 257
Lin LeMesurier, Jennifer, 95, 99–100, 104, 109
Living a Feminist Life (Ahmed), 246
Living Your Yoga (Lasater), 105, 115
Locklear, Nicole, 197n1
Loey Lane, 158
Lopiano, Donna, 83
Love, Meredith, 41, 42
Luckman, Susan, 62
Lunsford, Andrea, 257
Lyly, John, 139, 140, 141, 146n16
Lynn, Susan, 66
Lyvely, Chin, 21

Mack, Phyllis, 140
Mahmood, Saba, 144
maid, conotations of, 206
Maimon, Elaine, 216
Making Is Connecting (Gauntlett), 153
Manthley, Katie, 4
Marcus, Leah S., 145n3

Mardon, Rebecca, 151
Martorana, Christine, 7
Marwick, Alice, 151
Mastrangelo, Lisa, 205, 209, 211
material literacy, as artisanal epistemology, 12n4
Mathews, Kiernan, 226
Matzke, Aurora, 5, 11
McCracken, Jill, 5, 10, 181–82, 186, 197n3
McGrath, Shelley, 68
McGregor, Hannah, 51
McLeod, Susan, 209
Medalen, Linda, 85, 91
metis, 126, 127
#metoo movement, 247
Meyers, Laura, 251
Meyers, Nancy, 75, 78, 79, 80, 92n1
Micciche, Laura, 95, 103, 110
Milbrett, Tiffeny, 83
Millen, Lydia Elise, 158
Miller, Carolyn, 138, 145n6
Miller, Frank, 29
Miller, Hildy, 246–47, 257, 258
Miller, Susan, 223
mindfulness, 119, 121, 123, 125
miscarriage, remaking, 34–37
Molesworth, Mike, 151
Monroe, Kristen, 252
Monturori, Alfonso, 154, 155
Morgan, Alex, 73
Mountford, Roxanne, 78–79, 221, 222, 223
Moving Bodies (Hawhee), 12n3
Moxley, Joseph, 205
Mulvey, Laura, 88
muscle-building, 57, 68–69
My Pale Skin, 158

Najavitz, Lisa, 181
National Science Foundation (NSF), 227, 231
Nelson, Mariah Burton, 87, 88
Neubauer, Karen S., 11
Nganga, Christine, 247
Nicomachean Ethics, The (Aristotle), 3, 77
Nike, 83, 84, 87, 90
Nikki Tutorials, 158
Nimkulrat, Nithikul, 170–71
non-tenure-track faculty, 229, 230, 237–38, 251
Norris, Aaminah, 52
North, Stephen, 224
Norton, John, 141
Norton, Thomas, 145n7
Novotny, Maria, 4
Nowell, Alexander, 138
NSF. *See* National Science Foundation

O'Brien, Anne Marie, 20
Offerman, Michael, 234
Olson, Gary, 205
Olympic women's basketball team (1996), 84–85
Ozyurt, Saba, 252

Pang, Alex Soojung-Kim, 106
Park, Linda, 34
"patriarchal unconscious," 52
Pearce Center for Professional Communication (Clemson University), 164
Peary, Alexandria, 120, 125
Peitho (journal), 260
Pender, Kelly, 115, 122, 124
Penn State Conference on Rhetoric and Composition, 97
Perna, Laura W., 230
Perryman-Clark, Staci, 247, 257
perzine, 44
Peterson, Owen, 163
Pfau, Thomas, 174
Phan, Michelle, 154
Phelps, Louise Wetherbee, 215
Philips, John, 138, 141
phronesis, 3, 4, 12n1
physical bodies: and ethos, 73–74; homophobic perceptions, 73; sport and, 73
Pickering, Sir William, 136
Piepmeier, Alison, 42, 43
Pinellas County Jail (PCJ), 177, 183
Pinellas County Sheriff's Office Program Services, 184–85
Pinterest, 152
Plant, Sadie, 62
Play of Patient Grissell, The (Philips), 138, 141
Poltergeist (film), 27
Power of Making (Greenlees and Jones), 5

Queens Matter in Early Modern Studies (Levin), 146n16

Rankins-Robertson, Sherry, 5
Redefine Pretty, 158
Red Tent, The (Diamant), 180, 181
Red Tent Women's Initiative (Red Tent), 10; circle, 179, 180; display participants' artwork, 195; experiences in jail and Red Tent gatherings, 188–90; as feminist rhetoric creates community and change, 195–96; feminist rhetorics, 178–81; impact on individuals and community, 193–95; inductive movement, 179–80; introduction, 177–81; participant agreement,

196–97; at Phoenix, Arizona, 192–93; physically changed spaces, 194–95; in Pinellas County Jail, 186–88; quotidian rhetoric, 185–86; room in jail, 190–91; sensing differences, 190–92; serves nonviolent female offenders from prisons and jails, 183–85; voices and experiences, 192–93; women in community, 186–88; works with Pinellas County Sheriff's Office Program Services, 184–85
Regendering Delivery (Buchanan), 78
Rewriting Success in Rhetoric and Composition Careers, 227
Reynolds, Nedra, 41, 49
Rhetorica in Motion (Scheel and Rawson), 124
Rhetorical Bodies (Selzer and Crowley), 12n3, 97
Rhetorical Feminism and This Thing Called Hope (Glenn), 245
rhetorical strategies, 48–55
Rhetorics and Poetics in Antiquity (Walker), 92n2
Rhoades, Georgia, 257
Rhode, Barbara, 180
Ribero, Anna, 247
Rich, Adrienne, 212, 216
Riley, Kristine, 178
Ripped Goddess, 8, 57–71; CrossFit vs., 66–67; feminine fitness vs., 64–67; members of, 57, 59, 60, 68, 70–71; online identities, 62; overview, 57–60; practices and products of, 65, 67; as public, 60–61; women's fitness in public, 61–64; women's muscle as normative and nonnormative, 68–69
"ripped goddesses," 8
risks and rewards, 228–32
Ritchie, Joy, 96, 97
Robertson, Sherry Rankin, 11
Rodriguez, Javier, 36
Rodriguez-Connal, Luisa, 222
Ronald, Kate, 96, 97, 257; yoga practice, 120–21, 123
Rose, Shirley, 205, 209, 211, 254, 257
Rowe, Aimee Carrillo, 49–50
Royster, Jacqueline Jones, 79, 82, 257
Ruddick, Sara, 121
Rule, Jill Mattuck, 3
Rutgers, Mark, 217n3
Ryan, Kathleen J., 8, 75, 78, 79, 80, 92n1, 209, 254
Ryden, Wendy, 96
Ryerson, Rachael, 7

Sabre, 28–29
Sackville, Thomas, 141
Saga, 7, 18; abjection of female reproductive body in, 19, 22; Alana breastfeeding Hazel in, 33; Alana giving birth to Hazel in, 23; breastfeeding, normalize, 27–33; Hazel breastfeeding, 32; princess robot giving birth, 26; remaking miscarriage, 34–37; taboos of childbirth, 22–27
sankalpa, 115
Satchidananda, Sri Swami, 125
Schell, Eileen, 222
Schuster, Julia, 71
Scurry, Briana, 83, 85, 91
Seeking Safety (Najavitz), 181
Selfe, Cynthia, 257
selfless introspection, 49, 53, 54
Selzer, Jack, 12n3, 97, 99
service, conotations of, 206–7, 210
Severson, Andrea, 9–10
Shakespeare, William, 137
Sharpe, Kevin, 136
Shaughnessy, Mina, 216
Shellenberger, Loren, 8
Sheridan, Harriet, 216
Sidney, Sir Philip, 138, 141, 142, 146n26
situated ethos, 76–77, 82–86
Smith, Craig, 77
Smith, Pamela, 12n4
Smitherman-Clark, Carey, 5, 11
Sophie's Choice (Styron), 173
Sotirin, Patricia, 125
Spelman, Elizabeth, 12n3
Spider-Woman, 29, 36
Spillane, Sunny, 170
Sports Illustrated, 84, 86
Staley, Dawn, 84
Standridge, Emily, 10
Stanley, Jessamyn, 40
Stanley, Liz, 175
Staples, Fiona, 18, 22, 23, 27–37; answered Dorman's comments, 31; representing breastfeeding, 29. *See also Saga*
Starr, Patrick, 158
Steinem, Gloria, 258–59
Stolley, Amy Ferdinandt, 209
Strickland, Donna, 209
Stubbs, John, 137, 142
Stuller, Jennifer, 17
Styron, William, 173
Subramaniam, Ram, 178
Sugg, Zoe, 151
"suicidal obsession," 212
Survey of Earned Doctorates (SED), 225
Swavola, Elizabeth, 178

Tang, Nyma, 158
Tarule, Jill Mattuck, 237
Taylor, Shelley, 180
"teacher lore," 224
Teaching Rhetorica: Theory, Pedagogy, Practice (Ronald and Ritchie), 96
Teaching to Transgress (hooks), 256
techne, 3, 4, 122
Teeth (film), 27
Tending Instinct, The (Taylor), 180
Texas Christian University (TCU), 95, 100, 107, 112
The Thing (film), 27
Thomas, M. Carey, 207
Tilney, Edmund, 139
Title IX, 73, 81, 92n4
Tokio, Dina, 158
traditional doctorate, 226–27
Tragedy of Gorboduc, The (Norton and Sackville), 141
transgression, 61–64
Trower, Charlese, 5, 10, 181–83, 188
Tumanov, Vladamir, 197n4
Tyler, Imogen, 19, 23, 26, 28

Ulrich, Laurel Thatcher, 5, 145n8
Ussher, Jane, 21

Vaughan, Brian K., 18, 22, 23, 25, 27–37; representing breastfeeding, 29; responded to Dorman, 31. *See also Saga*
Venturini, Tisha, 83

WAC. *See* writing-across-the-curriculum
Walker, George, 242n2
Walker, Jeffrey, 92n2
Walmsley, Roy, 183–84
Walsdorf, Kristie, 66
Wambach, Abby, 73
Weber, Daneryl, 11
Weiser, Irwin, 209
Wenger, Christy I., 8, 95, 98, 99, 100, 108, 121; as WPA, 123–24; writing program, pressure of, 126–27
Wentworth, Thomas, 142
White, Edward, 254
WID. *See* writing-in-the-disciplines
Wills, Katherine V., 229
Winfree, L. Thomas, 184
Winzenburg, Stephen, 233
Wolf, Naomi, 152
Wolff, Alexander, 84
women's fitness in public, 61–64
women's muscle as normative and nonnormative, 68–69

Women's Professional Lives in Rhetoric and Composition (Flynn and Bourelle), 228
Women's Sports Foundation, 83
Women's Ways of Making It in Rhetoric and Composition, 221, 223
Women's World Cup, 2015, 73
Wright, Ashley "Tiyumba," 40
Wright, Sam, 68
Wrigley, Ted, 252
writing-across-the-curriculum (WAC), 204, 209, 216
writing-in-the-disciplines (WID), 204, 209
writing program administrators (WPAs), 10–11, 115, 117, 120, 123, 128, 203–17; as academic leaders, 215; applying feminist administration, 253–56; current status of, 204–9; feminist mentoring practices, leading with, 259–61; feminist studies of, critique of, 209–13; funding challenge, 127; gender distribution, 205; job market for, 10; leadership, 203; mentoring as, 256–59; perceptions on service, 204–9; practicing yoga as, 128–29; responding as female administrators, 249–53; self-care, 116; skills and scholarship potential of, 204; sole writing expert, 260; thoughtful judgments as, 129; undervaluing of, 205–6; ways of making arguments, 249–53; ways of making knowledge, 253–56; ways of making sense, 256–59; well-being of, 9; women, redefining as university leaders, 213–17; yoga as techne, 130
Writing Program Administrators Workshop, 260
Wu, Hui, 10
Wysocki, Anne, 98

Yancey, Kathleen Blake, 5, 10, 256–57
yoga, 9, 115–30; *arkana dhanurasana*s, 124; awareness and inner peace, 127–28; benefits of, 116, 126; bodyfulness, 122, 125; definition, 122; epistemological and ethical possibilities, 115; as feminist techne, 117–24; as means of feminist intervention, 125–29; *metis*, 126, 127; mindfulness, 119, 121, 123, 125; and resilience, 125–26; sense of identity and attention, 117–18. *See also* Yoga-Zen Writing
Yoga Minds, Writing Bodies (Wenger), 98
Yoga Sutras of Patanjali, 125
Yoga-Zen Writing, 95, 100–102; Course English 10803, 111–12; "Mantra Essay," 103, 106, 108; "Mediated Argument Essay," 106, 109

You Look Disgusting (video), 158
YouTube, 9, 150–60; Creator Studio, 157; female creators on, 158; Fleur de Force on, 9–10, 150, 152, 154, 156–60

Zen Buddhism, 100
zine, feminist, 39–47, 50–51
Zoella, 154

www.ingramcontent.com/pod-product-compliance
Lightning Source LLC
Chambersburg PA
CBHW031059080526
44587CB00011B/752